AF897507

NATURAL PERCEPTION

Images of nature abound in the practice of international environmental law, but their significance in law is unclear. Drawing on visual jurisprudence, and interpretative methods for visual art, this book analyses photographs for their representations of nature's aesthetic value in treaty processes that concern world heritage, whales and biodiversity. It argues that visual images should be embraced in the prosaic practice of international law, particularly for treaties that demand judgements of nature's aesthetic value. This environmental value is in practice conflated with natural beauty and ethical and cultural values, and displaced by economic and scientific values. Interpretations of visual images can serve instead to critique and conceive sensory, imaginative and emotional appreciations of nature from different cultural perspectives as proposed by philosophers of environmental aesthetics. Addressing questions of value and the visual, this landmark book shows how images can be engaged by nations to better protect the environment under international law.

DR ALICE PALMER is a Senior Lecturer and Director of the Art and Law Program of the Institute for International Law and the Humanities at Melbourne Law School. She writes on law and image with a focus on the visual arts, drawing on her work in international environmental law.

Natural Perception

ENVIRONMENTAL IMAGES AND AESTHETICS IN INTERNATIONAL LAW

ALICE PALMER
University of Melbourne

CAMBRIDGE
UNIVERSITY PRESS

CAMBRIDGE
UNIVERSITY PRESS

Shaftesbury Road, Cambridge CB2 8EA, United Kingdom

One Liberty Plaza, 20th Floor, New York, NY 10006, USA

477 Williamstown Road, Port Melbourne, VIC 3207, Australia

314–321, 3rd Floor, Plot 3, Splendor Forum, Jasola District Centre, New Delhi – 110025, India

103 Penang Road, #05–06/07, Visioncrest Commercial, Singapore 238467

Cambridge University Press is part of Cambridge University Press & Assessment, a department of the University of Cambridge.

We share the University's mission to contribute to society through the pursuit of education, learning and research at the highest international levels of excellence.

www.cambridge.org
Information on this title: www.cambridge.org/9781009350075

DOI: 10.1017/9781009350105

First published 2023
First paperback edition 2026

A catalogue record for this publication is available from the British Library

ISBN 978-1-009-35012-9 Hardback
ISBN 978-1-009-35007-5 Paperback

For my family

The Wurundjeri People of the Kulin Nation are the first owners of the lands and waters that inspired this book. I pay my respects to all Aboriginal and Torres Strait Islander Elders – past, present and emerging – and am hopeful that the *Uluru Statement from the Heart* will lead to the lawful acknowledgement of their continuing sovereignty.

First Nations peoples are advised that this book contains the names and images of Aboriginal and Torres Strait Islander people who have passed away.

Contents

Figures

Cover illustration: Danie Mellor, Story Place (*gambunu Wiinggina*) 2022, Infra-red photograph. Courtesy the artist and Tolarno Galleries, Melbourne and N.Smith Gallery, Sydney

Acknowledgements

My family has been vital to this book. My parents gave me and my sister a life with art, and a love of the environment, both of which have carried me through my work as a lawyer, and my years as a parent. My partner and our children conjured time, space and inspirations for this project. Also supportive have been my friends. Sundhya Pahuja has deftly straddled the roles of friend and mentor, and Emma Cornall and Carolina Lasén Diaz have been attentive allies throughout. I thank them and the many other friends who have helped to shape my thoughts for this book. Some friends are also colleagues. Sam Johnston has encouraged me with ideas and introduced me to people responsible for making international environmental law work. And I am greatly indebted to my other guides in international legal practice, Philippe Sands KC and Jacob Werksman.

Professor Alan Boyle and Professor Emily Brady were generous in meeting with me to discuss my ideas for international environmental law. People who make and think about art have been expert interlocutors, with many kindly providing me with images for inclusion in the book. Their thinking for art greatly expanded mine for law. Chapters 5 and 6 of this book are based on my previous publications 'Legal dimensions to valuing aesthetics in World Heritage decisions' (2017) 26(5) *Social & Legal Studies* 581 and 'Image and art in the *Whaling in the Antarctic Case*' in Jani McCutcheon and Fiona McGaughey (eds.), *The Research Handbook on Art and Law* (Northampton: Edward Elgar, 2020) 408. I sincerely thank the peer reviewers of those publications.

With the support of an Australian Government Research Training Program Scholarship (formerly an Australian Postgraduate Award), the doctoral research on which this book is based was undertaken at the Melbourne Law School. I am grateful to Kirsty Gover, Margaret Young, Dale Smith and Peter Rush for their thoughtful advice, and to Rebecca Croser, Jessica Cotton and

Domingo Córdoba of the MLS Office for Research. Staff from the MLS Law Library and other libraries have gladly facilitated my quest for information. The dedicated assistance of Sylvia Seldon, Belinda Nemec and the MLS Academic Research Service, particularly Daniel Beratis, was invaluable in bringing this book to completion. My fellow teachers and colleagues, my students and cohorts of graduate researchers have animated my thinking in myriad ways. Laura Petersen provided special support as we shared a desk of our own through parallel preoccupations in life. I am also grateful to the examiners of the thesis for their generous comments.

Which brings me to the two people at Melbourne Law School most often in conversation with me on the matters of image, aesthetics and international environmental law: Lee Godden and Shaun McVeigh. They have blended provocation and encouragement to guide my reading, writing and looking with law both during and beyond my doctorate to the writing of this book. Their contributions have been considered and radical. They have been caring yet critical collaborators in my task of making international environmental law work well to do good things. I am deeply grateful to Lee and to Shaun for everything they have done for me and will sorely miss the excuse of this book to ask for the close attention they have so willingly given to my thinking around law.

Finally, I am grateful to Tom Randall and Gemma Smith at Cambridge University Press, and to Aiswarya Narayanan, for their enthusiastic reception and assistance with this book project.

1

In the Frame

An Introduction

FIGURE 1.1. 'Picture 22. Ecotourism: … H.R.H. Prince Philip visits Sierra Chincua', 1988, in Mexico, *World Heritage Site Nomination Document*, p. 55. Photo: Carlos Gottfried.

I've never seen swarming butterflies. I've been in fields with dozens about. And I've picked my way cautiously over butterflies listing on the walkway in their enclosure at the Melbourne Zoo. But the winter destination for the Monarch Butterfly in Mexico looks to me, from this photograph (Figure 1.1), to be another thing altogether. For here, I see them gathering in flocks, their iridescent wings making a deciduous autumn of evergreen firs. While still more, in their thousands, fly every which way. From this photograph, I feel the air pulsing from their festive movement, I hear the percussive rhythm of their wings and I inhale the coniferous scents stirred in their carnival. I imagine my enchanted self, there, one of those people, in this photograph, hands on hips, gazing in wonder at those butterflies.

My response to this photograph describes an aesthetic appreciation of the natural environment that has been theorised in the philosophy of environmental aesthetics.[1] This is a form of aesthetic appreciation that has been distinguished from theories of aesthetic value of the arts.[2] But the photograph comes from another discipline – international environmental law, a specialism of international law that includes treaties agreed between nation states to protect the environment.[3] Specifically, the photograph is one of several images contained in a document of the Mexican government nominating the Monarch Butterfly Biosphere Reserve for recognition under the *World Heritage Convention*.[4] The Mexican property was ultimately inscribed in the World Heritage List on the basis of 'aesthetic' and 'natural beauty' values.[5] The treaty protects natural properties deemed by the World Heritage Committee to be of 'outstanding universal value' from these and other points of view.[6] It is, however, not clear what, if any, bearing the photographs in Mexico's nomination document had on the World Heritage Committee's determination of aesthetic value.

This image set me on a path of analysing for this book many more photographs used by nation states in the international processes created to protect the environment's aesthetic value under international law. My analysis has two aims. First, to consider how the environment's aesthetic value is represented in the photographs. In addition to the *World Heritage Convention*, I examine photographic images used in decision-making processes of two other treaties that demand an understanding of the

[1] See Brady, 'Aesthetic value, nature, and environment', 186; Carlson, 'Ten steps', 13. In Section 1.1, I discuss other vantages of aesthetic appreciation, including critical perspectives.

[2] See generally Levinson, 'Philosophical aesthetics', 3.

[3] See generally Sands and Peel, *Principles of International Environmental Law*; Boyle and Redgwell, *Birnie, Boyle and Redgwell's International Law and the Environment*; cf. Alam et al. (eds.), *International Environmental Law and the Global South*. See also Rajamani and Peel, 'International environmental law', 1.

[4] *Convention for the Protection of the World Cultural and Natural Heritage*, Paris, 16 November 1972, in force 17 December 1975, 1037 UNTS 151. See further Chapter 5.

[5] Article 2, ibid. For inscription, see World Heritage Committee, *Monarch Butterfly Biosphere Reserve (Mexico)*, Decision 32 COM 8B.17, UN Doc. WHC-08/32.COM/24Rev.

[6] Article 2 of the *World Heritage Convention* refers to aesthetic, scientific, conservation or natural beauty points of view as elements of 'outstanding universal value'; properties can be listed on the basis of multiple criteria, and as a mix of natural and cultural heritage: World Heritage Committee, *Operational Guidelines for the Implementation of the World Heritage Convention*, UN Doc. WHC.21/01, paras. [46] (mixed properties) and [77] (criteria).

environment's aesthetic value: The *Whaling Convention*,[7] and the *Biodiversity Convention*.[8] My second aim is to understand the relationship between the photographic images and the decisions of international bodies that judge the environment's aesthetic value under those treaties.[9] Finding no official account of the aesthetic values represented in the photographs, I go on to develop my own. I critique conceptions of the environment's aesthetic value that are conflated with singular notions of natural beauty typical of landscapes in Anglo-American and Western European art.[10] I then propose understandings of the environment's aesthetic worth that are sensitive to the likely plural conceptions of aesthetic value among the many nations that commit to international environmental treaties.

I turn to the photographs because I see them as representing the environment's aesthetic value in ways not acknowledged in the prosaic practice of international environmental law.[11] These ways matter for law. A clear understanding of what it means to value the environment on an 'aesthetic' basis might matter to compliance with those treaties that invoke the value by their terms and in their practice.[12] But a recognition that meanings of aesthetic value may be derived from photographic representations also goes to the integrity of the treaty processes that admit them. Proper legal procedure demands that those projections of aesthetic value be acknowledged by international bodies for any part they may play in the decisions that emerge from the processes that make, implement and enforce international environmental law.[13]

The trouble is that orthodox practices of international law lack the concepts and means to see more than facts from photographs.[14] And so it is that I come

7 *International Convention on the Regulation of Whaling*, Washington, 2 December 1946, in force 10 November 1948, 161 UNTS 72.

8 *Convention on Biological Diversity*, Rio de Janeiro, 5 June 1992, in force 29 December 1993, 1760 UNTS 79. See 'values' in Conference of the Parties to the *Convention on Biological Diversity*, *The Strategic Plan for Biodiversity*, UN Doc. UNEP/CBD/COP/DEC/X/2, annex para. [13].

9 On judgment and judgement as it relates to aesthetics in law, see generally Manderson, 'Judgment in law and the humanities'. In this book, 'judgment' refers to legal judgment and 'judgement' refers to aesthetic judgement.

10 On landscape and natural beauty, see generally Kemal and Gaskell (eds.), *Landscape, Natural Beauty and the Arts*, p. 1. For eco-critical perspectives, see Braddock and Irmscher (eds.), *A Keener Perception*.

11 On words and meaning, see d'Aspremont, 'Wording in international law'. Cf. Rose, Wewerinke-Singh and Miranda, 'Primal scene to anthropocene'.

12 For a political science perspective, see Mitchell, 'Compliance theory', 887.

13 See generally Kingsbury, 'Global environmental governance', 63. See also Voigt (ed.), *International Judicial Practice on the Environment*.

14 See Chapter 6.

to rely on aestheticians – aesthetic philosophers, scholars of art history and criticism, artists and art practitioners – in my analysis of images for law. Theirs is a field that is expert both in concepts of the environment's aesthetic value, and in ideas and methods that can be employed in the task of understanding images as representations of such concepts.[15] I show in the book the ways in which images of the environment's aesthetic value are already there in the photographs used by states in the decision-making processes of international environmental treaties. As static images of natural environments judged as having aesthetic value, photographs are well suited to the demands of a legal process that documents reasons for decisions.[16] It is just that the photographs are not yet being seen in those processes for their meanings.[17] Understood and analysed as representations, the photographs could be embraced as forms of legal argument, interpretation and judgment in international law.

Ultimately, this book combines different vantages on aesthetics – the philosophy of environmental aesthetics, together with aesthetic theories and methods for the visual arts – to analyse images for critical meanings of the environment's aesthetic value relevant to international environmental treaties. This is the book's very specific ambition. But there is a broader ambition for my analysis too. By employing aesthetic ideas and methods to analyse photographs as representations, the book points to the ways in which meanings could be made from images for the administration of international laws more widely. The result is a unique jurisprudential account of aesthetic meanings and methods, engaging in an interdisciplinary examination of image for international law. It draws from different philosophies of aesthetics, and legal theories of image, to give significance to the aesthetic value of the environment in international environmental law.[18] My findings in the book also equip the practice of international law in general with aesthetic methods for making, and critically analysing, meanings from photographs in international decision-making. In so doing, I contribute to a reorientation of the contemplation of aesthetic value for jurisprudents and practitioners of international environmental law.[19]

15 See Chapter 4.
16 See Chapter 5.
17 See generally Douzinas and Nead, 'Introduction', 1.
18 See Chapter 4. Cf. on image and international law, Goodrich, 'The international signs law', 365; Miles, 'Painting international law as universal'; Miles, 'Visuality of a treaty'; Charlesworth, 'The travels of human rights', 173; Palmer, 'Absent images of international law', 91.
19 Cf. Gillespie, *International Environmental Law, Policy and Ethics*, 2nd edn. See further Chapter 2.

In this first chapter, I explain what lies within the frame of my inquiry in the book. I briefly demonstrate how my different aesthetic vantages can shape understandings of the environment's aesthetic value, before providing an outline of how those vantages intersect throughout the book. My conception of the terms 'aesthetic', 'image' and 'international environmental law' are explained there. I conclude the chapter with an explanation of the materials and scholarly orientations that guide my analysis of the environment's aesthetic value for international law.

1.1 AESTHETIC VANTAGES

There are many vantages from which to understand aesthetic values from an image of the environment. Below I consider vantages in the philosophy of environmental aesthetics, aesthetic philosophy of visual art, and the practice of international environmental law, to highlight differences in and among them.

1.1.1 *Environmental Aesthetics*

My description of the photograph submitted by Mexico to the World Heritage Committee at the outset of this chapter (Figure 1.1) is a reflection on a sensorial experience shaped by my imagination, emotion and my knowledge, informed by personal experiences and cultural influences. From the photographs, I imagine the sights, sounds, touch and scents of the place in ways personal to me. This is the aesthetic value of 'subjectivists' in the philosophy of environmental aesthetics.[20] For those philosophers, aesthetic value is a personal or intuited value understood differently by different people. My aesthetic imagining of swarming butterflies in terms of delight, for example, could be viewed by others with a sense of dread – the furtive movement of the insects a disquieting sign of looming disaster.[21] In contrast, some philosophers have argued that knowledge, including scientific knowledge, is integral to the aesthetic value of the environment.[22] These 'objectivists' say that an aesthetic sensibility informed by scientific insight – a sense of awe arising from the knowledge of the migratory feat of the butterflies, for example – draws on objective information that is not personal to any one individual.[23]

[20] Also described as 'non-cognitivists', see Brady, *Aesthetics of the Natural Environment*, p. 87. For non-cognitivist appreciation of butterflies, see p. 135; cf. p. 138.

[21] See generally Brady, *The Sublime in Modern Philosophy*.

[22] See, for example, Allen Carlson's 'Natural environmental model' in Carlson, *Aesthetics and the Environment*, p. 6. On positive aesthetics, see p. 72.

[23] On objectivist and subjectivist orientations, see ibid., p. xix.

Environmental aestheticians work within a broader field of Western aesthetic philosophy that includes theorists, historians, critics and practitioners in the arts.[24] However, scholars of environmental aesthetics debate the relationship between first-hand aesthetic experiences of the natural environment, on the one hand, and the aesthetic appreciation of images that is analysed in, for example, art theory and practice, on the other hand. From the vantage of some philosophers of environmental aesthetics, aesthetic concepts for the arts, such as 'natural beauty', can inform, but do not alone determine, aesthetic sensations in the natural environment.[25]

1.1.2 *Aesthetics of Visual Art*

Despite a resurgence in scholarship on aesthetics of the natural environment taking hold in the 1960s,[26] the arts, including visual art, have been the principal focus of Western aesthetic philosophy since the nineteenth century.[27] An aesthetic analysis of the photograph in Mexico's World Heritage nomination document as an artwork – as opposed to the *in situ* appreciation of the environment depicted in the photograph – could take any number of approaches.[28] The photograph could be appreciated aesthetically for such things as its formal qualities, its signs and its symbols. For example, the photograph has a nostalgic, saturated hue. From this I might wonder if the butterflies are now lost to us, another casualty of the Anthropocene.[29] Equally, I could question whether the image has been altered – a wash skilfully added, contrasts manipulated – to emphasise the supernatural powers of the insects.

There are different ways in which the image might also be analysed for its many contexts.[30] I might for example discover that the photograph has been cropped so that we do not see the crowd of tourists alighting a bus outside the frame. I might also see it as a depiction of natural beauty, or of the sublime or even of the picturesque – all terms of art with particular meanings that have

[24] See generally Levinson, 'Philosophical aesthetics', 3.

[25] See, for example, Kemal and Gaskell, 'Nature, fine arts, and aesthetics', 1. See further Section 2.2.1.

[26] See Hepburn, 'Contemporary aesthetics'; Carlson, 'Ten steps', 13. See further Chapter 2.

[27] See, for example, Stecker, *Aesthetics and the Philosophy of Art*, p. 3. See generally Fisher, 'Environmental aesthetics', 667.

[28] I describe here different aesthetic methods developed in Chapters 5–7.

[29] On threats, see, for example, World Heritage Committee, *Monarch Butterfly Biosphere Reserve*. See also World Heritage Centre, 'Sadness and concern'. On 'anthropocene', a contested term for a current geological era of human-induced change, see, for example, Jagodzinski (ed.), *Interrogating the Anthropocene*.

[30] See generally Davies and Alperson, *The Philosophy of Art*.

FIGURE 1.2. Diana Thater, *Untitled Videowall (Butterflies)*, 2008. Installation view at the ICA Watershed, Boston, 2018. © Diana Thater. Courtesy the artist and David Zwirner. Photo: Kerry McFate.

evolved in aesthetic philosophy in respect to landscape art.[31] I could also assume a critical view of the image, including an eco-critical view informed by artworks and art history, as well as by natural history and socio-political critique, extending to matters relevant to First Nations peoples and matters of colonialism.[32]

The video installation *Untitled Videowall (Butterflies)* (Figure 1.2), by artist Diana Thater, for example, is a contemporary artwork that enables a critical comparison with Mexico's photograph. Thater's work shows monarch butterflies on screens underfoot. It speaks to human constructions and framings of nature: Recorded, dissected, enlarged and illuminated, nature is visible and resilient.[33] However, the technological intervention also isolates, divides and renders nature surreal and superficial. The viewers of the work seen here

[31] See Brady, *Aesthetics of the Natural Environment*, p. 32.

[32] See Braddock and Irmscher (eds.), *A Keener Perception*. Cf. Elkins, *The End of Diversity in Art Historical Writing*. See further Chapter 4. In this book, 'First Nations' is used interchangeably with 'Indigenous' peoples while the *Biodiversity Convention* refers to 'indigenous' communities and their knowledges.

[33] Cf. Godden, 'Preserving natural heritage'.

look down, not up, they are looking in, not out, as they themselves perform the disassociation of humans from nature. The artwork beckons them in a critical contemplation of a human/nature divide.[34]

Referencing Thater's artwork in my aesthetic analysis of Mexico's photograph submitted to the World Heritage Committee, I might note the separation between humans and nature evident in the distinct protections of natural and cultural heritage under the *World Heritage Convention*.[35] So it is that the people in Mexico's photograph gaze upon nature as a curiosity, they are visitors to an alien world from which they stand apart. But *Untitled Videowall (Butterflies)* invites viewers to see past divisions where the natural world in Mexico's photograph is whole, and the butterfly migration from Canada and the United States to Mexico takes place without regard for walls or political borders. Although it should be observed that these are no ordinary people absorbed by nature in Mexico's photograph. The man to the right is Prince Philip, the late consort of the British Queen. A monarch gazing on monarchs. His pate aglow with beneficence. What might he have seen when he looked down his upturned nose as Empire?[36]

1.1.3 *International Environmental Law*

The vantages of aesthetic philosophers evident from an analysis of Mexico's photograph of the Monarch Butterfly Biosphere Reserve are different from each other – their perspectives on the environment and on images of the environment can differ. It is, however, not clear that any of those views corresponds to the vantage point of international environmental lawyers in their understanding of the legal qualities and outcomes of World Heritage determinations of outstanding universal value from an 'aesthetic' point of view, for the purposes of Article 2 of the *World Heritage Convention*.[37]

Mexico's photograph is included in the nation state's nomination document to the World Heritage Committee,[38] and it has been published under the 'gallery' tab dedicated to the property in the online World Heritage List.[39] However, the status of the photograph as a source of international law, or for

[34] On Diana Thater's engagement with environmental subject matter, see, for example, Ballard, 'Portfolio: Diana Thater'.

[35] Articles 1 and 2 of the *World Heritage Convention*. See Chapter 5.

[36] See Chapter 7. See further MacKenzie, *The Empire of Nature*, p. 202.

[37] See, for example, Redgwell, 'Article 2 definition of natural heritage', 64. See also Gillespie, 'Ethical considerations', 217.

[38] Mexico, *World Heritage Site Nomination Document*.

[39] World Heritage List, *Monarch Butterfly Biosphere Reserve (Mexico)*.

international treaty interpretation, which might elaborate on the meaning of aesthetic value for the treaty, is not certain: Such sources are commonly derived from written texts.[40] A more likely source then for understanding the aesthetic point of view adopted for the treaty is the Statement of Outstanding Universal Value endorsed by the World Heritage Committee in its decision to inscribe the property.[41] It explains the aesthetic and natural beauty values for the Monarch Butterfly Biosphere Reserve in the following terms:

> The overwintering concentration of the monarch butterfly in the property is the most dramatic manifestation of the phenomenon of insect migration. Up to a billion monarch butterflies return annually, from breeding areas as far away as Canada, to land in close-packed clusters within 14 overwintering colonies in the oyamel fir forests of central Mexico. The property protects 8 of these colonies and an estimated 70% of the total overwintering population of the monarch butterfly's eastern population.[42]

The superlatives, numbers and percentages expressed in the Statement of Outstanding Universal Value could be seen to speak to measures and comparison consistent with the vantage of an aesthetic philosophy tied to science. There is, however, no mention of the 'aesthetic' or 'natural beauty' points of view posited in the treaty and referenced in the criterion against which the property was assessed. The measured bureaucratic prose provides little insight into the aesthetic qualities of the natural phenomenon that has been afforded the World Heritage imprimatur and consequent protection under the *World Heritage Convention*.[43]

1.2 INTERSECTING VANTAGES

These three different vantages on aesthetic value – the philosophy of environmental aesthetics and of the arts, and the practice of international environmental law – are examined in Chapters 2 to 4, and then employed through case studies of my three treaties in Chapters 5 to 7, before I conclude the book with Chapter 8. Each chapter features an artwork 'exhibit' that I analyse from aesthetic perspectives to introduce the themes addressed, and the methods of

[40] In accordance with the *Vienna Convention on the Law of Treaties*, Vienna, 23 May 1969, in force 27 January 1980, 1155 UNTS 331. On written sources, see Gardiner, *Treaty Interpretation*, p. 255. See further Section 3.5.1.

[41] World Heritage Committee, *Monarch Butterfly Biosphere Reserve*.

[42] World Heritage Committee, *Monarch Butterfly Biosphere Reserve (Mexico)*, Statement of Outstanding Universal Value.

[43] Cf. reference to sounds, ibid. See further Chapter 5.

analysis applied, in the relevant chapter. Together with artworks that are also featured within the chapters, the images make an exhibition: They 'tell a story alongside the text but do not illustrate it directly'.[44]

1.2.1 *Scholarship and Practice on Aesthetics and Image*

Chapters 2 to 4 explain and examine different approaches to understanding the term 'aesthetic' in aesthetic philosophy, and in the philosophy and practice of law. Chapter 2 outlines the principal themes of the philosophy of environmental aesthetics before examining the ways in which scholars of international environmental law have characterised aesthetic value as an environmental value. I explain conceptions of the 'natural environment' and 'nature' in terms of environmental aesthetics, paying particular attention to the scholarship of Emily Brady, a prominent philosopher of environmental aesthetics whose integrated theory of environmental aesthetics informs my characterisation of the aesthetic value of the environment through the remainder of the book.[45] The chapter then addresses scholarship on international environmental law that has examined the 'aesthetic' value of the environment protected under the terms of several international environmental treaties. Scholars recognise aesthetic value as one of several environmental values motivating states in their international agreement to protect the environment. Several associate aesthetic value with natural beauty and most conceive of environmental values in terms of the philosophy of environmental ethics as opposed to the philosophy of aesthetics that I employ in the book.[46]

The practice of international environmental law, as a specialist discipline of international law, relies on customary rules of treaty interpretation to construct meanings for terms in international treaties.[47] In Chapter 3, I employ these doctrinal methods of treaty interpretation to define 'aesthetic' value for the three international treaties that form the basis of my case studies in Chapters 5 to 7: The *World Heritage Convention* and the *Biodiversity Convention*, in which 'aesthetic' value is an express term, and the *Whaling Convention* where, for reasons I explain, aesthetic value informs the interpretation of the treaty. This orthodox approach to treaty interpretation is a 'vantage' point available in international environmental law to construct meanings for the environment's

[44] Tsing, *The Mushroom at the End of the World.*
[45] For Brady's scholarship, see further Section 2.2.3.
[46] See Section 2.3.2.
[47] Codified in the *Vienna Convention.* See generally Gardiner, *Treaty.*

'aesthetic' value. My doctrinal analysis of the 'aesthetic' value protected by international environmental treaties develops meanings associated with the sensorial appreciation theorised in environmental aesthetics. However, the practice of the states parties to the treaties is suggestive of aesthetic values that are conflated with natural beauty, cultural value and ethical concerns.[48]

As explained earlier, the orthodox sources contemplated in the service of treaty interpretation are written texts.[49] However, the practices of international bodies that are suggestive of agreed meanings of aesthetic value under the three treaties are replete with photographs of the environment.[50] In Chapter 4, I consider the relevance of image to international environmental law as I prepare to analyse the photographs of the natural environment used in international environmental treaty processes that protect aesthetic value. It is here that I explain the distinction made in aesthetic philosophy between graphic images and other visual images such as optical, verbal, mental or perceptual images.[51] After reviewing the literature on aesthetic philosophy of the arts, I describe the legal scholarship on aesthetics, and the specific treatments of 'image' in what is known as visual jurisprudence, alternatively described by Desmond Manderson as 'imaginal law'.[52] Jurisprudents of aesthetics maintain that the iconoclasm of the European Reformation shifted law's authority from the emotionally encumbered images of the Catholic Church to the dispassionate authority of the posited word.[53] Most of this theoretical work has been from the perspective of *domestic* law, specifically common and civil law, with only some scholars addressing the relationship between *international* law and aesthetics.[54] They do not appear to have combined understandings of image in the aesthetic philosophy for the arts, with the distinct study of environmental aesthetics, to analyse the concept of aesthetic value as an expression of international environmental law.[55] This is the task I undertake in the remaining chapters.

48 See Chapter 3.

49 See Section 1.1.3.

50 See Section 1.2.2.

51 Mitchell, *Iconology*, p. 10. See further Chapter 4. References to 'graphic' image refer to form as opposed to e.g. vivid images.

52 Manderson, 'Introduction: Imaginal law', 4, citing Bottici, *Imaginal Politics*.

53 See, for example, Douzinas and Nead, 'Introduction', 8.

54 See Chapter 4. Cf. literary perspectives in Morgan, *The Aesthetics of International Law*; O'Connell, *The Art of Law in the International Community*; Simpson, *Sentimental Life of International Law*.

55 Cf. Palmer, 'Legal dimensions'; Palmer, 'Image and art in the *Whaling in the Antarctic Case*', 408. On environmental law more broadly, see Richardson, Barritt and Bowman, 'Beauty'; Richardson, *The Art of Environmental Law*.

1.2.2 *Aesthetic Value of the Environment in Photographs*

Chapters 5 to 7 examine understandings of aesthetic value from images used in decision-making processes of my three case study treaties: The 1972 *World Heritage Convention*; the 1982 amendment to the 1946 *Whaling Convention* to ban commercial whaling;[56] and the 1992 *Biodiversity Convention*. The environments valued for their aesthetic qualities under the treaties represent an evolution spanning decades in international environmental law from the protection of species and spaces to systems.[57] That the parties to the treaties represent a diverse range of aesthetic traditions is also relevant to my analysis of different cultural appreciations of the environment's aesthetic value: Each treaty has a large number of states parties from different regions of the world.[58]

In Chapter 5, I analyse from the perspective of environmental aesthetics and art theory, two forms of image created in the process of inscribing natural properties in the World Heritage List for their aesthetic value under the *World Heritage Convention*: Verbal images in the Statements of Outstanding Universal Value endorsed by the World Heritage Committee; and photographs submitted by states parties in nominations of natural properties to the World Heritage List. There I find that the World Heritage Committee is uncritical in its use of concepts and methods associated with aesthetic theory and unclear about the role of photographs in determinations of aesthetic value under the *World Heritage Convention*. I argue that a reasoned determination of aesthetic value should engage concepts and methods developed in aesthetic philosophy to evaluate the aesthetic value of natural properties nominated for inscription on the World Heritage List. Recourse to aesthetic philosophy would include understanding and accounting for the role of photographs as representations of aesthetic value in the decision-making process under the treaty, as well as providing an aesthetic basis for interpreting those representations. These are representations of aesthetic value that nominating nation

56 Clause 10(e) of the schedule to the *Whaling Convention*. See International Whaling Convention, 'Verbatim record', 19–24 July 1982, 72, 86. I use the term 'ban' rather than 'moratorium'. See further Chapter 6.

57 See, for example, Sands and Peel, *Principles of International Environmental Law*, 21.

58 As at 30 June 2022, the *World Heritage Convention* and *Convention on Biological Diversity* have near universal membership of 194 and 196 parties, respectively: United Nations Educational, Scientific and Cultural Organisation, 'World Heritage Convention: States Parties', whc.unesco .org/en/statesparties; United Nations Treaty Collection, 'Depository: Status of treaties', treaties .un.org. The contracting members of the *Whaling Convention* have fluctuated, made up as at 30 June 2022 of 88 states: See www.state.gov/depositary-status-lists.

states claim is 'outstanding and universal', and that the World Heritage Committee might ultimately judge to be so. And behind the claims and judgements of aesthetic value is an interpretation represented in the image.

Chapter 6 progresses away from judgements of aesthetic value in the administration of an international environmental treaty to representations of the environment's aesthetic value in the context of enforcement. Specifically, it undertakes an aesthetic analysis of the photographic images submitted by the parties to the International Court of Justice (ICJ) in the *Whaling in the Antarctic* case.[59] That dispute, between Australia and Japan, concerned an exception to bans on whaling for scientific research under the *Whaling Convention*.[60] The chapter identifies the photographs of whales used in the ICJ proceedings before considering their potential role as evidence and as rhetoric. For this purpose, I characterise rhetoric as a legitimate means of legal argument.[61] I explain that the formal practice of the ICJ is limited to conceptions of photographic images as evidence. Like my analysis in connection with the *World Heritage Convention*, my findings in Chapter 6 show again that the capacity for photographs to convey meanings relevant to decisions made under international treaties is not acknowledged in the formal practices of the international bodies authorised to make those decisions. To appreciate the rhetorical significance of the photos, I argue that aesthetic theory must be employed first to understand the photographs as representations of aesthetic values rather than records of fact – something physical or manifest in 'reality'.

In Chapter 7, I consider the extent to which photographs used in the institutional work of the *Biodiversity Convention* contribute to an understanding of aesthetic value and its relationship to the cultural value of biodiversity also protected under the treaty. Through an analysis of photographs used in the fourth *Global Biodiversity Outlook* (GBO-4),[62] I find that representations of biodiversity values are incoherent, suggesting fragmented meanings of aesthetic values as scenic beauty, wilderness, culture and subsistence. Expert advisors to the parties to the treaty have recognised that the aesthetic value of biodiversity cannot be reduced to the economic valuations of biodiversity common to parties' assessments of biodiversity values.[63] I argue that a critical

59 *Whaling in the Antarctic (Australia v. Japan; New Zealand intervening) (Judgment)* [2014] ICJ Rep 226.

60 Article VIII of the *Whaling Convention*.

61 See generally Scobbie, 'Rhetoric, persuasion, and interpretation', 61. See further Chapter 6.

62 Secretariat of the *Convention on Biological Diversity*, *Global Biodiversity Outlook 4*.

63 See, for example, Leadley et al., *Progress towards the Aichi Biodiversity Targets*, p. 12.

aesthetic analysis of photographs of biodiversity can serve to articulate pluralised appreciations of biodiversity in terms not associated with economic gains for the state. This would, I maintain, assist understandings of biodiversity values that the parties identified through their Aichi Targets as fundamental to implementing the *Biodiversity Convention*.[64]

1.2.3 *Representations in Images for International Law*

The concluding Chapter 8 returns to the aims of the book to reflect critically on the environment's aesthetic value represented in photographs in the processes of international environmental treaties. Noting that international bodies making decisions under the three treaties examined in the book conflate and displace aesthetic value in favour of other environmental values, I consider these bodies at risk of having compromised the integrity of their decision-making processes and, ultimately, the protection of the environment.

I conclude that photographs of the environment submitted in international decision-making processes should be used to conceive aesthetic appreciation of the environment in ways important for all nation states. Such a conception would encapsulate a sensorial experience of the natural environment that is shaped by imagination, emotion and knowledge from different cultures.[65] But it would also reflect critical perspectives that understand aesthetic value as related but distinct from other environmental values such as natural beauty, cultural value and ethical value.[66] I maintain that, interrogated through images, the aesthetic value of the natural environment could be judged properly, together with other environmental values, to justify the cooperative efforts of a plurality of states in environmental protection.

In Chapter 8, I also address the broader consequences of my analysis to consider ways of working with aesthetic method in the practice of the three treaties and in international law more widely. I maintain that international law has not developed concepts or methods for understanding photographic images as representations with meanings relevant to legal interpretation and judgment. I conclude that aesthetic methods must be repurposed to identify images in the decision-making processes of international law and to articulate their role and significance in the making, implementation and enforcement of international law.

64 Ibid.

65 See generally Brady, *Aesthetics of the Natural Environment.*

66 For example, Braddock and Irmscher (eds.), *A Keener Perception*. Cf. Elkins, *The End of Diversity in Art Historical Writing.*

1.3 MATERIALS AND ORIENTATIONS

This book provides a jurisprudential account of aesthetics for the practice of international environmental law.[67] In this task, I assume an interdisciplinary orientation in law and the humanities,[68] using aesthetic philosophy to examine the doctrinal forms, conduct and methods of international law. In part, I take up for international law the challenge articulated by Kreitner, Rosenberg and Tomlins: 'Use of arts as sources and as theory in legal history awaits explanation, theorization, even introduction.'[69] But I also engage the less prominent field of the philosophy of environmental aesthetics which, I explained earlier, concerns the natural environment, as distinct from the aesthetic theories on representations of the environment in the arts that are more commonly referenced in legal scholarship on aesthetics.[70] These encounters of different scholarly orientations explain the range of primary materials across disciplines, as well as some points of distinction among scholars and practitioners in the different disciplines, that are relevant to my analysis.

1.3.1 *Primary Materials from International Law and the Visual Arts*

The principal objects of my inquiry are photographs that have been used by nation states in decision-making processes of international bodies relevant to the environment's aesthetic value. They are: Inscriptions of natural properties on the World Heritage List by the World Heritage Committee in its administration of the *World Heritage Convention*;[71] the judgment of the ICJ in *Whaling in the Antarctic* in its adjudication of a dispute between Australia and Japan under the *Whaling Convention*;[72] and the decision of the Conference of the Parties agreeing to the 'Aichi Targets' for the implementation of the *Biodiversity Convention*.[73] My analysis relies on a combination of treaty texts, formal rules governing the decision-making processes of the

[67] On concepts of 'jurisprudence' in both modern and postmodern terms, see Douzinas, Warrington and McVeigh, *Postmodern Jurisprudence*.

[68] See, for example, Sarat, Anderson and Frank (eds.), *Law and the Humanities*; Stern, Del Mar and Meyler (eds.), *The Oxford Handbook of Law and Humanities*. Cf. Douzinas, 'A short history of the British critical legal conference'.

[69] Kreitner, Rosenberg and Tomlins, 'Arts and the aesthetic'.

[70] See Section 1.1.1.

[71] Article 11 of the *World Heritage Convention*.

[72] *Whaling in the Antarctic*.

[73] Leadley et al., *Progress towards the Aichi Biodiversity Targets*.

relevant bodies, and legal decisions arising from those processes. Aspects of the 'environment' depicted in the photographs and valued for their aesthetic value under the three treaties are, respectively, natural properties, whales and biological diversity. The photographs are featured in: Documents submitted by states parties nominating natural properties to the World Heritage Committee for inscription;[74] written and oral submissions to the ICJ by the states parties to the *Whaling in the Antarctic* dispute; and *GBO-4*,[75] a report that is periodically commissioned for the Conference of the Parties to the *Biodiversity Convention* from scientific and policy experts.[76] Table 1.1 summarises these different features of the three case studies.

In identifying and analysing artworks for this book, my focus has been on visual art from collections of art museums, and featured in art exhibitions, in Australia, Europe, the United Kingdom and the United States.[77] In particular, I have been guided in my selection of visual art by the expert opinion of art historians, critics and curators, evident from academic literature and curatorial selections for exhibitions.[78] Artworks referenced include paintings, drawings, prints and mixed-media sculptural installations as well as audio-visual works. I rely on historical and contemporary works in different genres from artists born and working in countries in Africa and Europe and from Australia, Colombia, India, Japan, the United Kingdom and the United States. Images of select artworks are featured in the book.

1.3.2 *Points of Distinction among Theories and Practices*

This book highlights and develops several points of distinction for the philosophy and practice of international environmental law, visual jurisprudence, and the philosophy of environmental aesthetics. For international

74 *WHC Operational Guidelines*, UN Doc. WHC.21/01.

75 Secretariat of the *Convention on Biological Diversity*, *Global Biodiversity Outlook* 4.

76 Conference of the Parties to the *Convention on Biological Diversity*, *Report of the Second Meeting of the Conference of the Parties to the Convention on Biological Diversity*, UN Doc. UNEP/CBD/COP/2/19. For the fifth iteration, see Secretariat of the *Convention on Biological Diversity*, *Global Biodiversity Outlook* 5.

77 Including: National Gallery of Victoria, Trienniel 2021; *May You Live in Interesting Times*, Biennale Arte 2019 (58th International Art Exhibition) Venice, Italy; *Viva Arte Viva*, Biennale Arte 2017 (57th International Art Exhibition) Venice, Italy; *All the World's Futures*, Biennale Arte 2015 (56th International Art Exhibition) Venice, Italy; *Skulptur Projekte Münster 2017*, Münster, Germany; *Learning From Athens*, Documenta 14, Kassel, Germany, 2017. I attended exhibitions at a range of museums and galleries in Europe and Britain (Berlin, Edinburgh, Paris, London, Marseille, Venice) and in Australia and New Zealand (Adelaide, Brisbane, Hobart, Perth, Melbourne and Greater Victoria, Sydney, Auckland, Wellington).

78 On artistic merit, see, for example, Davies, *The Philosophy of Art*, p. 23. See also Levinson, 'Artistic worth and personal taste'; Schama, *Wordy*.

TABLE 1.1. *Features of the case studies on World Heritage, whales and biodiversity*

		World Heritage	Whales	Biodiversity
Features	International environmental treaty	1972 *World Heritage Convention*	1982 amendment to 1946 *Whaling Convention*	1992 *Biodiversity Convention*
	Aesthetic value as a treaty term	Express in Article 2 definition of 'natural heritage'	Informs ban on commercial whaling in Schedule	Express in preamble
	Decision under treaty	Inscriptions of natural properties to World Heritage List, various years	Judgment in *Whaling in the Antarctic* case, 2014	Decision agreeing to Aichi Targets, 2010
	International body making decisions	World Heritage Committee	International Court of Justice	Conference of the Parties
	Supporting documentation containing photographs	Nomination files of parties	Written and oral submissions of parties	Fourth Global Biodiversity Outlook, 2014
	Institutional rules on use of photographs	Guidelines of the World Heritage Committee	Rules of evidence	None identified from the public record

environmental law, the book attends to 'aesthetic' value as an environmental value at a time when it has received relatively little attention in the scholarship on international environmental law.[79] As explained earlier, that scholarship has focused on environmental ethics.[80] For scholars of environmental values

79 Cf. Gillespie, *International Environmental Law, Policy and Ethics*, 1st and 2nd edns. See further Chapter 2.

80 Note I do not engage theories of wild law relevant to 'intrinsic' values: See, for example, Maloney and Burden (eds.), *Wild Law: In Practice*. See discussion of 'Wild Law' as a function of 'ecolegality' in Davies, *Asking the Law Question*, p. 451. Cf. Davies, 'Consciousness of trees'.

in international environmental law, I conceive of 'aesthetic' value as a term of law to be interpreted in accordance with the international rules of treaty interpretation in a manner sensitive to environmental aesthetics and eco-critical theory. In contrast to most philosophers of international environmental law,[81] my theoretical foundation for this task is aesthetic philosophy rather than environmental ethics.

In my treatment of international environmental law, I move between doctrine and theory. I shift from dogmatic international law as a system of legal sources, to jurisprudence as a normative endeavour that relates to the proper conduct of law.[82] Inevitably, I come up against tensions between those approaches. I am aware of international legal theory critical of international environmental law as a statist vehicle that promotes the economic interests of the minority of rich states over environmental protection in the majority of poorer, often formerly colonised, developing states that constitute the Global South.[83] I nevertheless maintain normative aspirations for an international law capable of protecting the environment on a global and fair basis.[84] I advocate for a conception of the environment's 'aesthetic' value protected by treaties that can be valued by all nation states that are party to those treaties – albeit on a relative, pluralised basis – in ways articulated by philosophers of environmental aesthetics, and determined by means developed by scholars and practitioners of the visual arts.[85]

This book also extends jurisprudential scholarship on law and aesthetics – specifically visual jurisprudence – to international law, as opposed to law in domestic settings. But in contrast to scholars of visual jurisprudence, I develop a theory of image for law that relies not only on aesthetic understandings of art but which also borrows from the aesthetic philosophy of environmental aesthetics to interrogate images of the environment.[86] Visual jurisprudents might wonder at my conception of image as 'record' for the purposes of doctrinal approaches to evidence: They might conceive of images as always 'representation', regardless of the purpose served by a photographic image in

81 See Chapter 2.
82 On the relationship between practice and theory, see generally Orford and Hoffmann, 'Introduction', 1; Bianchi, *International Law Theories*. See also Cass, 'Navigating the newstream'.
83 See generally Natarajan, 'Third world approaches', 207; Humby, 'Evaluating the value'; Mickelson, 'South, north'.
84 See Prost and Torres Camprubí, 'Against fairness?'. See generally d'Aspremont, *International Law as a Belief System*.
85 See Maskit, 'On universalism', 41.
86 Cf. Ben-Dor (ed.), *Law and Art*.

legal process.[87] I contend, however, that the very particular confluence of the three aesthetic vantages addressed in this book – aesthetics of art, environmental aesthetics, and the environment's aesthetic value as a term of law – requires me to entertain different roles for image in light of those different vantages in the practice of international environmental law.

I am, in the book, proposing meanings of aesthetic value and methods by which such meanings might be developed from aesthetic scholarship for law and legal practice. There is for my purposes no study necessary in any empirical sense of how international bodies may have in fact formed meanings of the environment's aesthetic value from photographs in determinations reached under the relevant treaties. I maintain that images have persuasive potential as rhetoric but I do not set out to prove, in ways that psychological studies might, that persuasion is manifest in the decisions of international bodies.[88] But my attention to photographs of the environment does also beg questions for other theories taking hold in international law that rest on various understandings of materiality.[89] The photographs may take a physical form; and they have a complex relationship to the physical environment caught by the camera's lens.[90] One such theoretical orientation, 'new materialism', has particular relevance to matters of the environment in international law as it extends conceptions of materiality to the non-human.[91] But it, like other possible lines of inquiry raised by the many issues I interrogate in this book, remains a matter for further study.[92] It is, for now, the convergence of vantages on aesthetics as they relate to the visual in international environmental law that is my focus.

Finally, the book develops a practical application for scholarship on environmental aesthetics. As noted earlier, philosophers of environmental aesthetics generally assert that the aesthetic value of the environment is different from the aesthetic appreciation of art. As such, my analysis of the environment's aesthetic value from photographs, in ways analogous to the aesthetic appreciation of visual art, would likely be problematic for environmental

87 For example, Peter Goodrich argues that images cannot be 'depictions of the real': Goodrich, 'Imago decidendi', 14. See further Goodrich, 'Retinal justice'.

88 Compare scholarship on visual image in environmental activism: See, for example, Dunaway, *Seeing Green*; Gulliver et al., 'Testing the impact of images'; O'Neill and Smith, 'Climate change and visual imagery'.

89 See generally Kang, 'Law's materiality', 453; West, 'Feeling things'; Vadi, 'Power, law and images'. See also select contributors to Hohmann and Joyce (eds.), *International Law's Objects*.

90 See, for example, Chapter 5.

91 See Davies, *Law Unlimited*, p. 57.

92 See, for example, Grear et al. (eds.), *Posthuman Legalities*. Cf. Davies, Godden and Graham, 'Situating property'. Cf. also Duvic-Paoli, 'Trees', 504.

aestheticians. Philosophers of environmental aesthetics are, however, interested in identifying opportunities for their theories to be applied in institutional practices of environmental evaluation.[93] The book invites those philosophers to adapt their theories to the practice of using photographs of the natural environment in international legal processes that judge aesthetic value.[94] It is to this philosophy of 'environmental aesthetics' that I now turn in Chapter 2.

[93] Described as 'empirical' and 'speculative' aesthetics in Drenthen and Keulartz, 'Introduction', 1. See also Sepänmaa, 'From theoretical to applied environmental aesthetics', 87.

[94] For example, extending environmental hermeneutics for physical environments to photographs. On physical environments, see Drenthen, 'Environmental hermeneutics', 162.

2

The Environment's 'Aesthetic' Value

EXHIBIT: TARYN SIMON, *PAPERWORK AND THE WILL OF CAPITAL* (2015)

FIGURE 2.1. Taryn Simon, 'Agreement between Switzerland and the United States of America for Cooperation to Facilitate the Implementation of FATCA, Bern, Switzerland, 14 February 2013. *Phoenix roebelenii*, Miniature Date Palm, Costa Rica, *Antirrhinum majus*, Snapdragon, Spain, *Veronica spicata*, Spiked Speedwell, Kenya, *Phalaenopsis amabilis*, Moth Orchid, Venezuela, *Anemone coronaria*, Poppy Anemone, Italy, *Gypsophila paniculata*, Baby's Breath, Kenya, *Rosa × hybrida*, Hybrid Tea Rose, Kenya, *Paperwork and the Will of Capital*', 2015. Pigmented concrete press, dried plant specimens, archival inkjet prints, text on herbarium paper, and steel brace, 11.1 × 56.4 × 78.1 cm. © Taryn Simon. Courtesy Gagosian.

American artist Taryn Simon's mixed media work, *Paperwork and the Will of Capital,* comprises three elements: Text, photographs and flowers.[1] There is the text of instruments that effected the adoption of treaties on a range of matters with economic consequence. Different texts are displayed on multiple plinths under vitrines positioned around a room. One vitrine (Figure 2.1) shows the text for the adoption of the *Agreement between Switzerland and the United States of America for Cooperation to Facilitate the Implementation of FATCA* [Foreign Account Tax Compliance Act]. The subjects of other treaties featured in the installation range from sport to refugees. In addition to the texts, there are photographs of floral arrangements recreated from archival photographs of the ceremonial signings of the adoption instruments. Finally, there are the flowers themselves – pressed, dried and sewn to the page opposite the texts.

The pressed blooms stand out, literally, from their herbarium paper, the processed plant matter on which they have been displayed. Flattened yet raised, appreciable assemblages, in some cases heads without stems or leaves without stalks, the flowers have colour and texture to draw the eye, where they flutter and waft. Their dusky tones remember a springtime gone. And not just whimsy. You can see the insects they mimic. They are arranged on the page like a botanical drawing, not a true likeness but truth itself, caught and categorised in scientific stagecraft. The photograph opposite has caught the flowers too. Yet there they have been styled for pageantry. A florist, an artist no less, has used colour, form and shape to determine their position in the 'impossible bouquet'.[2] The flowers still shine brightly there, in the here and now, a crest to the fêted text. A text as dull as they come. Paperwork piled high, an archive emblematic of law's drudge. A testament to a pact between sovereigns, united adherents to progress, consumption and wealth. All on a pedestal of concrete – not clay – framed and contained, such that the economic project that is international law may never falter.

Taryn Simon's work presents many of the themes debated among philosophers of environmental aesthetics.[3] The work leaves me thinking about science and sensation as grounds for aesthetic judgement. I wonder whether my appreciation of the flower display is all the better for knowing that a flower imitates insects to attract them in the task of pollination. But I not only see the dried flowers; in my mind's eye, I also hear them rustle and smell their dusty stamens; their faded hues remind me of times past, flowers pressed between

1 Gyalui (ed.), *La Biennale di Venezia*, p. 406.

2 See Taryn Simon, *Paperwork and the Will of Capital.*

3 See, for example, Drenthen and Keulartz (eds.), *Environmental Aesthetics.*

the pages of books from my childhood. Then I ponder the distinctions between aesthetic judgement of the environment and of art. The arrangement to the left is creative, the arrangement to the right is botanical. They are also created, constructed, fabricated. Perhaps neither is environmental if the environment is none of those things. Then I contemplate artifice in nature, with the ceremonial endeavour of humans to one side of the vitrine and the 'other' nature on the paper pile opposite.

There is more though. Simon's work reveals the sharp edges between international law and the natural environment: The stacked paper is working or worked or work, rendering the environment – a tree – a resource for the printed word of law, celebrated with flowers, preserved on the page.

2.1 INTRODUCTION

My analysis of Taryn Simon's *Paperwork and the Will of Capital* (Figure 2.1) speaks to ways of understanding the aesthetic value of the natural environment, and the different orders of nature constructed through science, economics, law and, indeed, art. In this chapter, I contemplate constructions of the environment's 'aesthetic' value for international environmental law, including as an express term of the *World Heritage Convention* and *Biodiversity Convention*.[4] To situate my discussion of the relevant legal scholarship, I begin the chapter with an overview of themes addressed among philosophers of environmental aesthetics.[5] I then describe scholarly treatment of the expressions of the environment's aesthetic value in international environmental law. Noting that the legal scholarship has generally adopted a philosophical approach informed by environmental ethics and its attendant theories of value,[6] I then consider issues arising for international environmental law from the characterisations of aesthetic value among philosophers of environmental aesthetics. I observe that none of the legal scholars has analysed the meaning of 'aesthetic' value where it is a term of a treaty in accordance with international legal rules of treaty interpretation, an exercise I undertake later in Chapter 3.

4 *Convention for the Protection of the World Cultural and Natural Heritage*, Paris, 16 November 1972, in force 17 December 1975, 1037 UNTS 151; *Convention on Biological Diversity*, Rio de Janeiro, 5 June 1992, in force 29 December 1993, 1760 UNTS 79.

5 See Fisher, 'Environmental aesthetics', 667. See also Brady, 'Aesthetic value, nature, and environment', 186.

6 See, for example, Gillespie, 'Ethical considerations', 217. See Section 2.3.2.

2.2 AESTHETIC VALUE IN ENVIRONMENTAL AESTHETICS

Anglo-American philosophers typically describe the contemporary philosophy of environmental aesthetics as having developed through stages from the eighteenth century to the present.[7] The Western European philosophical school of 'aesthetics' that emerged in the eighteenth century distinguished the Platonic conception of beauty inherent in the object from the sensorial appreciation of objects by the human subject.[8] Immanuel Kant was influential in the development of an aesthetic philosophy that inquired into such subjective appreciation of objects, including objects from the natural environment.[9] However, Georg W F Hegel's early nineteenth-century *Æsthetik* is described as having largely displaced nature from the field of aesthetic philosophy, putting the objective appreciation of the arts at the core of philosophical scholarship.[10] So began what Jonathan Maskit facetiously calls the 'dark ages', where nature and the environment had a limited place in aesthetic philosophy.[11] It is this conception of aesthetic philosophy that has dominated since, focused on theoretical, critical and historical accounts of the arts in ways I address in Chapter 4.[12]

A further phase in the evolution of environmental aesthetics came with the publication of Ronald Hepburn's 'Contemporary Aesthetics and the Neglect of Natural Beauty' in 1966.[13] Hepburn was concerned that the focus of aesthetic philosophy on art objects had neglected the different form of aesthetic appreciation that comes from the immersive experience of the natural environment. Contemporary philosophers, working under the mantle of 'environmental aesthetics', have since examined the multi-sensory appreciation of the environment, one that is dynamic and extends beyond the visual to all senses – sight, sound, smell, touch and taste.[14] The scholarship

7 Maskit, 'On universalism', 41. Cf. Carlson, 'Ten steps', 13.

8 See Guyer, 'History of modern aesthetics', 25. See also Carlson, *Nature and Landscape*, p. 8.

9 Kant, *Critique of Judgment*. See further Brady, *Aesthetics of the Natural Environment*, p. 8.

10 Hegel, *The Introduction to Hegel's Philosophy of Fine Art*. See Carlson, *Nature and Landscape*, p. 4.

11 Exceptions include Arthur Schopenhauer, Friedrich Nietzsche and Martin Heidegger: See Maskit, 'On universalism', 42. Other exceptions include George Santayana, RG Collingwood, John Dewey, Paul Ziff, Frank Sibley and JO Urmson: See Brady, *Aesthetics of the Natural Environment*, p. 48.

12 See Saito, 'Environmental directions', 171. The conception of aesthetics as related to the arts is maintained in jurisprudential scholarship on law and aesthetics, as explained in Chapter 4.

13 Hepburn, 'Contemporary aesthetics', 285.

14 See, for example, Budd, 'Aesthetics of nature'; Brady, 'Aesthetic value, nature, and environment', 186.

of two philosophers, Emily Brady[15] and Allen Carlson,[16] provides an illustrative account of this field of Anglo-American environmental aesthetics.[17] Both have themselves provided comprehensive reviews of the philosophical literature while also positing their own models of environmental aesthetics. Both agree that an aesthetic appreciation of the natural environment is different from aesthetic characterisations of the arts.[18] They also seek a formulation of environmental aesthetics that has something as its basis that can be communicated in common terms rather than being peculiar to an individualised appreciation of the environment. This dimension to their thinking is, I explain later, particularly relevant to legal process.[19] However, their respective theories of environmental aesthetics highlight some of the tensions among philosophers of environmental aesthetics concerning characterisations of 'objective' criteria grounded in such things as scientific knowledge, and 'subjective' impressions of non-expert individuals. A discussion of these themes, as framed in large part by Brady and Carlson, and critiqued by Jonathan Maskit, follows.

2.2.1 *Environmental Aesthetics on the Arts*

When Ronald Hepburn returned aesthetic philosophy to the contemplation of the environment, he argued that appreciating the natural environment was an altogether different philosophical exercise from appreciating art.[20] Unlike art, he said, the environment's aesthetic quality 'is always provisional, correctible by reference to a different, perhaps wider context, or to a narrower one realized in greater detail'.[21] Hepburn was adamant in his claim that a love of the natural environment could not be understood in the same way as a love of

[15] Brady, *Aesthetics of the Natural Environment*, p. 1. See also Brady, 'Imagination and the aesthetic appreciation of nature'; Brady, *The Sublime in Modern Philosophy*.

[16] Carlson, *Aesthetics and the Environment*. See also Carlson, *Nature and Landscape*.

[17] On differences between analytic philosophy associated with Anglo-American scholarship and continental philosophy, see Maskit, 'On universalism', 47. Maskit highlights the work of scholars working in languages other than English, mostly German language scholars. Cf. Xue, 'Two types of a doctrine'.

[18] Carlson, *Aesthetics and the Environment*, p. 129. Brady, *Aesthetics of the Natural Environment*, pp. 69–70.

[19] Brady, *Aesthetics of the Natural Environment*, p. 191; Carlson, *Aesthetics and the Environment*, p. 54. As explained below, Maskit does not characterise their scholarship in these terms: See Maskit, 'On universalism', 51. The capacity for communicating aesthetic value in common terms is addressed in Section 2.2.3.3.

[20] See Hepburn, 'Contemporary aesthetics', 285. See discussion in Brady, *Aesthetics of the Natural Environment*, pp. 86, 103ff; Carlson, *Aesthetics and the Environment*, p. 5.

[21] Hepburn, 'Contemporary aesthetics', 524. Cf. my discussion of 'eco-criticism' later in Chapter 4.

art. Both Carlson and Brady agree.[22] For Brady, without artistic context or artistic meaning directing appreciation, a person has more freedom in appreciating the natural environment.[23] In Carlson's opinion, the assimilation of art and environment appreciation 'is both a theoretical mistake and an appreciative pity.'[24] Other philosophers take a similar view. Yrjö Sepänmaa considers the two aesthetics to have a 'common ancestry' from which they deviate,[25] while Yuriko Saito argues that 'art-centred' aesthetics is not equipped to account for the breadth of environmental aesthetics.'[26] Robert Elliot understands the appreciation of nature as antithetical to aesthetic judgements of art.[27] At the extreme, Don Mannison claims that the natural environment, absent 'artifactualisation' or crafting by humans, cannot be the subject of aesthetic appreciation at all.[28]

In distinguishing between the appreciation of the environment and art, Allen Carlson subscribes to a notion of 'positive aesthetics'.[29] Carlson understands all environments as being capable of positive aesthetic appreciation through scientific knowledge so long as they are 'untouched' or 'natural'.[30] This likely excludes from positive aesthetic appreciation places polluted, destroyed or otherwise changed by humans in a manner constituting an 'aesthetic affront'.[31] However, the concept of positive aesthetics raises several issues for debate. First, the use of science as a basis for aesthetic judgement can still produce contested outcomes. Forests ravaged by wildfire are judged negatively because they represent 'a truncated system of growth',[32] yet natural science and traditional knowledges might also understand them to have positive associations of renewal. Second, a narrow conception of the natural environment for aesthetic appreciation as one free from human impact or

[22] Brady, *Aesthetics of the Natural Environment*, p. 52. Carlson is drawn, however, to 'objective' bases for art appreciation: Carlson, *Aesthetics and the Environment*, p. 6, and further at pp. 42–7, 93, 121–2.
[23] Brady, *Aesthetics of the Natural Environment*, p. 15.
[24] Carlson, *Aesthetics and the Environment*, p. 115.
[25] See Sepänmaa, 'The two aesthetic cultures', 39.
[26] See Saito, 'Environmental directions', 171.
[27] Elliot, *Faking Nature*, p. 94; on art that mimics nature, see p. 89.
[28] Mannison, 'A prolegomenon', 212.
[29] Carlson, *Aesthetics and the Environment*, p. 72.
[30] Ibid. ('untouched' and 'virgin'), pp. 49, 51 ('natural'), 12 ('pristine' nature).
[31] Ibid., p. 151. Cf. Brady, *Aesthetics of the Natural Environment*, 246–7. See also Sibley, 'Some notes on ugliness', 190; Saito, 'The aesthetics of unscenic nature', 101. See generally Kieran, 'Aesthetic value'.
[32] Meeker, *The Comedy of Survival*, cited in Carlson, *Aesthetics and the Environment*, p. 75.

influence has been criticised by Emily Brady and other scholars.[33] Those scholars maintain that all environments are under human influence.[34] Whether described as 'natural' and 'wild', or 'managed' and 'cultivated', all environments are culturally constructed or imagined, including those few places on earth that humans cannot access.[35] Natural science also dictates this. The interdependent nature of ecosystems means that no part of the globe is free from the impacts of human pollution. Third, philosopher Janna Thompson criticises Carlson's theory of positive aesthetics for failing to differentiate between different natural environments: The object of appreciation in positive aesthetics extends to microscopic and 'uncharismatic' species, such as mould or invertebrates, making it an undiscerning concept. Thompson argues that when it comes to allocating resources for environmental protection, it is necessary to distinguish between environments more worthy of protection than others.[36]

In contrast to aesthetic philosophers who differentiate between the aesthetic appreciation of art and the environment, Janna Thompson entertains an aesthetic philosophy of the natural environment that is analogous to the arts.[37] She and others are not convinced of the demarcation between the aesthetics of nature and art.[38] The aesthetic philosophy developed for the arts provides a basis for aesthetic judgement of environments that can be communicated and argued – and which can differentiate between natural environments that do or do not merit protection by the state. Thompson considers aesthetic judgement as capable of distinguishing valuable environments – wild or managed – from environments that lack aesthetic value.[39] Thompson's view has, in turn, been criticised for its reliance on expertise and its exclusion of personal affect or response to the environment.[40] Addressing this, another approach linking art and the environment is offered by Arnold Berleant.[41] He argues for the 'naturalisation' of aesthetics, whereby art is judged on the same terms as nature as opposed to judging nature on the same terms as art. Specifically, he offers an account of 'participatory aesthetics' that recognises the role of the

33 Brady, *Aesthetics of the Natural Environment*, p. 100. See also Thompson, 'Aesthetics and the value of nature'.
34 See further Vogel, *Thinking Like a Mall*.
35 Brady, *Aesthetics of the Natural Environment*, p. 54.
36 Thompson, 'Aesthetics and the value of nature'.
37 Ibid.
38 See also Cooper, 'The intimacy of art and nature', 85.
39 Thompson, 'Aesthetics and the value of nature'.
40 See generally Brady, *Aesthetics of the Natural Environment*, pp. 199–200. On problems of 'expert knowledge', pp. 200, 206.
41 Berleant, 'The aesthetics of art and nature', 228.

'appreciator' in the construction of aesthetic appreciation, whether applied to nature or to art.[42]

Despite the different arguments that have been made in contemporary philosophy, the intimacy between visual art and the natural environment through such things as the concept of 'landscape' and 'environmental art' has played an important role in philosophical thinking on the environment and the place of humans in it.[43] The significance of this issue to the aesthetic value of the environment protected under international environmental law is explained later in Chapter 4 when I turn to discuss aesthetic philosophy as it relates to the arts and image.

2.2.2 *Aesthetic Value of the Environment as Sense or Sensibility*

Despite their agreement on the distinction between the natural environment and the arts for the purposes of aesthetic appreciation, Emily Brady and Allen Carlson take different approaches to matters of objectivity and subjectivity in environmental aesthetics. Emily Brady describes the discussion of such matters among philosophers of environmental aesthetics as falling on a spectrum between 'cognitive' and 'non-cognitive' appreciation of the natural environment.[44] Her categorisation of philosophical theories conforms, to some extent, to Allen Carlson's 'objectivist' and 'subjectivist' groupings.[45] The categories of both correspond in a very general way to, on the one hand, reasoned explanation (an object's sense), and intuited impressions (a subject's sensibility), on the other hand.[46] Below I explain views in the philosophy of environmental aesthetics on objectivity, subjectivity and the need for common grounds for appreciation. Those views are relevant in ways addressed later in Section 2.3 to my analysis of aesthetic value in international environmental law.

For Emily Brady, 'cognitive' understandings of an aesthetic experience of the environment are tied to the human subject's knowledge of the environ-

[42] Ibid., 238–41. See also Berleant, *Aesthetics and Environment.*

[43] Mitchell, *Landscape and Power.* See also Rolston, 'Landscape from the eighteenth century'; Osborne, 'The use of nature in art'.

[44] Brady, *Aesthetics of the Natural Environment*, p. 86.

[45] Carlson, *Aesthetics and the Environment*, pp. xviii–xix. The dichotomy is also described as: 'narrative' (knowledge) and 'ambient' (perception): See Foster, 'The narrative and the ambient'; and non-conceptualists and conceptualists: See Moore, 'Appreciating natural beauty as beautiful', 215, quoted in Maskit, 'On universalism', 45.

[46] Maskit offers an alternative to dichotomous categories: See Maskit, 'On universalism', 46.

mental 'object'.[47] Cognitive approaches posit a rational basis for understanding aesthetic value that inheres in the environment rather than in the person having the aesthetic experience of the environment. In Brady's view, the theories of Holmes Rolston III and Marcia Eaton fall under this cognitive category of environmental aesthetics,[48] while Allen Carlson's 'natural environmental model' is particularly illustrative of this category, one that he himself calls an 'objectivist' approach.[49] Carlson understands nature to be appreciated in light of human knowledges of it, particularly knowledge gained through the natural sciences.[50] Information about glacial forces that form rock, biological processes that turn leaves from green to orange, or the genetic coding of migration routes in animals, could be knowledge that is significant to aesthetic appreciation.[51]

Brady contrasts these models in environmental aesthetics with 'non-cognitive' theories that describe a range of sensory responses to the natural environment, placing the human subject's response to the environment to the fore.[52] Brady describes Ronald Hepburn, among others, as falling under the banner of 'non-cognitive' environmental aesthetics.[53] She includes philosophical models developed respectively by Arnold Berleant, Noël Carroll, Stan Godlovitch and Yuriko Saito in this category.[54] Brady applauds them for 'their awareness that aesthetically valuing nature involves bringing ourselves to the natural world as *cultural* beings'.[55]

Allen Carlson is critical of non-cognitive theorists, what he calls 'subjectivist' models of environmental aesthetics.[56] For him, subjectivist conceptions of aesthetic experiences of the environment are problematic for their attachment

[47] See generally Brady, *Aesthetics of the Natural Environment*, pp. 87–8.

[48] Brady, *Aesthetics of the Natural Environment*, p. 87.

[49] Carlson, *Aesthetics and the Environment*, p. 11. On Carlson's 'natural environmental model', see Brady, *Aesthetics of the Natural Environment*, p. 89.

[50] Carlson refers to 'common sense' but the natural sciences are more typically his reference for 'knowledge': Carlson, *Aesthetics and the Environment*, pp. 11–12, 72.

[51] Carlson refers to knowledge of 'categories of nature': Ibid., pp. 62, 89–90.

[52] Brady says it is a misconception that non-cognitive models are weighted towards the subject: Brady, *Aesthetics of the Natural Environment*, p. 111.

[53] Ibid., p. 87.

[54] Ibid.

[55] Ibid., pp. 115–6. Jonathan Maskit characterises Yuriko Saito's scholarship as addressing culture: Maskit, 'On universalism', 54, discussed in Section 2.2.3.5. On relevance to international law, see Section 2.4.3.

[56] Carlson, *Aesthetics and the Environment*, pp. xviii–xix.

to the individual, rendering aesthetic appreciation 'trivial and fanciful'.[57] A scientific basis for the aesthetic appreciation of the natural environment is, by contrast, 'serious'.[58] Betraying his frustration with philosophical models that are so deferential to personal experience as to be arbitrary or 'subjective whims',[59] Carlson praises aesthetics philosopher Yrjö Sepänmaa for recognising that 'not all nature either can or should be all things to all human beings'.[60]

Like Carlson, Emily Brady is not satisfied with non-cognitive theories. From her perspective, they are difficult to communicate or describe in terms of 'shared' features.[61] She says, '[i]f beauty is in the eye of the beholder, then it could be argued that there is no way to arbitrate between personal opinions'.[62] But nor is Brady satisfied with cognitive or objective characterisations of aesthetics.[63] She considers, for example, that Allen Carlson goes too far in giving priority to Western science over other forms of knowledge, which would include Indigenous knowledge.[64] She also considers it wrong to characterise science as objective.[65] Philosopher Malcolm Budd is even more emphatic in his condemnation of science-centric models of environmental aesthetics: '[E]ven someone who realizes that the structure of a bat's head is extraordinarily well-suited to the task of sonar emission and detection is unlikely to derive much, if any, aesthetic satisfaction from simply looking at such a head with this knowledge in mind.'[66]

Despite a range of views represented among philosophers of environmental aesthetics, Jonathan Maskit notes a common normative premise in the scholarship that 'there are better and worse ways to approach natural environments and that one requires something more than just what meets the senses in order to judge well.'[67] As I will address later, he criticises much of this scholarship for failing to account for cultural perceptions of the environment beyond the English-speaking world.[68]

57 Ibid., p. 11. Brady describes Carlson's objection to 'empty' appreciation: *Aesthetics of the Natural Environment*, p. 111. Cf. Hepburn, 'Trivial and serious'.

58 Carlson, *Aesthetics and the Environment*, p. 9.

59 Ibid., p. 12.

60 Ibid., p. 10.

61 Brady, *Aesthetics of the Natural Environment*, pp. 94ff.

62 Ibid., pp. 111–12.

63 Ibid., p. 112.

64 Ibid., p. 100.

65 Ibid., p. 94.

66 Budd, 'Objectivity and the aesthetic value of nature', 270; see also Budd, *The Aesthetic Appreciation of Nature*. Cf. Rolston, 'Does aesthetic appreciation of nature need to be science-based?'. See also Matthews, 'Scientific knowledge'.

67 Maskit, 'On universalism', 44.

68 Ibid., 41–2.

2.2.3 *Brady's Integrated Aesthetic Model as a Hybrid of Objective and Subjective Approaches*

Concerned that philosophical models wedded to one or other extreme of the subjective and objective binary are misplaced, Emily Brady developed a hybrid understanding of environmental aesthetics that she named the 'integrated aesthetic' model.[69] This model is defined by a multi-sensory experience and 'disinterested' engagement with the surrounding environment shaped by imagination, emotion and knowledge.[70] Brady promotes a conception of the natural environment's aesthetic value as an engaged, relational, contextual and non-instrumental appreciation that can be communicated among people.[71] Below I describe each of these elements in detail. In ways explained in later chapters, Emily Brady's integrated aesthetic model informs much of my consideration of how the environment's aesthetic value could be conceived for international law.

2.2.3.1 Hybrid of Subject and Object

Emily Brady is sympathetic to non-cognitive, subjectivist approaches in environmental aesthetics. However, she appreciates that aesthetic value must be capable of expression in a public policy context with reference to relatable concepts rather than singular experiences. For this, she sees merit in the intentions of scholars who have developed cognitive models. So, for Brady, the situations of object *and* subject guide appreciation. Her account of aesthetic value is a hybrid theory bringing together 'the particularity of individual aesthetic appreciation with a distinctive kind of objectivity of justification'.[72]

Brady wants to describe the environment's aesthetic value in terms that can be adopted, for example, in the management of national parks, or for the development of land, where aesthetic value might be one of several environmental values identified for protection in public policy. She is concerned that in British policy on the environment, 'aesthetics appears to be given less attention because it is simply considered less important'.[73] The environment's aesthetic value is considered in policy terms, Brady observes, to be 'lightweight,

[69] Brady, *Aesthetics of the Natural Environment*, pp. 120–3; on objectivity and subjectivity, p. 231.
[70] Ibid., pp. 120, 146, 185.
[71] Ibid., pp. 3–4.
[72] Brady, *Aesthetics of the Natural Environment*, p. 231.
[73] Ibid., p. 225.

less 'serious' than the scientific or the ethical, and associated with luxury, or what we do in our leisure time'.[74] She wants to address a tendency to dismiss aesthetic value in public policy as unimportant because it is subjective, which she maintains is not how Britons, for the purposes of her example, typically understand their aesthetic encounters with the environment.

2.2.3.2 Multi-Sensory and Contextualised Engagement

Emily Brady acknowledges a range of meanings for natural environments and nature, referencing Kate Soper's distinction between understandings of nature as 'real' and inclusive of humans, and understandings of nature as a cultural construct, apart from humans.[75] For Brady's theory, natural environments comprise non-human life and surrounds, but they are not exclusive of humans or necessarily free from human impacts or intervention.[76] Brady's aesthetic value of such natural environments by the humans in it is multi-sensory. She maintains that people appreciate their environments in aesthetic terms through all their senses. She considers that '[v]isual qualities, sounds, tactile qualities, olfactory and gustatory qualities, all may enable us to identify the aesthetic feel of a place'.[77]

What Brady calls 'human ocularcentrism' in government evaluations of aesthetic appreciation of the environment is linked, she suggests, to the quest for objectivity in aesthetic judgements of the environment.[78] For seeing-is-believing. But a focus on visual qualities in the environment fails, Brady says, to comprehend the complexity of an immersive aesthetic appreciation. To limit aesthetic appreciation to the visual leaves aesthetic value vulnerable to claims of triviality – aesthetic value as a superficial and dispensable value.[79] To the sensory channels of appreciation, Brady adds context – of imagination, emotion and knowledge – as informing the aesthetic experience of the environment.[80] Imagination, she says, 'enables us to adopt several different perspectives, as well as entirely new ones',[81] reaching 'beyond the beliefs and knowledge that we rely upon for day-to-day living'.[82] Associated with expressive

74 Ibid.
75 Ibid., p. 52, citing Soper, *What Is Nature?*. See also Godden, 'Preserving natural heritage'.
76 Brady, *Aesthetics of the Natural Environment*, pp. 53, 58–9.
77 Ibid., p. 237.
78 Ibid., pp. 227–8.
79 On 'environmentalism of the poor', see Section 2.4.3.
80 Brady, *Aesthetics of the Natural Environment*, p. 146.
81 Ibid., p. 147.
82 Ibid., p. 149.

qualities in the environment, emotion is not, Brady suggests, an idiosyncratic element of environmental appreciation.[83] Finally, knowledge is understood for Brady's purposes as a cultural construct that includes scientific, traditional and inexpert knowledge.[84]

2.2.3.3 Shared and Disinterested Appreciation

Emily Brady's aesthetic value is shared and can be communicated.[85] Although Brady considers subjectivity to be important to capturing the significance and pluralised appreciation of the environment's aesthetic value, she acknowledges that it is problematic in a policy context where a shared or common basis for understanding the environment's aesthetic qualities is required in the public management of the environment. Brady observes that environmental values characterised as objective – such as the ecological value of habitat for rare species – are given more weight in environmental management.[86]

So it is that Emily Brady tempers subjective elements in her environmental aesthetic with the aid of the Kantian concept of 'disinterestedness'.[87] This is the idea that if an object is appreciated with no sense of it being useful to the subject, the subject can undertake an assessment of environmental experience that is not driven by self-interest.[88] Brady maintains that disinterestedness 'supports appreciation that is sensitive to the particularities of the experience [of the environment] and works positively to shift focus away from the self and towards aesthetic qualities for their own sake, rather than as a means to fulfilling some personal or practical goal'.[89] Allen Carlson's model also relies on disinterestedness to make a case for objective appreciation.[90] However, Brady does not see the concept as inimical to pluralised, place-based appreciations of the environment.[91] She acknowledges and considers significant subjective inputs to the aesthetic experience,[92] but maintains that

83 Ibid., p. 183.
84 Ibid., pp. 183–6.
85 Ibid., p. 206. Cf. discussion of landscape tastes: Section 4.2.1.
86 Brady, *Aesthetics of the Natural Environment*, p. 225. See also John Benson, 'Aesthetic and other values'.
87 Brady, *Aesthetics of the Natural Environment*, pp. 34, 128ff, citing Kant, *Critique of Judgment*.
88 Brady, *Aesthetics of the Natural Environment*.
89 Ibid., p. 141.
90 Carlson, *Aesthetics and the Environment*, p. 120.
91 Brady, *Aesthetics of the Natural Environment*, p. 132; Carlson, *Aesthetics and the Environment*, pp. 7, 23ff.
92 Brady, *Aesthetics of the Natural Environment*, pp. 185–6.

disinterestedness filters out idiosyncratic appreciation that is anathema to consensus.[93] This means that, while sensorial perception of the natural environment informed by an individual's imagination, emotion and knowledge is the basis for describing aesthetic value, 'disinterestedness' works in Brady's model to extract from subjective appreciation elements that can be communicated to other people. Once communicated, people can agree on which elements are shared among a community of people. These, in turn, form the basis of public decisions informed by assessments of aesthetic value.

I maintain that Emily Brady's efforts to develop an understanding of aesthetic value that can be communicated in public decision-making could be adapted for assessments of the environment's aesthetic value under international law.[94] It is however not clear from Brady's model how, as a practical matter, disinterestedness can be institutionalised in public decision-making. I return to this point when I come to consider the application of her theory to decision-making in international law.[95]

2.2.3.4 Distinct and Non-Instrumental Value

Emily Brady distinguishes aesthetic value of the environment from other environmental values. She characterises aesthetic value as a non-instrumental value, different from, for example, instrumental environmental values such as scientific value.[96] In her critique of Allen Carlson's model of environmental aesthetics, Emily Brady is concerned that if aesthetics is tied so intimately to science, it becomes indistinguishable from the scientific or 'ecological' values identified by governments as also relevant in conservation policy.[97] She is also determined to distinguish aesthetic value from 'hedonistic' amenity or a form of recreational value.[98] The Kantian conception of disinterestedness, she maintains, allows for an understanding of aesthetic value that is not tied to

[93] Ibid., p. 6. The relevance of disinterestedness to practice is addressed in Section 8.2.2.
[94] Brady, *Aesthetics of the Natural Environment*, pp. 224ff. On applied philosophy generally, see Sepänmaa, 'From theoretical to applied environmental aesthetics', 87. See also the description of 'speculative' aesthetics in Drenthen and Keulartz, 'Introduction', 1. I do not in this book examine the literature on landscape assessments in planning policy: See, for example, Porteous, *Environmental Aesthetics*.
[95] See Section 8.2.2.
[96] Brady, *Aesthetics of the Natural Environment*, p. 23.
[97] Ibid., p. 99.
[98] Ibid., p. 129.

human self-interest and, as such, is different from instrumental environmental values.[99]

However, Emily Brady's work to distinguish aesthetic value from other environmental values also extends to drawing distinctions within the sphere of non-instrumental environmental values. Specifically, she examines the relationship between aesthetic value and ethical value. Ethical value in this sense is an object of inquiry in moral philosophy that includes normative understandings of right and wrong.[100] Ethical questions concerning the environment have been addressed under the mantle of environmental ethics, 'the study of the ethics of human interactions with and impacts on [nature's] systems', including normative ethics and meta-ethics.[101] Brady argues that aesthetics and ethics are distinct, but related.[102] She promotes aesthetic philosophy as an alternative to moral philosophy concerned with ethics but says that the differences between ethics and aesthetics can be exaggerated, with ethics associated with 'abstract rules and universal principles' and aesthetics pitched as 'reactive', 'subjective and particular'.[103] Brady entertains a role for aesthetic value in environmental ethics whereby an aesthetic appreciation of the environment can lead to a sense of care for the environment.[104] Understood in this way, she maintains that aesthetic value is not subordinated to ethical value and that it merits consideration in policy apart from ethical value from the vantage of aesthetic philosophy.[105] I will return to the relationship between environmental ethics and philosophies of environmental aesthetics in my discussion of environmental values in international environmental law in Section 2.3. There I explain the ways in which the study of environmental ethics is often engaged in the philosophical inquiry of international and domestic environmental law.[106]

99 Ibid., p. 101; see also p. 23.

100 Ibid., pp. 246, 254. See generally Gardiner and Thompson (eds.), *Oxford Handbook of Environmental Ethics.*

101 Attfield, *Environmental Ethics*, p. 15. See also Elliot, *Environmental Ethics*; Callicott, *Earth's Insights*.

102 Brady, *Aesthetics of the Natural Environment*, pp. 254–5; see also Maskit, 'On universalism', 54, quoting Martin Seel, *Eine Ästhetik der Natur* (Suhrkamp, 1991), 342.

103 Brady, *Aesthetics of the Natural Environment*, pp. 255, 229.

104 Ibid., 260; see also Nathalie Blanc, 'Ethics and aesthetics', 149; Bannon, 'Re-envisioning nature'.

105 See also Brady, 'Aesthetic value, nature, and environment', 194.

106 See generally Gillespie, *International Environmental Law, Policy and Ethics*, 2nd edn; Gillespie, 'Ethical considerations', 217. On the relevance of environmental ethics to political movements of environmentalism, see Brown and Eckersley, 'International political theory', 3.

2.2.3.5 Plural and Relative Values Informed by Culture

Ultimately, I understand Emily Brady to be describing an aesthetic value that I describe for this book as exquisite and profound. Exquisite in the sense that an environment's aesthetic value connotes a distinctive and, to some extent, ineffable affect in a person that is distinct from a natural beauty conceived for the arts;[107] profound in the sense that its apprehension is significant, meaningful, or important to a community of people – as opposed to merely trivial, hedonistic, empty or superficial.[108] As such, it is an environmental value that is meaningful: It has meaning and the meaning is one that matters – although different environments might be meaningful in aesthetic terms in different ways, and for different reasons, for different people and communities.

Aesthetic philosopher Jonathan Maskit is critical of philosophers of environmental aesthetics for failing to account for cultural relativism in the aesthetic appreciation of the environment. He describes the theories of the majority of philosophers in environmental aesthetics, including Emily Brady, as proponents of universalism in the Kantian tradition.[109] He distinguishes those philosophers from others whom he calls 'cultural historicists': A minority of philosophers who are aware of the temporal and cultural constructions of concepts – such as 'human' and 'nature' – in their theories of environmental aesthetics.[110] He identifies in this minority certain philosophers from Finland and Germany, and two scholars in America who have looked at aesthetic questions relevant to Japan.[111] Maskit's concerns are similar to those that motivate eco-critical scholars discussed in Chapter 4 of this book.[112]

As noted above, however, Emily Brady maintains that her integrated aesthetic model and other non-cognitivist models of environmental aesthetics provide for cultural pluralism.[113] In trying to marry the tensions between the non-cognitivist (subjectivist) and cognitivist (objectivist) models, she emphasises that common approaches to understanding the aesthetic value of the environment need not come at the expense of recognising appreciations of place as culturally situated. Indeed, as discussed later in Chapter 4, she is mindful of the ways in which historical philosophies of environmental value

[107] On ineffability in philosophy, see Jonas, *Ineffability and Its Metaphysics.*

[108] Brady, *Aesthetics of the Natural Environment*, p. 111.

[109] Maskit, 'On universalism', 48–51.

[110] Ibid., 47.

[111] Ibid., 51–4.

[112] See generally Braddock and Irmscher (eds.), *A Keener Perception.*

[113] Brady, 'Aesthetic value, nature, and environment'; on knowledge as culture, see also Brady, *Aesthetics of the Natural Environment*, pp. 100–1.

such as American Transcendentalism promoted as universal concepts that should have been properly understood for their cultural specificity.[114] This incorporation of pluralised understandings of aesthetic value in Emily Brady's integrated aesthetic model is important for my later examination of how such a value might be properly conceived for the many nation states that are parties to international environmental treaties.[115]

2.3. AESTHETIC VALUE IN INTERNATIONAL ENVIRONMENTAL LAW

The 'aesthetic' value of the environment protected under international environmental treaties has been the subject of only limited scholarly inquiry. Where they characterise 'aesthetic' value as synonymous with beauty, recreation and landscape, these legal scholars raise issues similar to those debated among philosophers of environmental aesthetics. Here I explain where the term 'aesthetic' is expressed as an environmental value in international environmental law and how it has been characterised in international legal scholarship. Later, I analyse those characterisations in light of philosophies of environmental aesthetics.[116]

2.3.1 *Expressions of Aesthetic Value in Treaties*

In his opening address to the First International Ornithological Congress in Vienna in 1884, Dr Bernard Altum distinguished himself from his ornithological colleagues by contemplating interstate protection of birds not only for their economic usefulness to agriculture as insectivores but in terms of their 'aesthetic' value too.[117] His proposed scheme of aesthetic value comprised form, colour and shape, movement and musical powers.[118] Altum's proposal was quashed.[119] The treaty that eventually emerged, the 1902 *Convention to Protect Birds Useful to Agriculture*,[120] made no mention of aesthetic value.

[114] See Brady, *Aesthetics of the Natural Environment*, p. 44.
[115] See Brady, *Aesthetics of the Natural Environment*, p. 185. Cf. Scholtz, 'Animal culling', 16.
[116] Note in Chapter 4 I address, as a separate concern, the discussion of law and aesthetics in terms of the arts.
[117] Herman, *International Convention for the Protection of Birds Concluded in 1902*, p. 61.
[118] Ibid., p. 61.
[119] Ibid., p. 63.
[120] *Convention to Protect Birds Useful to Agriculture*, Paris, 19 March 1902, in force 6 December 1905.

However, at least as early as 1933, states agreed to concerted action to preserve wildlife for, among other reasons, its 'esthetic interest'.[121]

Today, several international environmental treaties expressly assign aesthetic importance to particular species and habitats.[122] Aesthetic value is often listed as one in a constellation of environmental values that include scientific, economic, cultural and ethical values of environmental protection.[123] Aesthetic value has been extended to specific species, such as polar bears,[124] and groups of species, such as migratory birds and migratory wildlife in general.[125] Aesthetic value has also been assigned in international law to places and spaces, including the habitats and migratory paths of fauna.[126] Aesthetic value as an environmental value has been expressed in different parts of treaties – including as part of their commitments as well as in their preambles, their definitions and annexes. And these different modes of expression would be relevant to any interpretation of the term done for international environmental law in accordance with orthodox principles of treaty interpretation.[127]

Examples of international treaties specifically protecting the aesthetic value of the environment through express commitments include the *World Heritage Convention*[128] and the *Antarctic Protocol*.[129] As explained in this book's introduction, article 2 of the *World Heritage Convention* defines natural heritage to include 'natural features consisting of physical and biological formations or groups of such formations, which are of outstanding universal value from the aesthetic or scientific point of view'.[130] The definition of natural heritage is central to decisions of the World Heritage Committee to inscribe a natural

[121] Article 2(1) of the *Convention Relative to the Preservation of Fauna and Flora in Their Natural State*, London, 8 November 1933, in force 14 January 1936, 172 LNTS 241.

[122] See generally Gillespie, *International Environmental Law, Policy and Ethics*, 2nd edn, pp. 68, 72ff. My focus in this section is primarily multilateral treaties although I also reference select bilateral and regional treaties with restricted membership.

[123] van Heijnsbergen, *International Legal Protection*, p. 56.

[124] See, for example, preamble of the *Agreement on the Conservation and Management of the Alaska-Chukotka Polar Bear Population*, Washington, 16 October 2000, in force 23 September 2007, 40 ILM 397.

[125] See, for example, third tiret of the preamble of the *Convention on the Conservation of Migratory Species of Wild Animals*, Bonn, 6 November 1979, in force 1 November 1983, 1651 UNTS 333.

[126] See, for example, second tiret of the preamble and Articles I, V, VII of the *Convention on Nature Protection and Wildlife Preservation in the Western Hemisphere*, Washington, 12 October 1940, in force 1 May 1942, 161 UNTS 193.

[127] In accordance with the *Vienna Convention*. See Chapter 3.

[128] Article 2 of the *World Heritage Convention*.

[129] Article 3 of the *Protocol on Environmental Protection to the Antarctic Treaty*, Madrid, 4 October 1991, in force 14 January 1998, 2941 UNTS 3.

[130] Article 2 of the *World Heritage Convention*.

property on the World Heritage List,[131] a vehicle created under the treaty to protect the 'outstanding universal value' of specific environments. The *Antarctic Protocol* states in article 3 that 'the intrinsic value of Antarctica, including its wilderness and aesthetic values and its value as an area for the conduct of scientific research' shall be one of the 'fundamental considerations in the planning and conduct of all activities in the Antarctic Treaty area'.[132] It further provides that 'activities in the Antarctic Treaty area shall be planned and conducted so as to avoid ... degradation of, or substantial risk to, areas of biological, scientific, historic, aesthetic or wilderness significance'.[133] Several regional treaties also protect the environment's aesthetic value through substantive treaty provisions in Africa, the Western Hemisphere, the South Pacific, the Wider Caribbean Region and in the Mediterranean.[134]

International treaties that recognise aesthetic value in their preambular introductions include the *Convention on the International Trade in Endangered Species*,[135] the *Biodiversity Convention*,[136] and the *Bonn Convention*.[137] The preamble to the *Convention on the International Trade in Endangered Species*, for example, refers first to the concept of 'beauty', recognising that 'wild fauna and flora in their many beautiful and varied forms are an irreplaceable part of the natural systems of the earth which must be

131 Article 11, ibid.

132 Article 3 of the *Antarctic Protocol*.

133 Article 3(2)(b)(vi), ibid.

134 See, for example, preamble and Articles III and VI of the *African Convention on the Conservation of Nature and Natural Resources*, Algiers, 15 September 1968, in force 16 June 1969, 1001 UNTS 3; Article 12 and annexes of the *African Convention on the Conservation of Nature and Natural Resources* (Revised), Maputo, 11 July 2003, in force 23 July 2016; second tiret of the preamble and Articles I, V and VII of the *Convention on Nature Protection and Wildlife Preservation in the Western Hemisphere*, Washington, 12 October 1940, in force 1 May 1942, 161 UNTS 193; preamble and Article II of the *Convention on the Conservation of Nature in the South Pacific*, Apia, 12 June 1976, in force 26 June 1990, [1990] ATS 41; preamble and Articles 4 and 17 of the *Protocol Concerning Specially Protected Areas and Wildlife to the Convention for the Protection and Development of the Marine Environment of the Wider Caribbean Region*, Kingston, 18 January 1990, in force 17 June 2000, 2180 UNTS 101; Articles 4 and 8 and annex I of the *Protocol Concerning Specially Protected Areas and Biological Diversity in the Mediterranean*, Barcelona, 10 June 1995, in force 12 December 1999, 2102 UNTS 181; Article 11 of the *Protocol on Integrated Coastal Zone Management in the Mediterranean*, Madrid, 21 January 2008, in force 24 March 2011, 2742 UNTS 197. See also Article 13 of the ASEAN *Agreement on the Conservation of Nature and Natural Resources*, Kuala Lumpur, 9 July 1985.

135 Second tiret of the preamble of *Convention on International Trade in Endangered Species of Wild Fauna and Flora*, Washington, 3 March 1973, in force 1 July 1975, 993 UNTS 243.

136 First tiret of the preamble of the *Convention on Biological Diversity*.

137 Third tiret of the preamble of the *Convention on the Conservation of Migratory Species of Wild Animals*.

protected for this and the generations to come'.[138] It then goes on to state that the parties are '[c]onscious of the ever-growing value of wild fauna and flora from aesthetic, scientific, cultural, recreational and economic points of view'.[139] In a list that is similar to the values of wildlife animals identified in the preamble to the *Bonn Convention*, the *Biodiversity Convention* states in its preamble that its parties are '[c]onscious of the intrinsic value of biological diversity and of the ecological, genetic, social, economic, scientific, educational, cultural, recreational and aesthetic values of biological diversity and its components'.[140] Some regional agreements protecting the environment, such as Council of Europe's *Convention on the Conservation of European Wildlife and Natural Habitats*,[141] also mention aesthetic value in their preambles.

In contrast to treaties making express reference to aesthetic value, some treaties refer to other environmental values without including aesthetic value among them. The preamble to the *Ramsar Convention*, for example, makes no mention of aesthetic value when it states that the parties are 'convinced that wetlands constitute a resource of great economic, cultural, scientific, and recreational value, the loss of which would be irreparable'.[142] Other treaties may be seen to invoke environmental values with reference to concepts such as 'common' interest or concern.[143] The *Whaling Convention* recognises the 'interest of the nations of the world' and 'common interest' in whale stocks.[144] The *Climate Change Convention* refers to the changing climate and its adverse effects as a 'common concern of humankind'.[145] The aesthetic value of the environment is not expressed in these treaties but, in Chapter 3,

[138] Second tiret of the preamble of the *Convention on International Trade in Endangered Species of Wild Fauna and Flora*.

[139] Ibid.

[140] First tiret of the preamble of the *Convention on Biological Diversity*; see also second tiret of the preamble of the *Convention on the Conservation of Migratory Species of Wild Animals*.

[141] Third tiret of the preamble of the *Convention on the Conservation of European Wildlife and Natural Habitats*, Bern, 19 September 1979, in force 1 June 1982, ETS No. 104. See also fourth tiret of the preamble of the *Agreement on the Conservation of African-Eurasian Migratory Waterbirds*, The Hague, 15 August 1996, in force 1 November 1999, 2365 UNTS 203.

[142] Third tiret of the preamble of the *Convention on Wetlands of International Importance Especially as Waterfowl Habitat*, Ramsar, 2 February 1971, in force 21 December 1975, 996 UNTS 245.

[143] See Brunnée, 'Common areas'.

[144] *International Convention on the Regulation of Whaling*, Washington, 2 December 1946, in force 10 November 1948, 161 UNTS 72.

[145] First tiret of the preamble of the *United Nations Framework Convention on Climate Change*, New York, 9 May 1992, in force 21 March 1994, 1771 UNTS 107.

I explain how aesthetic appreciations of whales might inform a legal interpretation of the *Whaling Convention*.[146]

2.3.2 *Scholarly Characterisations of Aesthetic Value for International Law*

Philosophers of international environmental law have typically examined the normative foundations of international environmental law in terms of ethics or moral philosophy.[147] Critical approaches to values in international environmental law have given particular attention to the position of developing countries and the Global South.[148] But where legal scholars make specific mention of aesthetic value, they have largely done so in the broader context of 'environmental values' – the scientific, economic, ethical and cultural values listed in treaties.[149] Some of the few scholars of international environmental law who have examined the meaning of 'aesthetic' value as a term posited in international treaties are discussed below.[150] They typically equate aesthetic value with natural beauty, describing it as a subjective and instrumental value that is perceived visually in terms of 'landscape'. It is, however, difficult to identify any consensus among them on the meaning of aesthetic value in international environmental law.

2.3.2.1 Qualities of Aesthetic Value

International environmental law scholar Alexander Gillespie has undertaken an extensive study of environmental values in international environmental law that includes a specific and detailed analysis of aesthetic value.[151] Referencing

[146] See Section 3.4.

[147] Stone, 'Ethics and international environmental law', 291; Weiss, 'International environmental law'; Nickel and Magraw, 'Philosophical issues', 453–71; Fitzmaurice, 'Some reflections', 89–110.

[148] See generally Mickelson, 'South, north'; Humby, 'Evaluating the value'; Pahuja, 'Conserving the world's resources?', 398; Humphreys and Otomo, 'Theorizing international environmental law', 797; Natarajan and Khoday, 'Locating nature'. On critical perspectives of environmental law generally, see Philippopoulos-Mihalopoulos, 'Critical legal thinking', 18.

[149] See generally Gillespie, *International Environmental Law, Policy and Ethics*, 2nd edn. Discussed in Section 2.3.2.1.

[150] Discussed in this section. Cf. domestic environmental law: See, for example, Jenkins, 'In defence of natural beauty'; Richardson, Barritt and Bowman, 'Beauty: A lingua franca'; Richardson, *The Art of Environmental Law*; Fisher, 'Can the law protect landscape values?'; Costonis, *Icons and Aliens*. I discuss scholars who employ aesthetics for the arts in their analysis of environmental law and international environmental law in Section 4.4.2.

[151] Gillespie, *International Environmental Law, Policy and Ethics*, 2nd edn. See also his summary of aesthetic value in Gillespie, *Conservation, Biodiversity and International Law*.

a contested characterisation of environmental values as either anthropocentric or non-anthropocentric, he maintains that aesthetic value is considered in anthropocentric terms as useful to humans.[152] Aesthetic value, he says, 'is one of the foremost justifications for protecting the environment'.[153] Gillespie describes aesthetic value in terms of 'natural beauty', though variously defined,[154] and as a 'subjective' value.[155] In a previous edition of this important work, he maintained that efforts to identify an objective system of 'formal visual qualities' for aesthetic responses to the environment had been 'unsuccessful'.[156]

Legal scholars Catherine Redgwell and Werner Scholtz respectively discuss aesthetic value in relation to specific treaties. In the context of world natural heritage, Redgwell relates aesthetic value to 'natural beauty', describing them both as 'subjective'.[157] Commenting on the World Heritage Committee criterion that references both aesthetic and natural beauty values,[158] she explains that 'there does not exist a universal classification system for "aesthetic importance" or "natural beauty"'.[159] She nevertheless observes that 'aesthetic value must reside in more than the local population to satisfy the requirements of the [World Heritage] Convention'.[160] Werner Scholtz not only considers aesthetics in terms of beauty and subjectivity, he explicitly rejects what he terms 'aesthetic objectivism' in favour of pluralised conceptions of value. Discussing aesthetic value in the context of international laws protecting biodiversity, he states:

> It is, of course, probable that most of society may agree on the aesthetic appeal of a certain object. This agreement may exist at the local, national or international level. But even this form of consensus must not be viewed as evidence of aesthetic objectivism. It is merely the product of convention which may be coined in appropriate circumstances as society's taste.[161]

Equated with natural beauty and subjectivity, aesthetic value has also been characterised as an instrumental value. For legal scholars like Alexander Gillespie, aesthetic value is a way of valuing the environment for its usefulness to humans, as an anthropocentric value.[162] Instrumental values possibly

[152] Gillespie, *International Environmental Law, Policy and Ethics*, 2nd edn, p. 13.
[153] Ibid., 68.
[154] Ibid., 76–80.
[155] Ibid., 68.
[156] Alexander Gillespie, *International Environmental Law, Policy and Ethics*, 2nd edn, p. 87.
[157] Redgwell, 'Article 2 definition of natural heritage', 73.
[158] Article 2 of the *World Heritage Convention*. See discussion in Chapter 3.
[159] Redgwell, 'Article 2 definition of natural heritage', 73.
[160] Ibid.
[161] Scholtz, 'Animal culling', 16.
[162] Gillespie, *International Environmental Law, Policy and Ethics*, 2nd edn, p. 13.

equate to 'extrinsic' or 'utilitarian' values.[163] Legal scholar Pieter van Heijnsbergen distinguishes economic from non-economic values within the overall category of instrumental values, assigning aesthetic value to the realm of 'non-economic' concerns.[164] As a non-economic value, aesthetic value is categorised by van Heijnsbergen in the company of scientific, cultural, recreational and educational values, among others.[165]

There are, however, some differences among legal scholars as to the ways in which instrumental values can be distinguished from either inherent or intrinsic values of the environment.[166] Consistent with the work elsewhere of one of its authors,[167] *Lyster's International Wildlife Law* categorises aesthetic value as an 'inherent value', distinct from instrumental and intrinsic values.[168] Specifically, it provides that inherent value 'is that which an entity possesses of itself, by virtue not of its utility, but of its mere existence' distinct from 'intrinsic' value, which is also the value that an entity possesses 'for itself, regardless of the interests or utility of others'.[169] Michael Bowman couples 'aesthetic' with recreational considerations, contrasting both aesthetic and recreational values with 'utilitarian' concerns.[170] Lynda Collins also associates the environment's aesthetic value with 'the intangible, quality-of-life values inherent in natural environments',[171] and both JE Schaffner and Werner Scholtz take the view that aesthetic value is an inherent value of the environment.[172] However, James Nickel and Daniel Magraw potentially have a different perspective. They describe 'the experience of beauty' as 'intrinsically valuable' and suggest that in the view of some scholars the natural systems and objects are a constitutive rather than instrumental part of that experience.[173] If they, like Catherine Redgwell,[174] consider 'natural

163 See Brady, *Aesthetics of the Natural Environment*, 23. On axiology, see further Hirose and Olson, 'Introduction to value theory'.
164 See van Heijnsbergen, p. 56.
165 Ibid.
166 See Fosci and West, 'In whose interest?', 55; in philosophical literature, see Hargrove, 'An overview of conservation and human values', 227.
167 See Bowman, 'Biodiversity, intrinsic value', 41–61. Cf. Callicott, 'On the intrinsic value of nonhuman species'.
168 Bowman, Davies and Redgwell, *Lyster's International Wildlife Law*, p. 61.
169 Ibid., p. 62. See also Bowman, 'Biodiversity, intrinsic value'.
170 Bowman, 'Law, legal scholarship', 13.
171 Collins, 'The United Nations, human rights', 242. Note Collins also associates aesthetic value with beauty and Indigenous culture, 242.
172 See Schaffner, 'Value, wild animals and law', 8; Scholtz, 'Ethical and humane use', 77.
173 Nickel and Magraw, 'Philosophical issues', 464.
174 Redgwell, 'Article 2 definition of natural heritage'.

beauty' to be the same as 'aesthetic' value, they would likely support the classification of aesthetic value as an intrinsic value.

Consistent with understandings of aesthetic value as natural beauty, legal scholars have also emphasised the visual dimension of aesthetic value. Michael Bowman and his co-authors of *Lyster's International Wildlife* for example explain that:

> From an aesthetic point of view, [inherent] value may reside in any entity capable of being the subject of sensual appreciation. Clearly, plants and animals may satisfy this criterion, either individually or collectively, though the emphasis in the latter case is likely to fall upon aesthetically appreciable assemblages (notably flocks, herds, landscapes and vistas), rather than upon ecologically significant collectivities such as species, communities or ecosystems. Once again, such value is not restricted to living entities, but extends to inanimate features of the landscape, including mountains, lakes and rivers, and even to transient or intangible elements such as clouds, sunsets and rainbows.[175]

Despite the initial reference to 'sensual appreciation' in this quote,[176] the explanation is weighted to visual appreciation. Terms such as 'appreciable assemblages' and 'landscape' features indicate an understanding of aesthetic value in ways seen.

2.3.2.2 Reconciling Variable Accounts of Aesthetic Value

Scholarship on aesthetic value in international environmental law appears united in its reliance on axiology, the theory of values in philosophy.[177] Value theory is relevant to many philosophies to examine what is deemed good or bad, but it is well-developed in moral philosophy and theories of ethics, including environmental ethics.[178] A division between 'new' and 'old' environmental ethics, for example, is central to Alexander Gillespie's framing of environmental values for international environmental law.[179] Considerations of values in terms of instrumentality contrasted with the intrinsic, or subjectivity contrasted with objectivity, are concepts derived from axiology that the

[175] Bowman, Davies and Redgwell, *Lyster's International Wildlife Law*, p. 68.
[176] Ibid.
[177] On axiology, see Hirose and Olson, 'Introduction to value theory'. See also Keller (ed.), *Environmental Ethics*.
[178] See Gardiner and Thompson, *Oxford Handbook of Environmental Ethics*.
[179] Gillespie, *International Environmental Law, Policy and Ethics*, 2nd edn, p. 2. See further Gillespie, 'Ethical considerations', 217. Cf. Redgwell, 'Life, the universe and everything', 71.

legal scholarship reviewed for this book has applied to characterise 'environmental' values for international law.

There is, however, no apparent consensus on the meaning of aesthetic value for the various treaties that use the term. Possibly common to all the scholars reviewed is an understanding that aesthetic value is 'subjective'. It might also be commonly viewed as being judged in visual terms.[180] But little more is clear. Aesthetic value is variously described in the legal scholarship as anthropocentric and instrumental as well as non-economic, inherent and possibly intrinsic.[181] And while common associations are made with natural beauty, landscape and recreational values, it is not necessarily clear how distinctions between those values would be made for international law. As explained in the next section of this chapter, these elements are difficult to reconcile with the discipline of international law so often conceived for doctrinal purposes as objective and premised on common agreement among nation states.[182]

2.4 REVISITING AESTHETIC VALUE FOR INTERNATIONAL ENVIRONMENTAL LAW

Few characterisations of the environment's aesthetic value for international environmental law identify concerns and debates from perspectives of philosophers of environmental aesthetics.[183] Below I reference those perspectives to highlight issues arising in the conception of aesthetic value for international environmental law. Specifically, I consider conflations with other environmental values deemed trivial; the irregularity of subjectivity in international law; and concerns about the hegemony of values deemed universal. For reasons explained, I rely principally on arguments developed by aesthetic philosopher Emily Brady to develop an understanding of aesthetic value that takes account of considerations particular to international environmental law.

[180] Bowman, Davies and Redgwell, *Lyster's International Wildlife Law*, p. 68.

[181] See Gillespie, *International Environmental Law, Policy and Ethics*, 2nd edn; Redgwell, 'Article 2 definition of natural heritage'; van Heijnsbergen, *International Legal Protection*; Bowman, Davies and Redgwell, *Lyster's International Wildlife Law*.

[182] See generally Bianchi, *International Law Theories*; Orford and Hoffmann (eds.), *The Oxford Handbook of the Theory of International Law*. Discussed later in Chapter 4.

[183] Gillespie does not explicitly discuss the philosophy of 'environmental aesthetics' but he cites, for example, to Carlson and Brady: See Gillespie, *International Environmental Law, Policy and Ethics*, p. 68. On the significance of environmental aesthetics to international environmental law, see Palmer, 'Legal dimensions'.

2.4.1 *Aesthetic Value as Indistinct and Trivial*

The emphasis in international environmental legal scholarship on the visual dimensions of aesthetic value, evidenced for example in references to 'flocks', 'herds' and 'vistas' beset by 'sunsets and rainbows',[184] risks conflations with particular understandings of natural beauty – an environmental value that the *World Heritage Convention* identifies for protection as distinct from aesthetic value.[185] And once associated with natural beauty, aesthetic value might be cast for the purposes of international environmental law and policy as an hedonistic, incidental luxury that pales in comparison with other environmental values also protected by treaties, such as scientific concerns for ecosystem collapse, or ethical concerns for the survival of species, including humans.[186]

With her integrated aesthetic model, Emily Brady seeks to address what she describes as a trivialisation of aesthetic value in public policy that comes from conflations with natural beauty. She posits that 'a critical understanding of environmental aesthetics helps to correct the common view that aesthetics has only to do with values such as prettiness, beauty or attractiveness'.[187] A critical perspective disassociates aesthetic value from 'scenery' models of nature appreciation tied to the visual in British and European landscape conventions from the eighteenth and nineteenth centuries. As was explained in Section 2.2, Emily Brady and other philosophers of environmental aesthetics have instead developed complex accounts of the aesthetic value of the natural environment that extend beyond philocaly – a love of beauty – and the idea of wilderness as visual appreciation.[188] Theirs is a multi-sensory appreciation of the environment that does not privilege the visual in aesthetic experience.

Once expanded to take in other senses engaged in an aesthetic appreciation of the environment – along with sight also smell, sound, touch – aesthetic value can be more readily distinguished from other environmental values protected under international environmental law, and be less susceptible to being trivialised.

[184] Bowman, Davies and Redgwell, *Lyster's International Wildlife Law*; see various quotes above in Section 2.3.2.1.

[185] Article 2 of the *World Heritage Convention*.

[186] Brady, *Aesthetics of the Natural Environment*, p. 225. See Section 2.2.3.1.

[187] Ibid., p. 229.

[188] Ibid., p. 46 (on American transcendentalism). See also Cronon, 'The trouble with wilderness', 471–99. Cf. Woods, *Rethinking Wilderness*; Robyn Bartel et al. (eds.), *Rethinking Wilderness and The Wild*.

2.4.2 *Subjective Aesthetic Value an Irregularity in 'Objective' International Law*

The conception of aesthetic value among scholars of international environmental laws in subjective terms is consistent with models of environmental aesthetics identified by Emily Brady as 'non-cognitive' theories, and by philosopher Allen Carlson as 'subjectivist' accounts of aesthetic appreciation.[189] Alexander Gillespie, for example, understands the environment's aesthetic value as a 'relative' value.[190] Catherine Redgwell notes the lack of a 'universal classification system' for aesthetic value in the context of the *World Heritage Convention*.[191] And Werner Scholtz and Lynda Collins respectively also characterise the environment's aesthetic value as subjective, with Scholtz specifically rejecting 'aesthetic objectivism'.[192]

However, the practice of international environmental law is grounded in an expectation of objectivity.[193] To be sure, that expectation has long been a feature of sound criticism in international legal theory.[194] But it has persisted nonetheless, fuelled by positivist pretensions in the broad practice of international law, including those directed at environmental protection.[195] By this account, an objective international law is an expression of the will of sovereign states, quarantined from partisan or subjective influences. Any environmental values expressed in treaties are values on which all parties, at least for doctrinal purposes, are agreed and thus capable of objective determination.[196]

In this context, aesthetic value is at risk of being overshadowed in the administration of international environmental treaties by values that can be quantified or otherwise 'objectified' by forms of reductive valuation. Economic or scientific values of the environment are for example promoted for the objective 'rational' methods by which they are described. Alexander Gillespie observes that environmental values that can be reduced to economic values can then be compared with each other.[197] He notes that 'the costs and benefits that are more difficult to measure, and harder to attribute economic

[189] See Section 2.2.2.
[190] Gillespie, *International Environmental Law, Policy and Ethics*, 2nd edn, p. 76.
[191] Redgwell, 'Article 2 definition of natural heritage'.
[192] Scholtz, 'Animal culling'; Collins, 'The United Nations, human rights'.
[193] See, for example, Orford and Hoffmann, 'Introduction', 4.
[194] See Bianchi, *International Law Theories*, p. 21. Cf. p. 135. See also Bianchi, *Theory and Philosophy of International Law*.
[195] See Kammerhofer, 'International legal positivism', 407.
[196] On *pacta sunt servanda*, see Shaw, *International Law*, p. 788.
[197] Gillespie, *International Environmental Law, Policy and Ethics*, 2nd edn, p. 27.

data to, tend to be ignored or undervalued'.[198] *Lyster's International Wildlife* states that 'reliable methods of comparison and quantification' such as economic valuation are adopted for the purposes of prioritising different values – one environmental value as against another environmental value, and all environmental values as against non-environmental values – in the service of 'sustainable development'.[199] It describes the ways in which aesthetic appeal can be characterised in financial terms,[200] recognising, as does Gillespie, that not all aspects of aesthetic value are capable of being expressed in monetary or commodified terms.[201]

These issues of measure and comparison are at the root of concerns for those philosophers in environmental aesthetics who seek to develop 'cognitive' or 'objectivist' foundations for the aesthetic appreciation of the environment.[202] For Allen Carlson, for example, if scientific knowledge of natural species and natural spaces drives aesthetic appreciation, it provides common ground for the appreciation of the natural environment.[203] The sonar capacities of a bat's head, to respond to Malcolm Budd quoted earlier, would be significant to the aesthetic appreciation of the bat.[204] Having concerns about using science as a common ground, however, Emily Brady co-opted the concept of 'disinterestedness' in her quest for a theory of environmental aesthetics that can be communicated for the purposes of comparison in a policy setting.[205] In Janna Thompson's view – a view that I will return to in subsequent chapters of the book – it is the aesthetic criteria of art that provide a common framework for evaluation of the aesthetic value of the environment.[206]

International law's practised orientation towards objectivity might drive Redgwell's observation that 'aesthetic value must reside in more than the local population to satisfy the requirements of the [World Heritage] Convention'.[207] As discussed further in Chapter 5, the *World Heritage Convention* is by its terms premised on objectivity – it protects 'outstanding universal value' in natural and cultural heritage determined in accordance with scientific

198 Ibid., p. 26.
199 Bowman, Davies and Redgwell, *Lyster's International Wildlife Law*, pp. 78–9.
200 Ibid., p. 63.
201 Ibid., p. 79; Gillespie, *International Environmental Law, Policy and Ethics*, 2nd edn, p. 40.
202 See Section 2.2.2.
203 Carlson, *Aesthetics and the Environment*, p. 9.
204 Budd, 'Objectivity and the aesthetic value of nature', 270.
205 Brady, *Aesthetics of the Natural Environment*, p. 141.
206 Thompson, 'Aesthetics and the value of nature'.
207 Redgwell, 'Article 2 definition of natural heritage'. Cf. Scholtz, 'Animal culling'.

method.[208] Yet, by virtue of being multilateral arrangements among many nation states, all treaties that protect the environment for its aesthetic value are confronted in practice with locating aesthetic value in an objective framework – or at least a framework that provides for the articulation of the value in terms that can be understood by all parties as a unified concept that is distinct from other environmental values.[209] This concerns international treaties that express aesthetic value but it applies too where a legal claim is made on the basis that aesthetic value informs the interpretation of a treaty – as I will argue in Chapter 3 in the context of interpreting the *Whaling Convention*.[210]

2.4.3 *Hegemony of Objectified Aesthetic Value*

Any move away from subjectivism towards objectivism in the characterisation of aesthetic value could still be problematic for the practice of international environmental law. In the case of international law applied among states, the 'objectification' of aesthetic value could have the effect of universalising for all states parties to a treaty a culturally specific understanding of aesthetic value. Referencing the paradigm of 'environmentalism of the poor', critical scholarship has addressed the hegemonic effect of environmental movements bound to the specific ideas of natural beauty and wilderness developed in Europe and Britain and embraced in the United States.[211] Aesthetic value is seen as what might be called a 'full belly' luxury.[212] An aesthetic value 'objectified' as natural beauty might only constitute a value construct of rich, industrial, former colonising states that is applied by all states under the guise of universalism.[213] And that particular framing might be one that works against the natural environment. In his book *Law and Nature*, for example, David Delaney suggests that '[i]n stories about progress, development, civilization, and socialization, law is frequently cast by social theorists as that which marks the break, and therefore, that which makes humans distinctively *human*. As such, law is commonly figured as antinature, and it is this opposition to nature that makes law.'[214]

[208] Articles 1 and 2 of the *World Heritage Convention*.
[209] On treaty interpretation, see Chapter 3.
[210] See Section 3.4.2.
[211] See Cronon, 'The trouble with wilderness', 471, cited in Maskit, 'On universalism'.
[212] See generally Guha, *Environmentalism*; Guha, 'Radical American environmentalism. See discussion in Gillespie, *International Environmental Law, Policy and Ethics*, 2nd edn, p. 77. See also Nixon, *Slow Violence*, p. 5.
[213] See generally Pahuja, *Decolonising International Law*.
[214] Delaney, *Law and Nature*, p. 24.

It is not certain that Emily Brady's integrated aesthetic model would address such concerns if adopted for characterisations of aesthetic value in international environmental law. As explained above in Section 2.2, aesthetic scholar Jonathan Maskit does not appear to credit Brady and the non-cognitivist scholars she applauds as having situated aesthetic appreciation in a cultural context.[215] By her own description, however, Brady is a proponent of cultural pluralism, describing her understanding of the 'knowledge' that contributes to aesthetic appreciation in terms of 'commonsense, folk and other cultural knowledges, including scientific knowledge'.[216] Her reliance on the Kantian concept of disinterestedness is contrived by her to remove idiosyncratic judgements of value for the purposes of aesthetic evaluations in policy. This does not, she maintains, detract from an acknowledgement of pluralised aesthetic experiences of the environment that are spatially and culturally situated.[217] In this sense, Emily Brady's model of environmental aesthetics could be properly employed to avoid universalising a singular aesthetic in international environmental law. Yet, following her model, variances between states in their culturally specific articulation of the environment's aesthetic value could be accepted within a common framework for evaluation of the value. How disinterestedness could be institutionalised for this purpose, however, is not clear.[218] It might be that, in the context of judgements of aesthetic value under treaties, aesthetic value is significant for all states but significant in different ways explored in Chapters 5 to 7.

2.5 CONCLUSION

Consideration of the environment's aesthetic value in scholarship on international environmental law has largely examined environmental values from the philosophical perspective of environmental ethics.[219] It typically presents aesthetic value in terms of axiological categories, describing it as a subjective and instrumental value that is associated with environmental values such as natural beauty, recreation and scenic values.[220] Distinctions between aesthetic

[215] Maskit, 'On universalism'.
[216] Brady, *Aesthetics of the Natural Environment*, p. 185.
[217] Ibid. See also Brady, *The Oxford Handbook of Environmental Ethics.*
[218] See Chapter 8.
[219] See, for example, Gillespie, *International Environmental Law, Policy and Ethics*, 2nd edn; Gillespie, 'Ethical considerations', 217.
[220] See Section 2.3.2.2.

value and other environmental values have not been explained in this literature. I maintain that this characterisation in legal scholarship of the environment's aesthetic value is problematic for international environmental law. Aesthetic value might be seen as trivial and subjective, conflated with other values, or passed off as objective, leaving it to carry no, or too much, weight in the decisions of international communities to protect the environment.[221]

The characterisation of the environment's aesthetic value by scholars in international environmental law contrasts with that of philosophers of environmental aesthetics. Philosophers such as Emily Brady understand aesthetic value in terms of a multi-sensory engagement with the natural environment, shaped by imagination, emotion and knowledge, including knowledge from different cultures.[222] From Emily Brady's perspective, the environment's aesthetic value can be conceived in a way that is manifestly important to people while also allowing for pluralised, place-based aesthetic significance in ways some philosophers might describe as subjective. However, in her integrated aesthetic model, the situations of object *and* subject guide appreciation in an aesthetic approach that 'emphasises the engaged, relational and contextual character of environmental appreciation and preserves a kind of non-instrumentalism through the concept of disinterestedness'.[223]

Brady's philosophical account of environmental appreciation evokes what I am calling an 'exquisite' and 'profound' affect, which makes aesthetic value distinct from other environmental values. It is an environmental appreciation that is also a product of culture. Such conceptions of the environment's aesthetic value among philosophers of environmental aesthetics, including Emily Brady, are appropriate characterisations of aesthetic value for international law. As exquisite and profound, it is both distinct from other environmental values protected by international environmental treaties and important for protection by the international community of states that make international environmental law. That it is sensitive to cultural variations makes Brady's model of environmental aesthetics relevant to constructions of aesthetic value for the different nation states that are party to international treaties that protect the environment for its aesthetic value.[224]

It is, however, not clear if such a characterisation of the environment's aesthetic value would correspond with meanings of aesthetic value where it is

[221] Cf. issues of 'ugly' but ecologically significant environments in Gillespie, *International Environmental Law, Policy and Ethics*, 2nd edn, p. 79; Brady, *Aesthetics of the Natural Environment*, p. 229; Brady, 'The ugly truth'.

[222] See Section 2.2.3.

[223] Brady, *Aesthetics of the Natural Environment*, p. 3; see also p. 120.

[224] See Section 2.2.3.5.

expressed as a term of a treaty or is otherwise informing the interpretation of treaties that protect the environment. In Chapter 3, I will employ international rules of treaty interpretation to develop legal definitions of the term 'aesthetic' value in the context of three treaties: The *World Heritage Convention*,[225] the *Biodiversity Convention*[226] and the *Whaling Convention*.[227] There I will consider the extent to which meanings of the environment's 'aesthetic' value, developed from orthodox sources of treaty interpretation for each treaty, correspond to understandings of aesthetic value in the philosophy of environmental aesthetics. I contend that the term 'aesthetic' value expressed in international environmental treaties is a term subject to legal interpretation.[228] In international legal practice it would be interpreted in accordance with doctrinal rules of treaty interpretation, including those prescribed by the *Vienna Convention on the Law of Treaties*.[229] Under those rules, words in a treaty are to be interpreted in good faith in accordance with the ordinary meaning in context and in light of the treaty's object and purpose.[230] The same word can have a different meaning in different treaties and in different parts of the same treaty.[231] Enforcement of a treaty might turn on interpretation of a term,[232] and if treaty powers are exercised under a misapprehension of meaning, the exercise of those powers by officers authorised to make decisions under the treaty might be unlawful.[233]

[225] *World Heritage Convention*; see Chapter 5.
[226] *Convention on Biological Diversity*; see Chapter 7.
[227] *Whaling Convention*; see Chapter 6.
[228] See further Chapter 3.
[229] *Vienna Convention on the Law of Treaties*, Vienna, 23 May 1969, in force 27 January 1980, 1155 UNTS 331.
[230] Article 31(1), ibid.
[231] On different meanings of the same term in an instrument, see Gardiner, *Treaty Interpretation*, p. 209.
[232] See Chapter 6.
[233] See Chapter 5.

3

Legal Interpretation of Aesthetic Value

EXHIBIT: WILLIAM WYLD, *MANCHESTER FROM KERSAL MOOR* (1852)

FIGURE 3.1. William Wyld, *Manchester from Kersal Moor*, 1852. Watercolour, 32 × 49 cm. Royal Collection Trust. *Source*: Wikimedia Commons.

William Wyld's *Manchester from Kersal Moor* (Figure 3.1) provides a remarkably contemporary vision despite portraying a landscape from two centuries past. In the distance, the golden glow of a sunset blends to a bruised hue in the haze of emissions from chimney stacks, spires of industrialisation threatening to overcome the church steeples in their midst. A river encircles the eponymous moor, a border to the unkempt countryside outside the city limits. A dank but not unpleasant smell rises with heat from muddy banks. A family atop a hill in that unwieldly foreground might be missed but for the cardinal red of the woman's skirts. There a mother's gaze appears caught by her infant while an attentive dog looks on and a protective father looks out. Long, end-of-day shadows extend from darkening trees as night falls. Bleats and tweets are reedy in the cooling air.

Is the man watchful or distracted? Whether his gaze is one of awe or concern is not clear. It is a spectacular scene, commissioned by Britain's Queen Victoria.[1] Not knowing then what we know now of the impacts that fossil fuel emissions would wreak on the world – the chimneys were built on cotton mills powered by coal-fired steam engines[2] – the painting might well be seen as a secular homage to the might of 'man', a sacrilegious celebration of human ingenuity and the taming of both nature and God. Seen today, it resembles contemporary New Delhi, Los Angeles or Beijing, bathed in the unabated smog of consumption.[3] Or this is a dystopian vision: Hell's fires burn while that mighty man looks on, beguiled or complacent, so happy with his lot that he cannot see beyond the brilliant palette that backgrounds his domestic contentedness.

3.1 INTRODUCTION

My description of William Wyld's painting *Manchester from Kersal Moor* (Figure 3.1) uses aesthetic methods developed for the analysis of visual art to articulate different understandings of the environment's aesthetic value. Multiple meanings arise from my analysis. Some of those understandings relate to conceptions of aesthetic value among philosophers of environmental aesthetics that I described in Chapter 2.[4] A multi-sensory engagement with the environment is suggested, for example, by sounds, smells and sights. My perception of the depicted environment is shaped by my imagination, emotion and knowledge. Other elements in my description suggest an aesthetic appreciation relevant to the arts, including eco-critical perspectives on history and environmental concerns of the current day.[5]

1 Royal Collection Trust, 'Manchester from Kersal Moor'.
2 Hills, *Power in the Industrial Revolution*, pp. 10, 139, 149.
3 See World Health Organisation, *Global Ambient Air Quality Database*.
4 See Section 2.2.2. Note I address different aspects of the relationship between art and the environment's aesthetic value in Section 2.2.1 and in Section 4.3.2.
5 See Section 4.3.3.

Later in Chapter 4, I will discuss art methods and their relevance to my analysis of the environment's aesthetic value from photographs in international decision-making processes. First, I will here engage international law's doctrinal methods for interpreting terms in treaties to understand the meanings of the environment's aesthetic value that might be decided in international legal practice. Where expressed as a treaty term, or otherwise informing the implementation of a treaty, 'aesthetic' value is a legal term that would be interpreted in accordance with international rules of treaty interpretation.[6] In this chapter, I employ different methods of treaty interpretation to develop meanings of 'aesthetic' value for three international treaties:[7] The *World Heritage Convention* and the *Biodiversity Convention*, both of which protect the environment's aesthetic value through their express terms; and the *Whaling Convention*, which, I argue here, protects aesthetic value through an amendment to ban commercial whaling.

As was the case for my aesthetic analysis of Wyld's *Manchester from Kersal Moor*, a range of meanings, and methods for constructing meanings, can arise from treaty interpretation in international law. Employing literal, contextual and teleological approaches, as well as intentional and evolutive techniques,[8] I conclude in this chapter that the orthodox sources and methods for interpreting treaties produce a variable account of the meanings of the environment's aesthetic value. For reasons explained earlier,[9] I maintain that Emily Brady's integrated aesthetic model is an appropriate reference from which to develop meanings of the environment's aesthetic value for international law. Brady's model understands aesthetic value as distinct from other environmental values, and important for consideration in its own right, yet sensitive to cultural variations.[10] This is a conception of the environment's aesthetic value that is proper as a matter of doctrine, and as a matter of critical understandings of environmental aesthetics, for protection under international treaties by

6 See, for example, Gardiner, *Treaty Interpretation*. See also Aust, *Modern Treaty Law and Practice*. Cf. critical interpretation of international law: See generally Bianchi, Peat and Windsor, *Interpretation in International Law*.

7 *Convention for the Protection of the World Cultural and Natural Heritage*, Paris, 16 November 1972, in force 17 December 1975, 1037 UNTS 151; *International Convention on the Regulation of Whaling*, Washington, 2 December 1946, in force 10 November 1948, 161 UNTS 72; *Convention on Biological Diversity*, Rio de Janeiro, 5 June 1992, in force 29 December 1993, 1760 UNTS 79.

8 Explained in Section 3.3.

9 See Section 2.4.

10 See generally Brady, *Aesthetics of the Natural Environment*.

diverse nation states.[11] It is, however, not readily conceived through the orthodox sources of interpretation in international law.

3.2 TREATY INTERPRETATION UNDER INTERNATIONAL LAW

The making, implementation and enforcement of international treaties agreed between sovereign states are functions of international legal practice that rely on the interpretation of terms in those treaties.[12] Public international law has developed rules for interpreting treaties that are largely codified in the 1969 *Vienna Convention on the Law of Treaties* ('*Vienna Convention*').[13] The meaning of treaty terms is constructed for the purposes of the practice of international law in accordance with a range of techniques. The oft-cited Article 31(1) of the *Vienna Convention* provides for treaty interpretation to be 'in good faith in accordance with the ordinary meaning to be given to the terms of the treaty in their context and in the light of [the treaty's] object and purpose'.[14] Treaty interpreters may also look to evidence of such things as subsequent practice, historical intention and 'evolutive' meanings to construct meanings for treaty terms.[15] The act of treaty interpretation in accordance with these rules has been variously characterised as the application of legal rules,[16] reference to guidance,[17] part of the 'atmosphere' lying around the law,[18] derived from the 'climate of opinion',[19] and a 'social practice' between like-minded people.[20] Jan Klabbers suggests that treaty interpreters should be guided by 'humility, acquiescence, integrity and candour'.[21] Iain Scobbie argues that legal texts 'need to have an identifiable meaning, or [a] range of

[11] See Section 2.4.

[12] See generally Sands and Peel, *Principles of International Environmental Law*; Bodansky, Brunnée and Hey, 'International environmental law', p. 1. Cf. Koskenniemi and Leino, 'Fragmentation of international law?'.

[13] *Vienna Convention on the Law of Treaties*, Vienna, 23 May 1969, in force 27 January 1980, 1155 UNTS 331. See Gardiner, *Treaty Interpretation*, p. 16.

[14] Article 31(1) of the *Vienna Convention*.

[15] For issues arising from different techniques, see Gardiner, *Treaty Interpretation*, pp. 460ff. Note Maarten Bos identifies the methods as grammatical, historical, systematic, teleological and sociological: Bos, 'Theory and practice', part II, 136. Cf. Jan Klabbers, who limits the methods to textual, historical and teleological: Klabbers, *International Law*, pp. 57–8.

[16] Allott, 'Language, method and the nature of international law', 133.

[17] Bos, 'Theory and practice', part I, 21.

[18] Ibid., part II, 170.

[19] Johnstone, 'Treaty interpretation', 376.

[20] Klabbers, *International Law*, p. 59.

[21] Klabbers, 'Virtuous interpretation', 37. See also Hosseinnejad, 'On the nature of interpretation', 225–49.

acceptable meanings, because the practice of law is an instrumental activity aimed at practical outcomes'.[22] With all this in mind, below I make general observations about the relevance of aesthetic value to the three treaties analysed in this chapter before undertaking in later sections a detailed analysis of the term in accordance with interpretative rules.

Interpretation is relevant to developing meanings of the express terms of treaties, as well as to terms implied. Two of the treaties examined in this book make express mention of aesthetic value although to different juridical effect. The use of the term 'aesthetic' as an element of 'outstanding universal value' in the definition of 'natural heritage' under the *World Heritage Convention* pertains to determinations of World Heritage status. The *Biodiversity Convention* identifies aesthetic value in its preamble as a value of biological diversity. As a term in the preamble, aesthetic value would, under the rules of treaty interpretation, inform the implementation of the substantive commitments but it is not a provision that itself takes the form of a substantive commitment.[23] As noted earlier, the *Whaling Convention* contains no express mention of aesthetic value. I will discuss later in this chapter how aesthetic value might nevertheless be relevant to the interpretation of the ban on commercial whaling and exceptions to the ban.[24]

There is seemingly no authoritative interpretation by an international court or tribunal of the term 'aesthetic' value as it relates to the environment under these international environmental treaties.[25] Enforcement proceedings that would require judicial interpretation of such treaties are not common. However, the task of interpreting international environmental treaties is not limited to judges: Various officers, including diplomats and civil servants, engage in acts of interpretation in the course of making and implementing international environmental treaties.[26] A range of officials and bodies have functions mandated by the treaties under the authority of the states parties that require them to form a view on the meaning of the treaty terms. Both the *World Heritage Convention* and the *Biodiversity Convention* have what is called 'universal' membership, in the sense that almost all of the world's nations are bound by their terms, with 194 and 196 states parties, respectively.[27]

22 Scobbie, 'A view of Delft', 63–4.
23 On preambles, see Gardiner, *Treaty Interpretation*, pp. 205–6. Discussed in Section 3.3.1.3.
24 Clause 10(e) of the schedule to the *Whaling Convention*.
25 Dupuy and Viñuales, *International Environmental Law*, pp. 299–300, 328–30.
26 Ibid. See also Rosenne, 'Conceptualism as a guide', 441.
27 See United Nations Educational, Scientific and Cultural Organisation, 'World Heritage Convention: States parties'; United Nations Treaty Collection, 'Depository: Status of treaties'.

The membership of the *Whaling Convention* is 88 contracting states but it has fluctuated over time.[28]

Orthodox sources for interpretation take the form of the written word, expressed for example in the text of the treaty, in authoritative references such as dictionaries, and documents generated in the course of the parties' governance of their treaty commitments.[29] An understanding of those governance arrangements is needed to identify those sources. In a form of 'international administration',[30] outstanding universal value under the *World Heritage Convention* is determined through a long-standing but evolving decision-making process. The process for inscribing properties on the World Heritage List is initiated through state nominations, then informed by expert evaluations, and decided by the World Heritage Committee – a body of experts elected by the states parties to the treaty.[31] The administration of the states parties' commitments under the *Biodiversity Convention* is overseen by a governing body, the Conference of the Parties (COP), supported by a network of subsidiary bodies.[32] States parties, known as contracting members, are each represented in the International Whaling Commission, the governing body created by the *Whaling Convention* to develop scientific studies of whale stocks and manage whale fisheries.[33]

Each 'object' of aesthetic appreciation could produce different meanings of aesthetic value because the rules of treaty interpretation dictate that terms be interpreted in their context.[34] The three treaties differ in terms of the aspects of the natural environment valued for their aesthetic qualities. The *World Heritage Convention* protects natural areas, features and formations of natural areas (natural properties);[35] the *Biodiversity Convention* protects natural

[28] See United States Department of State, 'Status lists for treaties'.

[29] See, for example, Gardiner, *Treaty Interpretation*, pp. 81 (interpretative material generated in making treaties), 255 (written documentation of subsequent practice). Cf. on written sources of law as opposed to sources for interpretation: Staubach, *The Rule of Unwritten International Law*.

[30] As opposed to 'distributed' or 'network' administration: See Kingsbury, 'Global environmental governance as administration', 63.

[31] Article 8 of the *World Heritage Convention*.

[32] Article 23, ibid.

[33] The International Whaling Commission's work is supported by committees of experts, including the Scientific Committee: Article III.4 of the *Whaling Convention*.

[34] Article 31 of the *Vienna Convention*.

[35] Article 2 of the *World Heritage Convention*. Note that properties can be a mix of natural and cultural heritage: See Section 3.3.1.2.

systems (biological diversity) for their aesthetic qualities;[36] and the *Whaling Convention* protects species of wild animals (whales and other cetaceans).[37]

As explained later in this chapter, treaty interpretation can take account of meanings that have evolved over time: Meanings intended by the negotiators of a treaty might be changed by such things as explicit agreement on interpretation,[38] the subsequent practice of states under the treaty or,[39] more controversially, evolving expectations of the international community prevailing at the time of interpretation.[40] For these reasons, it is relevant that the treaties were made and are implemented at different times. Two decades separate the *World Heritage Convention* adopted in 1972 and the *Biodiversity Convention* adopted in 1992. The *Whaling Convention* was first adopted in 1946, then amended in 1982 to ban commercial whaling,[41] before being enforced in 2014 in a decision of the International Court of Justice.[42] Various changes over time might inform the legal interpretation of treaties. For example, the conception of the environment for treaties has evolved with scientific developments, shifting from species to their habitats and, ultimately, the ecosystems that render all species and habitats interdependent.[43] Different political and cultural interests are also represented over time in ways that might be relevant to an evolutive interpretation of a treaty. International relations have evolved from a period dominated by the interests of the rich countries of the 'North' to one influenced by the environmental concerns of the poor or 'developing' nations of the 'Global South'.[44]

All of these factors could be relevant to the crafting of meanings of 'aesthetic' value in accordance with the international rules of treaty interpretation. Next, I analyse the meaning of the environment's aesthetic value as an express term of the *World Heritage Convention* and the *Biodiversity Convention*. The meaning of aesthetic value for the *Whaling Convention* is examined in

36 Preamble of the *Convention on Biological Diversity*.

37 Coverage of cetacean species is contentious: See Fitzmaurice, *Whaling and International Law*, pp. 50–1.

38 Article 31(4) of the *Vienna Convention* (special meaning).

39 Article 31(3)(b), ibid.

40 See, for example, evolutive interpretation: Section 3.3.4. On 'time factors in treaty interpretation', see Gardiner, *Treaty Interpretation*, p. 292.

41 Clause 10(e) of the schedule to ibid. (commercial whaling ban). See International Whaling Commission, 'Verbatim Record', 19–24 July 1982, 72, 86.

42 *Whaling in the Antarctic (Australia v Japan; New Zealand intervening) (Judgment)* [2014] ICJ Rep 226.

43 See, for example, 'History' in Sands and Peel, *Principles of International Environmental Law*, p. 21. See also Davies, Godden and Graham, 'Situating property within habitat'.

44 Mickelson, 'South, north'; Humby, 'Evaluating the value'.

Section 3.4 before I return in Section 3.5 to all three of the treaties to consider matters arising from the use of written sources in a doctrinal account of the meaning of aesthetic value for international law.

3.3 AESTHETIC VALUE AS EXPRESS TERM: NATURAL HERITAGE AND BIODIVERSITY

As explained previously,[45] the environment's aesthetic value is an express term of both the *World Heritage Convention* and the *Biodiversity Convention*. Agreed under the auspices of the United Nations Educational, Scientific and Cultural Organization (UNESCO) in 1972, the *World Heritage Convention* creates an international system for the protection of natural and cultural heritage that is of 'outstanding universal value'. An 'aesthetic' point of view is one of four that informs the concept of 'outstanding universal value' of natural environments. Specifically, Article 2 of the treaty defines 'natural heritage' to include 'natural features consisting of physical and biological formations or groups of such formations, which are of outstanding universal value from the aesthetic or scientific point of view'.[46] Under the treaty, the outstanding universal value of natural sites is also protected from 'conservation' or 'natural beauty' points of view.

Like the *World Heritage Convention*, the *Biodiversity Convention* also expressly protects 'aesthetic' value. The treaty was adopted in 1992 to protect biological diversity, an attribute of healthy natural environments – often shortened to 'biodiversity' – which is defined in the treaty to mean 'the variability among living organisms'.[47] In the preamble to the treaty, the parties identify the values underlying their pact as applying to 'biological diversity' and to 'its components'. As explained in Chapter 2, the first tiret of the preamble states that the parties are '[c]onscious of the intrinsic value of biological diversity and of the ecological, genetic, social, economic, scientific, educational, cultural, recreational and aesthetic values of biological diversity and its components'.[48] The *Biodiversity Convention* combines the objectives of conserving biodiversity, sustainably using biodiversity's components, and sharing 'benefits' such as medicines and agricultural products derived from genetic resources.[49] To these ends, states parties undertake a range

45 See Section 2.3.1.

46 Article 2, ibid. Natural heritage is defined separately from 'cultural heritage', which also refers to aesthetic value: Article 1 of the *World Heritage Convention*. Discussed in Section 3.3.1.2.

47 Article 2 of the *Convention on Biological Diversity*.

48 Preamble, ibid.

49 Article 1, ibid.

of initiatives such as the establishment of natural reserves known as 'protected areas'.[50]

In this section, I interpret the environment's 'aesthetic' value as an express term of the two treaties in accordance with international rules of treaty interpretation. Ultimately, I find that none of the interpretative techniques provides a clear meaning of aesthetic value as it applies to natural heritage or biodiversity. Textual approaches to interpreting terms in light of the ordinary meaning, context and treaty object and purpose might support a broader understanding of aesthetics as 'perception of the senses' as opposed to 'beauty'. However, subsequent practice of the parties to the treaties suggests that aesthetic value is conflated with other environmental values. Aesthetic value is conflated with natural beauty in the administration of the *World Heritage Convention*, and with cultural value under the *Biodiversity Convention.* Whether this subsequent practice qualifies as a source of interpretation or constitutes interpretation that is misconceived is not clear.[51] The meaning intended by the negotiators of the treaties is not apparent from the preparatory documents for the treaties and, while evolutive interpretation would support looking to characterisations of aesthetic value in the contemporary philosophy of environmental aesthetics, that approach might be seen to subvert the parties' intentions. The techniques of treaty interpretation do, however, reveal complexities in the understanding of aesthetic value of the environment that are not necessarily recognised in some of the practices under the treaties. A detailed explanation of my analysis follows.

3.3.1 *Treaty Text: Ordinary Meaning in Context and in Light of Object and Purpose*

The text of a treaty is the source for techniques of treaty interpretation contemplated in Article 31(1) of the *Vienna Convention* that have been described as 'literal', 'contextual' and 'teleological' approaches.[52] No technique takes precedence over another.[53] For reasons explained here, it is possible to conclude that 'aesthetic' value, as it relates to either natural heritage under the *World Heritage Convention* or biodiversity under the *Biodiversity Convention*, has a meaning associated with broad dictionary

50 Article 8, ibid. (protected areas).

51 See Chapter 8.

52 Gardiner, *Treaty Interpretation*, pp. 161–2; 460.

53 Ibid., p. 162. Cf. Aust, saying Article 31 gives preference to textual technique: Aust, *Modern Treaty Law and Practice*, p. 209.

definitions associated with 'perception by the senses'. This approach would give aesthetic value a meaning that is distinct from the dictionary references to 'beauty', and from other environmental values mentioned in those treaties. An understanding of aesthetic value in terms of sensorial perception would be consistent with an aesthetic appreciation of the environment contemplated in the philosophy of environmental aesthetics that I explained in Chapter 2. My application of textual techniques of treaty interpretation to the term 'aesthetic', as expressed in the *World Heritage Convention* and the *Biodiversity Convention*, is explained in detail below.

3.3.1.1 Literal Interpretation

The search for the literal or 'ordinary' meaning of a treaty term typically starts with reference to dictionaries.[54] Where used as an adjective, the *Oxford English Dictionary* defines 'aesthetic' to mean '[o]f or relating to the perception, appreciation, or criticism of that which is beautiful'.[55] In relation to a thing, 'aesthetic' means 'in accordance with principles of artistic beauty or taste; giving or designed to give pleasure through beauty; of pleasing appearance'.[56] In the *Macquarie Dictionary*, 'aesthetic' means: 'relating to the sense of the beautiful or the science of aesthetics'.[57] In contrast, the *New Oxford American Dictionary* meaning is confined to beauty, defining 'aesthetic' as 'concerned with beauty or the appreciation of beauty' or 'giving or designed to give pleasure through beauty; of pleasing appearance'.[58] Finally, a meaning of 'aesthetic' noted by the *Oxford English Dictionary* as obsolete is '[o]f or relating to perception by the senses; received by the senses'.[59] This meaning is linked to the historical meaning of aesthetic as a noun that references the usage by eighteenth-century German philosopher Immanuel Kant and 'the

[54] Gardiner, *Treaty Interpretation*, pp. 186ff.
[55] *OED Online.*
[56] Ibid.
[57] *Macquarie Dictionary Online* defines aesthetic as:
Adjective 1. relating to the sense of the beautiful or the science of aesthetics.
2. having a sense of the beautiful; characterised by a love of beauty.
Noun 3. a philosophical theory as to what is aesthetically valid at a given time.
4. an artistic expression, viewed as reflective of a personal or cultural ideal of what is aesthetically valid.
[58] Stevenson and Lindberg, *New Oxford American Dictionary.*
[59] *OED Online.*

science of sensory perception'.[60] It explains that '[m]odern usage of the word and its family largely reflects [Alexander] Baumgarten's use',[61] as distinct from Immanuel Kant.

Reference can be made to dictionaries in the negotiating or authorised languages of the treaty.[62] The *World Heritage Convention* was negotiated in both English and French,[63] and both it and the *Biodiversity Convention* can be read in several authorised languages.[64] In a definition that resonates with that of the *Oxford English Dictionary*, the *Dictionnaire de l'Académie française* defines 'esthétique' as '[q]ui est motivé par la perception et la sensation du beau' ['[t]hat which is motivated by perception and a sense of beauty'].[65] However, the dictionaries do not necessarily specify the object of appreciation or specifically address the meaning of aesthetic as it relates to the environment. Here, specialist dictionaries or encyclopaedias could be instructive.[66] The *Routledge Encyclopedia of Philosophy* describes the study of 'aesthetics' in relation to the environment as extending 'beyond the narrow confines of the art world and beyond the appreciation of works of art to the aesthetic appreciation of human-influenced and human-constructed as well as natural environments'.[67]

In summary, these sources suggest a variety of meanings, ranging from a narrow conception of 'beauty' associated with the arts to broader definitions linked to 'perception by the senses', and a combination of both. The broader and purportedly obsolete definitions of 'aesthetic' associated with 'perception' and the 'senses' resonate with the characterisation of aesthetic value by contemporary philosophers of environmental aesthetics.[68]

3.3.1.2 Contextual Interpretation

The possibility of different meanings for aesthetic as either synonymous with 'beauty' or otherwise relating to 'perception by the senses' could be clarified by

60 Ibid.
61 Baumgarten's use of the word was purportedly derived from the Greek *aisthētikos*: Ibid.
62 Article 33 of the *Vienna Convention*; see also Gardiner, *Treaty Interpretation*, pp. 413ff.
63 See negotiating documents in English and French language: World Heritage Centre, 'Documents: Establishment of the *Convention*'.
64 Article 30 of the *World Heritage Convention*: Arabic, English, French, Russian and Spanish; Article 42 of the *Convention on Biological Diversity*: Arabic, Chinese, English, French, Russian and Spanish.
65 *l'Académie française* (tr. Author).
66 Article 33 of the *Vienna Convention*; see also Gardiner, *Treaty Interpretation*, pp. 413ff.
67 Carlson, 'Environmental aesthetics'. See also Carlson, 'Nature: Contemporary thought'.
68 See Section 2.2.

an examination of context. Resort to context in treaty interpretation includes the term's grammatical context as well as the treaty as a whole.[69] The different context of a term in a given treaty means that the same word can have different meanings within the one treaty and between different treaties.[70]

In both treaties, the term 'aesthetic' applies to different aspects of the environment to which other values are attached. In the context of the definition of 'natural heritage' in Article 2 of the *World Heritage Convention*, the term 'aesthetic' concerns the value attached to 'natural features'.[71] Under Article 2, these elements may also be assessed to be of 'outstanding universal value' from a 'scientific point of view'. As noted earlier, the *World Heritage Convention* identifies other points of view – conservation and natural beauty – in the definition of natural heritage. But those points of view apply to elements of the environment that are different from those elements to which an 'aesthetic' point of view is applied. In the *Biodiversity Convention*, 'aesthetic' is one of several adjectives describing the value of 'biological diversity and its components'.[72] The other adjectives denoting different values of biological diversity are: Ecological, genetic, social, economic, scientific, educational, cultural, recreational. These values are identified separately from 'intrinsic value of biological diversity'. As noted earlier, biological diversity is defined in the treaty as 'the variability among living organisms'.[73] However, the concept of biological diversity, and the attribution of values to it, is contested in both legal and philosophical literature,[74] making it difficult to draw any definitive conclusions from that aspect of the term's context.

That the objects of aesthetic value in the treaties are elements of the natural environment would mean that the literal meaning of aesthetic value established from dictionaries as 'beauty' could be understood in the more specific terms of 'natural beauty'. However, an interpretative maxim of international law known as the 'principle of effectiveness' requires that no treaty term be rendered redundant by interpretation.[75] By this reasoning, if a treaty referred to 'white and all the colours of the rainbow', the 'colours' of the rainbow would be interpreted to exclude white. The principle of effectiveness would

69 Gardiner, *Treaty Interpretation*, p. 197.
70 Ibid., p. 209.
71 Article 2 of the *World Heritage Convention*.
72 First tiret of the preamble of the *Convention on Biological Diversity*.
73 Article 2, ibid.
74 See generally Bowman, 'The nature, development and philosophical foundations', 5; Dawson, 'What is the value of biodiversity?', 93, 107. See further Section 7.3.1.2.
75 The Latin maxim *ut res magis valeat quam pereat*: Gardiner, *Treaty Interpretation*, pp. 168, 179ff.

mean that 'aesthetic' must have a meaning that is different from the other 'points of view' in Article 2 of the *World Heritage Convention*, including a meaning that is different from the 'natural beauty' point of view. Under the *Biodiversity Convention*, 'aesthetic' would need to be interpreted to have a meaning different from the other values listed with it in the preamble. The preamble does not list 'natural beauty', so 'aesthetic' value under the *Biodiversity Convention* could mean natural beauty without flouting the rule on effectiveness. It would, however, need to be distinguished from other values that are expressed in the treaty such as 'cultural' and 'recreational' values, and 'intrinsic' value too.[76]

The context extends to the whole agreement. In the case of the *World Heritage Convention*, the term 'aesthetic' is also used in the definition of 'cultural heritage'. Article 1 defines three kinds of cultural heritage properties, including 'sites' that are 'works of man or the combined works of nature and man, and areas including archaeological sites which are of outstanding universal value from the historical, aesthetic, ethnological or anthropological point of view'.[77] Properties can be inscribed as a mix of natural and cultural heritage.[78] The different contexts for the term 'aesthetic' in the respective definitions would suggest different meanings, justifying an understanding of the term for natural heritage as one distinct from the aesthetic value of built environments.

The context also includes annexes. Article 7 of the *Biodiversity Convention* requires parties to '[i]dentify components of biological diversity important for its conservation and sustainable use having regard to the indicative list of categories set down in annex I'.[79] Annex I refers explicitly to only four of the values of biodiversity listed in the preamble – namely social, economic, cultural or scientific values. There is no mention of 'aesthetic' value in the annex. States are however guided to identify ecosystems and habitats containing 'wilderness'.[80] It could be argued that the terms 'aesthetic' and 'wilderness' should be read in the context of each other, with each informing the other's meaning.[81]

76 First tiret of the preamble of the *Convention on Biological Diversity*. See Section 2.3.1. See also discussion of 'instrinsic' value of biodiversity in Section 7.3.1.2.

77 Article 1 of the *World Heritage Convention*.

78 World Heritage Committee, *Operational Guidelines for the Implementation of the World Heritage Convention*, UN Doc. WHC.21/01, paras. [46] (mixed properties), [77] (criteria).

79 Article 7 of the *Convention on Biological Diversity*.

80 Annex I, ibid.

81 See discussion of 'wilderness' in Section 7.3.1.2.

To summarise, the context of the term 'aesthetic' in the two treaties suggests a definition of aesthetic that is different from other environmental values expressly stated. In the case of the *World Heritage Convention*, 'aesthetic' would be different from 'natural beauty' and other points of view on natural heritage, and different from the 'aesthetic' value of cultural heritage. I argue that this favours the dictionary definition of 'aesthetic' described above as 'perception by the senses', distinct from aesthetic value in the arts.[82] In the case of the *Biodiversity Convention*, a contextual interpretation requires that the 'aesthetic' value of biodiversity be distinguished from other biodiversity values, including cultural value.[83] However, given that there is no mention of 'natural beauty' in that treaty, context does not exclude a narrow dictionary definition associated with 'beauty' as distinct from sensorial perception in general. Context might also mean that the 'aesthetic' value of biodiversity is informed by, or that it informs, the term 'wilderness' in annex I to the *Biodiversity Convention*.

3.3.1.3 Purposive Interpretation

The teleological or purposive technique of reading a term in light of a treaty's 'object and purpose' will include reference to any stated objectives, including any in the preamble.[84] In practice, there is little if any distinction between the 'object' and the 'purpose'.[85] The purpose of the *World Heritage Convention* is apparent in at least two paragraphs of the preamble, stating that 'deterioration or disappearance of any item of the cultural or natural heritage constitutes a harmful impoverishment of the heritage of all the nations of the world'[86] and 'that parts of the cultural or natural heritage are of outstanding interest and therefore need to be preserved as part of the world heritage of mankind as a whole'.[87] It could be argued that the international significance assigned by the parties to cultural and natural heritage warrants a broad interpretation of 'aesthetic'. This favours the broader literal definition of aesthetic described above as 'perception by the senses'.[88]

The term 'aesthetic' appears in the preamble of the *Biodiversity Convention*, that part of the treaty that can itself describe a treaty's object and purpose. The

[82] See Section 2.2.1.
[83] In Chapter 7, I discuss the relevance of this argument to Indigenous knowledges.
[84] Article 31(1) of the *Vienna Convention*.
[85] Gardiner, *Treaty Interpretation*, p. 214.
[86] Second tiret of the preamble of the *World Heritage Convention*.
[87] Sixth tiret of the preamble, ibid.
[88] See Section 3.3.1.1 (dictionaries).

interpretation of terms in the substantive parts of the treaty could depend on the meaning of 'aesthetic' value in the preamble as part of context and as part of the object and purpose.[89] Terms in the preamble must also be interpreted in light of their object and purpose. In the *Biodiversity Convention*, the objectives are expressly stated in Article 1 to concern biodiversity conservation, the sustainable use of the commercially valuable components of biodiversity, and the sharing of 'benefits' derived from the exploitation of genetic resources. As suggested in connection with the *World Heritage Convention*, it could be argued that the international significance assigned by the parties to biological diversity warrants a broad interpretation of 'aesthetic' offered by literal interpretation, favouring sensual perception over natural beauty.

The possibility of understanding the environment's aesthetic value in terms distinct from natural beauty is, as explained next, not necessarily supported by the practices of the states parties in their administration of the two treaties.

3.3.2 *Subsequent Practice*

Article 31(3) of the *Vienna Convention* describes other sources that interpreters of treaties can look to, including '[a]ny subsequent practice in the application of the treaty which establishes the agreement of the parties regarding its interpretation'.[90] In his treatise on treaty interpretation, Richard Gardiner describes 'subsequent practice' as 'what can be shown to have been done systematically or repeatedly in implementation and application of a treaty'.[91] Gardiner goes on to explain the circumstances in which decisions of organisations might satisfy these requirements. He explains that:

89 On preamble as a source for object and purpose, see Gardiner, *Treaty Interpretation*, p. 213.

90 Article 31(3)(b) of the *Vienna Convention*. Maarten Bos suggests that subsequent practice is part of context: Bos, 'Theory and practice', part II, 145. I do not consider in this chapter related agreements, either as subsequent agreement (Article 31(3)(a) of the *Vienna Convention*) or other agreements on the same subject matter (for purposes either of 'context', 'relevant rules of international law', or supplementary means of interpretation: Articles 31(1), 31(3)(a) or 32 of the *Vienna Convention*). Aust says, in relation to Article 32, '[o]ne may also look at other treaties on the same subject matter adopted either before or after the one in question that use the same or similar terms': Aust, *Modern Treaty Law and Practice*, p. 220. Note that none of the following related agreements refers to 'aesthetic' value: *Convention for the Safeguarding of the Intangible Cultural Heritage*, Paris, 17 October 2003, in force 20 April 2006, 2368 UNTS 3; *Cartagena Protocol on Biosafety to the Convention on Biological Diversity*, Montreal, 29 January 2000, in force 11 September 2003, 2226 UNTS 208; *Nagoya Protocol on Access to Genetic Resources and the Fair and Equitable Sharing of Benefits Arising from Their Utilization to the Convention on Biological Diversity*, Nagoya, 29 October 2010, in force 12 October 2014, 3008 UNTS 3.

91 Gardiner, *Treaty Interpretation*, p. 254. See also Moloo, 'When actions speak louder than words'.

> [W]here states by treaty entrust performance of activities to an organization, how those activities are conducted can constitute practice under the treaty; but whether such practice establishes agreement of the parties regarding the treaty's interpretation may require account to be taken of further factors. These may include assessment of the powers of the organ acting in the matter, the potential for any other body in the organization to control the organ, [or] the manner in which states parties to the treaty participate in the activities of the organization.[92]

Below I explain in detail the different practices in the application of each treaty that might establish 'the agreement of the parties' regarding the interpretation of aesthetic value for the *World Heritage Convention* and *Biodiversity Convention*. In summary, subsequent practice does not appear to clarify the meaning of 'aesthetic' value for either the *World Heritage Convention* or the *Biodiversity Convention*. If anything, it tends to contradict the conclusion from the literal, contextual and teleological approaches to interpretation used above.[93] I used those approaches to construct a meaning of aesthetic value associated with 'perception by the senses', which was distinct from other environmental values expressly mentioned in the treaties and consistent, to some extent, with the 'aesthetic' value conceived in the philosophy of environmental aesthetics. However, as explained next, subsequent practice appears in some cases to have conflated aesthetic value with other values, such as with 'natural beauty' in the case of the *World Heritage Convention*, and with 'cultural value' in the case of the *Biodiversity Convention*.

3.3.2.1 Subsequent Practice under *World Heritage Convention*

The determination of the 'outstanding universal value' of natural properties under the *World Heritage Convention*, including a determination from an aesthetic point of view, follows a process of state nominations, expert evaluations and Committee decisions.[94] Although the World Heritage Committee comprises only twenty-one of the states parties to the *World Heritage Convention*,[95] its decision-making authority derives from the treaty,[96] and it makes decisions on behalf of the parties as a whole. As such, any 'subsequent practice' of the parties as to the meaning of the term 'aesthetic' can be gleaned

92 Gardiner, *Treaty Interpretation*, p. 281.
93 See Section 3.3.1.
94 Article 2 of the *World Heritage Convention*. See Section 3.2.
95 Article 8 of the *World Heritage Convention*.
96 Article 11, ibid. See *Rules of Procedure of the World Heritage Committee*, UN Doc. WHC-2015/5.

from the guidance and decisions of the World Heritage Committee.[97] In particular, the World Heritage Committee has produced and regularly updates *Operational Guidelines for the Implementation of the World Heritage Convention* ('*Operational Guidelines*'). They detail the policies and procedures that are applied in the administration of the treaty.[98] Agreed by the World Heritage Committee, they would be an authoritative indication of the subsequent practice of the parties to the *World Heritage Convention* in their interpretation of the treaty. The *Operational Guidelines* provide that, to be of 'outstanding universal value', a property must conform to one or more of the stated criteria.[99] Under criterion (vii), the outstanding universal value of natural heritage contemplates environments that 'contain superlative natural phenomena or areas of exceptional natural beauty and aesthetic importance'.[100]

The Secretariat for the World Heritage Committee generates resource manuals that might also be indicative of 'subsequent practice'.[101] A 2011 World Heritage Resource Manual on 'Preparing World Heritage Nominations' guides the states parties to the *World Heritage Convention* on the characteristics contemplated by criterion (vii).[102] The *Resource Manual* provides that the aesthetic importance of natural heritage is distinct from considerations of aesthetics in connection with cultural heritage.[103] It indicates that nominated properties should be compared with properties previously inscribed under criterion (vii), including a 'comparison of measurable indicators of scenic value.'[104] It is, however, not clear whether 'scenic

97 See World Heritage Committee, *Operational Guidelines*, UN Doc. WHC.21/01.

98 World Heritage Committee, *Operational Guidelines*, UN Doc. WHC.21/01. Cf. World Heritage Committee, *World Heritage Policy Compendium*.

99 World Heritage Committee, *Operational Guidelines*, UN Doc. WHC.21/01, para. [77]. Other criteria discussed below.

100 World Heritage Committee, *Operational Guidelines*, UN Doc. WHC.21/01, para. [77]. The term 'aesthetic' was introduced into the equivalent criterion in 1994: See World Heritage Committee, *Operational Guidelines for the Implementation of the World Heritage Convention*, UN Doc. WHC/2/Revised, February 1994, para. [44(a)(iii)]. The criteria for natural and cultural heritage were later combined so natural criterion 44(a)(iii) became Outstanding Universal Value criterion 77(vii): World Heritage Committee, *Operational Guidelines for the Implementation of the World Heritage Convention*, UN Doc. WHC. 05/2, para. [77(vii)]. The requirement of integrity attached to criterion (vii) was changed from 'outstanding aesthetic value' to 'Outstanding Universal Value': At para. [92].

101 See above discussion of Gardiner, *Treaty Interpretation*, p. 254.

102 World Heritage Centre, 'Preparing World Heritage nominations', 40.

103 Ibid.

104 Ibid.

value' relates to either or both 'natural beauty' and 'aesthetic importance' in criterion (vii).[105]

If determined by the World Heritage Committee to have 'outstanding universal value' on the basis of one of the criteria in the *Operational Guidelines*, a nominated property may be 'inscribed' on the World Heritage List by a decision of the World Heritage Committee.[106] Inscriptions are to be accompanied by a Statement of Outstanding Universal Value.[107] Individual instances of the application of criterion (vii) justified in Statements of Outstanding Universal Value could constitute 'subsequent practice' of the parties' interpretation of the term 'aesthetic'. Individual applications of criterion (vii) evidenced by Statements of Outstanding Universal Value are examined later in Chapter 5, where I explain that a study of the application of the criterion found that quantitative and scientific values typically prevail over natural beauty and aesthetic importance in justifications of that criterion.[108]

3.3.2.2 Subsequent Practice under *Biodiversity Convention*

Several sources could be seen to document the subsequent practice of the parties to the *Biodiversity Convention* as to the meaning of aesthetic value. Decisions of the treaty's governing body, the COP, could be evidence of meanings for treaty terms. However, the capacity of such COP decisions to 'establish the agreement of the parties' is not clear.[109] In any event, they do not appear to have addressed the meaning of aesthetic value of biodiversity in its own right. Later in Chapter 7, I consider the mention of biodiversity values in general terms in the Aichi Biodiversity Targets, agreed by a COP decision.[110] Other COP decisions mention aesthetic value in the context of naming all the values of biodiversity.[111]

[105] See Chapter 5.

[106] The Committee considers nominations and the recommendations of the Advisory Bodies at its annual meetings and decides whether or not to include the property in the World Heritage List: Article 11(2) of the *World Heritage Convention*; World Heritage Committee, *Operational Guidelines*, UN Doc. WHC.21/01, para. [153].

[107] Statements of outstanding universal value are adopted in World Heritage Committee decisions to inscribe properties on the World Heritage List: World Heritage Committee, *Operational Guidelines*, UN Doc. WHC.21/01, paras. [154], [157].

[108] IUCN, *Study on the Application of Criterion (vii)*, pp. 57–8. See Section 5.3.3.2.

[109] On legal status of decisions of governing bodies, see Brunnée, 'COPing with consent'. See also Morgera and Tsioumani, 'Yesterday, today, and tomorrow'.

[110] Conference of the Parties to the *Convention on Biological Diversity*, *The Strategic Plan for Biodiversity*, UN Doc. UNEP/CBD/COP/DEC/X/2, annex. See Section 7.2.1.

[111] See, for example, Conference of the Parties to the *Convention on Biological Diversity*, *Resource Mobilization*, UN Doc. UNEP/CBD/COP/DEC/XII/3. Cf. discussion of aesthetic services as

Reports of international organisations endorsed by the COP could also be relevant to establishing 'subsequent practice'. Several such reports refer to the aesthetic value of biodiversity as a cultural service of ecosystems. The *Millennium Ecosystem Assessment*,[112] for example, is referenced in COP decisions made under the *Biodiversity Convention*.[113] It explains that ecosystem services can be clustered in terms of provisioning, regulating and supporting services as well as 'cultural' services.[114] Ecosystem services are described to include such things as the purification of water, the protection of land from erosion, the propagation of food sources, the absorption of carbon dioxide, and medicinal properties.[115] In the context of cultural ecosystem services, the *Millennium Ecosystem Assessment* refers to 'beauty or aesthetic value in various aspects of ecosystems, as reflected in the support for parks, scenic drives, and the selection of housing locations'.[116] In its assessment of aesthetic value, the *Millennium Ecosystem Assessment* notes:

> Natural environments are an important source of aesthetic pleasure for people all over the world. The high aesthetic value of nature is reflected in many areas of human behaviour, such as the use of plants and flowers as decorative elements in interiors, the use of computer screensavers depicting natural environments, and the demarcation of 'scenic routes'.[117]

part of cultural value in Conference of the Parties to the *Convention on Biological Diversity, Impact Assessment*, UN Doc. UNEP/CBD/COP/DEC/VIII/28; values of biodiversity in Conference of the Parties to the *Convention on Biological Diversity, Incentive Measures (Article 11)*, UN Doc. UNEP/CBD/COP/DEC/9/6. Cf. also different conceptions of aesthetic value in Posey, *Cultural and Spiritual Values of Biodiversity*.

[112] Millennium Ecosystem Assessment, *Ecosystems and Human Well-Being: Synthesis*. Note reports of the Millennium Ecosystem Assessment were circulated to the parties to the *Convention on Biological Diversity* as UN documents, without photographs: See Millennium Ecosystem Assessment, *Summary for Decision Makers of the Biodiversity Synthesis Report*, UN Doc. UNEP/CBD/SBSTTA/11/7/Add.1; and with photographs: See, for example, Millennium Ecosystem Assessment, *Ecosystems and Human Well-Being: Biodiversity Synthesis*, circulated as UN Doc. UNEP/CBD/SBSTTA/11/INF/22).

[113] See, for example, Conference of the Parties to the *Convention on Biological Diversity, Ecosystem Approach*, UN Doc. UNEP/CBD/COP/DEC/VII/11; Conference of the Parties to the *Convention on Biological Diversity, Implications of the Findings of the Millennium Ecosystem Assessment*, UN Doc. UNEP/CBD/COP/DEC/VIII/9; Conference of the Parties to the *Convention on Biological Diversity, Ecosystem Approach*, UN Doc. UNEP/CBD/COP/DEC/IX/7; Conference of the Parties to the *Convention on Biological Diversity, Follow-Up to the Millennium Ecosystem Assessment*, UN Doc. UNEP/CBD/COP/DEC/IX/15.

[114] Millennium Ecosystem Assessment, *Ecosystems and Human Well-Being*, p. v.

[115] Ibid. Alternative conceptions of valuing biodiversity to ecosystem services are discussed in Section 7.2.2.

[116] Millennium Ecosystem Assessment, *Ecosystems and Human Well-Being*, p. 40.

[117] Millennium Ecosystem Assessment, 'Cultural and amenity services', 467.

The Economics of Ecosystems and Biodiversity (TEEB), an accounting framework for ecosystem services, is also endorsed by the COP.[118] It describes aesthetic value as 'aesthetic appreciation and inspiration for culture, art and design'.[119]

The reference to aesthetic value in descriptions of 'cultural services' suggests that, in the context of ecosystem services at least, 'aesthetic' value is understood as 'cultural'. I maintain, however, that this characterisation of aesthetic value does not assist in developing an interpretation of the term that is distinct from the 'cultural' value of biodiversity, a term that is also expressly identified in the preamble to the *Biodiversity Convention* and which is also capable of complex interpretations.[120] As explained earlier, all terms must be interpreted to have an effective meaning that is distinct from other terms in a treaty.[121]

Several technical and information reports on the values of biodiversity have been produced by the Secretariat of the *Biodiversity Convention*. Again, it is not clear that such publications would constitute 'subsequent practice' for the purposes of treaty interpretation. In any event, they make only limited if any mention of 'aesthetic' value. One publication, *An Exploration of Tools and Methodologies for Valuation of Biodiversity and Biodiversity Resources and Functions*, describes 'aesthetic benefits' as an 'intangible aspect of well-being'.[122] Another report, *Protected Areas in Today's World: Their Values and Benefits for the Welfare of the Planet*, notes that aesthetic value is relevant to all the case studies in the paper but does not elaborate how.[123] A report titled *The Value of Nature: Ecological, Economic, Cultural and Social Benefits of Protected Areas* makes no mention of aesthetic value.[124]

Evidence of subsequent practice for interpretative purposes could also include the national reports submitted by individual states parties under Article 26 of the *Biodiversity Convention*.[125] National reports commonly describe specific cases of treaty implementation, including mentions of aesthetic value in national laws and policies that implement the *Biodiversity*

[118] See, for example, Conference of the Parties to the *Convention on Biological Diversity, The Strategic Plan for Biodiversity*, p. 5.

[119] Sukhdev et al., *The Economics of Ecosystems and Biodiversity*, annex, p. 34.

[120] First tiret of the preamble of the *Convention on Biological Diversity*. See also Chapter 7.

[121] Gardiner, *Treaty Interpretation*, pp. 168, 179ff.

[122] Secretariat of the *Convention on Biological Diversity, an Exploration of Tools and Methodologies*, p. 16.

[123] Secretariat of the *Convention on Biological Diversity, Protected Areas in Today's World*, p. 95.

[124] Mulongoy and Gidda, *The Value of Nature*.

[125] Article 26 of the *Convention on Biological Diversity*.

Convention.[126] A comprehensive review of all of the national reports and jurisdictions that protect aesthetic value in laws and policies on biodiversity would be necessary to make a case for an agreed understanding among the parties on the meaning of aesthetic value in the treaty. However, an assessment of select national reports suggests that the variable meanings attributed to biodiversity's aesthetic value are unlikely to amount to an agreed definition.[127]

3.3.3 *Historical Intention*

In addition to the subsequent practice contemplated for interpretation in Article 31 of the *Vienna Convention*, Article 32 provides for 'supplementary means of interpretation' in some circumstances, including where meanings are 'ambiguous or obscure'. Historical documents generated in the negotiation of the treaty are the preparatory work (or '*travaux préparatoires*') that can be consulted to clarify meanings of terms.[128] Anthony Aust warns, however, that this is a source that is 'very seldom decisive'.[129] I consider the significance of this documentation for the meaning of aesthetic value in the *World Heritage Convention* and the *Biodiversity Convention* below. To summarise, it would appear that the distinction between 'aesthetic' and 'natural beauty' in the *World Heritage Convention* was intended by the negotiators. However, the reasoning behind the differentiation is not apparent from the negotiating documents. Other than suggesting that another agreement protecting wildlife was a precedent for the list of values associated with biodiversity,[130] the negotiating drafts of the *Biodiversity Convention* suggest no specific meaning for the term 'aesthetic' in the treaty's preamble. A historical approach to interpreting the term 'aesthetic' in the treaties does not exclude a broad

[126] See Secretariat of the *Convention on Biological Diversity*, 'National reports'.

[127] See, for example, references to biodiversity's 'aesthetic' value in *Convention on Biological Diversity* national reports: Antigua and Barbuda, 'First national report'; Georgia, 'Second national report', 46; Brazil, 'Fourth national report', 120; Canada '4th national report', 91; Kenya 'Fourth national report', 26; Kyrgyz Republic, 'Fourth national report', 16; Malta, 'Fourth national report', 17; Australia, 'Fifth national report', 4; Cambodia, 'The fifth national report', 18; Estonia, 'V national report', 17, 20; Indonesia, 'The fifth national report', 2; Lao People's Democratic Republic, 'Fifth national report', 19; Lebanon, 'Fifth national report', 50; Malawi, 'Fifth national report', 4; Maldives, 'Fifth national report', xii; Seychelles, 'Fifth national report', 4; Tuvalu, 'Fifth national report', xiv, 23; Uganda, 'Fifth national report', 16, 31; Yemen, 'Fifth national report', 2–3. All reports available at www.cbd.int/reports.

[128] Article 12 of the *Vienna Convention*.

[129] Aust, *Modern Treaty Law and Practice*, p. 219.

[130] *Convention on the Conservation of Migratory Species of Wild Animals*, Bonn, 23 June 1979, in force 1 November 1983, 1651 UNTS 333.

interpretation associated with perception of the senses. Nor does it explicitly support such a view.

The preparatory drafts of the *World Heritage Convention* are not helpful in clarifying the intended meaning of the 'aesthetic' point of view in the treaty's definition of outstanding universal value. One of the first drafts of the definition for 'natural heritage' for the *World Heritage Convention* incorporated 'great beauty' but contained no reference to aesthetic value.[131] A further draft created three categories of property in the definition and included the 'aesthetic' point of view for the first and third clusters of natural property.[132] Subsequent draft proposals saw the deletion of 'aesthetic' value from the third cluster of properties in natural heritage and reference to 'conservation or natural beauty' in its place, as evident in the final agreement.[133] A draft report at the conclusion of an expert meeting makes ambiguous reference to 'aesthetic' and 'natural beauty' as possibly synonymous.[134] The French delegation was responsible for the use of the term 'aesthetic' in relation to the definition of 'cultural heritage'. It proposed at one stage that the word 'artistic' should be deleted and replaced with 'aesthetic'. I speculate that this proposed change could have been to distinguish it from the use of 'aesthetic' in connection with natural heritage but no reasons for the change were provided in the document.[135]

Similarly, the preparatory drafts of the *Biodiversity Convention* are unclear as to the intended meaning of the 'aesthetic' value of biodiversity. The final wording of the preambular phrase in the *Biodiversity Convention* referencing 'aesthetic' value evolved from an earlier phrase in the first draft of the treaty stating: '*Conscious* of the ever growing environmental, ecological, genetic, scientific, aesthetic, recreational, cultural, educational, social and economic values of biological diversity and its components'.[136] This formulation appeared unchanged from the first until the penultimate final draft, when

[131] See United Nations Educational, Scientific and Cultural Organization ('UNESCO'), *Working Document Prepared by the Working Group: Draft Convention Concerning the Protection of Cultural and Natural World Heritage*, UN Doc. SHC-72/CONF.37/4.

[132] UNESCO, *Working Document Prepared by the Working Group II: Draft Convention Concerning the Protection of Cultural and Natural World Heritage*, UN Doc. SHC-72/CONF.37/8.

[133] UNESCO, *Drafting Committee*, UN Doc. SHC.72/CONF.37/RED/1.

[134] UNESCO, *Draft Report*, UN Doc. SHC.72/CONF.37/19, para. [13].

[135] UNESCO, *Projet d'amendement, présenté par la délégation de la France*, UN Doc. SHC.72/CONF.37/DR.21, 10 April 1972.

[136] Ad Hoc Working Group of Legal and Technical Experts on Biological Diversity, *Draft Convention on Biological Diversity*, UN Doc. UNEP/BIO.Div/WG.2/2/2.

'intrinsic' value was also included.[137] The first draft claims as the source for the phrase one of the *Elements for Possible Inclusion in a Global Framework Legal Instrument on Biological Diversity*.[138] There was, however, no reference in that source to aesthetic value or to many of the other values ultimately listed. An Explanatory Note in the first draft of the *Biodiversity Convention* explains that '[l]anguage and precedents from existing treaties have been drawn on when consistent with the elements and comments from delegations'.[139] Several legal instruments are listed in that Explanatory Note as source material, including the *Convention on the Conservation of Migratory Species of Wild Animals* ('*Bonn Convention*').[140] The *Bonn Convention* includes a list of values similar to that included in the first draft of the *Biodiversity Convention* so it was a likely precedent for the naming of 'aesthetic' as a value of biodiversity.[141] There is, however, no suggestion from the documentation that consideration was given to any difference between the valuing of biodiversity as opposed to migratory species on aesthetic grounds.

3.3.4 *Evolutive Interpretation*

Distinct from an analysis of historical intention, evolutive interpretation is another technique of treaty interpretation recognised as either derived from or additional to those contemplated in the *Vienna Convention*.[142] It is also known as an evolutionary, sociological or dynamic approach to the interpretation of treaties.[143] There is, however, debate among practitioners of international law as to whether evolutive interpretation is a sanctioned technique and, if so, what it entails.[144] Judges and adjudicators from a range of international courts

[137] Intergovernmental Negotiating Committee for a Convention on Biological Diversity, *Fifth Revised Draft Convention on Biological Diversity*, UN Doc. UNEP/Bio.Div/N7-INC.5/2.

[138] Ad Hoc Working Group of Experts on Biological Diversity, *Elements for Possible Inclusion in a Global Framework Legal Instrument on Biological Diversity*, UN Doc. UNEP/Bio.Div/WG.2/1/3.

[139] Ad Hoc Working Group of Legal and Technical Experts on Biological Diversity, *Draft Convention on Biological Diversity*, p. 2.

[140] Ibid, p. 4; *Convention on the Conservation of Migratory Species of Wild Animals*, Bonn, 23 June 1979, in force 1 November 1983, 1651 UNTS 333.

[141] Second tiret of the preamble of the *Convention on the Conservation of Migratory Species*.

[142] See generally Gardiner, *Treaty Interpretation*, pp. 467ff. See also Djeffal, *Static and Evolutive Treaty Interpretation*.

[143] See Gardiner, *Treaty Interpretation*, pp. 467ff. Note Bos identifies the 'sociological' method of treaty interpretation: Bos, 'Theory and practice', part II, 136.

[144] See further Bjorge, *The Evolutionary Interpretation of Treaties*; Dupuy, 'Evolutionary interpretation of treaties', 123; Fitzmaurice, 'Dynamic (evolutive) interpretation of treaties, part I'; Fitzmaurice, 'Dynamic (evolutive) interpretation of treaties, part II'; Arato, 'Subsequent practice and evolutive interpretation'.

and tribunals have recognised a degree of mobility in the meaning of treaty terms to reflect 'present-day conditions'.[145] And in his comprehensive text on international treaty interpretation, Richard Gardiner has proposed that evolutive interpretation might be justified in at least three circumstances: Advances not contemplated at the time the treaty was made; elaborations emerging from processes created by the treaty to develop the treaty; or developments in the legal system at large.[146]

Other scholars have also acknowledged the technique. Evolutive interpretation is an approach that appears to be contemplated by George Nolte of the International Law Commission who referred to the need for treaties to 'evolve according to the social needs of the international community'.[147] Maarten Bos describes the technique in terms of an interpreter exercising freedom in departing from an 'obsolete' written rule to ensure that it continues to 'correspond with the needs of society'.[148] Legal scholar Ian Johnstone has suggested that it is the international nature of the community of states parties to multilateral treaties as opposed to a small number of states that demands evolutive interpretation. Both the *World Heritage Convention* and *Biodiversity Convention* qualify as multilateral treaties.[149] Johnstone observed that '[m]ultilateral treaties and constitutional instruments (like the United Nations Charter) tend to be more open-textured than bilateral treaties, because they must capture a broader range of interests, concerns and understandings. The interpretive process tends to be more evolutionary as shared meanings are worked out over time.'[150]

However, some judges and scholars have been critical of evolutive interpretation as subverting the states' intentions when agreeing to treaty commitments. Referring to states parties, Sir Gerald Fitzmaurice has said: 'It would not be *their* treaty that would emerge from the fray, but another that someone else thought was the one they should have entered into.'[151] Aware of this concern, judges of the European Court of Human Rights have stressed, in the context of the Council of Europe's *Human Rights Convention*,[152] that evolutive interpretation 'does not allow entirely new concepts or spheres of

145 Gardiner, *Treaty Interpretation*, p. 472. See also Letsas, A *Theory of Interpretation*, p. 74.
146 Gardiner, *Treaty Interpretation*, p. 468.
147 Nolte, 'Treaties over time in particular', annex, p. 1 para. [1].
148 Bos, 'Theory and practice', part II, 137–8, citing Pitlo, *Evolutie in het privaatrecht*, p. 126.
149 See Section 3.2.
150 Johnstone, 'Treaty interpretation', 407.
151 Fitzmaurice, '*Vae victis*', 368.
152 *Convention for the Protection of Human Rights and Fundamental Freedoms*, Rome, 4 November 1950, in force 3 September 1953, 213 UNTS 222.

application to be introduced into the Convention: That is a legislative function that belongs to the member States of the Council of Europe.'[153]

Scholarship suggests that an evolutive interpretation would be appropriate in the cases of the *World Heritage Convention* and the *Biodiversity Convention*. For example, Catherine Redgwell has described the *World Heritage Convention* as 'the quintessential living treaty instrument',[154] linking changes effected by the World Heritage Committee's *Operational Guidelines* to 'new environmental legal concepts such as the conservation of biological diversity'.[155] An evolutive interpretation of the environment's aesthetic value would, I suggest, take account of developments in the philosophy of environmental aesthetics to support a broad meaning of aesthetic value associated with sensorial perception in the *World Heritage Convention* and the *Biodiversity Convention*.

As explained in Chapter 2, philosopher Ronald Hepburn's paper calling for a specific conception of aesthetics in relation to the natural environment was ground-breaking in the Anglo-American philosophical literature in 1966. Writing before the adoption of the *World Heritage Convention* in 1972 and the *Biodiversity Convention* in 1992, Hepburn's ideas were at odds with the mainstream philosophy of aesthetics that focused on the arts. The field of environmental aesthetics has, however, since acquired the support of a significant number of contemporary philosophers.[156] Philosophers such as Emily Brady describe aesthetic value of the environment in terms of sensorial experience shaped by imagination, emotion and knowledge.[157] Developments in the philosophy of environmental aesthetics would likely favour a shift from the dictionary conflations of aesthetic value and 'beauty' to a broader understanding of aesthetics as 'perception of the senses'. To the extent that Brady and other philosophers also advocate an understanding of aesthetic value that is culturally diverse,[158] their views would likely inform an interpretation that also acknowledges that the environment's aesthetic value manifests differently for different states parties to the treaties.

It is arguable that a contemporary understanding of the environment's aesthetic value derived from the philosophy of environmental aesthetics serves 'the social needs of the international community',[159] thereby justifying an

[153] *Feldbrugge v. Netherlands* (Appl. no. 8562/79), joint dissenting opinion, paras. [23]–[24].
[154] Redgwell, 'Article 2 definition of natural heritage', 66.
[155] Ibid, 67.
[156] See Section 2.2.2.
[157] See generally Brady, *Aesthetics of the Natural Environment*.
[158] See Section 2.2.3.5.
[159] Nolte, 'Treaties over time in particular'.

evolutive interpretation of the term for doctrinal purposes. However, whether developments in the philosophy of environmental aesthetics would warrant evolutive interpretation of the treaties on the basis of what Richard Gardiner calls 'advances not contemplated at the time the treaty was made'[160] is not clear. I maintain that such developments in philosophy would be relevant but the contested nature of evolutive interpretation as a technique means it is far from certain that treaty interpreters would be compelled to reach such a conclusion.

3.4 AESTHETIC VALUE INFORMING INTERPRETATION: WHALES

Unlike the treaties protecting the aesthetic value of natural heritage and biological diversity examined in Section 3.3, the *Whaling Convention* does not refer to the aesthetic value of whales in its express terms. It was agreed in 1946 to create a system for the preservation of certain whale species as a resource for human use: The treaty's preamble recognises 'the interest of the nations of the world in safeguarding for future generations the great natural resources represented by the whale stocks' and expresses the desire of the states parties 'to establish a system of international regulation for the whale fisheries to ensure proper and effective conservation and development of whale stocks'.[161] The treaty could appear from this preambular language to be motivated by a range of environmental values that concern either keeping whales in the oceans or taking them out.[162]

An ethical responsibility to keep whales in the oceans is apparent, for example, from the treaty's preambular claim that parties are conserving whale stocks for 'future generations'. This is not ethics concerning the whales but people – it is a value based on a perceived ethical responsibility to unborn humans, so that they might also benefit in unstated ways from whale stocks in the future.[163] However, the preamble also refers to exploiting whales for their 'economic and nutritional' values for present generations, evoking both commercial and subsistence values associated with harvesting whales.[164] Allowances made in the treaty for scientific research are indicative of the scientific value of whales (whether in or out of the oceans), while exceptions

[160] Gardiner, *Treaty Interpretation*, p. 468.
[161] Preamble of the *Whaling Convention*.
[162] On dual purpose, see *Whaling in the Antarctic* at para. [56].
[163] See Fitzmaurice, *Whaling and International Law*, p. 177.
[164] Preamble of the *Whaling Convention*.

for 'aboriginal' whaling are related to cultural and subsistence values of whaling.[165]

I argue that additional environmental values – not expressed in the treaty – are also relevant to an interpretation of the terms of the *Whaling Convention*. This would include the interpretation of the ban on commercial whaling that was introduced into the treaty by an amendment agreed in 1982.[166] The *Whaling Convention* allows for amendments to be made to the treaty by a three-fourths majority of the members of the governing body, the International Whaling Commission.[167] Amendments bind all parties unless, within a fixed period of time, individual parties lodge formal objections.[168] In 1982, the International Whaling Commission achieved the requisite majority vote to amend the treaty to set commercial catch limits of whales at zero, with an anticipated review of that limit at a later time.[169] The new provision was effective from the 1985/1986 whaling season.[170] Several members lodged objections and continued whaling unbound by the amendment.[171] Japan was bound by the ban but continued to allow whaling 'for purposes of scientific research', purportedly under an exemption in Article VIII of the treaty.[172] In 2014, Australia successfully challenged Japan's reliance on the exemption before the International Court of Justice.[173] Following several failed attempts to see the ban lifted, Japan withdrew from the *Whaling Convention* effective from July 2019.[174]

Relying on the international rules of treaty interpretation, I explain in this part how the aesthetic value of whales could inform the interpretation of the ban on commercial whaling and the exemptions to it, including the exemption for scientific whaling.[175]

165 Article VIII and the schedule, ibid. See Fitzmaurice, *Whaling and International Law*, p. 234.
166 See Section 3.2.
167 Articles III and V of the *Whaling Convention*.
168 Article V(3), ibid.
169 Clause 10(e) of the schedule, ibid.
170 Note other restrictions are also included: See, for example, Cl. 7(b) of the schedule to the *Whaling Convention*.
171 See for example n * of Cl. 10(e) of the schedule to the *Whaling Convention*. Note in particular that: Norway and the Russian Federation lodged and maintained objections to the moratorium; Iceland made a reservation to it after leaving then rejoining the treaty in 2002; Canada withdrew from the *Whaling Convention*. See further Nagtzaam, *The Making of International Environmental Treaties*, p. 192.
172 Article VIII of the *Whaling Convention*.
173 *Whaling in the Antarctic*.
174 See United States Department of State, 'Status list for the *Whaling Convention*'.
175 I do not examine for the purposes of this chapter other bans on whaling and other exceptions to such bans under the *Whaling Convention*: See, for example, at Cl. 7(b) of the schedule.

3.4.1 *Aesthetic Value as a Reason for the Ban*

The decision to amend the *Whaling Convention* to ban commercial whaling was debated at meetings of the International Whaling Commission and its advisory bodies before and after the ban was introduced.[176] In their statements at the annual meetings of the International Whaling Commission, nation states invoked science in support of both the creation, maintenance and removal of the ban. Some members claimed that the science on whale stocks was too uncertain to justify any commercial whaling while others maintained that scientific evidence confirmed that certain whale populations would tolerate a resumption of the practice.[177]

Japan has described science as the only value justifying the ban that has united members of the International Whaling Commission.[178] However, values other than science are also apparent in statements of members. For example, several members have pointed in meetings to ethical concerns, particularly regarding inhumane methods for killing whales.[179] But Japan has also identified aesthetic value as a – in its view illegitimate – basis for the ban. During the debate that preceded the approval of the ban in 1982, Japan cited a representative of the Food and Agriculture Organisation as having stated that 'a justification for a complete cessation of whaling can be put forward on aesthetic or moral grounds but these are outside the terms of reference of the Commission.'[180] Supporting the ban, St Lucia pointed out that 'there were no provisions made at the time [the treaty was adopted in 1946] for the circumstances with which we are now confronted'.[181] It cited 'world public opinion' against whaling, evidenced by instruments and agreements made in the United Nations and other fora representing the world's nations.[182]

That the 'world public opinion' on whaling is influenced at least in part by aesthetic considerations is suggested by anthropologist Arne Kalland who describes a composite 'super-whale' as being common to many cultures around the world. The super-whale is a totemic blend of whale species that combines size, intelligence, song and beneficent tendencies in one

176 Fitzmaurice, *Whaling and International Law*, 66–76.
177 Ibid. See, for example, International Whaling Commission, 'Verbatim record', 19–24 July 1982.
178 International Whaling Commission, 'Verbatim record', 9–13 July 1979, 60 (Japan).
179 See, for example, International Whaling Commission, 'Verbatim record', 19–24 July 1982, 72 (Australia), 73 (United Kingdom), 78 (Antigua and Barbuda).
180 Ibid., 77 (Japan).
181 Ibid., 78 (St Lucia).
182 Ibid., 80 (St Lucia).

endangered animal.[183] Kalland argues that it has replaced the image of whale as a resource commodity.[184] The super-whale qualities are evident in a letter to the International Whaling Commission from then US President Ronald Reagan, read to a meeting prior to the introduction of the ban:

> Throughout human history, whales have evoked awe and wonder. They are the largest creatures ever to have lived on this earth; yet they are also among the most mysterious. It is this mysterious quality that gives whales their appeal and increased the importance of effective management that could assure whale populations for the future. ... I urge you to join with us and other people throughout the world to secure the protection of these magnificent creatures.[185]

President Reagan's invocation of awe and wonder is an aesthetic claim.[186] It is not unlike claims made by other state leaders when speaking to laws that prohibit whaling in their domestic jurisdictions.[187] Such descriptions of whales by states parties to the *Whaling Convention* adhere to elements of aesthetic value discussed by philosophers of aesthetics. Aesthetic value associated with expressive wild animals, including large mammals, has been recognised by philosophers of environmental aesthetics. Philosopher Emily Brady has, for example, argued that '[e]ngaging with expressive qualities [of wild animals] can deepen appreciation and open up new avenues that are not shallow but instead support respectful aesthetic valuing.'[188] However, some philosophers critique the aesthetic value placed on charismatic mammals (such as whales) at the expense of small or 'ugly' animals.[189]

As explained next, these records of debates among the members of the International Whaling Commission, and the views of scholars, would be relevant to a textual and evolutive interpretation of the *Whaling Convention*.

3.4.2 *Interpretative Techniques for the Ban*

The evocations of aesthetic value by the states parties to the *Whaling Convention* could be seen to inform a doctrinal interpretation of the treaty

183 See Kalland, *Unveiling the Whale*, p. 28. Cf. Fitzmaurice, 'Whale', 539.
184 See Kalland, *Unveiling the Whale*, p. 75.
185 International Whaling Commission, 'Verbatim record', 20 July 1981, 29 (USA).
186 See Section 4.2.1. See also Chapter 6.
187 See, for example, Commonwealth of Australia, *Parliamentary Debates*, House of Representatives, 4 April 1979, 1481 (Prime Minister Malcolm Fraser).
188 Brady, 'Aesthetic value and wild animals', 199.
189 Brady, 'The ugly truth'.

text – including of the express terms of the ban on commercial whaling, and of the exemptions to it. For reasons explained here, the protection of whales for their aesthetic value could be seen as an 'object and purpose' of the ban,[190] evident from material constituting supplementary means of interpretation.[191] It is also possible to apply an evolutive technique to invoke aesthetic value in the interpretation of the treaty.

3.4.2.1 Protection of Aesthetic Value as an Object or Purpose of the Ban

By virtue of it forming part of the ban's object and purpose, the aesthetic value of whales would be relevant to the interpretation of the ban on commercial whaling, and the exemptions to it, under the *Whaling Convention*. As already explained in connection with my interpretation of aesthetic value of natural heritage and biological diversity, Article 31 of the *Vienna Convention* provides that a treaty's object and purpose inform the interpretation of treaty provisions.[192] The object and purpose are apparent from the preamble and the treaty as a whole.[193] Aesthetic value is not expressly stated in the preamble or other provisions of the treaty and I do not maintain that it should be an implied term.[194] However, it is apparent from debates among the members of the International Whaling Commission described earlier,[195] that protecting whales for their aesthetic value was at least one of the ban's purposes.

According to Article 32 of the *Vienna Convention*, 'supplementary means of interpretation, including the preparatory work of the treaty and the circumstances of its conclusion' may be used to confirm or determine a meaning in certain circumstances. The debate of the ban is recorded in verbatim records and can be ascertained from materials relevant to individual states parties, such as the letter to the International Whaling Commission from the US President and other statements cited earlier.[196] Forming either part of the 'preparatory work' of the amendment to the treaty, or part of the 'circumstances of its conclusion', the verbatim records and materials concerning the aesthetic value of whales are supplementary means of interpretation for the

[190] Article 31(1) of the *Vienna Convention*; Gardiner, *Treaty Interpretation*, p. 211.
[191] Article 32 of the *Vienna Convention*; Gardiner, *Treaty Interpretation*, p. 347.
[192] Article 31(1) of the *Vienna Convention*; discussed above in Section 3.3.1.3.
[193] Gardiner, *Treaty Interpretation*, p. 218.
[194] See ibid., pp. 165–7.
[195] See Section 3.4.1.
[196] See International Whaling Commission, 'Verbatim record', 20 July 1981, 29 (USA); Commonwealth of Australia, *Parliamentary Debates*, House of Representatives, 4 April 1979, 1481 (Prime Minister Malcolm Fraser).

purposes of Article 32. Richard Gardiner explains that '[t]he circumstances which cause a treaty to be drawn up, affect its content, and attach to its conclusion, are all factors which are in practice taken into account [in interpretation]'.[197]

I maintain that the records of debate and other material are also relevant to the interpretation of terms in the ban that are not otherwise ascertained through an interpretation of the ordinary meaning of terms in their context and in light of the treaty's object and purpose. So by extension, aesthetic value would also inform the interpretation of the exemptions to the ban – such as the scientific exemption in Article VIII of the *Whaling Convention*.

3.4.2.2 Protection of Aesthetic Value through Evolutive Interpretation

In addition to the treaty's object and purpose, it is also possible to understand the terms of the ban and exemption in an evolutive way to have regard for aesthetic values of whales.[198] In its decision in *Whaling in the Antarctic* – discussed in detail in Chapter 6 – the International Court of Justice acknowledged that the *Whaling Convention* is 'an evolving instrument'.[199] Above I referred to understandings of the 'evolutive' technique of treaty interpretation as taking account of 'present-day conditions',[200] including 'the social needs of the international community'.[201] St Lucia referred in debate in the International Whaling Commission to a changed 'world public opinion'.

The verbatim records and other official statements of states parties to the *Whaling Convention* described earlier would be a relevant source of evolutive interpretation. However, not all parties bound by the amendment that introduced the ban on commercial whaling under the *Whaling Convention* indicated aesthetic grounds for the ban. As noted above,[202] scientific values are commonly referenced, and ethical values have also been invoked. I nevertheless maintain that the other values do not displace aesthetic value in the motivation of states supporting the moratorium but are additional to it. States parties have the option of objecting to amendments such that they are

197 Gardiner, *Treaty Interpretation*, p. 398.

198 See generally Smith, 'Evolving to conservation'; Young and Rioseco Sullivan, 'Evolution through the duty to cooperate'.

199 *Whaling in the Antarctic* at para. [45]. Cf. at paras. [3]–[4] (Ad Hoc Judge Charlesworth), para. [46] (Judge Yusuf). Discussed in Fitzmaurice, *Whaling and International Law*, p. 91.

200 Gardiner, *Treaty Interpretation*, p. 308. See Section 3.3.4.

201 Nolte, 'Treaties over time in particular'.

202 See Section 3.4.1.

not bound by them.[203] Where they opt to be bound, the concept of 'good faith', and the international legal principle of *pacta sunt servanda* require that the treaty terms be interpreted on the same basis for all the parties bound by it.[204] Japan's statements as to scientific value, during the debate on the ban, would not then exclude consideration of aesthetic value as a basis for the ban and exemptions to it.

It would also be relevant for the purposes of evolutive interpretation to refer to the philosophy of environmental aesthetics for a contemporary understanding of the aesthetic value of the environment.[205] Richard Gardiner explains that 'academic guides and studies are often used by courts and tribunals to assist them in analysis of text, preparatory work, comparative case law, and argument on controversial issues'.[206] Recourse to scholarship on the philosophy on environmental aesthetics would introduce pluralised meanings of the environment's aesthetic value associated with such things as sensation, imagination, emotion and knowledge from experience and culture.[207]

I will consider the implications of my arguments around aesthetic value in the *Whaling Convention* in Chapter 6. For now, I conclude only that aesthetic value is relevant to the interpretation of the *Whaling Convention* and that an understanding of that value as developed by philosophers of environmental aesthetics could be relied on to describe the aesthetic value of whales for that purpose.

3.5 SOURCES FOR TREATY INTERPRETATION

Doctrinal techniques for treaty interpretation rely on written sources.[208] As seen so far in this chapter, orthodox sources for treaty interpretation include materials such as the text of treaties augmented by dictionaries, documentation generated in and descriptive of subsequent practice, as well as written materials created in the course of treaty negotiations. For reasons explained below, I argue that the written sources that typically document meanings for

[203] See Section 3.4.

[204] On *pacta sunt servanda* and 'good faith', see, for example, Gardiner, *Treaty Interpretation*, p. 169.

[205] See Brady, 'Aesthetic value and wild animals'.

[206] Gardiner, *Treaty Interpretation*, p. 404.

[207] See Brady, *Aesthetics of the Natural Environment*. See generally Brady, 'Aesthetic value, nature, and environment', 186. See Section 2.2.2.

[208] See, for example, Gardiner, *Treaty Interpretation*, pp. 81 (interpretative material generated in making treaties), 255 (written documentation of subsequent practice). Cf. on written sources of law as opposed to sources for interpretation: Staubach, *The Rule of Unwritten International Law*.

law do not provide an adequate account of the meaning of aesthetic value in terms conceived in the philosophy of environmental aesthetics. Images, by contrast, do.

3.5.1 *From Documents*

Like the scholarship on aesthetic value in international environmental law examined in Chapter 2, a doctrinal legal interpretation of the treaties using orthodox written sources provides a variable account of the environment's aesthetic value. It would be possible for certain interpretative techniques to draw from the philosophical scholarship on environmental aesthetics to develop a comprehensive understanding of aesthetic value for law. Earlier I explained, for example, the ways in which that scholarship could be engaged in a textual or evolutive interpretation of the three treaties. The philosophy of environmental aesthetics could be used to build on a broad definition of aesthetic value as 'perception by the senses' to describe a multi-sensory appreciation informed by imagination, emotion and knowledge.[209] However, other sources of interpretation – such as the documentation I identify as having been generated in the practice of the treaties – suggest accounts of aesthetic value wedded to natural beauty, and cultural and ethical values. This documentation of subsequent practice undermines a legal characterisation of aesthetic value that is both distinct from those other environmental values and profound in its significance in ways contemplated by philosophers of environmental aesthetics.[210]

The equivocal results from applying the international rules of treaty interpretation highlight the failings of such techniques in identifying clear meanings for treaty terms. Both legal practitioners and critical legal scholars would be unsurprised by such findings. Treaty interpretation is, after all, an 'art' dressed up as 'science'.[211] More specifically, *legal* science.[212] But these methods of interpretation are used in the practice of international law – they are themselves customary international law[213] – and, as such, they would be applied by interpreters of the terms in international environmental treaties to develop legal understandings of the term 'aesthetic'. Ultimately, to engage in the formalities of treaty interpretation is to do as nation states do, or at least to

[209] See Brady, *Aesthetics of the Natural Environment*. See Section 2.2.2.
[210] See Section 2.2.3.
[211] See Waldcock, 'Third report on the law of treaties', 54. See also Klabbers, *International Law*, p. 58.
[212] Merkouris, 'Introduction', 1.
[213] See Gardiner, *Treaty Interpretation*, p. 16.

do as states want to be seen to be doing: Using legal method to determine law.[214] One meaning might be identified from several as valid with reference to techniques of interpretation.

However, any interpreters of international environmental treaties engaging doctrinal techniques of interpretation to characterise the environment's aesthetic value are twice blighted in their task. They are limited in the ways that all doctrinal interpretations are constrained by textual ambiguity. But they are also limited in a more fundamental way in respect of the environment's aesthetic value – by the orthodox written sources of legal interpretation, and the techniques constructed for those sources.

3.5.2 *To Images*

The written documents typically used as a source for treaty interpretation contrast with the 'sources' relied on by philosophers of environmental aesthetics when they characterise the environment's aesthetic value. The principal source for philosophy is the physical environment itself, with imagination, emotion and knowledge, to greater or lesser degrees, shaping philosophical characterisations of the aesthetic value of that environment. Philosophers of environmental aesthetics contemplate an immersion in natural environments or physical experiences of the environment.[215] Such characterisations of the environment's aesthetic value, and critical perspectives on those views, were developed using aesthetic methods for the arts in my description of Wyld's *Manchester from Kersal Moor* (Figure 3.1) at the outset of this chapter.

Yet, in writing about the aesthetic value of the natural environment, philosophers of environmental aesthetics rely on images – images expressed in words, and images expressed graphically, such as in photographs.[216] These images are used by environmental aestheticians to characterise the aesthetic experience or value of the environment theorised in their scholarship. So, for example, Allen Carlson includes a photograph by Ansel Adams of *The Grand Tetons, Wyoming* in his discussion of whether the site is 'majestic' or 'dumpy'.[217] Also appealing to images, Emily Brady includes an evocative description of the 'magnificently sublime and harmonious' South Lewis, Harris and North Uist National Scenic Area in a case study on the

[214] See generally Allott, 'Language, method and the nature of international law'.
[215] See Section 2.2.1.
[216] See, for example, list of 'illustrations', including photographs, in Carlson, *Aesthetics and the Environment*, p. ix.
[217] Ibid., p. 56. The debate was also taken up by Parsons, 'Freedom and objectivity'; Budd, 'Objectivity and the aesthetic value of nature'.

environment's aesthetic value.[218] Understandings of the representations of the environment's aesthetic value in those images are formed by reference to the philosophy of environmental aesthetics. They could, I argue in Chapter 4,[219] also be developed through insights from aesthetic philosophy as it relates to the arts where aesthetic methods are used to interpret the images.

Images – expressed in words or graphically – are not formally recognised as orthodox sources of treaty interpretation. I have found that images such as those used by philosophers of environmental aesthetics are, however, apparent in the materials generated in practices under the three treaties.[220] As explained in my introductory chapter to this book, those images include photographs submitted by states parties under the *World Heritage Convention* in nominations of natural properties to the World Heritage List,[221] photographs of whales and whale parts submitted to the International Court of Justice by parties to a dispute under the *Whaling Convention*,[222] and photographic images of the environment used in documentation that informs decisions of the COP to the *Biodiversity Convention*.[223] In the remainder of this book, I consider the relevance of those and other images to understandings of the meaning of the environment's aesthetic value for decisions made under the three treaties.

3.6 CONCLUSION

It is conceptions of aesthetic value in the philosophy of environmental aesthetics that, I have argued in Chapter 2,[224] should inform meanings of aesthetic value for international environmental law. However, a reliance on written sources, and the use of techniques designed for written sources, in the course of doctrinal interpretations of treaties, will inevitably compromise an understanding of the environment's aesthetic value. In later chapters, I argue that extending the sources of interpretation to include images, particularly photographic images, is both lawful and desirable to construct meanings of

[218] See Brady, *Aesthetics of the Natural Environment*, p. 240.

[219] See Section 4.3.2.

[220] See, for example, site visits for treaty decision-making processes: See Section 5.5.1. Cf. Becker and Rose, 'Investigating the value of site visits'.

[221] See Chapter 5.

[222] *Whaling in the Antarctic*. See further Chapter 6.

[223] For example, Secretariat of the *Convention on Biological Diversity*, *Global Biodiversity Outlook 4*.

[224] See Section 2.4.

the environment's aesthetic value for international environmental law in terms contemplated by philosophers of environmental aesthetics.[225]

With an extension of sources would come an extension of interpretative techniques. And in ways contemplated next in Chapter 4, aesthetic concepts and methods for the visual arts are relevant to the conception and analysis of such images for international law and legal practice. There I describe the different techniques developed in the aesthetic philosophy of the arts to analyse photographs, identifying possible concerns for using images to analyse the environment's aesthetic value from the perspective of environmental aesthetics, before closing with an examination of the understandings of image in legal theory known as visual jurisprudence or 'imaginal law'.[226]

[225] See, for example, Emily Brady's integrated aesthetic model: Brady, *Aesthetics of the Natural Environment.*

[226] Manderson, 'Introduction: Imaginal law'. See Chapter 4.

4

Images and Aesthetics for International Environmental Law

EXHIBIT: PIERRE HUYGHE, *AFTER ALIFE AHEAD* (2017)

FIGURE 4.1. Pierre Huyghe, *After ALife Ahead*, 2017. Sculptural environment, mixed media. Skulptur Projekte Münster, Germany. © Pierre Huyghe. Photo: Alice Palmer.

In 2017, French artist Pierre Huyghe took over a disused ice-skating rink in the German town of Münster to create a large-scale sculptural environment called *After ALife Ahead* (Figure 4.1).[1] Huyghe had partly removed a concrete floor to excavate a pit of clay. At first glance, it was a mining site that had displaced the natural environment. On further inspection, it was an archaeological dig, uncovering natural artefacts. Seemingly random pools of eutrophic, snail-inhabited water edged a maze of walking paths. Visitors were invited to navigate a post-Apocalyptic scene of concrete shards and termite-like 'hills' that housed living bees. Crabs lurked in a small aquatic acropolis atop a mound of earth while overhead skylights opened and closed intermittently to allow the bees to move between the cool dark interior and the hot bright world outside. Fetid odours filled the cavernous space while a soundscape of drips, clanks, buzzing and whispers encroached on the cathedral silence.

The variability of life was subtle and artificially manipulated in the work but, ultimately, biology was ingenious, adapting in the task of survival. Drained of colour, the space and its elements nevertheless exhibited diversity in tones, shapes and scale. From the high canopy to the subterranean pools, contrasts and variety might have indicated a healthy environment. Charismatic, domesticated animals placed in the artwork – peacocks white so that they too were robbed of colour – had gone rogue, apparently taking flight never to return,[2] giving way to lesser known wild species of insects, molluscs and crustaceans. Malignant microorganisms, fed with oxygen, flourished in a box at the edge of the excavation, a reminder of nature's irreverent course. The skating rink, constructed on an environment it had destroyed, was itself decaying to bear new life, good and bad, life in a cycle that would in turn die or be evicted when the artwork was ultimately demolished.

The artwork's dominant medium of clay, a malleable and often-times transitional material used by sculptors in the process of making more durable creations in metals, embodies both art practice and the earth's raw material. It was nature constructed by humans. But the artwork demonstrated to me how such a fecund place can appear, on the surface, empty of life, upsetting visual expectations of biodiverse environments. It extended the understanding of aesthetic values of biodiversity beyond classical concepts of beauty and exceptionalism to new forms of appreciation, disrupting one aesthetic with its proposal of another. I could be nostalgic for the lost aesthetic while also appreciating Huyghe's novel take on the ecological elements and processes

1 *Skulptur Projekte Münster 2017*.

2 Joe Lloyd, 'Skulptur Projekte Münster 2017'.

that comprise the variability of life. I noted, however, that even this life is fragile, its extinction anticipated from its inception.

4.1 INTRODUCTION

Relying on philosopher Emily Brady's conception of the environment's aesthetic value,[3] I argued in Chapter 2 that the aesthetic value protected under international environmental law should be understood in terms of a multisensory experience shaped by imagination, emotion and knowledge, including Western science and other cultural knowledges. Brady's conception of aesthetic value is, however, at odds with the meaning I constructed from written sources using methods of treaty interpretation in Chapter 3. In treaty practice, aesthetic value has been conflated with natural beauty, cultural value and ethical values of the environment – all related but distinct from characterisations of aesthetic value for Brady's integrated aesthetic model.[4] However, my description of Pierre Huyghe's sculptural installation *After ALife Ahead* (Figure 4.1) shows how aesthetic analysis of an artwork can be used to develop an aesthetic understanding of the natural environment informed by the philosophy of environmental aesthetics. I maintain that these same methods of analysis can be employed in the task of analysing photographic images of the environment for their meanings of aesthetic value to interpret the meaning of aesthetic value for international law.

In this chapter, I examine scholarship on the arts as it relates to the environment, before explaining the ways in which the arts have been engaged in the analysis of law, and its relationship to image, and the visual. In the process, I introduce aesthetic concepts for the arts that I later develop in my analysis of photographs in treaty processes in Chapters 5 through 7.

4.2 AESTHETICS IN ART ON THE NATURAL ENVIRONMENT

The natural environment analysed by philosophers of environmental aesthetics such as Emily Brady and Allen Carlson is not the mainstream concern of contemporary aesthetic philosophy.[5] Since the nineteenth century, the principal focus of the philosophy of aesthetics in Western Europe and Britain has been the arts.[6] Over time, aesthetic scholarship for the arts has evolved to

[3] Emily Brady, *Aesthetics of the Natural Environment*, pp. 120, 146, 185. Note discussion of environmental aesthetics in connection with quarry, p. 239.

[4] Ibid. See Section 2.2.3.

[5] See Section 2.2.1. See further Carlson, 'Ten steps', 13.

[6] Levinson, 'Philosophical aesthetics', 3.

define, describe, analyse, critique, interpret and judge creative expression in its many forms.[7] It has been grandly claimed by one such scholar, Elizabeth Grosz, that all arts 'are linked to the birdsong'.[8] Indeed, it has been demonstrated how artistic renditions of the environment – prehistoric cave and parietal art, ancient Chinese landscapes, Australian First Nations representations of Country, Western European landscapes from medieval, classical and Romantic periods, twentieth-century photographs of American 'wilderness', as well as modern and contemporary reflections on environmental subjects – can capture or dictate the complexity of the aesthetic experience and value of the natural environment.[9] The 'arts' for these purposes encompasses a broad range of creative endeavours, including literature and poetry, visual art in its many media, as well as music and the performing arts such as theatre and dance.[10] However, in this part, I consider different ways in which aesthetic scholarship has conceived the relationship between the environment and *visual art*. I discuss landscape as a genre of visual art before looking at categories of 'environmental art', and the politically motivated 'ecological art', as forms of what I am calling for the book 'art of the environment'. My discussion of these categories helps to situate my discussion of aesthetic methods in Section 4.3.

4.2.1 *Landscape and Nature*

Art historian Kenneth Clark writes that the 'rise and development since the middle ages [of landscape painting] is part of a cycle in which the human spirit attempted once more to create a harmony with its environment'.[11] The arts have long been a source of 'idealisations of nature'.[12] It is however through landscape painting, since the eighteenth century, that artists and aesthetic philosophers in Europe and Britain have developed the concepts of 'natural beauty', the 'picturesque' and the 'sublime'.[13] These concepts, and the landscape tastes they have inspired, are described below.

Philosophical theories of the environment's aesthetic value, including contemporary environmental aesthetics, rely on a concept of natural beauty variously conceived. In the eighteenth century, Western European

7 See generally Davies and Alperson, *The Philosophy of Art*.
8 Grosz, *Chaos, Territory, Art*, p. 12, cited in Lange-Berndt, 'White cube ecologies', 82.
9 See Matilsky, *Fragile Ecologies*, p. 4; Schama, *Landscape and Memory*. Cf. Brady, *Aesthetics of the Natural Environment*, p. 15. Cf. Section 2.2.1.
10 Stecker, 'Definition of art', 136; Danto, *What Art Is*.
11 Clark, *Landscape into Art*, p. 17.
12 Brady, *Aesthetics of the Natural Environment*, p. 30.
13 Ibid., p. 39. See also Brady, *The Sublime in Modern Philosophy*.

philosophical understandings of beauty included the beauty of nature. Yet the objects contemplated for aesthetic appreciation were not necessarily conceived in terms of the natural and unnatural.[14] Aesthetics philosopher Emily Brady explains that 'natural beauty', as understood in European and British painting prior to the eighteenth century, largely corresponded to neo-classical renditions of pastoral beauty – smooth, uniform, symmetrical and serene.[15] Nature loved was a becalmed nature, tended and fruitful; nature unkempt was, Marjorie Hope Nicolson maintains, a place of gloom.[16]

Separate from 'natural beauty', is a concept of the environment as 'picturesque'.[17] Emily Brady describes the concept of the 'picturesque' in European and British landscape painting as connoting qualities of 'roughness' and ruggedness, 'sudden variation' and asymmetry, as well as 'irregularity' and changes in the environment over time.[18] 'Picturesque scenery' is, Brady says: '[B]roken and undulating with variety, including water, for example a lake with 'savage banks' and a surface broken rather than smooth, perhaps with a pattern in the water from the wind, or the fast-flowing water of waterfalls and whitewater.'[19] Buildings feature in picturesque scenes but as ruins. The scene is framed – tourists to the British countryside were directed to use a 'Claude glass' to tint and frame a natural landscape so that it might be better observed.[20] Nature's temporality, imperfections and expressiveness were prized in the picturesque.[21]

Reacting to the objectification of nature as 'picturesque', the nineteenth-century Western European Romantic movement conceived humans as at one with nature. Emily Brady explains that Romantics did not see humans as detached and reasoned observers of nature but imaginative and emotional subjects in nature.[22] Romanticism took elements of the picturesque and magnified them through the 'sublime', the philosophical concept accounting for awe and fear arising from a sense of nature being beyond human control and capacities.[23] Romanticism would extend from Europe and Britain to the

[14] See Maskit, 'On universalism', 41.
[15] See, for example, Brady, *Aesthetics of the Natural Environment*, 41.
[16] Nicolson, *Mountain Gloom and Mountain Glory*, cited in Brady, *Aesthetics of the Natural Environment*, p. 35.
[17] Brady, *Aesthetics of the Natural Environment*, pp. 39–40.
[18] Ibid.
[19] Ibid., p. 40.
[20] See Carlson, *Aesthetics and the Environment*, p. 45.
[21] See Brady, *Aesthetics of the Natural Environment*, p. 41.
[22] Ibid., p. 43.
[23] Abrams, *The Mirror and the Lamp*. See further Brady, *The Sublime in Modern Philosophy*.

invaded frontierscapes of the Americas, Africa and Australia.[24] By the twentieth century, the 'American Transcendentalism' of Henry David Thoreau and Ralph Waldo Emerson had, Brady explains, fostered a concept of 'wilderness' that echoed the themes of Romanticism.[25] Their philosophies would later inform twentieth-century conservation laws in the United States and other countries inspired by the wilderness ethos,[26] with various critiques of such concepts still energising scholars today.[27]

Scholars and artists have observed a convergence of landscape-style tastes in people's appreciation of the natural environment around the world.[28] In their painting *America's Most Wanted*, artists Vitaly Komar and Alexander Melamid created a visual composite of what Americans surveyed in 1993 expected of a pleasing painting – a 'dishwasher-sized' landscape in blue hues with water, animals and people at leisure.[29] The results for the majority of the other thirteen countries surveyed – mostly European nations but China, Kenya and Russia were also included – suggested that a 'World's Most Wanted' would look strikingly similar to the American ideal.[30]

Responding to the Komar and Melamid project, art critic Arthur Danto concluded that '[t]he 44 percent-blue landscape with water and trees must be the a priori aesthetic universal'.[31] Landscapes in art are built on visual precedents in art: Landscape conventions developed in art in Europe and Britain mirror landscape aesthetics that evolved in Asia, particularly China and Japan, from the tenth century.[32] Those conventions were adopted in colonial landscapes.[33] But Danto blamed popular media – the scourge of calendar images circulated around the world – for propagating ubiquitous visions of nature that art had long left behind.[34] Others have attributed a universal preference for

24 See generally Fitter et al., 'Landscape'. See also Ian Potter Museum of Art, *Not as the Songs of Other Lands*.
25 Brady, *Aesthetics of the Natural Environment*, pp. 45–7.
26 See Cronon, 'The trouble with wilderness'. See Chapter 2.
27 See generally Bartel et al. (eds.), *Rethinking Wilderness and The Wild*. See discussion in Chapter 7.
28 See Mitchell, *Landscape and Power*.
29 Wypijewski, *Painting by Numbers*, pp. 2, 7.
30 Countries surveyed in an initial phase from 1993 were: China, Denmark, Finland, France, Iceland, Kenya, Russia, Turkey, Ukraine and the United States, gathering opinions from almost 2 billion people: Ibid., pp. 2, 89. Germany, Italy, The Netherlands and Portugal were subsequently polled: See Dia Art Foundation, '*Most wanted* and *least wanted* paintings'.
31 Danto, 'Can it be the "most wanted painting"', 124, 137.
32 See Whitfield, 'Landscape: China, People's Republic of'. See also Munsterberg, *The Landscape Painting of China and Japan*.
33 For example, Bonyhady, *Images in Opposition*.
34 Danto, 'Can it be the "most wanted painting"', 137.

particular qualities in natural environments to human evolution.[35] Aesthetic philosopher Denis Dutton apportioned responsibility for the harmonisation of landscape conventions to both nature and nurture.[36]

For aesthetic philosophers Emily Brady and Allen Carlson,[37] it is the picturesque and Romantic conceptions of nature developed through the arts that survive today in 'landscape' or 'scenery' models in nature conservation and restoration policy.[38] Both of those scholars consider the contemporary incarnations of these aesthetic concepts from the arts as inadequate to the task of environmental aesthetics.[39] Brady criticises the 'picturesque' movement for its 'impoverished' aesthetic experience of nature, marred by human-centred standards, limited framing, two-dimensional flatness and a bias towards the visual.[40] As explained earlier, environmental aesthetics understands environmental appreciation instead in terms of all senses.[41]

4.2.2 *Environmental Art*

Despite its apparent ubiquity, the eighteenth- and nineteenth-century conceptions of landscape in Europe and Britain are only one of the many ways in which the natural environment has been conceived in the practices of visual art around the world. Art scholar and curator Barbara Matilsky posits that 'artists throughout history have sought metaphors in nature to help define human existence'.[42] Matilsky suggests that periods of 'environmental stress' have provoked major artistic developments.[43] She traces these developments in art through social history, commencing with an awareness of critical species, surmised from cave paintings for hunter-gatherer societies. A concern for the impact of agriculture on the natural environment is evident later, she maintains, in artistic imagery of sacred trees from Mesopotamia and Mayan peoples.[44] She concludes her historical survey with the responses to urbanism and industrial intensification evident in landscape painting in Europe and its colonies, as well as in China and Japan. For Matilsky, the

[35] See e.g. Rampley, *The Seductions of Darwin*; Walsh et al., *On the Origin of Art*.
[36] Dutton, *The Art Instinct*, p. 31.
[37] See Section 2.2.2.
[38] See Brady, *Aesthetics of the Natural Environment*, p. 43.
[39] Ibid., pp. 225ff. See also Carlson, *Aesthetics and the Environment*, 46–7; on environmentalism of the poor, see Section 2.4.3.
[40] Brady, *Aesthetics of the Natural Environment*, pp. 42; 228–9.
[41] See Section 2.2.
[42] Matilsky, *Fragile Ecologies*, p. 4.
[43] Ibid., p. 5.
[44] Ibid.

response of contemporary artists to the environmental stresses of the Anthropocene era marks another significant development in artistic expression.[45]

In describing the subject of her inquiry, Matilsky refers to a broad category of 'environmental art' that reflects 'a wide range of approaches to nature'.[46] In one sense, her understanding of 'environmental art' includes the art that Allen Carlson also contemplates under the same term: Forms of 'earth art', 'earthworks' or 'Land Art' that creates art from the natural environment.[47] Much cited North American examples of Land Art include Robert Smithson's *Spiral Jetty* (1970), Michael Heizer's *Double Negative* (1970) and Christo's *Running Fence, Sonoma and Marin Counties, California* (1972–76).[48] This form of art has been controversial for its destructive impact on the environment from which it is created.[49] These interventions in the environment could be distinguished from works such as Agnes Denes' tree stand at the City West Sewage Plant in Altona, Melbourne, *A Forest for Australia* (1998),[50] or Alan Sonfist's *Time Landscape: Greenwich Village, New York* (planted 1978), which are situated in urban places to 'present' rather than 'alter' the environment.[51] British artists such as Richard Long, David Nash, Andy Goldsworthy, and in some respects, Barbara Hepworth, could also be termed environmental artists, with their works made from, in or of environmental elements and situated in national parks or natural settings.[52]

However, it is possible that a category of environmental art extends to all manner of artworks that engage, or could be understood to engage, environmental subject matter. James Morrison's painting, *Sepik River* (2012) (Figure 4.2), for example, can be seen on one level in terms of natural beauty. Landscape and seascape have merged, the coral fish and crustacean habitat drained and joined to the land by the hint of a saltwater crocodile nudging into the frame. Vivid and varying colours appear hyperreal, yet they are true to the species. The colours and layering are, literally, outstanding. This is

[45] See Braddock and Ater, 'Art in the anthropocene'; Heartney, 'Art for the anthropocene era'; Miles, *Eco-Aesthetics*.
[46] Matilsky, *Fragile Ecologies*, p. 36.
[47] Carlson, 'Is environmental art an aesthetic affront', 150. See also Art & Design Magazine: Art & Design Profile No. 36, *Art and the Natural Environment*.
[48] See Ross, 'Gardens, earthworks, and environmental art', 158.
[49] See, for example, Brady, 'Aesthetic regard for nature'.
[50] See Buchanan, 'Agnes Denes' public sculpture neglected'.
[51] Matilsky, *Fragile Ecologies*, p. 37; Carlson, *Aesthetics and the Environment*, p. 160.
[52] See, for example, sculpture parks Domaine du Muy, France; Grizedale Sculpture, UK; Jupiter Artland, Scotland; Kröller-Müller Museum and sculpture garden, The Netherlands; Louisiana, Denmark; Skulptur I Pilane, Sweden. Cf. Fisher, 'Environmental aesthetics', 667, 674.

FIGURE 4.2. James Morrison, *Sepik River*, 2012. Oil on linen, 100 × 100 cm. Private collection. © James Morrison. Courtesy Darren Knight Gallery, Sydney.

'wilderness', humans are absent, but all eyes are on the human viewer, staring out from the frame. Henri Rousseau's nineteenth-century whimsy is invoked too with the vibrant crowding of exotic flora and fauna.[53]

Yet critical elements can also be constructed from the painting. Animals native also to Australia meet with the flora edging the Sepik River in Papua New Guinea, the colony within the colony. The other's other, empire twice removed, the river itself once named for a German Empress. The Royal spoonbill of Oceania substituted for the Roseate spoonbill of the Amazon. It is not the only species seemingly at home yet out of place in the Sepik – the Golden Conure, also from the Amazon, would be unlikely to meet in the wild

[53] See, for example, Rousseau, *Exotic Landscape*, 1908.

the Cassowary lurking at a distance in the foliage. The ubiquitous wader, possibly a godwit or curlew, migrates vast distances between the hemispheres. Displaced animals belonging in a foreign place. The river of the title is unseen in the image, though it is perhaps its dry bed that hints at a lost habitat. A river that connects ecosystems, eventually flowing to the Bismarck Sea, the oceans that challenge territorial borders. The mottled purple serpent – the river animated in Indigenous law stories – snakes through the image as a riparian proxy. Drought-resistant succulents meet tropical vines but behind, layers below, is a possible hint of European foliage.

4.2.3 *Ecological Art*

Also included in Matilsky's notion of environmental art is what she calls 'ecological art'.[54] This, she says, refers to artworks that 'relate to ecology by respecting nature and establishing a reverent relationship between the viewer and the earth.'[55] Matilsky's conception of 'ecological art' appears similar to that of Linda Weintraub who identifies 'eco-artists' as those who address their art 'from the vantage point of a sustainable planet'[56] as opposed to others who might use or reference the environment in their work. Ecological art is directed at raising awareness about the state of the environment and advocating change.[57] It is art that is motivated by a belief that: 'Art and fiction can change the world, and they can also increase the significance that nature has in the human world.'[58]

Matilsky and Weintraub identify several artists, mostly North American, who could be termed eco-artists.[59] There are, however, many others from around the world who could also be named as such.[60] Exhibitions and art festivals have showcased art featuring human impacts on the environment. The Australian art association, CLIMARTE, for example, has initiated a regular festival of art projects responding to climate change.[61] The

54 Matilsky, *Fragile Ecologies*, p. 56; see also Simus, 'Environmental art and ecological citizenship', 101; Wallen, 'Ecological art'.
55 Matilsky, *Fragile Ecologies*, p. 37.
56 Weintraub, *To Life!*, p. 9.
57 See Demos, 'Contemporary art and the politics of ecology'; Curtis, 'Creating Inspiration'. See generally Edelman, *From Art and Politics*; Brown, *Art and Ecology Now*; Demos et al., *The Routledge Companion*.
58 Haapala, 'The interplay of works of art and natural phenomena', 54. See also Finchett-Maddock and Lekakis, 'Introduction', 1.
59 See Matilsky, *Fragile Ecologies*, pp. 57–8.
60 See Demos, 'Contemporary art and the politics of ecology'; Nnamdi, Gomba and Ugiomoh, 'Environmental challenges and eco-aesthetics'.
61 See, for example, Abrahams, Johnson, and Gellatly (eds.), *Art+Climate=Change*; Johnson and Gellatly (eds.), *Art+Climate=Change II*.

University of Melbourne's Ian Potter Museum of Art hosted the exhibitions *Nature/Revelation*, *EXIT* and Liam Gillick's *Some significant equations* as part of the respective CLIMARTE festivals in 2015, 2017 and 2019.[62] 'Artwise' curators in Britain has been involved in exhibitions concerning endangered species and fragile environments.[63] At the 56th Venice Biennale of 2015, Artwise worked with the Heydar Aliyev Foundation to mount an environmentally themed exhibition in the Azerbaijan Pavilion, while the environment and environmental crises were the subject of art in several of the other national pavilions and the international exhibition that year.[64] Environmental issues were also the subject of several works in the Venice Biennales of 2017 and 2019,[65] and in *Documenta 14* and *Skulptur Projekte Münster 2017*.[66] The exhibition *In the Balance: Art for a Changing World* at Sydney's Museum of Contemporary Art in 2010 is another example of curated collections of art directed at environmental activism.[67] Contemporary art reflecting on environmental destruction, pollution and extinction was also a strong feature of the National Gallery of Victoria Triennial 2020, and the 23rd Biennale of Sydney (2022), titled *rīvus*, was dedicated to rivers, wetlands and other water ecosystems.[68]

The political instrumentalism of ecological art is highlighted through exhibitions that are staged in conjunction with international meetings responsible for implementing and developing international protections for the environment. CarbonArts, for example, has been active in presenting exhibitions of art in association with treaty processes concerning the environment.[69] A world-wide ArtCOP21 was held in 2015 to coincide with the negotiations in Paris of a new agreement under the *United Nations Framework Convention on Climate Change*.[70] Artist Janet Laurence was one of the artists included in that art festival. Her work *Deep Breathing: Resuscitation for the Reef*

62 See CLIMARTE, 'Arts for a safe climate'.

63 See Artwise Curators, *Here Today*.

64 See Bracker (ed.), *Vita Vitale*; Wiseman and Chomley, 'Wrong way time'.

65 See Margutti (ed.), *Viva Arte Viva*; Margutti (ed.), *May You Live in Interesting Times*.

66 See Latimer and Szymczyk (eds.), *The Documenta 14 Reader*; Skulptur Projekte Münster 2017, www.skulptur-projekte-archiv.de/en-us/2017.

67 *In the Balance: Art for a Changing World*; see also arts programme at Glenorchy Art and Sculpture Park (GASP), Tasmania.

68 See National Gallery of Victoria, *Triennial*; José Roca, *rīvus*.

69 See, for example, CarbonArts-World Health Organisation, *Breathe*. See also art for World Environment Day: UN Environment, '12 art installations to be unveiled'; World Environment Day, 'Turning air pollution into art'.

70 *United Nations Framework Convention on Climate Change*, New York, 9 May 1992, in force 21 March 1994, 1771 UNTS 107. See ARTCOP21; CLIMARTE, 'Art provokes and inspires'.

FIGURE 4.3. Janet Laurence, *Deep Breathing: Resuscitation for the Reef*, 2015–16 (detail, still). Installation view, Artists 4 Paris Climate COP21, Muséum national d'Histoire naturelle, Paris, 2015, corals, pigment, acrylic, boxes, laboratory glass, film projections, various wet specimens, specimens from the collections of the Muséum national d'Histoire naturelle. © Janet Laurence. Courtesy the artist.

(Figure 4.3) was a sculptural installation comprising natural specimens of coral placed among mirrors, blown glass, petri dishes, vials and beakers, some upended, mimicking the coral in their chaotic protrusions, rounded shapes and diverse sizes. The objects, joined by threads and hoses, were encased in Perspex to create *Wunderkammers*,[71] cabinets of curiosities that in sixteenth-century Europe displayed myriad objects not yet subject to modern scientific classification. The work 'curated' the environment in all the senses of that word. The world created was primordial and wondrous, one that preceded Western science, but which might be saved by it. Here, an ecosystem is preserved as a memory, to be studied as a curiosity unknown to a future world. A Romantic environmental aesthetic, distinct from scientific value, is, literally, put on a pedestal, where reverence might translate to care.

Janet Laurence is among several artists working in Australia who have for decades positioned their work in relation to environmental conservation in

[71] Kent, 'Janet Laurence: *After Nature*'.

ways that might satisfy Matilsky's categorisation of ecological art.[72] Lauren Berkowitz, who uses recycled materials in her work as 'an act of regeneration',[73] has for example consistently addressed environmental themes in her work. Artists such as Fiona Hall and Mandy Martin have also used their artwork as a vehicle for environmental activism.[74] Martin painted the scars from open-cut mining and nuclear fuel towers with the expressive swipes and smudges of European Romanticism,[75] while Fiona Hall's representation of Australia at the 56th Venice Biennale in 2015 included many works speaking to environmental issues that have long occupied a place in her work.[76]

To identify the work of such artists as ecological art under a broader category of environmental art raises several long-debated concerns for the 'political' in aesthetic philosophy for the arts.[77] That art can engage and provoke popular and ultimately national and international policy debate on environmental causes has been claimed or observed for example by historian Finis Dunaway and other scholars, such as Tim Bonyhady, who have had a particular interest in environmental movements leading to law reform.[78] Historically, drawings by Thomas Moran from which he painted *Grand Canyon of the Yellowstone, 1872* were said to be instrumental in the decision to legislate the area as a national park in the United States.[79] Artists such as Nicholas Chevalier were commissioned by governments in the nineteenth century to undertake 'pictorial surveys' of colonised lands that would be the subject of legislative intervention.[80] For the twentieth century, the photographs of Peter Dombrovskis in Australia and of Ansel Adams in the United States are often cited for having influenced law and policy on environmental management.[81] Their photographs are, arguably, what aesthetic philosopher John Fisher calls 'nature art', exhibiting a 'favourable regard to nature' that 'inspires appreciation of nature'.[82] With respect to contemporary art, a study

72 See, for example, Couacaud, *After Nature*; Davis, Owen and Unsworth, *Venice Biennale 1978*.
73 Berkowitz, 'Work'; see Wilson, 'Lauren Berkowitz's fragile structures'.
74 See, for example, an event featuring artists Fiona Hall AO and Mandy Martin among others: 'Art climate ethics: what role for the arts?'.
75 See Haynes, *Mandy Martin*; Soboslay, 'Mandy Martin: Eco-worrying'.
76 Michael (ed.), *Fiona Hall*.
77 See Goehr, 'Art and politics', 471; Bishop, *Artificial Hells*. See also Manderson, 'Here and now'.
78 See Dunaway, *Seeing Green*. See also Bonyhady, *Places Worth Keeping*.
79 See Miller, 'The fate of wilderness', 85.
80 See Tipping, 'Chevalier, Nicholas (1828–1902)'.
81 See CLIMARTE Festival 2019, '*Peter Dombrovskis: Journeys into the Wild*'; Dunaway, 'The ecological sublime'.
82 Fisher, 'Environmental aesthetics', 673.

on the psychological impacts of art in ArtCOP21 also suggests a link to political action aimed at law reform and other action on climate change.[83]

To the extent that such artists articulate a political intention for their works, they might rightly be identified as eco-artists for Weintraub's purposes. However, visual art depicting the natural environment could be analysed for its ecological import even if the artist has not positioned their work as such. With a work like James Morrison's *Sepik River* (Figure 4.2), for example, it is possible to see how any environmental art could be understood as a political intervention that might ultimately be reflected in law. An artist's intentions – political or otherwise – do not determine the meanings that any one viewer might take from their artworks.[84]

In Chapters 5 through 7, I examine photographs of the natural environment for their significance to understandings of the environment's aesthetic value. In those chapters, I rely on scholarship of art theorists to describe, analyse and attribute significance to the photographs in decision-making processes of international bodies. As I explained in the first chapter of this book, aesthetic scholarship for the visual arts is the field of expertise I rely on to develop meanings from images in international law. I do not set out to demonstrate in fact that the photographs were intended by states parties, or have been understood by decision-makers, as depicting a specific characterisation of the environment's aesthetic value. As explained later, if those photographic images were to be recognised as having a formal role in decision-making processes of international bodies, it would be for states to articulate the significance of those images, and for decision-makers to explain how they relate to their decisions.[85]

4.3 ANALYSING THE ENVIRONMENT'S AESTHETIC VALUE FROM ART

Nelson Goodman's *The Languages of Art* advances an aesthetic theory that understands visual representation as 'denotation' construed in accordance with conventions – habits or schemes for interpretation that are acquired by a viewer of the image through life or study.[86] Meaning can be ascribed in myriad ways but I understand aesthetic analysis to organise those meanings in a manner that can be communicated and replicated by others. But to interpret

83 See Sommer and Klöckner, 'Does activist art have the capacity'. See also Robidoux and Kovacs, 'Public art as a tool'; Gulliver et al., 'Testing the impact of images'.

84 See further Livingston, 'Intention in art', 275.

85 See Section 8.3.

86 Goodman, *Languages of Art*. See also Eldridge, *An Introduction to the Philosophy of Art*, p. 32.

the denotations of environmental photographs in terms of the environment's aesthetic value, using conventions known to the study and practice of visual art, raises several questions for aesthetic philosophy. These include the conception of photographs as representation, understandings of the environment's aesthetic value from photographic representations, and eco-critical approaches to those understandings in the study and practice of visual art. I will consider each in turn below.

4.3.1 *Photography as Representation*

To analyse a photograph with aesthetic conventions for visual art requires a conception of the photographic image as representation.[87] However, scholars of aesthetics have historically debated whether photographs are more properly conceived as 'transparent' windows to the physical place or thing depicted.[88] Some scholars maintain that photographs are a replication of what would have been seen with the naked eye by any person there in the place and time it was taken. From this perspective, my photograph of Pierre Huyghe's *After ALife Ahead* (Figure 4.1) is a kind of true-to-life presentation of the artwork.

André Bazin, for example, maintained that photographic images 'are the object itself'.[89] Roger Scruton took the view that photographs were a substitute for their subject.[90] Contrasting photography with painting, Scruton said 'if one finds a photograph beautiful, it is because one finds something beautiful in its subjects. A painting may be beautiful, on the other hand, even when it represents an ugly thing.'[91] Kendall Walton described the notion of representation in photography in terms of 'transparency' whereby the viewer of a photographic image sees through the image to the object in it.[92] This position was maintained by one of the pioneers of photography, Louis Daguerre, who was quoted to say: 'The daguerreotype is not merely an instrument which serves to draw nature... [it] gives her the power to reproduce herself.'[93] This despite the fact that early photographs of landscapes were created from spliced

87 See Fisher, 'Environmental aesthetics'.
88 See Warburton, 'Photography', 614. See also Stecker, 'Definition of art', 190–2.
89 Bazin, 'The ontology of the photographic image', reprinted in Bazin, *What is Cinema?*, pp. 9, 14, cited in Warburton, 'Photography', 615.
90 Scruton, 'Photography and representation', 111, cited in Warburton, 'Photography', 616.
91 Ibid., 114, quoted in Warburton, 'Photography', 617.
92 Walton, 'Transparent pictures'.
93 Louis Daguerre quoted in Savedoff, *Transforming Images*, p. 48.

negatives, in order that the land or the sky was neither under-, nor overexposed.[94]

The commitment to photography as verisimilitude has, however, been contradicted by critical scholars who argue instead that photographs are a mediated image. Joel Snyder and Neil Walsh Allen, for example, state:

> The notion that a photograph shows us "what we would have seen had we been there ourselves" has to be qualified to the point of absurdity. A photograph shows us "what we would have seen" at a certain moment in time, *from* a certain vantage point *if* we kept our head immobile and closed one eye *and if* we saw the equivalent of a 150-mm or 24-mm lens *and if* we saw things [in the colour and printed format of the photograph].[95]

Barbara Savedoff concurs with Snyder and Allen, though she acknowledges that something of the belief in photographic mimesis is never quite abandoned by a critical viewer, giving photographs a quality that is distinct from other forms of representational art.[96] Trevor Pateman discusses the difference in terms of photograph as 'record' and as 'art',[97] while Patrick Maynard speaks of 'detection' and 'depiction'.[98] Finis Dunaway, in contrast, expresses little tolerance for this debate, stating:

> While modern cultural critics fretted over the reproduction of reality, wondering if images estranged viewers from the physical world, environmental reformers expressed little anxiety over the status of nature in an age of mechanical reproduction. Their enthusiasm for the camera rested on the belief that it could elicit an emotional response in spectators, awakening them to the beauty of nature and arousing their concern for its protection.[99]

Adopting the view of critical scholars such as Snyder and Allen, and Savedoff, it is possible to contemplate photographs as representation – pictures or images available for aesthetic reflection and analysis, rather than as purported verisimilitude. And, as representation, photographs can be understood, I maintain, in conceptual terms, including those that underscore philosophical theories of environmental aesthetics like those of Emily Brady or Allen Carlson.

94 Ibid., p. 87.
95 Snyder and Allen, 'Photography, vision and representation', 151–2; see also Warburton, 'Seeing through "seeing through photographs"'; Mitchell, *The Reconfigured Eye*.
96 See Savedoff, *Transforming Images*.
97 See Pateman, 'Photography', 138.
98 Patrick Maynard, *The Engine of Visualization*.
99 Dunaway, *Natural Visions*, p. xviii.

4.3.2 *Representation of the Environment's Aesthetic Value*

In Chapter 2, I explained the ways in which philosophers of environmental aesthetics have distinguished aesthetic appreciation of the natural environment from that of the arts. There I explain that aesthetic philosophers, such as Emily Brady or Allen Carlson, maintain a distinction between the appreciation of art and of the environment that might be seen to preclude the use of aesthetic concepts and methods of analysis for the arts to characterise the environment's aesthetic value.[100] However, in a reorientation of this view, aesthetic philosopher John Fisher asks, 'can we experience nature aesthetically (albeit indirectly) or experience the aesthetic properties of nature through appreciating nature art'?[101] Referring to Allen Carlson's defence of an aesthetic appreciation of the natural environment distinct from that of art, Fisher observes:

> Carlson's argument raises the question whether we can experience the beauty of a natural environment by appreciating the beauty of a photograph of that environment. However, might not nature art exhibit how a part of nature actually appeared at a certain moment from a certain point of view? Even though limited and incomplete, why must a representation be seen as necessarily unable authentically to exhibit some of the aesthetic qualities of the represented objects or scenes?[102]

Arguments offered by other philosophers in favour of appreciating the environment in terms analogous to art do not necessarily address the issues raised by Fisher's question. For example, Janna Thompson's understanding of the environment in aesthetic terms contemplates an artistic analysis of the environment 'in situ' as opposed to an analysis of art representing the environment.[103] However, responding to Fisher's provocation, I maintain that it is possible to describe an aesthetic appreciation of nature from photographic images of the environment. At the very outset of Chapter 1 of this book, I described a photograph of the Monarch Butterfly Biosphere Reserve (Figure 1.1) that had been included in a nomination file of the Mexican government submitted to the World Heritage Committee.[104] The form and expressive qualities of the photograph, combined with my personal experiences and amateur knowledge of biology, allowed me to describe an aesthetic

[100] See Section 2.2.1.
[101] Fisher, 'Environmental aesthetics', 674.
[102] Ibid., 667, 674.
[103] Thompson, 'Aesthetics and the value of nature'. See Section 2.2.1.
[104] Mexico, *World Heritage Site Nomination Document*.

appreciation of the environment in ways informed by the philosophy of environmental aesthetics.

I am, for the purposes of my analysis, viewing the photographic image as a static proxy for the environment that is valued on an aesthetic basis under the treaty, the *World Heritage Convention*. This relies in part on me making meaning from place in ways contemplated by philosophers of environmental hermeneutics. Martin Drenthen explains that '[e]nvironmental hermeneuticists have shown that humans understand themselves not just through texts and narratives but also through the meaningful places in which they find themselves'.[105] He concludes that: 'By explicating the interpretational base of our being-in-the-world and articulating those pre-existing meanings and interpretations that already play a role in how we act and think, hermeneutics will force us to have a second look at the meanings we often take for granted.'[106] As I attempt in this book to develop meanings of the environment's aesthetic value from photographs for legal process, I make the same assumptions for interpretation as environmental hermeneuticists. But I come full circle, relying on aesthetic methods for the arts, to understand the aesthetic value of the environment in terms of the philosophy of environmental aesthetics, looking to photographic images for my interpretation of an appreciation of place.

An understanding of the environment's aesthetic value developed from a photograph will, however, be affected by the aesthetic quality of the image. In my description of Pierre Huyghe's *After ALife Ahead* (Figure 4.1) at the beginning of this chapter, I explained how the work represented an environmental sensibility – an aesthetic evocation in art of an aesthetic appreciation of the environment that I could describe in words. Yet my description of the work was based on my physical experience of it, when I was immersed in the material 'environment' of the artwork at the time of my visit. As a sculptural environment in a physical space, it engaged all my senses. But the photograph that I took of the work does not capture the complexity of the space, or the senses and ideas on the natural environment that my visit activated: The low-resolution image shows only part of the work, it is backlit and the foreground is out of focus. Had I relied only on the photograph to describe an aesthetic appreciation of the environment created by the work, it is not certain that I would have formulated the aesthetic experience in the same way. To work as a representation of the environment's aesthetic value, the photograph of the artwork would itself need to be of an aesthetic quality that allows a Babushka

[105] Drenthen, 'Environmental hermeneutics', 162, 170. See also Felski, *Hooked*.
[106] Ibid., 171. See further Clingerman et al. (eds.), *Interpreting Nature*.

doll-style appreciation of the image, as an appreciation of the artwork, as an appreciation of the environment.

4.3.3 *Eco-Critical Approaches to Representations*

Consistent with the positions of Snyder and Allen, and with Savedoff, I maintain that the same kinds of aesthetic concepts and methods used to analyse a landscape painting can be applied to analyse photographs of the environment.[107] I employed several such methods in the introductory chapter to this book to describe Mexico's photograph of the Monarch Butterfly Biosphere Reserve (Figure 1.1). One of the 'conventions' or techniques that I used to give significance to the photograph was that of using other images – in that case from the contemporary artwork of Diana Thater (Figure 1.2) – to articulate a narrative about nature and the place of humans in nature. It is an approach or method of aesthetic analysis that generates meaning from visual connections.[108] It situates images in the context of visual histories or precedents, as well as socio-political contexts, to develop understandings of the subject matter portrayed in, or suggested by, an artwork.[109]

These approaches or methods for analysing visual art can be critical in the sense of undertaking an eco-critical analysis of the art through the lens of social and natural history with the intention of exposing 'false assumptions' about the state of the environment 'while pointing the way to a more sustainable future'.[110] For example, my discussion of Mexico's photograph of the Monarch Butterfly Biosphere Reserve (Figure 1.1) introduced socio-political matters of empire and environmentalism. Similarly, in my analysis of Pierre Huyghe's *After ALife Ahead* (Figure 4.1), I was directed by the work to think about elements that make an environment 'natural' – not focused on the bright colours, symmetrical patterns or melodious sounds associated with a neo-classical natural beauty. And it made me reflect critically on human imaginings of nature, as well as the seemingly dogged insistence of nature to carry on regardless of human disruption – as if we do not matter. The turn to eco-criticism among scholars of aesthetics has been focused in large part on

[107] On strategies for understanding art generally, see Eldridge, *An Introduction to the Philosophy of Art*, p. 128.
[108] See Manderson, 'Introduction: Imaginal law', 3, citing Panofsky, *Studies in Iconology* and Gombrich, *Art and Illusion*.
[109] See Levinson, 'Aesthetic contextualism', 17.
[110] Ibid., 19.

literature,[111] however, those theories have also been transposed to visual art.[112] Art historians Alan Braddock and Christoph Irmscher refer to eco-critical art history as a 'probing and pointedly ethical integration of visual analysis, ecocultural interpretation, and environmental history' that 'pays sharper attention to the environmental embeddedness of art within a world that is both stubbornly real and infinitely vulnerable'.[113]

An eco-critical analysis could be seen then as one aimed at social or political change in ways contemplated for critical theory by Bernard Harcourt. Harcourt has emphasised the task of contemporary critical thought as one of critical praxis with 'the ultimate aim of changing the world'.[114] Eco-critical analysis is, however, not limited to images produced by artists who actively engage law and policy on environmental protection to make what Barbara Matilsky calls ecological art.[115] It can also be applied to analyse images depicting the natural environment without a stated political or social purpose. It is, in this way, available for the analysis of photographs used by nation states in the processes that make decisions under international environmental treaties. The nature and meaning of images in law, and the role of conventions from aesthetic philosophy in defining and translating images for law, has occupied the scholarship of legal theorists in ways discussed in the next part of this chapter.

4.4 AESTHETICS OF IMAGE AS ART IN LAW

So far in this chapter, my focus has been on the aesthetic value of the environment in terms of the aesthetic philosophy of the arts. I now turn to understandings of aesthetic philosophy in law. Formulations of 'aesthetics' in law are principally in the domain of legal theory or 'jurisprudence' – the philosophical study of law done well.[116] Jurisprudents have engaged aesthetic

[111] See, for example, Glotfelty and Fromm (eds.), *The Ecocriticism Reader*; Garrard, *Ecocriticism*; Hiltner (ed.), *Ecocriticism*.
[112] See, for example, Braddock and Irmscher, *A Keener Perception*.
[113] Ibid., p. 4. See also Braddock, 'From nature to ecology', 448; Braddock, 'Ecocritical art history'.
[114] Harcourt, *Critique and Praxis*, p. 18.
[115] See further Matilsky, *Fragile Ecologies*, p. 4. See also Weintraub, *To Life!*, p. 9; Miles, *Eco-Aesthetics*.
[116] See generally Gearey, *Law and Aesthetics*. On meanings of jurisprudence, see, for example, Davies, *Asking the Law Question*, p. 1. Cf. jurisprudence as 'a training in *persona* and office': Dorsett and McVeigh, 'The persona of the jurist; Genovese, McVeigh and Rush, 'Lives lived with law', 2. See also McVeigh, 'Jurisprudent of London' (jurisprudence as it relates to place); Barr, A *Jurisprudence of Movement*: p. 58 ('minor jurisprudence' of movement).

philosophy in the interdisciplinary study of law and humanities.[117] Their conception of aesthetics is associated with the philosophical study of the arts, adapted in the main to theorise several aspects of common and civil law traditions, including the place of image in law.[118] Jurisprudential scholarship on image and law has been named such things as legal iconography,[119] visual jurisprudence,[120] and imaginal law.[121]

In the main, scholars of law and the visual conceive images in graphic forms as manifestations of law and legal authority despite – or in spite of – a preponderance of the prosaic word in written texts and the verbal languages of law.[122] Scholars Costas Douzinas and Lynda Nead, among others, observe that a one-time intimacy between law and image dissipated in seventeenth-century Anglo-European law, evolving away from visual emblems towards written text, as an iconoclastic secular state wrenched legal authority from the Roman Catholic Church.[123] Image in forms graphic or as 'painted words' was seen as circumspect, possibly anathema, to law.[124] Douzinas and Nead together with other scholars of visual jurisprudence have, however, challenged the presumed sovereignty of the word in law.[125] As explained below, several scholars have examined the extent to which image was ever exiled from the legal domain, highlighting the myriad ways in which images as graphic or literary devices continue to populate legal form and thinking.

Legal theorists addressing the place of image in law have called for visual literacy, or visual competence, in legal method and legal education.[126] Those charged with making and applying the law, these scholars suggest, should recognise and understand the role of image in law. Legal methods and sources must be expanded to openly encompass aesthetic understandings of image. There is, otherwise, a risk that justice will be undone by image. Legal theorist

[117] See Sarat, Anderson and Frank (eds.), *Law and the Humanities*; Del Mar and Goodrich (eds.), *Legal Theory and the Humanities*; Stern, Del Mar and Meyler (eds.), *The Oxford Handbook of Law and Humanities*; Goodrich, 'Law by other means'; Goodrich, 'Jurisliterature and transgression'.

[118] See, for example, Douzinas and Nead, 'Introduction', 1; Gearey, *Law and Aesthetics*, p. 25. See also Petersen, 'Foot notes. Reflections on method and form'.

[119] Douzinas and Nead, 'Introduction', 11.

[120] Sherwin, 'Visual jurisprudence'.

[121] Manderson, *Imaginal Law*.

[122] See Douzinas, 'The legality of the image'. See generally Goodrich and Hayaert (eds.), *Genealogies of Legal Vision*.

[123] See, for example, Douzinas and Nead, 'Introduction', 8.

[124] Ibid.

[125] Ibid.

[126] See Sherwin, *Visualizing Law in the Age of the Digital Baroque*, p. 40; Bańkowski, Del Mar and Maharg (eds.), *The Arts and the Legal Academy*; Manderson, 'Bodies in the water'.

Peter Goodrich, for example, points to the interpretive significance of graphic images reproduced in judgments of United States courts.[127] Legal scholar Richard Sherwin highlights the risk of context being excluded by the selective framing of photographs or videos proffered in evidence before courts.[128] He also describes the emotive powers of image as a potential source of bias, where a photographic or video image informs legal judgments but is not recognised as having done so.[129] Peter Rush and Andrew Kenyon critique verbal imagery in case law as betraying the bias within judgments.[130] Alison Young warns that law's ignorance of artistic conventions can lead to 'misjudgements' of images,[131] while Costas Douzinas points to the common law's problematic engagement with the aesthetics of art.[132] Katherine Biber and Mehera San Roque describe images that are 'troubling in what they say about law' and that 'cause trouble for law'.[133]

As will be explained in this section, image is, for the purposes of scholarship on law and the visual, variously defined. It has included visual art and other graphic images as distinct from images apparent in law's literary or metaphorical language.[134] Although possibly dominated by scholars of the common law,[135] theoretical approaches to the visual are also being engaged in an analysis of public international law. However, reference to the arts, including visual art, in scholarship concerning international environmental law has not necessarily been situated in theories of visual jurisprudence.

4.4.1 *Images for Law*

The 'images' analysed in jurisprudential scholarship on law and aesthetics assume myriad forms that I identify and interrogate for my analysis of

[127] Goodrich, 'Imago decidendi', 14. See also Porter, 'Taking images seriously'; Goodrich, 'Retinal justice'. Cf. Moran, *Law, Judges and Visual Culture*.

[128] Sherwin, *Visualising Law in the Age of the Digital Baroque*, pp. 38–42.

[129] Ibid., p. 39.

[130] Rush and Kenyon, 'Alter egos', 1.

[131] Young, 'Aesthetic vertigo', 20.

[132] On *Whistler v. Ruskin* (High Court of Justice, Huddleston J, 1878), see Douzinas, 'The legality of the image', 827–30.

[133] Biber and San Roque, 'The trouble with pictures', 2. See also Biber, 'Photographs and labels'.

[134] See generally Silbey, 'Images in/of Law'. See also Farley, 'Imagining the law', 292; Behrmann, 'Law, visual studies, and image history'. Cf. Hanne and Weisberg (eds.), *Narrative and Metaphor in the Law*.

[135] For different descriptions of the field of law and visual scholarship, see, for example, Behrmann, 'Law, visual studies, and image history'; Mulcahy, 'Eyes of the law'. Older reviews include Dahlberg, Stierstorfer and Carpi (eds.), *Visualizing Law and Authority*; Petroski, 'Visual legal commentary', 671; Sherwin, 'Introduction: Law, culture, and visual studies', iv.

photographs of the natural environment used in international treaty processes. In the book, I assume vantages of different disciplinary orientations – international law, philosophy of art and philosophy of environmental aesthetics – to attribute different conceptions of image to the different roles of the photographs in the decision-making processes under treaties. For reasons related to my earlier discussion of representation,[136] I use for the typology of images espoused by art historian WJT Mitchell to interrogate the photographs in those treaty processes.

WJT Mitchell explains that image can be understood as 'optical' projections, 'mental' memories, 'graphic' representations, 'verbal' metaphors and 'perceptual' associations.[137] Each, Mitchell explains, is characterised in terms of different intellectual disciplines. His conception of 'graphic' images pertaining to the disciplines of art and design is particularly important for my examination of photographs used in international treaty processes. Broadly construed, Mitchell's graphic image would likely extend to a wide range of visual arts, including photography. I maintain, however, that Mitchell's conception of graphic image would also extend to graphic images in law, including the photographs used in international legal processes that I identify and examine in this book. Mitchell's graphic image would include, for example, ancient legal emblems,[138] photographic and video evidence,[139] graphic images in judgments,[140] and comic book-style illustrations in legal contracts.[141] It would also include the visual art used by visual jurisprudents to interrogate law and legal concepts.[142] The term graphic here goes to form, not to the vivid or explicit nature of the image.

Mitchell's graphic image in terms of art and design is different from his 'optical' image, associated with the study of physics and aligned with light on material objects and spaces. It is the projection on the eye of an image created by light reflected off a physical surface. The 'optical' image is what is elsewhere described by aesthetic philosopher Jacques Rancière as a 'naked'

[136] See Section 4.3. See generally Mitchell, 'Pictorial turn', 230.
[137] Mitchell, *Iconology*, p. 10. See also Douzinas, 'A legal phenomenology of images', 247; Del Mar, 'Thinking in images'.
[138] Goodrich, *Legal Emblems*. See also Haldar, 'The tongue and the eye', 152. Cf. Widener and Weiner, *Law's Picture Books*.
[139] See Sherwin, *Visualising Law in the Age of the Digital Baroque*; Biber and San Roque, 'The trouble with pictures'.
[140] See Goodrich, 'Imago decidendi'. See also Porter, 'Taking images seriously'; Goodrich, 'Retinal justice'.
[141] See Keating and Andersen, 'A graphic contract'. Cf. Giddens, *On Comics and Legal Aesthetics*.
[142] See, for example, Manderson, *Danse Macabre*; Young, 'Aesthetic vertigo'.

image.[143] Mitchell's 'mental' image is associated with psychology, referring to memories and ideas. Mitchell's 'verbal' image refers to metaphorical or descriptive images associated with literature or literary theory – those images for international law that are analysed for example by scholars Ed Morgan, Mary-Ellen O'Connell and Gerry Simpson, among others.[144]

The catch-all 'perceptual' image in WJT Mitchell's typology is the most abstract form in his image family. He says it captures the 'strange creatures that haunt the border between physical and psychological accounts of imagery'.[145] It might be characterised as a combination of each of his other forms of image; it is possibly that image conceptualised in linguistic theory as 'signs' – the confluence of a concept and an utterance.[146] It is perhaps perceptual images that Richard Sherwin describes as 'quickly activat[ing] patterns of seeing and feeling that we have internalized from a lifetime of watching.'[147] Art historian Simon Schama explores image in terms of landscape and memory, possibly like Mitchell's perceptual image, arguing that landscape is a cultural construct developed over time and in the context of a particular place – it is a socialised but personal sense of place.[148] Perceptual image might also be the kind of image contemplated by social scientist Sheila Jasanoff when she described an image of humanity in the popular imagination derived from a graphic image – the first photograph of Earth from space.[149]

WJT Mitchell's typology of image does not include a perspective from the discipline of law. While scholars of visual jurisprudence do not necessarily define 'image' in their examination of law and aesthetics, some have made distinctions that correlate with part of Mitchell's typology such that image for law's purposes could assume any and all of the disciplinary orientations Mitchell identifies. Costas Douzinas and Lynda Nead, for example, refer to 'painted words' and 'iconophilic text' in a manner likely contemplated in Mitchell's 'verbal' image.[150] Writing elsewhere, Douzinas describes three

[143] Rancière, *The Future of Image.*

[144] Morgan, *The Aesthetics of International Law*; O'Connell, *The Art of Law in the International Community*; Simpson, *Sentimental Life of International Law*. In respect of film and international law, cf., for example, Corten et al., A *Critical Introduction to International Law*; Ainley, Humphreys and Tallgren, 'International criminal justice on/and film'; Rush and Elander, 'Working through the cinematography'.

[145] Mitchell, *Iconology*, p. 10.

[146] See de Saussure, 'Nature of the linguistic sign', 75.

[147] Sherwin, *Visualising Law in the Age of the Digital Baroque*, p. 2.

[148] Schama, *Landscape and Memory*. See also on memory Schama, *Wordy*.

[149] Jasanoff, 'Heaven and Earth', 31; Klaver 'Landscapes of the environmental imagination', 135; Buell, *The Environmental Imagination*. Cf. Morgan, *Images at Work*.

[150] Douzinas and Nead, 'Introduction', 8.

forms of image: The object of vision, mental representations and works of art.[151] His 'object of vision' might be understood for Mitchell's purposes as an optical image and his 'works of art' as included in Mitchell's graphic images. Douzinas' 'mental' representations possibly relate to Mitchell's mental images for psychology but they might also incorporate the 'perceptual' in Mitchell's family of images. Douzinas explains his distinction between images in the following terms:

> Watching a fishing boat pass in the tranquil waters of a Greek island in August, imagining a fishing boat pass while cloistered in the austere environs of a central London office and seeing a painting of a fishing boat in a gallery are experientially different activities; all three are enabled however by the same specular operation, the support and continuity the image offers to consciousness. We are not able to 'see' or recognise the painting of the fishing boat without the memory and imagination of a fishing boat; nor would we be able to 'see' or recognise a fishing boat passing by without the imagistically supported words that refer to 'fishing', 'boat' or the 'sea'.[152]

In a comprehensive review of the field of aesthetic jurisprudence occupied with image – what he calls 'imaginal law' – Desmond Manderson conceives of image in at least two ways: Conceptual and physical.[153] His conceptual images are abstractions while his physical images – possibly Mitchell's graphic images – are 'artworks, photographs, representations, and the like'.[154] Elsewhere Manderson describes image as inclusive of 'mental image' but different from 'imagination or the imaginary',[155] while Peter Goodrich refers to images in terms of 'rhizomic connections'.[156]

While Douzinas' trio of images, and Manderson's binary of the conceptual and physical image, correspond to elements of Mitchell's typology of images, neither quite corresponds to the distinctions I make in this book to explain the understandings of photographic image from the vantages of international law, art theory and the philosophy of environmental aesthetics. As I explain in detail in Chapters 5 through 7: International law's treatment of photographs, as proxies for reality, correspond to Mitchell's optical image; art theory could characterise the photographs in terms of Mitchell's graphic images; while the philosophy of environmental aesthetics might be seen to adopt Mitchell's

151 Douzinas, 'Legal phenomenology', 247.
152 Ibid.
153 Manderson, 'Introduction: Imaginal law', 3, 4.
154 Ibid.
155 Manderson, *Danse Macabre*, 16–17.
156 Peter Goodrich, 'Retinal justice', 246.

perceptual image or no image at all. But as I use a specific kind of graphic image – visual art – to develop understandings of the environment's aesthetic value projected from photographs, I will in the next part consider the ways in which art, particularly visual art, has been conceived for legal scholarship.

4.4.2 *Image as Visual Art in Law*

The use of aesthetic method by scholars to engage visual art in understandings of law is instructive for my analysis of photographs as representations of the environment's aesthetic value. Art has been characterised in many ways in the study of law and aesthetics or, more broadly, law and humanities. It is described by Costas Douzinas and Lynda Nead in terms of 'law's art' and 'art's law',[157] while Jani McCutcheon and Fiona McGaughey conceive of 'law in art' and the 'art in law'.[158] Christine Haight Farley adds prepositional variety with her consideration of the 'law of art' and the 'art of law' before providing a detailed assessment of the variety of ways in which art encounters law under the moniker 'art law'.[159] The interdisciplinary scholarship addresses different art forms. It ranges from the many scholars who engage literature and literary devices for law,[160] to the relatively few scholars who have for example examined law in connection with other arts such as music.[161] Relevant to my analysis of photographic images for this book is the legal scholarship that uses aesthetic theory and methods developed for visual art in a theoretical examination of law.[162]

In my examination of the photographs used in decision-making processes that evaluate the environment's aesthetic value under international environmental treaties, I draw on concepts employed in the study of law and aesthetics. My examination of photographic images with reference to methods of art theory, and to visual artworks, leads me to rely on the insights of those law and aesthetics scholars who have attended specifically to visual art as images in or

[157] Douzinas and Nead, 'Introduction', 11.
[158] McCutcheon and McGaughey, 'Introduction', 1.
[159] Farley, 'Imagining the law'. The law of art includes law's regulation of the arts: See, for example, Phillips, 'The dilemma of artistic works', 1–13; McCutcheon and Skead, 'The art of crime'. The art of law includes law's methods or 'theatre': See, for example, Haldar, 'The tongue and the eye'; Schlag, 'The aesthetics of American law'. Cf. Bagnall, *Law as Art*.
[160] See, for example, Sarat, Anderson and Frank (eds.), *Law and the Humanities*. See also Kennedy, 'Critical legal theory', 124.
[161] See, for example, Manderson, *Songs without Music*; Parker, *Acoustic Jurisprudence*; Ramshaw, *Justice as Improvisation*.
[162] See, for example, Manderson, *Danse Macabre*; Young, 'Aesthetic vertigo'. See also Doherty, 'Susanna the slut'.

for the law. Desmond Manderson organises the scholarship on law and image as inclusive of art, describing it in terms of visual representations of law, visual technologies in law, and aesthetic critiques of law where 'image' includes visual art.[163] Manderson undertakes aesthetic analyses of visual art to interrogate, for example, the temporal elements of common law,[164] concepts of justice,[165] and, more specifically, Australia's law and policy on asylum seekers.[166] Alison Young engages visual art to examine law and legal concepts, describing in the process the different acts of writing, making and being art.[167] Katherine Biber and Mehera San Roque also consider visual art in relation to law,[168] as does Laura Petersen.[169] Leslie Moran, among others, has examined the visual for law in respect of court architecture.[170]

These scholars demonstrate ways in which aesthetic method can be adapted to give significance to visual representations for law. Like them, I use in Chapters 5 through 7 concepts and methods developed in the aesthetic contemplation of visual art. The objects of my analyses are, however, not works of art in a formal sense. They are photographic images created or used in decision-making processes of international law. My examination of photographic images nevertheless approaches them as I might works of art, employing aesthetic methods, including reference to visual artworks, to develop meanings of the environment's aesthetic value for international environmental law.

Scholars writing on the particular field of international environmental law have not necessarily situated their engagement with aesthetics within the scholarship on law and image. Scholars assuming Third World Approaches to International Law have incorporated aesthetic elements into their analysis of international environmental law. Stephen Humphreys and Yoriko Otomo, for example, analyse the cultural origins of international environmental law with reference to Romantic poetry in nineteenth-century Britain.[171] They are critical of the influence of Romanticism on the development of international environmental law but they do not engage legal theory on aesthetics in their

[163] Manderson, 'Introduction: Imaginal law'. See Silbey, 'Images in/of law'.
[164] Manderson, *Danse Macabre*, p. 16.
[165] See, for example, Manderson, 'Force of wall'. Note also Huygebaert et al. (eds.), *The Art of Law*.
[166] Manderson, 'Bodies in the water'. See also Manderson, 'Not drowning, waving', 159.
[167] See, for example, Young, 'Aesthetic vertigo', 1.
[168] See, for example, Biber and San Roque, 'The trouble with pictures', 2.
[169] See, for example, Petersen, 'Foot notes. Reflections on method and form'.
[170] See, for example, Moran, *Law, Judges and Visual Culture*.
[171] Humphreys and Otomo, 'Theorizing international environmental law', 797.

critique.[172] Legal scholars Usha Natarajan and Kishan Khoday also examine cultural histories of international environmental law relying in large part on an anthropological perspective as opposed to aesthetic sources.[173] International environmental law scholar, Michael Bowman, dismisses claims of Romantic influence in what he calls international 'wildlife' law but he does not invoke aesthetic theory in that task.[174]

There is, however, particular guidance for my analysis of image from those legal scholars who have used visual art as a basis for their examination of international law in a general sense, or for other fields of international law such as human rights. For example, Kate Miles analyses visual art among other images to construct a visual archive that, she argues, constitutes legal discourse, legal argument and legal reality for international law.[175] Hilary Charlesworth has examined the photographic and other images that formed part of the UNESCO Human Rights Exhibition 1950–1953 for the narratives of universalism and progress that shape international human rights law.[176] Others have engaged specific artworks to interrogate concepts of international law.[177] The concepts interrogated, and the methods engaged for these considerations of visual art, suggest particular insights from images for international law as a domain of law that might also be relevant to an examination of image for international environmental law.

There might also be guidance on concepts and methods for images of the environment in law from those legal scholars who have used visual artworks to analyse environmental law in domestic spheres. For example, proponent of critical thinking in environmental law,[178] Andreas Philippopoulos-Mihalopoulos, has written about the 'solar balloon',[179] a creation of Argentinian-born architect turned artist Tomás Saraceno who has collaborated with a multi-disciplinary team to make air balloons, for transporting

[172] Ibid., 805–10.

[173] Natarajan and Khoday, 'Locating nature', 583–5, citing Argyrou, *The Logic of Environmentalism*.

[174] Bowman, 'Law, legal scholarship', 13. Cf. Stephens, 'What is the point', 121.

[175] Miles, 'Visuality of a treaty'. See also Miles, 'Painting international law as universal'.

[176] Charlesworth, 'The travels of human rights', 173. See also Palmer, 'Absent images of international law', 91.

[177] See, for example, Joseph, 'Art and human rights law', 389; Roele, 'We are making a new world', 227; d'Aspremont and De Brabandere, 'Paintings of international law', 331.

[178] See Philippopoulos-Mihalopoulos, 'Critical legal thinking', 18; Philippopoulos-Mihalopoulos, 'The sound of a breaking string'.

[179] Philippopoulos-Mihalopoulos, 'Lighter-than-air'.

people, that are powered by the sun.[180] Philippopoulos-Mihalopoulos provides an account of Saraceno's solar balloon referencing the geological era of the Anthropocene, a concept he posits as a concept of 'law'. This treatment of Saraceno's creation applies critical legal theory to an art object – albeit engineered to function as a viable form of transport – aimed at addressing climate change.

Elsewhere, in a contribution to *Law and Ecology: New Environmental Foundations* edited by Philippopoulos-Mihalopoulos,[181] Mark Halsey examines the protection of natural heritage from a perspective of critical legal studies. He discusses famous artworks – icons of cultural heritage such as Jackson Pollock's *Blue Poles* and Leonardo da Vinci's *Mona Lisa* – to draw analogies in his critical analysis of natural heritage.[182] Also engaging art in the analysis of environmental law, Afshin Akhtar-Khavari analyses the concept of environmental justice with reference to Edvard Munch's *The Scream*.[183] David Schorr has used art and art history to narrate the development of environmental law addressing atmospheric pollution.[184] Benjamin Richardson has examined the use of art and art practice as community participation in environmental protection.[185]

These legal scholars have examined concepts in environmental law, to varying extents and in different ways, through visual art. They have used aesthetic representations to interrogate or narrate environmental law. Few directly reference scholars of jurisprudence on law and aesthetics to explain or justify their methodology but they do demonstrate how the arts can be employed to interrogate issues specific to environmental law.[186] Viewed together, their approaches to engaging visual art in the analysis of environmental law demonstrate a variety of ways in which the jurisprudence on law and aesthetics can intersect critical thinking on environmental law. It is, however, notable that the 'aesthetic' value of the environment as a term expressed in international environmental law has received limited attention in the legal literature from the perspective of aesthetic philosophy – as it

180 Saraceno, *Aerocene*; Saraceno, 'Studio Tomás Saraceno'. See also Tomás Saraceno in Margutti, *May You Live in Interesting Times*.
181 See Mark Halsey, 'Majesty and monstrosity', 214.
182 Ibid., 216.
183 Akhtar-Khavari, 'Fear and ecological (in)justice'.
184 Schorr, 'Art and the history of environmental law'.
185 Cf. Richardson, 'Climate change law'; Richardson, Barritt and Bowman, 'Beauty'; Richardson, 'Aesthetics and environmental law'; Richardson, *The Art of Environmental Law*.
186 Halsey, 'Majesty and monstrosity'.

relates to the arts or to the environment.[187] The environment's aesthetic value as a legal or policy concept in a more general sense has instead been addressed largely from a doctrinal perspective in legal scholarship on domestic planning and land use laws,[188] and, as explained in Chapter 2, from the perspective of legal philosophy concerned with environmental ethics.[189]

4.5 CONCLUSION

The conceptions of aesthetics in law identified and examined in this chapter are different from understandings of aesthetic value that I considered from legal perspectives in the previous chapters. In Chapter 2, I explained how scholars such as Alexander Gillespie have contemplated aesthetic value as one of several environmental values that are the foundation of international environmental law. Gillespie and others have associated the environment's aesthetic value with natural beauty and subjective judgement within a broader context of environmental ethics. Noting that such scholars of international environmental law have not analysed the term 'aesthetic' with reference to international legal principles of treaty interpretation, I proceeded in Chapter 3 to develop a doctrinal account of aesthetic value for international environmental treaties that relies on the written sources of interpretation typically consulted for the interpretation of international law. My account pointed to both narrow conceptions of aesthetic value as synonymous with natural beauty and with cultural and ethical values of the environment. This contrasts with philosophers of environmental aesthetics such as Emily Brady who have characterised aesthetic value as distinct from, though related to, these values of the environment.[190]

These conceptions of 'aesthetic' value in the philosophy of international environmental law, and in my doctrinal account of treaty interpretation, are different from the understanding of aesthetics for the field of visual jurisprudence explained in this chapter. Scholars of what Desmond Manderson has called 'imaginal law' have focused on aesthetic conceptions developed for the arts.[191] They have not addressed questions of aesthetic value as it concerns the natural environment in the specific case of international environmental law.

187 Cf. Gillespie, *International Environmental Law, Policy and Ethics*, 2nd edn; Richardson, *The Art of Environmental Law*.
188 See, for example, Costonis, 'Law and aesthetics'.
189 See, for example, Gillespie, *International Environmental Law, Policy and Ethics*, 2nd edn. See Chapter 2.
190 Brady, *Aesthetics of the Natural Environment*. See Chapter 2.
191 Manderson, 'Introduction: Imaginal law'.

I will nevertheless draw from their use of aesthetic methods for the arts applied to law – in the work, for example, of Desmond Manderson, Alison Young and Kate Miles – to develop aesthetic understandings of the photographs used in treaty decision-making to determine aesthetic value. My examination of photographs of the environment in international treaty decision-making for this book extends the work of these legal scholars to understand image in terms of the environment's aesthetic value.

Separately, the different conceptions of aesthetic value for law explored in legal scholarship provide an incomplete account; together, however, they highlight the complexities that arise in the contemplation of the environment's aesthetic value for international environmental law. It is to these complexities that I now turn, analysing in the following chapters photographs of the environment used in the decision-making processes to develop meanings of aesthetic value for international environmental treaties. I look to photographs in part because I consider that, from a jurisprudential perspective, their role in international environmental decision-making demands examination and explanation. Aesthetics for the arts and visual jurisprudence is important to this analysis. But I also do this to better understand meanings of the environment's aesthetic value for international environmental law. My identification and examination of the photographs presented to the international bodies could have instrumental applications in treaty interpretation and implementation that I identify in my concluding Chapter 8. However, by paying close attention to the photographs used in the decision-making processes under the treaties, I contribute to the jurisprudential understanding of graphic image in international law more broadly too.

5

Valuing Aesthetics of World Natural Heritage

EXHIBIT: WANGECHI MUTU, *THE END OF CARRYING ALL* (2015)

FIGURE 5.1. Wangechi Mutu, *The End of carrying All*, 2015 (still). Three-screen animated video (colour, sound), 10 minutes, looped. © Wangechi Mutu. Courtesy Gladstone Gallery, New York, Victoria Miro, London and Susanne Vielmetter, Los Angeles.

Most people were standing to watch Wangechi Mutu's animated video installation *The End of carrying All* (Figure 5.1).[1] I chose to sit on the floor, arms around my shins and chin resting on my knees, as I stared at the three large screens, mesmerised by the woman climbing a hillside. Wrapped in floral

1 Cf. Van Veeren, 'Layered wanderings', 488.

print fabric, a Kenyan khanga perhaps, she climbed with purpose but her pace was ponderous: She had somewhere she needed to be but she had things on her mind too. Literally. On her head she carried a basket of what appeared, at least at first, to be fruit and vegetables, a bag of grain. She swatted insects about her legs and adjusted her dress as distant mountain peaks came into view. Birds occasionally passed in flocks and she occasionally passed a tree. A distinctively fan-shaped tree of East Africa, a tangle of branches with only dabbles of leaves, trees still sparse in Kenya despite all the efforts of planting urged by Wangari Maathai. The wind howled, birds squawked, locusts swarmed. And all around her an amber glow emanated from a sky soon to sleep or to wake.

Up and up she went, sashaying as if to a song. And, as she climbed, the cornucopia atop her head grew. Soon her basket contained a sneaker, a bicycle wheel, a satellite dish and an oil rig. A prairie barn expanded into an electric lit skyscraper. Her back bent as she laboured under the increasing weight on her head. With the wind came ominous tolls of church bells and the siren sounds of an urban streetscape. A sleeping sky it was – the orange faded to black. As she neared the top of the hill – a precipice – her load metamorphosed into a sluggish formless phosphorescing beast that consumed her, pitching over the edge into the abyss as the hillside erupted and a nuclear light engulfed the scene leaving the screens white. It was not as I wanted it to end for her but she seemed not to know it was coming. The film was on a loop. I stayed, sitting on the floor, to watch it again.

5.1 INTRODUCTION

Wangechi Mutu's *The End of carrying All* (Figure 5.1) addresses issues of ever-increasing consumption indifferent to the natural environment. Yet such concerns for sustainability, and differentiated responsibilities for environmental protection as between the rich North and the poor South, would come late to international environmental law. In this chapter, I consider how images of the environment might inform the protection of natural heritage under the 1972 *World Heritage Convention*.[2] That treaty was adopted in an era of environmental protection dominated by a largely Western preoccupation with preserving natural beauty absent humans, before a need for limits on consumption implied in the concept of 'sustainable development' would emerge in international environmental law.[3]

2 Article 2 of the *Convention for the Protection of the World Cultural and Natural Heritage*, Paris, 16 November 1972, in force 17 December 1975, 1037 UNTS 151.

3 Mickelson, 'South, north, international environmental law', 52. See also Gillespie, *The Long Road to Sustainability*.

My analysis and findings in this chapter address my specific question in the book on how images of the natural environment could be used to give significance to the environment's aesthetic value in international environmental law. I identify images of the natural environment, including photographs, which are submitted by states parties in their nominations of natural properties for World Heritage status. I then examine those images for meanings relevant to World Heritage determinations of the 'outstanding universal value' of natural heritage from an 'aesthetic' point of view.[4] In this task, I demonstrate ways in which environmental images can be used to articulate understandings of the environment's aesthetic value, using aesthetic methods developed for visual art.[5] I incorporate considerations in the philosophy of environmental aesthetics, where the environment's aesthetic value is understood by philosophers such as Emily Brady, in terms of multi-sensory experience shaped by imagination, emotion and knowledge.[6]

My attention to images, and my methods for analysing them, are also relevant to my broader question in the book around images in international law.[7] Environmental images are used in the process of inscribing natural heritage in the World Heritage List. I argue that they should be recognised by the World Heritage Committee as relevant to determinations of outstanding universal value from an aesthetic 'point of view'.[8] Even if they are properly characterised as subjective, aesthetic methods should be employed formally in the World Heritage inscription process as part of a thorough and responsible evaluation, and reasoned determination, of the natural environment's aesthetic value. Photographic images have a particular role in comprehending aesthetic value in the decision-making processes of an international body such as the World Heritage Committee.

This chapter describes in Section 5.2 the process and criteria used by the World Heritage Committee to inscribe natural heritage in the World Heritage List. I revisit matters that I explained for the purposes of my treaty interpretation in Chapter 3. Section 5.3 identifies the verbal and photographic images of the environment used in the inscription process of five World Heritage properties recognised for their natural beauty and aesthetic importance in Australia, Chad, China, Kenya and Mexico. In Section 5.4, I analyse the World Heritage images with reference to aesthetic methods for the arts and

4 *World Heritage Convention*, Article 2.
5 See Sections 4.3.2 and 4.3.3.
6 Brady, *Aesthetics of the Natural Environment*, pp. 237–8. See Section 2.2.3.
7 See Chapter 1. See also Section 4.4.
8 Article 2 of the *World Heritage Convention*.

the philosophy of environmental aesthetics. Section 5.5 considers the relevance of aesthetic method to future inscriptions of natural heritage in the World Heritage List on an aesthetic basis. Although I acknowledge that World Heritage decisions are highly politicised,[9] my focus here is law and legal process – recognising all the while the intimacy between law and politics, public international law being a much-lauded exemplar of that union.[10]

5.2 WORLD HERITAGE DETERMINATIONS OF AESTHETIC VALUE

As explained in previous chapters of this book, the *World Heritage Convention* protects natural heritage for its 'outstanding universal value' from, among others, an 'aesthetic ... point of view'.[11] The other points of view from which the outstanding universal value of natural heritage is judged under the treaty are science, conservation and natural beauty.[12] The consideration of the natural environment's aesthetic value is separate under the treaty from any assessment of the aesthetic value of 'cultural heritage'.[13] In this part, I recall the process for inscribing natural properties on the World Heritage List, elaborating on the criteria for consideration of the environment's aesthetic and other values by the World Heritage Committee.[14] This provides the background to my identification of images used in the inscription process.

5.2.1 *Process for World Heritage Inscription*

The inscription of properties on the World Heritage List is a threshold requirement in the implementation of the *World Heritage Convention*. Once listed, benefits such as assistance, including financial assistance, can be granted for the conservation and management of World Heritage properties under the treaty.[15] Sanctions – such as moving a property to the World

[9] See, for example, Maswood, 'Kakadu and the politics of World Heritage listing', 357; Cameron and Rössler, *Many Voices, One Vision*, pp. 236–8. In connection with cultural heritage, see Labadi, *UNESCO, Cultural Heritage, and Outstanding Universal Value*.

[10] See, for example, Koskenniemi, 'What is international law for?', 28. See also Koskenniemi, *From Apology*.

[11] Article 2 of the *World Heritage Convention*.

[12] Ibid.

[13] Ibid., Article 1 defines three kinds of 'cultural heritage', including 'sites' that are 'works of man or the combined works of nature and man, and areas including archaeological sites which are of outstanding universal value from the historical, aesthetic, ethnological or anthropological point of view'. See Section 5.5.1. See also Section 3.3.1.2.

[14] See also Section 3.3.2.1.

[15] Article 13 of the *World Heritage Convention*.

Heritage in Danger List and, ultimately, removal from the World Heritage List – can also arise where a state fails to protect a listed property.[16]

The *World Heritage Convention* establishes the World Heritage Committee, an international body of twenty-one experts elected by the states parties.[17] The World Heritage Committee inscribes properties of outstanding universal value in the World Heritage List and oversees the administration of benefits and sanctions.[18] Decisions of the World Heritage Committee to inscribe properties may require determinations of 'aesthetic' value.[19] Negative determinations of aesthetic value might arise in cases where properties are refused inscription, moved to the World Heritage in Danger List, or removed from the World Heritage List.[20] For the purposes of this chapter, however, I will limit my inquiry to the positive decisions to inscribe properties on the World Heritage List on an aesthetic basis.

The *Operational Guidelines for the Implementation of the World Heritage Convention* ('*Operational Guidelines*') is the principal document prescribing procedures for attaining and maintaining the World Heritage imprimatur.[21] It describes the process of inscription as commencing with tentative listing followed by nomination of properties by states parties. Evaluations undertaken by the International Union for Conservation of Nature (IUCN) inform the World Heritage Committee's assessment of the outstanding universal value of natural heritage.[22]

5.2.2 *Criteria for World Heritage Inscription*

The concept of 'outstanding universal value' is described in the *Operational Guidelines* as 'significance which is so exceptional as to transcend national boundaries and to be of common importance for present and future generations of all humanity'.[23] A finding of 'outstanding universal value' for any given property is determined by the World Heritage Committee on the basis of ten criteria for cultural and natural heritage contained in the *Operational*

16 Article 11(4), ibid.
17 Article 8(1), ibid.
18 Articles 11(2) and 13(6), ibid.
19 See Section 5.2.2.
20 See, for example, World Heritage Committee, *Great Barrier Reef (Australia)*, UN Doc. WHC-14/38.COM/16; Australia, *State Party Report on the Great Barrier Reef*, 25 November 2019 discussing impacts on 'natural beauty'.
21 World Heritage Committee, *Operational Guidelines*, UN Doc. WHC.21/01.
22 Ibid., para. [37].
23 Ibid., para. [49].

Guidelines. A property can be inscribed on the basis of one or more criteria,[24] and it can be inscribed in the World Heritage List as either cultural or natural heritage, or as a mix of both.[25] The *Operational Guidelines* require states parties nominating properties for World Heritage status to justify the application of the criteria to the nominated property both in its own right, and relative to other properties inscribed in the World Heritage List on the basis of the same criteria.[26]

Four of the World Heritage Committee's criteria for outstanding universal value relate to natural heritage. Three of those criteria appear to relate to the 'scientific' and 'conservation' points of view in the definition of natural heritage in the *World Heritage Convention*.[27] The remaining criterion – known as criterion (vii) – appears to correspond to the 'aesthetic' and 'natural beauty' points of view in that definition. It describes natural properties as having outstanding universal value if they 'contain superlative natural phenomena' or are 'areas of exceptional natural beauty and aesthetic importance' (criterion (vii)).[28]

The wording and numbering of what is now criterion (vii) have changed since its adoption by the World Heritage Committee in 1977.[29] Until the equivalent to criterion (vii) was amended in 1994 to include 'aesthetic importance',[30] its only reference to a point of view in the definition of natural heritage in the *World Heritage Convention* had been to 'natural beauty'.[31] More than half of the natural properties on the World Heritage List have been inscribed on the basis of criterion (vii) or its equivalent since 1977.[32] Only nine properties have been listed on the sole basis of criterion (vii),[33] three of which

[24] Ibid., para. [77].

[25] Ibid., paras. [45], [46].

[26] Ibid., para. [132.3].

[27] Ibid., paras. [77] (viii) ['major stages of earth's history']; (ix) [ecological and biological evolutionary processes]; and (x) [natural habitats for the conservation of biological diversity]. See discussion in Section 5.3.3.2.

[28] *Operational Guidelines*, UN Doc. WHC.21/01, para. [77].

[29] World Heritage Committee, *Operational Guidelines*, UN Doc. CC-77/CONF.001/8.

[30] World Heritage Committee, *Operational Guidelines*, UN Doc. WHC/2/Revised, February 1994, para. [44(a)(iii)].

[31] See, for example, World Heritage Committee, *Operational Guidelines*, UN Doc. WHC/2/ Revised, 27 March 1992, para. [36(a)(iii)].

[32] As at 30 June 2022, 146 properties out of 257 natural and mixed heritage sites had been identified under the *World Heritage Convention* to be of outstanding universal value for the purposes of criterion (vii): 'World Heritage List', whc.unesco.org/en/list.

[33] Eight properties are inscribed on the World Heritage List, ibid. A ninth property, Belarus Belovezhskaya Pushcha State National Park, had also been inscribed under the natural heritage criterion (iii) (equivalent to criterion (vii)): World Heritage Committee, *Report*, UN Doc. WHC-92/CONF.002/12, p. 37. It was, however, subsequently incorporated into another

were inscribed after 1994 when the criterion was amended to refer to 'aesthetic importance'.[34]

5.3 WORLD HERITAGE IMAGES OF AESTHETIC VALUE

In this part, I identify images of the environment's aesthetic value currently used in the documentation supporting the inscription of natural properties in the World Heritage List. In Chapter 4, I explained different forms of 'image'.[35] The images used in the World Heritage inscription process take the form of 'verbal' images in the descriptions of World Heritage properties. They also take the form of 'graphic' images, specifically photographs, submitted to the World Heritage Committee by the states parties in their files nominating natural properties for World Heritage status. Together, these are what I call 'World Heritage images'. I argue that the World Heritage images have juridical significance, or significance for law. However, the formal rules and practices of the World Heritage Committee do not explain whether, and if so how, images are relevant to determinations of natural beauty and aesthetic importance for the purposes of natural heritage criterion (vii). I maintain that a preference for purportedly objective methods has compromised the use of images in the evaluation of the environment's aesthetic value in the World Heritage inscription process.

I have limited my study of World Heritage images to the documentation of five properties inscribed on the World Heritage List. Three are natural heritage properties that were inscribed in the World Heritage List on the sole basis of criterion (vii), after 1994 when 'aesthetic importance' had been included: Monarch Butterfly Biosphere Reserve in Mexico;[36] Mount Sanqingshan National Park in China;[37] and Lakes of Ounianga in Chad.[38] The other two properties examined are examples of properties inscribed on

property inscribed under other criteria: World Heritage Committee, *Białowieża Forest (Belarus/Poland)*, Decision 38 COM 8B.12, UN Doc. WHC-14/38.COM/16.

[34] These were the 2008 inscriptions of the Monarch Butterfly Biosphere Reserve in Mexico and the Mount Sanqingshan National Park in China as well as the 2012 inscription of the Lakes of Ounianga in Chad. See in this section.

[35] WJT Mitchell describes 'image' in terms of graphic, optical, perceptual, mental and verbal images: WJT Mitchell, *Iconology*, p. 10. See Section 4.4.1.

[36] World Heritage Committee, *Monarch Butterfly Biosphere Reserve (Mexico)*, Decision 32 COM 8B.17, UN Doc. WHC-08/32.COM/24Rev.

[37] World Heritage Committee, *Mount Sanqingshan National Park (China)*, Decision 32 COM 8B.6, UN Doc. WHC-08/32.COM/24Rev.

[38] World Heritage Committee, *Lakes of Ounianga (Chad)*, Decision 36 COM 8B.7, UN Doc. WHC-12/36.COM/19.

the basis of criterion (vii) in combination with other criteria.[39] The Kenya Lakes System of the Great Rift Valley was inscribed as a natural heritage property in 2011 on the basis of three natural heritage criteria, including criterion (vii).[40] The Tasmanian Wilderness in Australia is a mixed cultural and natural heritage property first inscribed in 1982 and justified with reference to seven criteria, including all four of the natural heritage criteria.[41]

5.3.1 *Verbal Images in Descriptions of Outstanding Universal Value*

Nominations of properties for inscription in the World Heritage List must include a proposed Statement of Outstanding Universal Value ('OUV Statement').[42] Proposed OUV Statements must 'make clear why the property is considered to merit inscription on the World Heritage List'.[43] The World Heritage Committee adopts OUV Statements as part of its decision to inscribe properties in the World Heritage List.[44] OUV Statements are being adopted on a retrospective basis for properties, like the Tasmanian Wilderness, which were inscribed prior to 2007 when the practice of OUV Statements commenced.[45]

The descriptions of Chad's Lakes of Ounianga and Australia's Tasmanian Wilderness in World Heritage documentation contain particularly vivid verbal images. Inscribed in the World Heritage List in 2012, the OUV Statement for the Lakes of Ounianga states:

> The property represents an exceptional example of permanent lakes in a desert setting, a remarkable natural phenomenon which results from an aquifer and associated complex hydrological system **which is still to be fully understood**. The **aesthetic beauty** of the site results from a **landscape**

[39] 'World Heritage List'.

[40] World Heritage Committee, *Kenya Lake System in the Great Rift Valley (Kenya)*, UN Doc. WHC-11/35.COM/20.

[41] The Tasmanian Wilderness was inscribed under criteria (iii)(iv)(vi)(vii)(viii)(ix)(x): World Heritage Committee, *Western Tasmania Wilderness National Parks (Australia)*, UN Doc. CLT-82/CH/CONF.015/8. Note its name was subsequently changed: World Heritage Committee, *Tasmanian Wilderness (Australia)*, UN Doc. SC-89/CONF.004/12. Inscription under the equivalent criterion (vii) preceded the amendment to refer to 'aesthetic importance'.

[42] *Operational Guidelines*, UN Doc. WHC.21/01, para. [132].

[43] Ibid.

[44] Ibid., para. [154].

[45] The practice of adopting OUV Statements was introduced in 2005, effective from 2007, by World Heritage Committee, *Operational Guidelines*, UN Doc. WHC.05/2. On the process for retrospective OUV Statements for properties inscribed before 2007, see World Heritage Committee, *Reflection on the Preparation of the Next Cycle of Periodic Reporting*, UN Doc. WHC-07/31.COM/24.

> **mosaic** which includes **the varied coloured lakes with their blue, green and/or reddish waters**, in reflection of their chemical composition, surrounded by palms, dunes and **spectacular sandstone** landforms, all of it in the heart of a desert that stretches over thousands of kilometres. In addition, about one third of the surface of the Ounianga Serir Lakes is covered with **floating reed carpets whose intense green colour contrasts with the blue open waters**. Rock exposures which dominate the site offer a **breathtaking view** on all the lakes, of which **the colours contrast with the brown sand dunes separated by bare rock structures**. The **shape and distribution of the lakes**, combined with the effect of **the wind moving the floating vegetation in the lakes**, gives the impression of **"waves of water flowing in the desert"**.[46] [emphasis added]

The lyrical description of the Lakes of Ounianga is reminiscent of the description of the Tasmanian Wilderness provided by the nominating state, Australia. First inscribed in the World Heritage List in 1982, and subsequently amended, the Tasmanian Wilderness has been the subject of a protracted process for the drafting of a retrospective OUV Statement.[47] However, as explained below, the nomination and amending applications have included descriptions relevant to equivalent criterion (vii), and draft OUV Statements prepared by Australia contain references to the site's aesthetic qualities.

In its 1982 nomination of the Tasmanian Wilderness, for example, Australia referred to 'natural beauty', 'pristine wilderness' and 'aesthetically stimulating landforms'. It claimed, however, that '[i]n a region so diverse, wild, distinctive and spectacular it would be an arbitrary exercise to list particular landscapes as outstanding'.[48] In a later application to extend the site in 1989, Australia was more specific about the property's 'landscape' qualities. It referred for example to '[c]old, deep lakes . . . perched among the ranges like secret jewels', 'the magnificence of the rugged wilderness', 'wonderful views of the jagged skyline', 'soft, moist plains, contrasted with the heavy bulk of the ranges', and a 'diverse landscape' of 'classical grandeur'.[49] It also stated that '[a]lthough extinct, sightings of the thylacine . . . are still reported from the area'.[50]

[46] World Heritage Committee, 'Statement of Outstanding Universal Value' in *Lakes of Ounianga Inscription*.

[47] See World Heritage Committee, *Tasmanian Wilderness (Australia)*, Decision 42 COM 7B.61, UN Doc. WHC/18/42.COM/18, 4 July 2018. Note Australia, *State of Conservation of the Tasmanian Wilderness*, 2022.

[48] Australia, *Nomination of Western Tasmania Wilderness National Parks*, 18–19.

[49] Australia, *Nomination of the Tasmanian Wilderness*, Request.

[50] Ibid.

A draft retrospective OUV Statement for the Tasmanian Wilderness from 2010 is consistent with the language in Australia's original applications.[51] In relation to criterion (vii), it provides in part:

> The glaciated mountains of the property are aesthetically distinct and outstanding, with **red and gold to dark green tones** in their **blanket** of vegetation, the **dark tones** of their glacial lakes, their **silence** in calm weather and their **clamour** during storms. [. . .] Lowland areas with their **sweeping green-gold** buttongrass coat, **stark white** metamorphic rocks, **dark waters, patches of emerald** rainforest, terraces and flats and typically **dark skies** also present a landscape of outstanding **contrasts** and aesthetic distinction. [. . .] **Wild rivers carve** through rainforest or moorland uplands and gorges, **plunging** over waterfalls into **foaming eddies** before **snaking darkly under the lime green drapes of ancient** Huon pines and **moss-covered giant** tree ferns to the **lonely waters** of the area's south western shores and towards the lowlands to the north and east.[52] [emphasis added]

A further draft of the retrospective OUV Statement in 2015 is less expressive of aesthetic qualities.[53] It nevertheless refers to such things as 'rugged mountain ranges scattered with picturesque tarns', 'wild rivers churning' and 'serene Huon pine reflections'.[54]

The OUV Statement for the Mount Sanqingshan National Park in China references scientific facts, such as 'meteorological effects' and 'granite features'.[55] These are, however, expressly linked to verbal images of scenic quality and natural beauty. The site is described in the OUV Statement as 'landscape of exceptional scenic quality', with 'near and distant vistas', 'fantastically shaped pillars and peaks' and a 'serene atmosphere'. The 'natural beauty' of Mount Sanqingshan is said to derive 'from the juxtaposition of its granite features with the mountain's vegetation enhanced by meteorological conditions which create an ever-changing and arresting landscape'.[56]

The verbal images apparent in the descriptions of these World Heritage properties in Chad, Australia and China can be distinguished from the

51 Australia, 'Draft retrospective statement of Outstanding Universal Value', 2010.

52 Ibid.

53 Australia, 'Draft retrospective statement of Outstanding Universal Value', 2015.

54 Ibid. Note as at 30 June 2022, a revised draft retrospective Statement of Outstanding Universal Value was to be provided to the World Heritage Centre by Australia for consideration at the 45th meeting of the World Heritage Committee: Australia, *State of Conservation of the Tasmanian Wilderness*, 2022, p. 7.

55 World Heritage Committee, 'Statement of Outstanding Universal Value' in *Mount Sanqingshan Inscription*.

56 Ibid.

scientific and quantitative descriptions for the two other properties considered for this chapter. The paragraph dedicated to criterion (vii) in the OUV Statement for the Monarch Butterfly Biosphere Reserve is focused on quantitative superlatives and scientific facts, such as the numbers and percentages of butterflies migrating to the property each year.[57] I quoted the relevant paragraph in Chapter 1 of the book.[58] Similarly, the justification for the application of criterion (vii) to the Great Rift Valley also focuses on scientific information, highlighting geological and biological processes. It refers, for example, to 'massed congregations of birds on the shores of the lakes including up to 4 million Lesser Flamingos which move between the three lakes' and 'the steep escarpment of the Rift valley and associated volcanic features'.[59]

The emphasis on quantitative and scientific elements for the properties in Mexico and Kenya produces prosaic descriptions that are less expressive of verbal images than those for the other properties. I return to address this distinction later.[60] I note that there is nevertheless some reference to aesthetic concepts in the documentation for those two properties. The introductory paragraph of the OUV Statement for the Monarch Butterfly Biosphere Reserve, for example, refers to the beating wings of the butterflies sounding 'like light rain'.[61] The concentration of butterflies is described as 'dramatic'.[62] The OUV Statement for the Great Rift Valley refers to 'the landscape backdrop' and the 'outstanding wildlife spectacle'.[63]

As explained next, the verbal images in the OUV Statements for the five properties appear to correspond, to greater and lesser extents, with images of aesthetic value depicted in photographs that were submitted by the states parties in their nomination of the properties for inscription in the World Heritage List.

5.3.2 *Photographic Images in Nomination Files*

The nomination files for the five World Heritage properties examined in this chapter contained a variety of graphic images, including the photographs of

57 World Heritage Committee, 'Statement of Outstanding Universal Value' in *Monarch Butterfly Biosphere Reserve Inscription*.

58 See Section 1.1.1.

59 World Heritage Committee, 'Statement of Outstanding Universal Value' in *Great Rift Valley Inscription*.

60 See Section 5.3.3.2.

61 World Heritage Committee, 'Statement of Outstanding Universal Value' in *Monarch Butterfly Biosphere Reserve Inscription*.

62 Ibid.

63 World Heritage Committee, 'Statement of Outstanding Universal Value' in *Great Rift Valley Inscription*.

the sites reproduced below. I catalogue them here in this part before examining their juridical significance and analysing them from an aesthetic vantage in the parts that follow.

5.3.2.1 Monarch Butterfly Biosphere Reserve

In my introductory chapter (Chapter 1), I analysed a photograph that Mexico included in its nomination of the Monarch Butterfly Biosphere Reserve for World Heritage status (Figure 1.1).[64] It was one of 23 photographs included in the nomination file. Several were of butterflies, particularly butterflies en masse (e.g. Figure 5.2), but some also showed the landscape (e.g. Figure 5.3).

5.3.2.2 Mount Sanqingshan

China's World Heritage nomination file for Mount Sanqingshan contained sixty-eight photographs – in addition to 35 mm slides, a DVD, and a photo album.[65] Many of the still photographs depict the geological formations and flora and fauna described in writing in the nomination file. Some depict seasonal changes or meteorological effects such as 'Nanqing peak forest' (Figure 5.4). Most of the photographs have literal titles naming the place or describing the features depicted while others suggest aesthetic qualities such as 'Thousands peaks showing lovely scenery',[66] 'Colourful road amid cloud',[67] and 'Awfully stirring billows' (Figure 5.5).[68]

5.3.2.3 Lakes of Ounianga

Chad's nomination file for the Lakes of Ounianga contained sixty-one photographs of the area.[69] Most have detailed captions describing what is depicted (e.g. Figure 5.6). The captions for the photographs accompanying the description of natural beauty and aesthetic values include language such as 'striking beauty' and 'impressive view'.[70]

64 Mexico, *World Heritage Site Nomination Document.*
65 China, *Mount Sanqingshan National Park*, Nomination.
66 'Photo 2.52 Thousands peaks showing lovely scenery': Ibid., p. 66.
67 'Photo 2.58 Colourful road amid cloud': Ibid., p. 71.
68 Other photographs have titles suggesting spiritual experiences such as 'Photo 2.56 Sanqing divine light': Ibid., p. 70.
69 Chad, *Proposition d'Inscription*, iii–v (list) and annex. A.
70 'Photo 27: Des rochers formés par les vents. Les structures sont exceptionnelles et d'une beauté frappante' and 'Photo 29: Vue impressionnante vers le lac Boukou, direction de regard vers le Nord': Ibid., p. 24.

FIGURE 5.2. 'Picture 2. Monarch Clusters in an Oyamel Tree: Monarch butterflies display their full activity in the spring', 1999, in Mexico, *World Heritage Site Nomination Document*, p. 4. Photo: Carlos Gottfried.

5.3.2.4 Kenya Lakes System

Photographs, several of bird flocks (e.g. Figure 5.7), were included in Kenya's nomination file for the Great Rift Valley.[71]

5.3.2.5 Tasmanian Wilderness

At least two photographs accompanied Australia's nomination document for the Tasmanian Wilderness in 1982, and some photographs were included in the application to extend the area in 1989 (e.g. Figure 5.8).[72]

[71] Kenya, *Nomination Proposal: Kenya Lake System*.

[72] Australia, *Nomination of Western Tasmania Wilderness National Parks*, p. 10; *Nomination of the Tasmanian Wilderness*, Request, p. 131.

FIGURE 5.3. 'Picture 14. Transverse Neovolcanic Axis: Helicopter view with the Nevado de Toluca in the foreground, Popocatépetl and Iztaccíhuatl in the center, and between them, in the background, the Pico de Orizaba', 1995, in Mexico, *World Heritage Site Nomination Document*, p. 34. Photo: Carlos Gottfried.

FIGURE 5.4. 'Photo 2.48 Nanqing peak forest' in China, *Mount Sanqingshan National Park*, Nomination, p. 60.

FIGURE 5.5. 'Photo 2.59 Awfully stirring billows' in China, *Mount Sanqingshan National Park*, Nomination, p. 71.

FIGURE 5.6. 'Photo 7: Une dune se trouvant à droite et qui se jette dans le lac Yoan' [A dune featured on the right spills into the Yoan Lake] (tr. Author) in Chad, *Proposition d'Inscription*, p. 10. Photo: © Sven Oehm.

FIGURE 5.7. 'Figure 7 Lesser flamingo feeding in Lake Bogoria' in Kenya, *Nomination Proposal: Kenya Lake System*, p. 42. Photo: © NMK.

FIGURE 5.8. 'Plate 10 South East Cape from Pindars Peak', in Australia, *Nomination of the Tasmanian Wilderness*, Request, p. 131. Photo: G Dixon.

5.3.3 *Use of World Heritage Images*

World Heritage images could have juridical significance in the World Heritage inscription process in the sense that they could have meanings relevant to the decisions made in that process. As explained below, the World Heritage formally adopts OUV Statements containing verbal images and it requires the submission of photographs to substantiate nominations. I argue, however, that requirements under the *World Heritage Convention* for 'objective' methods of evaluation have compromised the reasoned use of images to represent the environment's aesthetic value in the World Heritage inscription process.

5.3.3.1 Juridical Significance of Images

The verbal images of World Heritage identified earlier appear in proposed and adopted OUV Statements.[73] As noted earlier, these are documents prepared by states to 'make clear why the property is considered to merit inscription on the World Heritage List'.[74] They may be amended, then ultimately adopted, by the World Heritage Committee as part of the decision to inscribe a nominated property in the World Heritage List.[75] As such, I maintain that the OUV Statements justify the World Heritage Committee's determination of outstanding universal value. They are statements of reasons like those that might be provided for the purposes of administrative law requirements in domestic jurisdictions.[76] Cumulatively and relative to other inscriptions, OUV Statements document the practice of the World Heritage Committee in its application of the criteria for outstanding universal value, constituting a form of precedent. This includes – at least since 1994 – the inscription of natural heritage for its 'aesthetic' importance, combined in the relevant criterion (vii) with 'natural beauty'.[77]

However, the formal rules and practices of the World Heritage Committee do not explain whether and, if so how, verbal images in the OUV Statements are relevant to determinations of 'natural beauty and aesthetic importance' for the purposes of natural heritage criterion (vii). They do not explain, for

[73] See Section 5.3.1.
[74] *Operational Guidelines*, UN Doc. WHC.21/01, para. [132].
[75] Ibid., para. [154].
[76] See generally Kingsbury, 'Global environmental governance', 63–84.
[77] Retrospective statements reflect the reasons at the time of inscription: ICOMOS et al., *Guidance on the Preparation of Retrospective Statements*, p. 8.

example, why natural beauty or aesthetic points of view are represented in the 'fantastically shaped' rocks of Mount Sanqingshan, the 'colour contrasts' of the Lakes of Ounianga and the Tasmanian Wilderness, or the 'massed congregations' and 'concentrations' of animals in the Kenya Lakes System or the Monarch Butterfly Biosphere Reserve.[78]

I argue that the photographic images used in the inscription process, as distinct from the verbal images,[79] also have juridical significance. They form part of the record of World Heritage nominations. The *Operational Guidelines* require states parties to provide 'documentation necessary to substantiate the nomination', including 'images of a quality suitable for printing'.[80] In addition, the format of nominations requires states to 'provide a sufficient number of recent images (prints, slides and, where possible, electronic formats, videos and aerial photographs) to give a good general picture of the property'.[81] To the extent that the photographs justify nominations of properties for World Heritage status, they attest to the conception of natural beauty and aesthetic value held by individual states parties for the purposes of criterion (vii). However, nominating states must also contextualise their justifications with reference to properties already listed on the basis of a given criterion.[82] I argue that the photographs form part of this comparative justification and, as such, they are a form of precedent. They are indicative of the practice of all the parties as to the meanings of 'natural beauty' and 'aesthetic' points of view in the definition of natural heritage.[83]

However, World Heritage rules on the use of photographs in the process of nominating properties for inscription in the World Heritage List make no specific mention of how the graphic images might be used to support reliance on criterion (vii). A *World Heritage Resource Manual* provides only limited guidance on the use of photographs in World Heritage nomination files.[84] It indicates that criterion (vii) contains two concepts. It says that the first concept (superlative natural phenomena) 'can often be objectively measured and assessed'.[85] Of the second concept (exceptional natural beauty and aesthetic

78 See Section 5.3.1.
79 See Section 4.4.1.
80 *Operational Guidelines*, UN Doc. WHC.21/01, para. [132].
81 *Operational Guidelines*, UN Doc. WHC.21/01, Annex 5 ('Properties for inscription on the World Heritage List' Nomination Format) para. [7a] p. 113. The World Heritage emblem is also protected: *Operational Guidelines*, UN Doc. WHC.21/01, part VIII.
82 *Operational Guidelines*, UN Doc. WHC.21/01, para. [132.3] ('comparative analysis').
83 See Section 3.3.2.1.
84 World Heritage Centre, 'Preparing World Heritage nominations', 121.
85 Ibid., 40.

importance) it says that it 'is harder to assess' but '[m]erely asserting these qualities without a robust supporting argument is insufficient'.[86] It adds that 'providing attractive photographs is inadequate'.[87] The *Resource Manual* advises that images giving a 'general picture of the property', in accordance with the *Operational Guidelines*, 'should portray the potential Outstanding Universal Value of the property, as well as its context'.[88] It further warns that '[p]oor quality images are of no use'.[89]

Ultimately, these rules do not explain the relevance of photographs to determinations of outstanding universal value on the basis of natural beauty or aesthetic points of view under Article 2 of the *World Heritage Convention*. The *Operational Guidelines* do not specify, for example, *how* photographs can 'substantiate the nomination',[90] or *how* they might 'give a good general picture of the property'.[91] The *Resource Manual* does not elaborate on *what* constitutes an 'attractive' photograph.[92] Nor does it explain *why* an 'attractive' photograph is inadequate to the task of justifying aesthetic value. It provides no guidance as to *why* or *how* '[p]oor quality images are of no use' in portraying 'the potential Outstanding Universal Value of the property'.[93]

The lack of formal guidance from the World Heritage Committee on how images can be used to represent the environment's aesthetic value is related, in ways I explain next, to the emphasis on 'objective' grounds in the practice of justifying 'outstanding universal value' under criterion (vii).

5.3.3.2 Objective Evaluation of Outstanding Universal Value

Natural heritage criterion (vii) is understood to contain two concepts: (1) superlative natural phenomena and (2) natural beauty and aesthetic importance. There is no further subdivision as between the terms 'natural beauty' and 'aesthetic importance': According to the *Resource Manual*, those terms together form part of the second concept.[94] States parties to the *World*

86 Ibid.
87 Ibid., 60.
88 Ibid., 121.
89 Ibid., 98.
90 *Operational Guidelines*, UN Doc. WHC.21/01, para. [132].
91 Ibid., annex. 5.
92 World Heritage Centre, *World Heritage Resource Manual*, p. 60.
93 Ibid., pp. 98, 121.
94 Ibid., p. 40. See Chapter 3 on the extent to which this conflation is consistent with treaty interpretation.

Heritage Convention have been advised to justify their nominations with respect to either or both of the two concepts.[95]

Led by author Nora Mitchell, an IUCN study of the application of criterion (vii) found a tendency in World Heritage documentation to rely on measurable elements to describe the 'superlative natural phenomena' mentioned in the first concept in criterion (vii).[96] Superlatives are used to refer to the longest river, the oldest trees, the deepest lake, the tallest mountain, the largest herd. The study observed that this first concept is not often distinguished from 'areas of exceptional natural beauty and aesthetic importance', the so-called second element of criterion (vii).[97] Research commissioned by the Australian Government found that where inscriptions are based on multiple natural heritage criteria, the descriptions for criterion (vii) generally replicate the descriptions for the natural sciences criteria (viii) to (x).[98] The report concluded that scientific values 'drive the nomination and inscription of properties'.[99] By this analysis, the descriptions in the OUV Statements for the Monarch Butterfly Biosphere Reserve and the Kenya Lakes System, both tending towards quantitative measures of aesthetics, are more representative of World Heritage justifications under criterion (vii) than the qualitative verbal images in the World Heritage documentation describing the natural beauty or aesthetic importance of the Lakes of Ounianga, Mount Sanqingshan and the Tasmanian Wilderness.[100]

The preference for measurable or objective features in the practice of describing properties for criterion (vii) appears consistent with the rules and guidance on the World Heritage determination process. The *Operational Guidelines* require the decisions of the World Heritage Committee to be based 'on objective and scientific considerations'.[101] The *Resource Manual* mentioned earlier emphasises the need for objective method with respect to aesthetic criterion (vii). It states that 'standards applied under this criterion are

95 Ibid.
96 IUCN, *Study on the Application of Criterion (vii)*, p. 21.
97 Ibid., p. 28.
98 Context Pty Ltd, *Defining the Aesthetic Values*, p. 10.
99 Ibid., p. 14. See also IUCN, *Study on the Application of Criterion (vii)*, p. 21. On science in international environmental law in general, see Johnston, 'The role of science'.
100 See Section 5.3.1.
101 *Operational Guidelines*, UN Doc. WHC.21/01, para. [23]. Scientific expertise of the Advisory Bodies also informs the decision-making process: Ibid para. [37]. See also IUCN, 'Terms of reference'.

expected to meet a global standard of proof'.[102] It indicates that nominated properties should be compared with properties previously inscribed under criterion (vii), including a 'comparison of measurable indicators of scenic value.'[103] These rules and guidance likely stem from the *World Heritage Convention* itself. The treaty states in its preamble that World Heritage shall be protected 'in accordance with modern scientific methods'.[104]

An advisory body to the World Heritage Committee,[105] the IUCN maintains that, in contrast to the first concept in criterion (vii), the evaluation of exceptional natural beauty and aesthetic importance 'tends to be more subjective'.[106] Participants at an IUCN workshop in 2005 'noted that "aesthetics" is a personal and emotionally based response (not just visual but including a range of senses and associative responses), and therefore the concept is rooted in a community/culture.'[107] They went further to say 'that application of this criterion has been previously mainly descriptive and often using a "Eurocentric" approach, and that there is a need to provide better guidance on its understanding and application.'[108]

The practice of evaluating outstanding universal value on 'objective' grounds, combined with the characterisation of natural beauty and aesthetic value as 'subjective', has undermined the evaluation of 'natural beauty' and 'aesthetic' points of view for the purposes of criterion (vii) and, ultimately, Article 2 of the *World Heritage Convention*.[109] The World Heritage Committee has no formal method for understanding these points of view – either together, or as distinct terms. Nor has it formally articulated a role for images in justifying natural beauty or aesthetic value. However, in ways I explained in Chapters 2 and 4, theories for understanding the environment's aesthetic value, and methods for identifying and analysing representations of that value through images, exist in the field of aesthetic philosophy. In the next part, I use aesthetic methods for analysing the arts, and considerations from the philosophy of environmental aesthetics, to develop meanings for an aesthetic point of view from the World Heritage images.

[102] World Heritage Centre, *World Heritage Resource Manual*, p. 40.
[103] Ibid.
[104] *World Heritage Convention*, preamble. The term 'scientific methods' is not defined and could extend beyond the natural sciences to social and other sciences.
[105] *Operational Guidelines*, UN Doc. WHC.21/01, para. [37]. See Section 5.2.1.
[106] IUCN, *Outstanding Universal Value Standards*.
[107] Ibid., p. 9.
[108] Ibid.
[109] Cf. Thorsell, 'Scenic natural beauty: How can it be judged?', 8.

5.4 AESTHETIC REFLECTIONS ON WORLD HERITAGE IMAGES

The images that I have identified in processes of World Heritage determinations of aesthetic value are significant in ways understood and debated among philosophers of aesthetics. In this part, I analyse the World Heritage images to reveal associations with aesthetic conventions prevalent in nineteenth-century Western European and British landscape art. I then undertake a critical analysis of the images in light of eco-critical theory. I close by considering the World Heritage images from the perspective of the philosophy of environmental aesthetics. Later in Section 5.5, I argue that aesthetic method and theories could be properly employed in future World Heritage inscription processes to identify and evaluate the aesthetic value of natural heritage from photographic images.

5.4.1 *Landscape Aesthetic in World Heritage Images*

Many of the verbal images of the five properties described above reflect the language of artistic movements that have explored the human experience of the natural environment.[110] Specifically, they recall the Romantic conceptions of natural beauty, the sublime and the picturesque developed through nineteenth-century Western European and British landscape that I explained in Chapter 4.[111] The OUV Statements of properties I identified earlier as being scientifically oriented contain verbal images that reflect artistic ideas of landscape. For example, the concentration of butterflies in the Monarch Butterfly Biosphere Reserve is described as 'dramatic'.[112] The OUV Statement for the Great Rift Valley describes natural beauty in terms of the 'landscape backdrop' and 'wildlife spectacle'.[113] However, the verbal images in the descriptions of Chad's Lakes of Ounianga, China's Mount Sanqingshan and Australia's Tasmanian Wilderness are particularly evocative of a Romantic landscape ideal. The Ounianga Lakes' varied and contrasting colours, the 'dominating' rocks, 'breathtaking views' and the mystery of a hydrological system 'still to be fully understood'[114] invoke the Romantic sublime. The description of Mount Sanqingshan refers to 'near and distant vistas' and

[110] See Section 5.3.1.
[111] See Section 4.2.1.
[112] World Heritage Committee, 'Statement of Outstanding Universal Value' in *Monarch Butterfly Biosphere Reserve Inscription*.
[113] World Heritage Committee, 'Statement of Outstanding Universal Value' in *Great Rift Valley Inscription*.
[114] World Heritage Committee, 'Statement of Outstanding Universal Value' in *Lakes of Ounianga Inscription*.

'a landscape of exceptional scenic quality'.[115] Such aesthetic concepts are also apparent in the 'red and gold to dark green tones' of vegetation, the 'silence' and 'clamour' of glacial lakes, 'stark white' rocks against 'dark waters', and carving wild rivers, plunging waterfalls and foaming eddies 'snaking darkly under the lime green drapes of ancient Huon pines and moss-covered giant tree ferns' of the Tasmanian Wilderness.[116] The mention there of the possibility that the exotic thylacine might have returned from the dead lends still further mystery to that enchanted place.

Indeed, the verbal images of the Tasmanian Wilderness could well describe the paintings of John Glover, a British-born artist who settled for a time in Australia in the nineteenth century. Glover painted scenes of both a real and imagined Tasmanian landscape in a European style.[117] His painting *A mountain torrent* (Figure 5.9) was done during his time in Tasmania but it is reputedly based on sketches made when he was still in Britain, possibly from the Welsh or Lakes Districts.[118] There jagged rocks are softened by the daubs of trees and shrubs while a raging river threatens to overwhelm the human figure perched precariously on a makeshift bridge. A wary – possibly more knowing – dog looks on. Though so small against the majestic mountainside, the plight of the figure in these indifferent surrounds attracts all the attention of an observer of the work.

The studies commissioned by IUCN, and by the Australian Government, of the application of criterion (vii),[119] support a conclusion that the Romantic language of the five properties is typical of properties inscribed for their natural beauty and aesthetic importance. Those studies found, for example, common references in the documentation generated throughout the inscription process to concepts of diversity, combination, abundance, contrast, dramatic impact, seasonal changes, weather and light effects, scale, majesty, depth, steepness and wilderness, as well as descriptions of landscapes that are said to be rising, falling, towering, scenic, spectacular, wild and 'free from human influence'.[120]

[115] World Heritage Committee, 'Statement of Outstanding Universal Value' in *Mount Sanqingshan Inscription*.

[116] Australia, 'Draft retrospective statement of Outstanding Universal Value', 2010.

[117] See also discussion of critical perspectives on Glover's work in Section 7.3.2.1.

[118] See Glover, *A mountain torrent*.

[119] See IUCN, *Study on the Application of Criterion (vii)*; Context Pty Ltd, *Defining the Aesthetic Values*.

[120] Context Pty Ltd, *Defining the Aesthetic Values*, p. 11. See also IUCN, *Study on the Application of Criterion (vii)*, p. 33.

FIGURE 5.9. John Glover, *A mountain torrent*, c. 1837. Oil on canvas on plywood, 74.5 × 112.5 cm. National Gallery of Victoria, Melbourne. The Joseph Brown Collection. Presented through the NGV Foundation by Dr Joseph Brown AO OBE, Honorary Life Benefactor, 2004. Photo: National Gallery of Victoria.

Viewed as depictions of landscape, the photographic images submitted by states in their nominations of the five properties exhibit the same qualities of natural beauty, the sublime and the picturesque that I have observed in connection with the verbal images.[121] The photograph of glacial lakes in the Tasmanian Wilderness (Figure 5.8), for example, shows the 'secret jewels' described in the nomination file to justify World Heritage inscription for the area's natural beauty. The jagged peaks of the Nevado de Toluca in Mexico's photograph (Figure 5.3) present a picturesque scene. The congregations – of butterflies in Mexico (Figure 5.2) or birds in Kenya (Figure 5.7) – are the prized assemblages of natural beauty as understood in nineteenth-century Europe and Britain.[122] However, the aesthetic conventions apparent in the photographic images are not exclusive to a Western European ideal of landscape. They are also reflected in ancient Chinese art.[123] The photographs of 'Nanqing peak forest' (Figure 5.4) and 'Awfully stirring billows' (Figure 5.5) included in China's nomination of Mount Sanqingshan evoke ancient

[121] See Section 5.3.1.
[122] Also adopted in scholarly descriptions of aesthetic value in international environmental law: See Section 2.3.2.
[123] See, for example, Whitfield, 'Landscape: China, People's Republic of'.

Chinese landscape conventions still referenced in the work of contemporary Chinese artists. For example, in a series titled *Pulse (Mountain)*, Chinese artist Cai Guo-Qiang shows splintered contours evocative of the mountain ridges that represent 'life force'.[124]

5.4.2 *Eco-Critical Approaches to World Heritage Images*

Much contemporary art addresses environmental concerns.[125] Using an 'eco-critical' approach, I can examine environmental images in the arts through the lens of ethics, in light of the social, political and natural sciences.[126] For example, I commenced this chapter with a description of Kenyan-born artist Wangechi Mutu's animated video, *The End of carrying All* (Figure 5.1). Set against a Romantic landscape, it critiques the economic models of sustained development in industrialised countries in the North and warns of the impacts of consumption on the natural environment. The woman climbing the hillside starts out by carrying her daily needs before her simple fare turns into an overloaded collection of modern trappings. The environment that once nourished her is destroyed by wealth. By her dress, by the trees, a viewer understands this to be East Africa. So it is that the transformation from subsistence to consumption – literally, in the end, as her load turns into an all-consuming beast – is set against the background of perpetual colonial exploitation.

A critical perspective can also be developed from the work of Ghanaian-born artist, John Akomfrah. His video installation *Vertigo Sea* juxtaposes archival, dramatic and documentary footage on a triptych of screens.[127] At several stages, it shows sea mammals – whales, seals – and polar bears, in colourful splendour and in black and white harpooned carnage. It also shows re-enactments of slaves tossed from boats to their death and asylum seekers drowned and washed ashore. The desecration of nature and the loss of human life play out together, leaving the viewer to reflect on where her sympathies – and those of the international community – lie. Akomfrah's subsequent work, *The Elephant in the Room – Four Nocturnes* (Figures 5.10 and 5.11), is another potent critique of historic concepts of natural beauty in art.[128] Also a video installation, it alternates spectacular scenes from Ghana's natural environment

[124] See further Ma, Cai and Hasegawa, *The Transient Landscape*.
[125] See Section 4.2.
[126] Braddock and Irmscher (eds.), *A Keener Perception*, p. 4. See Section 4.3.3.
[127] Akomfrah, *Vertigo Sea*. See Gyalui (ed.), *La Biennale di Venezia*.
[128] See Biennale Arte 2019, *Ghana Pavilion*.

FIGURE 5.10. John Akomfrah, *Four Nocturnes*, 2019 (still, elephants). Three-channel HD colour video installation, 7.1 sound, Ghana pavilion, 58th International Art Exhibition of la Biennale di Venezia, co-commissioned by the Ministry of Tourism, Arts and Culture of Ghana, Sharjah Art Foundation and Smoking Dogs Films with support from Lisson Gallery. © Smoking Dogs Films. Photo: Alice Palmer.

with images of people, displaced and migrating through a barren desert landscape. Akomfrah's work prompts questions about the relevance of international protections for charismatic animals to the lives of people fleeing war, persecution and poverty, matters of significance in the artist's country of birth.[129]

The critical perspectives evident in Mutu and Akomfrah's works could be contrasted with Romantic depictions of flora and fauna that can also be understood from contemporary environmental artworks.[130] UK artist Tacita Dean's *Majesty (Portrait)* (2006) pays homage to the ancient oak trees of Britain. The image depicts the significance of the tree and the artist's own sense of self and place.[131] Dean's exhibition *Landscape* includes works that

[129] See also Bracker (ed.), *Vita Vitale*.
[130] See, e.g., Leahy, McDonald and Wolseley, *John Wolseley: Heartlands and Headwaters*; Ian Potter Museum of Art, *Nature/Revelation*. Cf. Cai, *Falling Back to Earth*.
[131] Tacita Dean, 'Interview with artist' in *Majesty (Portrait)*, Paris, 2006.

FIGURE 5.11. John Akomfrah, *Four Nocturnes*, 2019 (still, desert). Three-channel HD colour video installation, 7.1 sound, Ghana pavilion, 58th International Art Exhibition of la Biennale di Venezia, co-commissioned by the Ministry of Tourism, Arts and Culture of Ghana, Sharjah Art Foundation and Smoking Dogs Films with support from Lisson Gallery. © Smoking Dogs Films. Photo: Alice Palmer.

depict natural wonders in a manner that evokes awe and mystery.[132] French-born artist Pierre Huyghe's video, *A Journey That Wasn't*,[133] documents his trip with fellow artists and scientists to Antarctica, showing a barren and inhospitable landscape in which humans are alien while penguins and seals belong. Yet the approaches in Dean and Huyghe's works, and in other contemporary works from artists addressing environmental issues from the perspective of the North, could also be understood as a critique of the Romantic ideals.[134] For example, artists Justy Phillips and Margaret Woodward challenge aesthetic conventions and explore the transportation of aesthetic ideals in nature from Britain to Australia in their work *Fall of the Derwent* (2015–16). In a performative element, they walked the rivers Derwent

[132] See Harris, Hollinghurst and Smith, *Tacita Dean*.

[133] Collection of Fondation Louis Vuitton, Paris. Exhibited at *Pierre Huyghe: TarraWarra International 2015*, TarraWarra Museum of Art, Australia.

[134] For example, Hall, *Wrong Way Time*; Simon, *Paperwork and the Will of Capital*; Laurence, *Deep Breathing: Resuscitation*.

in England's Lakes District, and in Tasmania, then documented their aesthetic experience of those places in written text. The text was published as a book, downloaded and generated in print from the project's website.[135] Each download was unique, the text arranged and extracted in different ways so the artists were not in control of the execution of their work: Its construction was 'random'. In written text, and in black and white with only a few photographs of a polluted waterway, the work does not present in the way of Glover's *A mountain torrent* (Figure 5.9). But it projects a highly evocative image of an aesthetic experience of place. As in Glover's work, a human figure is present in *Fall, Now a River* (Figure 5.12) from *Fall of the Derwent* – a man 'in a sweat-stained cornflower collar' – but the scale is small – a leech, a hook – more intimate, more personal and, possibly, truer to human experiences of the environment. It is also expressed as verbal images.

Looking upon the World Heritage images from an eco-critical perspective, I make three observations. First, the natural beauty and aesthetic points of view – two different points of view identified in Article 2 of the *World Heritage Convention* – have been treated as one, conflated in a Romantic landscape ideal. Second, the Romantic ideal is one that emerged in Western Europe and Britain in the nineteenth century. It is an aesthetic preference that is culturally and historically situated. Third, it idealises an environment absent humans. When I imagine humans into the environments depicted in the World Heritage photographs, I think on the various forms of sustenance that the environment provides, within limits, to all people. I see among the flocks of birds in the Kenya Lakes System (Figure 5.7), Mutu's woman, ascending and progressing but ultimately consumed by consumption itself. I consider the harm done to the environment by some humans, with consequences for other humans. Seeing sand dunes around Chad's Lakes of Ounianga (e.g. Figure 5.6), I reflect on Akomfrah's images of people displaced and deserted (Figure 5.11). In the images of Mexico's Monarch Butterfly Biosphere Reserve (e.g. Figure 5.3), I am aware of the effects of mining, and of climate change, on the butterflies and their habitat, and the risks to people who try to protect them.[136] I see in China's Mount Sanqingshan 'Nanqing peak forest' (Figure 5.4) environments constructed through culture, resonating today in artworks such as those by Cai Guo-Qiang.[137] Seeing the photograph of glacial lakes in the Tasmanian Wilderness (Figure 5.8), I am reminded of works by

[135] Phillips and Woodward, *Fall of the Derwent*.

[136] See, e.g., World Heritage Committee, *Monarch Butterfly Biosphere Reserve*, UN Doc. WHC/19/43.COM/18; IUCN, *Reactive Monitoring Mission Report*.

[137] See Ma, Cai and Hasegawa, *The Transient Landscape*.

FIGURE 5.12. Justy Phillips and Margaret Woodward, A Published Event, *Fall, Now a River*, 2016. Postcard printed on the occasion of *Fall of the Derwent* (2015–16), an experiment in hydrographic publishing, commissioned and presented by Glenorchy Art & Sculpture Park, lutruwita/Tasmania in 2016. 150 × 105 mm. Edition of 500. © Justy Phillips and Margaret Woodward. Courtesy the artists.

Phillips and Woodward (Figure 5.12), the migration and reorientation of aesthetic preferences for environments. I am conscious of how aesthetics transposed contributed to the displacement in Tasmania – and in other colonised places – of First Nations peoples and their own aesthetic conceptions of the environment.[138]

As explained earlier in Chapter 4, Romantic ideals about nature persist in art practice today.[139] Some scholars argue that the Romantic landscape ideal is universal – whether as a function of human evolution or because of the migration of aesthetic preferences with colonialism and globalisation.[140] However, eco-criticism cautions against universalism, promoting pluralised and context-driven understandings of the environment's aesthetic value.[141] On this basis, I maintain that the projection of a nineteenth-century Western European and British Romantic ideal of the environment in World Heritage images does not reflect an aesthetic preference commonly held today by all states parties to the *World Heritage Convention*. Nor is it a definition of aesthetic value that is necessarily supported by the international principles of treaty interpretation explained and applied in Chapter 3.[142] In Section 5.4.3, I examine the World Heritage images in light of the philosophy of environmental aesthetics to offer an alternative account of the environment's aesthetic value.

5.4.3 *Environmental Aesthetics*

In Chapter 2, I described a range of views among philosophers of environmental aesthetics as to whether aesthetic appreciation of the natural environment is developed through an objective, cognitive evaluation or a subjective, non-cognitive impression of the natural environment. I identified Emily Brady's integrated aesthetic model as a hybrid of these approaches.[143] She characterises the aesthetic value of the natural environment in the subjective terms of sensorial perception, shaped by imagination and emotion. But she also recognises that it is informed by knowledge, including Western scientific knowledge and different cultural knowledges, shared among a given epistemic community.[144]

138 See discussion in Chapters 7 and 8; see also Gough et al., *Fugitive History*.
139 See Section 4.2.2.
140 See Section 4.2.1.
141 Cf. Nixon, *Slow Violence*.
142 See Section 3.3.
143 Brady, *Aesthetics of the Natural Environment*; see further Section 2.2.3.
144 Brady, *Aesthetics of the Natural Environment*, pp. 237–8. For discussion of situated interpretations for law, see Iain Scobbie, 'A view of Delft', 63. See generally Waibel, 'Interpretive communities in international law', 147.

Together with other philosophers,[145] Brady's views on environmental aesthetics are critical of the Romantic ideal apparent in nineteenth-century Western European and British landscape art: Framing the environment and emphasising visual qualities does not offer a comprehensive account of the aesthetic appreciation of the natural environment suggested by her integrated aesthetic model.[146] In addition to developing a critical account, though, her aesthetic appreciation is also normative: She, along with other philosophers of environmental aesthetics, understands that there are ways in which the aesthetic value of the environment can be judged well.[147]

As explained earlier in Chapter 2, I understand Brady to be offering an account of aesthetic value that is exquisite and profound.[148] I take her model to incorporate ineffable affect and meaningful engagement. Hers is not a trivial luxury – it is an aesthetic value worthy of consideration on equal terms with other environmental values.[149] Taking account of critiques of aesthetic value as universal, Brady understands that different environments might be meaningful in aesthetic terms in different ways, and for different reasons, for different people and communities.[150] To my mind, she promotes a pluralised understanding of the environment's aesthetic value.

I consider that some of the World Heritage images can be understood to depict an exquisite and profound aesthetic value, yet shaped by cultural knowledges. In my introductory Chapter 1, for example, I described a photograph of Mexico's Monarch Butterfly Biosphere Reserve (Figure 1.1) in such terms. I maintain that other photographs submitted with the nominations of the five properties studied for this chapter could also be described in this way. Those photographs with expressive qualities – such as the image of swarming butterflies at the Monarch Butterfly Biosphere Reserve (Figure 1.1) or those of jagged peaks and billowing clouds at China's Mount Sanqingshan (Figures 5.4 and 5.5) – are well-placed for an analysis of an exquisite and profound aesthetic value. That the images might also present a Romantic ideal of nature does not preclude an understanding from another vantage, informed by scholars of environmental aesthetics. Yet it is the photographs – as opposed to the verbal images – that are best suited to a representation of the environment's aesthetic value for international legal process. I maintain that graphic images provide visual cues that can be described, using concepts and

[145] See, for example, Carlson, *Aesthetics and the Environment*, p. 45.
[146] See Brady, *Aesthetics of the Natural Environment.*
[147] See Maskit, 'On universalism', 44.
[148] See Section 2.2.3.5.
[149] See Section 2.2.3.2.
[150] See Brady, *Aesthetics of the Natural Environment.*

methods developed for the visual arts, to comprehend the environment's aesthetic value in complex ways contemplated in the philosophy of environmental aesthetics.[151]

My willingness to engage photographs to represent the environment's aesthetic value is, however, problematic for environmental aesthetics. Many philosophers of environmental aesthetics agree that the aesthetic appreciation of the natural environment is different from aesthetic appreciation of the arts. I explained their reasons in Chapter 2.[152] For many philosophers, there is a distinction between aesthetic judgement of an art object, created by a person, and the aesthetic experience that comes from being immersed in an environment that is naturally formed.[153] The reasons for disqualifying aesthetic methods for the arts from the aesthetic appreciation of the environment call into question my use of aesthetic concepts and methods, developed for the arts, to describe the environment's aesthetic value from photographs. I agree that the environment's aesthetic value judged from a photograph is not the same as judging aesthetic value in an environment. I argued earlier, however, that aesthetic methods for the arts can be employed to describe the environment's aesthetic value in terms contemplated in the philosophy of environmental aesthetics.[154] Like my description of the photograph of butterflies in the Monarch Butterfly Biosphere Reserve (Figure 1.1) in Chapter 1, aesthetic methods for the visual arts can describe a multi-sensory experience of a place, augmented by imagination, emotion and knowledge. And for reasons explained next, photographic images provide an approximation of the aesthetic experience of place in a form suited to institutional decision-making and international law.

5.5 AESTHETIC METHOD FOR WORLD HERITAGE DETERMINATIONS

An absence of guidance as to the significance of images – verbal and photographic – to determinations of outstanding universal value under the *World Heritage Convention* has allowed uncritical uses of images in ways that might be at odds with international law. In this part, I consider how aesthetic philosophy could be applied in the future practice of inscribing natural

[151] On visual art and the appreciation of nature, see Section 4.2. See also Tafalla, 'From Allen Carlson to Richard Long'.

[152] See Section 2.2.1.

[153] See ibid.

[154] See Section 4.3.2.

heritage in the World Heritage List. I advocate the continued use of images, particularly photographs, with formal guidance on how aesthetic method can be used to identify aesthetic values represented in those images. Aesthetic methods from the arts, and considerations from the philosophy of environmental aesthetics, should be used to give images meaning in the World Heritage inscription process. As I explain here, this can be done without falling foul of the international laws that govern the decision-making processes of international bodies such as the World Heritage Committee.

5.5.1 *Expert Guidance on Images of the Environment's Aesthetic Value*

Graphic images representing the environment's aesthetic value document the claims and determinations of 'outstanding universal' aesthetic value in a form that can be reproduced in the administrative processes mandated by the *World Heritage Convention*. Site visits, such as field evaluations by IUCN for nominated properties, form part of the inscription process and provide the immersive experience of physical environments contemplated for aesthetic appreciation in the philosophy of environmental aesthetics.[155] But absent such visits by all twenty-one members of the World Heritage Committee, decisions to inscribe properties in the World Heritage List are based 'on the papers' – papers that, by my account, currently include images, both verbal and graphic. The images are, I suggest, an institutional approximation of the first-hand appreciation of environmental spaces on which environmental aesthetics is premised.[156] They are a representation of the natural environment's aesthetic value protected by the treaty.

However, guidance on methods used to understand meanings of the environment's aesthetic value from these photographic images is necessary for the proper functioning of the decision-making processes. As explained in Chapter 3,[157] international rules require the interpretation of a term in a treaty in a way that makes it effective, including a meaning that is distinct from other terms in the treaty. As Article 2 of the *World Heritage Convention* refers separately to natural beauty and aesthetic points of view, those terms should not be conflated – they should, as a matter of treaty interpretation, be understood on their own terms. To support a reasoned process of inscription, the *Operational Guidelines* should be amended to address how

[155] See *Operational Guidelines*, UN Doc. WHC.21/01 annex 6 ('Evaluation Procedures of the Advisory Bodies for Nominations').

[156] Brady, *Aesthetics of the Natural Environment*. See Section 2.2.2.

[157] Section 3.3.1.2.

representations of aesthetic value differ from that of natural beauty. They should also be amended to explain how photographs can 'substantiate the nomination',[158] or how they might 'give a good general picture of the property',[159] with respect to an aesthetic point of view.

I argue that aesthetic concepts and methods for analysing visual art, and considerations in the philosophy of environmental aesthetics, can be used to guide states parties and the World Heritage Committee on representations in photographs relevant to determinations of 'outstanding' and 'universal' aesthetic value for the purposes of Article 2 of the *World Heritage Convention*. Acknowledging critiques of universalism, aesthetic methods and environmental aesthetics can be used to develop pluralised meanings of aesthetic value that are nevertheless of 'outstanding universal value' in the sense that they are exquisite and profound in ways tied to place and people.[160] Aesthetic methods and environmental aesthetics could also be used to explain how criterion (vii) could be applied in a manner that distinguishes between natural beauty and aesthetic points of view.

In this task, the World Heritage Committee could be guided by experts in aesthetic theories, methods and forms. The World Heritage Committee already has a process for drawing on aesthetic expertise for the purposes of justifying its criterion concerning the aesthetic value of cultural heritage.[161] Although the meaning of 'aesthetic' is likely different for cultural and natural heritage,[162] the way in which the World Heritage Committee engages aesthetic understandings in respect of cultural heritage could be instructive for natural heritage determinations. Properties nominated under cultural heritage criteria must meet 'conditions of authenticity' that are satisfied by reference to credible or truthful 'information sources' that permit the 'elaboration of the specific artistic, historic, social, and scientific dimensions of the cultural heritage being examined'.[163] The *Operational Guidelines* define 'information sources' as 'all physical, written, oral, and figurative sources, which make it

[158] *Operational Guidelines*, UN Doc. WHC.21/01 para. [132].
[159] Ibid., Annex 5 para. [7.a].
[160] See Section 5.4.3.
[161] See IUCN, *Study on the Application of Criterion (vii)*, p. 44. Note *Operational Guidelines*, UN Doc. WHC.21/01, paras. [31] (role of Advisory Bodies) [34] (role of International Council on Monuments and Sites in evaluation of the outstanding universal value of 'cultural heritage'). Both Art. 1 of the *World Heritage Convention* and *Operational Guidelines*, UN Doc. WHC.21/01, para. [77] (cultural heritage criterion (iii)) refer to the aesthetic outstanding universal value of cultural heritage.
[162] See Section 3.3.1.2.
[163] See *Operational Guidelines*, UN Doc. WHC.21/01, para. [84].

possible to know the nature, specificities, meaning, and history of the cultural heritage'.[164]

Such information sources could also be required by the World Heritage Committee for an aesthetic justification for natural heritage – sources prepared and identified by people expert in environmental aesthetics and aesthetic theory as it relates to representation and the natural environment. The World Heritage Committee already looks to ecologists and anthropologists for advice:[165] It can, I submit, also look to aesthetic philosophers.

5.5.2 *Using Art Methods for Images*

The verbal and graphic images arising from World Heritage inscriptions can be analysed from an aesthetic perspective even though they might not constitute 'art'. It is not clear that any of the photographs would amount to 'art' or even 'good' art: That would fall to contested positions in aesthetic theory.[166] The photographs are, however, at least for some schools of aesthetic thinking, representations available for aesthetic analysis.[167] That they might have been taken by an amateur photographer, and that they are incorporated into a document produced in the implementation of international law, does not exclude an understanding of that image as representation in aesthetic theory.[168] However, as explained in Chapter 4,[169] some images more than others lend themselves to aesthetic analysis. A preponderance of prosaic language, and emphasis on quantitative measures, in OUV Statements might undermine their relevance to understandings of the environment's aesthetic value. Similarly, the significance of the photographs to determinations of aesthetic value would be impacted by form and presentation. Many of the photographs for the Lakes of Ounianga are, for example, small and in a low resolution, making it difficult to appreciate the aesthetic qualities of the environment they represent.[170] In contrast, the photographs of Mount Sanqingshan National Park are large format and high resolution, making them better objects for aesthetic analysis.

The production of images suitable for aesthetic analysis – whether they are verbal or graphic images – requires resources. Writers, photographers and

164 Ibid., para. [84]. See also World Heritage Centre, *World Heritage Resource Manual*, p. 36.
165 See *Operational Guidelines*, UN Doc. WHC.21/01, paras. [34] (ICOMOS), [36] (IUCN).
166 See Levinson, 'Artistic worth and personal taste'.
167 See generally Savedoff, *Transforming Images*.
168 See further Section 4.2.3.
169 See further Section 4.3.2.
170 See, for example, six photos to a page in Chad, *Proposition d'Inscription*, p. 10.

graphic designers are among the many professionals needed to produce images that might support a determination of the environment's aesthetic value. Some nation states do not have the resources required to support expert representations of that value in verbal or graphic form in a nomination under the *World Heritage Convention*. In this respect, I note that Ghana does not have a property inscribed on the World Heritage List for its aesthetic value despite what might be deemed aesthetically valuable environments represented in John Akomfrah's *The Elephant in the Room – Four Nocturnes* (e.g. Figure 5.10).[171] The administration of nominations for World Heritage status already provides assistance to some states:[172] Assistance with justifications of aesthetic value could also promote the use of photographs representing aesthetic points of view.

5.5.3 *Legality of Aesthetic Method*

The World Heritage Committee is likely bound by the international 'principle of legality' requiring international bodies to act in accordance with the powers conferred on them by the states parties under a governing treaty.[173] In international legal practice, the World Heritage Committee would be an international treaty organisation and its accountability is arguably also extended under the *World Heritage Convention* to an international organisation of the United Nations, the United Nations Educational, Scientific and Cultural Organization (UNESCO).[174] As such, the principle of legality would apply to require the World Heritage Committee to conform to the 'internal law' of the treaty; and it might also require adherence to 'external' laws governing its decision-making.[175]

The requirements of the *World Heritage Convention* and the *Operational Guidelines* are, I maintain, internal laws that apply to the World Heritage Committee in deciding to inscribe properties to the World Heritage List. As noted earlier, the *World Heritage Convention* states in its preamble that 'an

[171] Ghana's 'Tentative List' of properties for nomination to the World Heritage Committee has, since 2000, included Kakum National Park (Assin Attandanso Reserve) (criteria (vii) and (x)) and Mole National Park ((vii)(viii)(ix)(x)): whc.unesco.org/en/tentativelists/state=gh.

[172] See World Heritage Committee, 'Upstream process', UN Doc. WHC/19/43.COM/9A.Rev.

[173] On the 'principle of legality', see Sands and Klein, *Bowett's Law of International Institutions*, p. 297. Cf. 'attributed competence' in Schermers and Blokker, *International Institutional Law: Unity within Diversity*, p. 166 para. [209].

[174] See Zacharias, 'The UNESCO regime', 1843.

[175] Sands and Klein, *Bowett's Law of International Institutions*, p. 297. See generally Kingsbury,'Global environmental governance'.

effective system of collective protection' of World Heritage properties shall be organised 'in accordance with modern scientific methods'.[176] Relatedly, the *Operational Guidelines* require the decisions of the World Heritage Committee to be based 'on objective and scientific considerations'.[177] Scientific expertise also informs evaluations of properties.[178] Assuming that aesthetic approaches to assessing the aesthetic value of nature are properly characterised as neither scientific nor objective,[179] and leaving aside the fact that science and scientific method have themselves long been impugned as subjective by critical scholars,[180] these internal laws could be seen to preclude the use of aesthetic methods and aesthetic forms such as images. However, the *Operational Guidelines* also require that appraisals made on behalf of the World Heritage Committee 'must be thoroughly and responsibly carried out'.[181] So even if aesthetic method is characterised as leading to subjective evaluations, I argue that it can, as a matter of doctrinal practice, be engaged in World Heritage determinations in a 'thorough' and 'responsible' appraisal. For the purposes of the treaty's internal law, experts advising the World Heritage Committee on aesthetic values can provide 'thorough' and 'responsible' appraisals of the aesthetic importance of natural heritage within the terms of the *Operational Guidelines* when they employ aesthetic methods and sources in those appraisals. 'Thorough' and 'responsible' appraisals would extend to developing informed understandings of critical approaches in aesthetic scholarship and considerations in the philosophy of environmental aesthetics.

General principles of international law, and other concepts of 'good' law,[182] likely also apply to the World Heritage Committee's determinations of aesthetic value as part of the external laws that govern international institutions. General principles of international law derived from 'global administrative law' require international institutions to reach reasoned decisions.[183] Reasoned determinations of the environment's aesthetic value by the World Heritage Committee would require an evaluation and explanation based on aesthetic theories and methods using aesthetic forms.

[176] Preamble of the *World Heritage Convention*. See Section 5.3.3.2.
[177] *Operational Guidelines*, UN Doc. WHC.21/01, para. [23].
[178] Ibid., para. [31] (role of Advisory Bodies). See also IUCN, 'Terms of reference'.
[179] Cf. Carlson, *Aesthetics and the Environment*.
[180] See, for example, Kitcher, *Science Truth and Democracy*.
[181] *Operational Guidelines*, UN Doc. WHC.21/01, para. [23].
[182] See generally Klabbers, 'The paradox of international institutional law'.
[183] See Kingsbury, 'Global environmental governance'. See also Kingsbury, 'The concept of "law" in global administrative law'; Kingsbury, Krisch and Stewart, 'The emergence of global administrative law'; Harlow, 'The quest for principles and values'.

Consistent with these internal and external laws, aesthetic method and aesthetic forms such as photographs can be used by World Heritage decision-makers without falling foul of the principle of legality.[184] I present this as a doctrinal legal argument in favour of aesthetic method. But it also applies inversely. A failure to engage aesthetic method in the World Heritage inscription process, or to explain the relevance of images required by the World Heritage Committee in the nominations of states parties, is not 'thorough' and 'responsible', or reasoned. Such failure is, I argue, contrary to international law.

5.6 CONCLUSION

In the introduction to their edited collection of essays on *Law and the Image*, Costas Douzinas and Lynda Nead describe verbal and graphic images, respectively, as 'painted words' and 'icons'.[185] They state that both forms of image were banished from the common law in the aftermath of the European Reformation 'as too worldly, too sensual and potentially corrupt, too contingent and transient'.[186] The rise of the secular state in seventeenth-century Western Europe has been described as pivotal to the development of modern international law.[187] But if the common law unease with images infected the founding of international law,[188] the extensive use of verbal and photographic images in the World Heritage inscription process suggests such qualms are not held today by the states parties to the *World Heritage Convention*. Persistent reservations about images and attendant anxieties about aesthetic practices in legal process might nevertheless explain the objective methods mandated by the treaty. They might also account for the lack of guidance on how the images used in the inscription process relate to determinations of aesthetic value by the World Heritage Committee.

Yet by its express reliance on an 'aesthetic' point of view in the definition of the outstanding universal value of natural heritage, the *World Heritage Convention* requires a determination – a judgement[189] – of aesthetic value. I argue that the World Heritage Committee is required by international law to rely on thorough and responsible appraisals of aesthetic value, and to make a reasoned determination as to the aesthetic value of any natural property it

184 Palmer, 'Legal dimensions to valuing aesthetics'.
185 Douzinas and Nead, 'Introduction', 8.
186 Ibid. See Section 4.4.1.
187 Neff, 'A short history of international law', 11.
188 See, for example, Morgan, *The Aesthetics of International Law*.
189 On 'judgement' in this context, see Manderson, 'Judgment in law and the humanities'.

inscribes in the World Heritage List.[190] The philosophy of environmental aesthetics has developed concepts and theories for evaluating the environment's aesthetic value. And such concepts and theories could be a proper foundation for a reasoned determination of the environment's aesthetic value under the *World Heritage Convention*. Photographs of those environments are required by the decision-making process that is governed by international law. Aesthetic theories and methods for the arts should be employed to understand the aesthetic value of natural heritage represented in those photographs, in a manner distinct from natural beauty and mindful of contemporary developments in the philosophy of environmental aesthetics and critical scholarship.

Aesthetic methods and sources adopted for World Heritage purposes might well serve other international legal regimes that protect environmental aesthetics, acknowledging the place of aesthetic value in the mix of values that motivate states to protect the environment through international law. In the next chapter, I analyse the relevance of aesthetic philosophy to the interpretation and enforcement of the *Whaling Convention*.

[190] See Section 5.5.3.

6

The Art of Image in the *Whaling in the Antarctic* Case

EXHIBIT: CAPTAIN BOOMER, *THE WHY OF THE WHALE* (2018)

FIGURE 6.1. Captain Boomer, *The Why of the Whale*, 2018. Sculptural installation and performance, Madrid. © Captain Boomer. Courtesy the artist. Photo: CiudaDistrito Acción cultural.

When a beluga whale was seen off-course in England's River Thames in September 2018,[1] it appeared to be a case of life imitating art: Just over a week before, the residents of Madrid had been bemused to find a sperm whale

[1] Hoare, 'The lonely Thames beluga whale'.

stranded in the Manzanares River. Only this was a model, titled *The Why of the Whale* (Figure 6.1), made by the Belgian art collective Captain Boomer. The model had already been sighted in other European cities, created by the artists to disrupt city life as a critique of the city's disruption of ecology.[2]

For Captain Boomer, the whale is ready-made for an aesthetic rendition intended to capture both awe and concern for the natural environment. The whale image is loaded with an aesthetic history from many cultures that lends itself to metaphor. From depictions of whales in prehistoric petroglyphs in Alaska, Norway and South Korea and in ancient Greek art,[3] to the dramatic scenes of whaling and sensitive characterisations of whales in visual and other arts seen around the world,[4] a composite 'super whale' has been cultivated in many nations as an aesthetic subject associated with other-worldly powers and human sensibilities.[5] Captain Boomer's model could migrate from one city to the next, a universal symbol of all that is wondrous in the natural environment and all that is at risk from human exploitation of it.

6.1 INTRODUCTION

In her treatise on the international regulation of whaling, international lawyer Patricia Birnie points out that the whale has long been the subject of artistic representations.[6] But she might well have said that it is the subject of legal representations too. Photographic images of whales were used in a dispute before the International Court of Justice ('ICJ' or 'the Court') in *Whaling in the Antarctic (Australia v. Japan; New Zealand intervening)* (*Whaling in the Antarctic*).[7] The ICJ ultimately agreed with Australia that Japanese whaling in the Southern Ocean violated bans on whaling under the 1946 *Whaling Convention*.[8] In the course of the proceedings, Australia presented photographs of bloody harpooned whales, while Japan submitted images of sanitised

[2] Captain Boomer, *The Why of the Whale*.

[3] Slijper, *Whales*, pp. 11–14.

[4] Ellis, *Men and Whales*.

[5] Kalland, *Unveiling the Whale*; cf. Fitzmaurice, 'Whale', 539.

[6] See Birnie (ed.), *International Regulation of Whaling*, p. 63.

[7] *Whaling in the Antarctic (Australia v. Japan; New Zealand intervening) (Judgment)* [2014] ICJ Rep. 226.

[8] *International Convention on the Regulation of Whaling*, Washington, 2 December 1946, in force 10 November 1948, 161 UNTS 72.

whale tissue in laboratory settings, in their submissions on the utility or otherwise of lethal methods in scientific research of whales.[9]

I argue that the blended character of photographs, as peddlers of truth in law and masters of construction in aesthetics, makes them curious artefacts in the assessment of the facts and laws contested in the *Whaling in the Antarctic* case. Yet neither the parties nor the ICJ explained the purpose of the photographs in the proceedings. In this chapter, I show how analysis of the images from the perspective of the arts can entertain matters raised in the philosophy of environmental aesthetics that are relevant to the interpretation of the *Whaling Convention*. The *Whaling Convention* makes no express mention of aesthetic value. However, as explained in Chapter 3, the aesthetic value of whales is one of the reasons the states parties adopted at least one of the bans on whaling that was at issue in the dispute – the ban or 'moratorium' on commercial whaling.[10]

An aesthetic understanding of the photographic images can illuminate the legal rhetoric employed by the parties in the *Whaling in the Antarctic* proceedings and explain how the aesthetic value of whales was invoked in their submissions. For this purpose, I characterise rhetoric as a legitimate persuasive element of legal argument before the ICJ,[11] and I rely on scholars such as Costas Douzinas and Lynda Nead in my conception of photographic images as legal rhetoric.[12] My analysis addresses my specific concern in the book about how images of the natural environment in photographs could be used to make aesthetic value meaningful in international environmental law. Additionally, my linking of the photographs and rhetoric relates to the broader implications my attention to graphic images might have for the practice of international law in general.

In Section 6.2, I describe the findings of the ICJ in *Whaling in the Antarctic* in the context of the debate over commercial whaling in the International Whaling Commission (IWC). In Section 6.3, I identify the photographs used in the proceedings and analyse their purpose in light of the rules generally applied to graphic images before the ICJ. I undertake an aesthetic analysis of the whale photographs used in the case in Section 6.4, referencing visual art in Australia and Japan, where whalers and whales alike are revered. I conclude

9 See Section 6.3.1.

10 Clause 10(e) of the schedule to the *Whaling Convention*. See also International Whaling Commission, 'Verbatim Record', 19–24 July 1982, 72, 86.

11 See, for example, Scobbie, 'Rhetoric, persuasion, and interpretation in international law', 61; see Section 6.3.3.

12 Douzinas and Nead, 'Introduction', 1.

the chapter with a discussion of aesthetics and the rhetorical function of photographs in proceedings before the ICJ.

6.2 ICJ DECISION IN CONTEXT

The ICJ's decision in *Whaling in the Antarctic* was a pivotal development in a long-standing debate over commercial whaling among the parties to the *Whaling Convention*. The debate began with a recommendation for a moratorium from the 1972 *United Nations Conference on the Human Environment* in Stockholm,[13] and coalesced around the 1982 decision of members of the IWC to place a ban or 'moratorium' on commercial whaling.[14] Following the ICJ's decision, Japan withdrew its consent to be taken to the Court in future whaling matters,[15] and resumed whaling in Antarctica under a new programme.[16] After a further announcement of its intention to withdraw from the treaty altogether, effective in 2019, Japan retreated to its own territorial waters to hunt whales.[17] In this part, I describe developments in the International Whaling Commission leading up to Japan's withdrawal from the *Whaling Convention*,[18] before summarising the decision of the ICJ in *Whaling in the Antarctic*. This introduces my examination in Section 6.3 of the photographs presented by the parties in the proceedings.

6.2.1 *Debate in the IWC*

The unveiling of Captain Boomer's whale model in Madrid on 14 September 2018 (Figure 6.1) corresponded with the final day of the IWC's 67th meeting far from Spain in the city of Florianópolis, Brazil.[19] On that day, the parties to the *Whaling Convention* passed a resolution reaffirming 'the importance in maintaining the moratorium on commercial whaling'.[20] The resolution, eponymously titled the 'Florianópolis Declaration', was not likely binding in international law.[21] The moratorium of which it speaks, however, is binding

[13] UN Conference on the Human Environment, *Report*, UN Doc. A/CONF.48/14/Rev.1, p. 12 ('Recommendation 33').
[14] Clause 10(e) of the Schedule to the *Whaling Convention*.
[15] Japan, *Declaration Recognizing as Compulsory the Jurisdiction of the ICJ*, 6 October 2015.
[16] International Whaling Commission, *Chair's Report of the 67th Meeting*, annex O.
[17] *Whaling Convention*; Japan, *Note Verbale*; see www.state.gov/depositary-status-lists.
[18] See generally Fitzmaurice, *Whaling and International Law*, p. 71.
[19] International Whaling Commission, *Chair's Report of the 67th Meeting*.
[20] International Whaling Commission, 'Florianópolis declaration' in International Whaling Commission, *Chair's Report of the 67th Meeting*, annex F, 8–9.
[21] See *Whaling in the Antarctic* at para. [46].

on states parties that have not objected to it. As I explained in Chapter 3, the parties to the *Whaling Convention* agreed in 1982 to amend the treaty to set catch limits for commercial whaling at zero. Some parties to the treaty objected to the ban that would become effective in the 1985/1986 season while others withdrew from the treaty altogether.[22]

In its opening statement to the Florianópolis meeting, Australia observed that '[t]he world has changed dramatically over the 70 years since the [*Whaling Convention*] was first agreed. People across the world now recognise the link between healthy whale populations and healthy oceans, and the many benefits from sustainable whale watching and other eco-tourism activities'.[23] The UK Minister of State for Agriculture, Fisheries and Food said of the Florianópolis Declaration that it had delivered 'a clear statement from anti-whaling nations on their vision for the future of the IWC; one that is rooted in conservation without the need for commercial or scientific whaling'.[24]

The endorsement of the moratorium at the IWC meeting in Florianópolis was a tin ear response to the long-time efforts of some IWC members, led by Japan, to remove the zero catch limit on commercial whaling from the *Whaling Convention*.[25] Following yet another failed attempt at the Florianópolis meeting to circumvent the moratorium with an amendment to the *Whaling Convention*,[26] Japan gave notice of its intention to withdraw as a party to the treaty effective in 2019.[27] Australia had been strident in its opposition to Japan's 'Way Forward' initiative at the meeting, its Commissioner to the IWC Nick Gales reportedly stating that 'the debate was not about human rights, "nor is it a debate about the important subject of global food security", but was a "business proposition" against which there were "legitimate environmental and welfare concerns"'.[28]

The conflict over the moratorium on commercial whaling evident from the Florianópolis Declaration, and Japan's 'Way Forward' initiative at the IWC's meeting in 2018, has been central to the so-called whale wars. The states parties are divided over the treaty's purpose of 'ensuring the conservation of all

22 See Cl. 10(e) of the Schedule to the *Whaling Convention*.
23 Ruston, 'Opening statement' in International Whaling Commission, *Chair's Report of the 67th Meeting*, annex D, 3–4.
24 Eustice, 'Outcomes from the 67th meeting'.
25 For an historical account, see Nagtzaam, *The Making of International Environmental Treaties*, p. 181ff.
26 Japan, 'The way forward' in International Whaling Commission, *Chair's Report of the 67th Meeting*, 9.
27 Japan, *Note Verbale*.
28 Commissioner Nick Gales quoted in Readfearn, 'Whaling vote'.

species of whales while allowing for their sustainable exploitation'.[29] The divisions had been poised for a legal resolution after Australia complained earlier to the ICJ in 2010 that Japan's killing of whales in Antarctica violated the moratorium and other bans in the *Whaling Convention*.

6.2.2 *The Decision in* Whaling in the Antarctic

In *Whaling in the Antarctic*, the ICJ considered whether Japanese whaling in the Southern Ocean complied with the *Whaling Convention*. At issue were annual whaling permits granted from 2005 by Japan under JARPA II, a research whaling programme allowing for the killing of minke, fin and humpback whales in the Southern Ocean bordering Antarctica.[30] The Court considered whether whaling pursuant to JARPA II was scientific whaling exempted under Article VIII of the *Whaling Convention* from restrictions on whaling prescribed in the treaty's Schedule. Article VIII allows any party to the *Whaling Convention* to 'grant to any of its nationals a special permit authorizing that national to kill, take and treat whales for purposes of scientific research'. It further provides that such whaling 'shall be exempt from the operation of this Convention'. Under the Schedule, 'an integral part' of the treaty,[31] several restrictions on whaling apply to parties that have not formally objected to them.[32] In particular, clause 10(e) of the Schedule provides for zero catch limits for commercial whaling of all whale species – the ban on commercial whaling discussed earlier – while clause 10(d) bans factory ship whaling of certain species other than minke whales and clause 7 (b) prohibits commercial whaling of all species in the Southern Ocean Sanctuary. Japan is subject to each of these restrictions.[33]

Before the ICJ, Australia argued that Japan's whaling under JARPA II was not for purposes of scientific research within the meaning of Article VIII. Lethal method – the killing of whales in order to harvest organs, tissue and other biological samples for analysis – was identified by Australia as being unnecessary for the collection of scientifically relevant information.[34] Japan contested this claim, producing data gathered from analyses of whale organs,

[29] *Whaling in the Antarctic* at para. [56], based on the preamble to the *Whaling Convention*.

[30] JARPA II is the abbreviation for *Plan for the Second Phase of the Japanese Whale Research Program under Special Permit in the Antarctic II*.

[31] Article I.1 of the *Whaling Convention*.

[32] Clause 10(e) of the Schedule to the *Whaling Convention*.

[33] Except that Japan could undertake commercial whaling of minke whales in the Southern Ocean Sanctuary if the whaling ban were lifted: Note to Cl. 7(b) of the *Whaling Convention*.

[34] 'Memorial of Australia', vol. I, *List of Figures*, vii and *List of Photographs*, viii.

such as the content of stomachs, that it said was relevant to scientific conclusions as to whale diet, or the presence of mercury from polluted seas.[35]

In its consideration of Article VIII, the ICJ considered first whether whaling under JARPA II 'involves scientific research' and, second, whether it is 'for purposes of' such research.[36] The Court was at pains to distinguish its 'objective' review of the relationship between the means and ends of Japan's whaling in Antarctica from a review of the ends themselves.[37] Professing that 'it is not called upon to resolve matters of scientific or whaling policy',[38] the Court maintained that '[t]he stated research objectives of a [whaling] programme are the foundation of a programme's design, but the Court need not pass judgment on the scientific merit or importance of those objectives in order to assess the purpose of the killing of whales under such a programme.'[39] Japan succeeded on the first but failed on the second part of the ICJ's analysis under Article VIII. As to the first part of its assessment, the Court considered that Japan's 'lethal sampling of whales can broadly be characterized as "scientific research".'[40] JARPA II's four stated research objectives combined with the systematic collection of data analysed by scientists was enough to satisfy the Court in its first line of inquiry. As to the second part of its assessment, however, the Court concluded that 'the evidence does not establish that the [JARPA II] programme's design and implementation are reasonable in relation to achieving its stated objectives'.[41] In addition to addressing issues around sample sizes,[42] the Court expressed concerns about JARPA II's limited analysis of non-lethal methods,[43] the open-ended time frame,[44] the limited scientific output[45] and the lack of cooperation with other research institutions.[46]

Finding that whaling not covered by Article VIII is subject to the Schedule's restrictions on whaling,[47] the ICJ decided that Japan's whaling under JARPA II was largely inconsistent with the relevant bans in the Schedule.[48]

35 'Counter-memorial of Japan', vol. I, various images throughout.
36 *Whaling in the Antarctic* at para. [67].
37 Ibid.
38 Ibid., para. [69].
39 Ibid., para. [88].
40 Ibid., para. [127].
41 Ibid., para. [227]; conclusions summarised at paras. [225]–[226].
42 Ibid., paras. [181], [195], [198]; see also ibid., para. [179].
43 Ibid., para. [144]; see also ibid. (Ad Hoc Judge Charlesworth).
44 Ibid., para. [216].
45 Ibid., para. [219].
46 Ibid., para. [222].
47 Unless constituting 'aboriginal subsistence whaling': Cl. 13 of the Schedule to the *Whaling Convention*.
48 *Whaling in the Antarctic* at paras. [231]–[233].

In granting relief to Australia, the Court ordered Japan to revoke existing permits under JARPA II and to refrain from issuing new permits under that programme.

6.3 REPRESENTATION OF WHALES BEFORE THE ICJ

In their written and oral submissions to the ICJ, the parties to the *Whaling in the Antarctic* dispute relied on a range of visual images to support their claims.[49] Scientific experts also incorporated visual material into their reports and oral testimony.[50] The visual images comprised maps, graphs and diagrams to illustrate the concepts employed in the submissions. Maps, for example, showed where the Japanese whaling was taking place,[51] graphs showed such things as whale meat production,[52] while diagrams included figurative representations of ecosystem relationships.[53] The submissions also included photographs of whales and whale parts. In this section, I identify the photographs used by the parties in their submissions to the ICJ before describing the ICJ rules and practice on the use of photographs in proceedings.

6.3.1 *Photographs Presented in the Case*

The subject-matter of the photographs proffered by the parties in the *Whaling in the Antarctic* proceedings was different: Australia presented photographs of Japan's whaling while Japan submitted images of scientific applications of whale tissue. In particular, Australia included eight photographs in its written submission to the ICJ of Japanese whaling in Antarctica.[54] The images appeared in the context of an 'overview' of Japan's whaling practices.[55] Australian officials had taken the photographs during 'direct observation' of Japan's whaling practices in the 2007/08 season. The text preceding the photographs explained that '[k]illing a large animal moving at high speed is difficult and the process may have a range of impacts upon the data that can be collected from the whale. These impacts include damage from the

[49] See 'Memorial of Australia', *List of Figures*, vii; 'Counter-memorial of Japan' contains over twenty explanatory graphic images, most of which are identified as 'figures'.
[50] See, for example, statement of Mr Marc Mangel (expert called by Australia), 15 April 2013.
[51] See, for example, figure 5 in 'Memorial of Australia', 90; 'Counter-memorial of Japan', 39.
[52] See, for example, figure 7 in 'Memorial of Australia', 106; figure 3-2 in 'Counter-memorial of Japan', 106.
[53] See, for example, figure 5-2 in 'Counter-memorial of Japan', 238.
[54] 'Memorial of Australia', *List of photographs*, viii; see also pp. 96–103.
[55] Ibid., 88.

FIGURE 6.2. 'Photo 4: A harpooned whale being hauled to the side of one of Japan's whale catcher boats' in 'Memorial of Australia', vol. I, 99.

exploding grenade to the body tissues and internal organs or vomiting by the whale which empties its stomach'.[56]

In the oral proceedings, Australia's images were used again in the course of counsel's description of Japan's whaling methods and the examination of an expert witness.[57] Australia projected its photographs on the two large screens flanking the Judges' Bench.[58] For one photograph (Figure 6.13), Australia's legal counsel benignly identified 'the gentleman ... with the rifle' ready to shoot a whale not yet dead from the harpoon.[59] In the next day's hearing, a close-up image of a harpooned minke whale (Figure 6.2) was described by Australia's then expert witness (later Australia's Commissioner on the IWC), Dr Nick Gales: 'You can see coming out from behind the minke whale's blowhole the harpoon head and it will be presumably bent as the rope comes through from the other side so the whale is being pulled to the bow of the

56 Ibid., 95 [3.61].

57 *Whaling in the Antarctic*, 'Verbatim record 2013/8', 11–12; *Whaling in the Antarctic*, 'Verbatim record 2013/10', 22 (Dr Nick Gales, expert called by Australia); *Whaling in the Antarctic*, 'Verbatim record 2013/19', 27 (images of two scientists).

58 *Whaling in the Antarctic*, 'Audio-visual record', 26 June 2013, 01:50; *Whaling in the Antarctic*, 'Audio-visual record', 27 June 2013, 00:23.

59 'Verbatim record 2013/8', 60 (Philippe Sands QC).

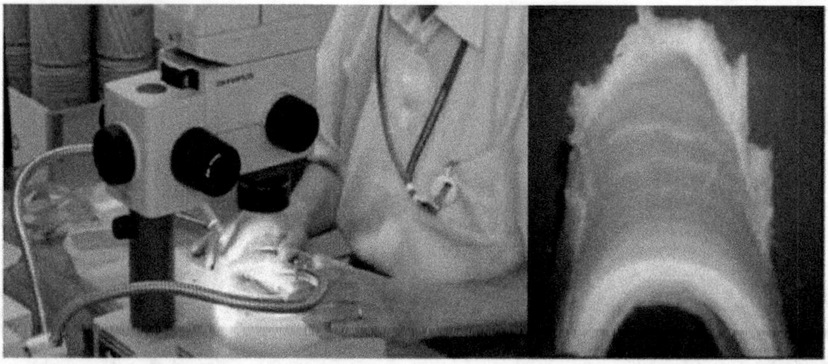

FIGURE 6.3. 'Photo 1 Earplug analysis' (attributed to Institute of Cetacean Research) in 'Counter-memorial of Japan', vol. I, 171.

ship'.[60] Photographs of non-lethal methods, including 'tagging', referenced in Dr Nick Gales' written statement to the Court, were also projected on the Court screens.[61]

In contrast to the Australian photographs, Japan's photographs included in its written submission on the necessity of lethal sampling could be seen to support its claims of scientific endeavour. Each 'photo' was a composite of two images. The source is identified as Japan's Institute of Cetacean Research. One of the images in a composite photograph (Figure 6.3) is of a scientist in a white lab coat testing indeterminate whale parts identified in the submission as 'ear plugs'.[62] The other image shows what is presumably the microscopic view of the ear plug tissue. Japan maintained that '[i]ndividual age is obtained by counting growth layers in the earplug which are formed in the external auditory meatus of baleen whales. . . . Because of its internal nature, the only way to access the earplugs is by lethal sampling.'[63] Another 'photo' in Japan's Counter-memorial (Figure 6.14) combines two images to depict scientific analysis of mercury in whale muscle,[64] with the accompanying text explaining that the testing for pollutants in whales requires lethal sampling.[65]

In the course of oral submissions, Japan presented a photographic montage of scientists purportedly working on board a whaling vessel, stating, 'Mr. President, I invite you to look at these photos. They show what the

60 'Verbatim record 2013/10', 22 (Dr Nick Gales).
61 Ibid.; see *Whaling in the Antarctic*, 'Statement by Dr Nick Gales', 32–3.
62 'Photo 1 earplug analysis' in 'Counter-memorial of Japan', 171.
63 Ibid.
64 'Photo 2: Analysis of mercury contained in muscle' in ibid., 177.
65 Ibid.

researchers do on board. Japan considers these activities to be scientific, but Australia does not share this point of view.'[66] The montage was included in the Judge's folder but neither the provenance of the images, nor the procedural grounds upon which the montage was included, are stated in the publicly available records of the proceedings. Elsewhere in its written submissions, Japan referenced but did not reproduce photographs of incidents in which ships belonging to the anti-whaling organisation Sea Shepherd Conservation Society 'rammed' Japanese whaling vessels.[67] In the oral proceedings, a photograph of two ships was projected on the court screens by counsel for Japan, described as showing a Sea Shepherd ship 'attacking' a Japanese scientific research vessel.[68] Counsel referred to the image in the context of Japanese claims that the reduced whale catch was due to the interference from Sea Shepherd as opposed to declining whale meat sales in Japan. It is not clear if the projected image was one of the photos referenced in the footnotes of Japan's Counter-memorial because the links to the website provided no longer function.

In its written decision, the ICJ reproduced one figure (Figure 6.4) that had been included in Japan's written submission to illustrate its process for determining whale catch sample size.[69] There was, however, no explanation for why this graphic image – one figure submitted by Japan out of several figures and photographs submitted by both parties – merited inclusion in the decision.[70] Indeed, there is no formal account of the relevance of any of the graphic images, photographic or otherwise, to the proceedings or the Judgment. In the next sections, I consider possible characterisations of the photographs in the proceedings as either evidence or rhetoric.

6.3.2 *Photographs as Evidence*

Presented in *Whaling in the Antarctic* in the context of factual submissions about lethal methods, the photographs could have been relevant to the proceedings as evidence. Neither the *Statute* nor the *Rules* of the ICJ make explicit mention of visual images or give directions on how they relate to legal

66 See *Whaling in the Antarctic*, 'Verbatim record 2013/13', 14; *Whaling in the Antarctic*, 'Verbatim record 2013/16', 28 (court tr. from French).

67 'Counter-memorial of Japan', 263 nn 729, 731.

68 *Whaling in the Antarctic*, 'Verbatim record 2013/12', paras. [75], [82].

69 *Whaling in the Antarctic* at para. [182], reproduced from 'Counter-memorial of Japan', 261 (attributed to Institute of Cetacean Research).

70 Cf. Porter, 'Taking images seriously'; Goodrich, 'Imago decidendi'; Goodrich, 'Retinal justice'; Rush, 'A sense of place with landmark judgments'.

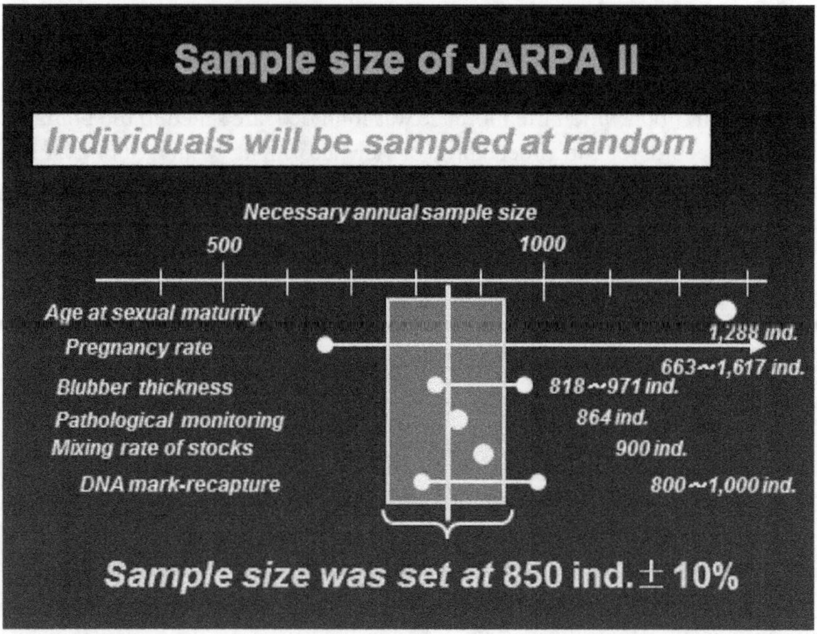

FIGURE 6.4. 'Figure 5-4. Necessary annual sample sizes for respective research items under JARPA II, which was calculated by the established statistical procedures' in *Whaling in the Antarctic* at para. [182].

process.[71] As a matter of practice, however, visual images such as maps, audio-visual material and photographs have been treated as evidence, received on the same basis as a 'document',[72] a term that is otherwise understood to refer to written materials.[73] The ICJ's apparent acceptance of the photographs in *Whaling in the Antarctic* is consistent with a long history of receiving graphic images as evidence in other cases.[74] In the first contentious case initiated in 1947, photographs of British ships destroyed by mines in the Corfu Channel were submitted in the pleadings.[75] Often presented by parties to prove

[71] *Statute of the International Court of Justice*, San Francisco, 26 June 1945, in force 24 October 1945, USTS 993; International Court of Justice, *Rules of Court*, 14 April 1978. This chapter does not extend to practices with visual images in other international adjudicatory fora: See, e.g., Amerasinghe, *Evidence in International Litigation*, p. 394.

[72] See Aguilar Mawdsley, 'Evidence before the ICJ', 547.

[73] 'Document' is not defined in the *ICJ Statute* or *ICJ Rules*. Documentary evidence generally includes written materials such as treaties, official records and diplomatic communications: Shaw, 'Documents in Support'.

[74] See Riddell and Plant, *Evidence before the ICJ*, p. 283; Valencia-Ospina, 'Evidence before the ICJ', 204.

[75] 'Memorial of the United Kingdom', *Corfu Channel (United Kingdom of Great Britain and Northern Ireland v. Albania)*, International Court of Justice, 30 September 1947, Annex 8 [16].

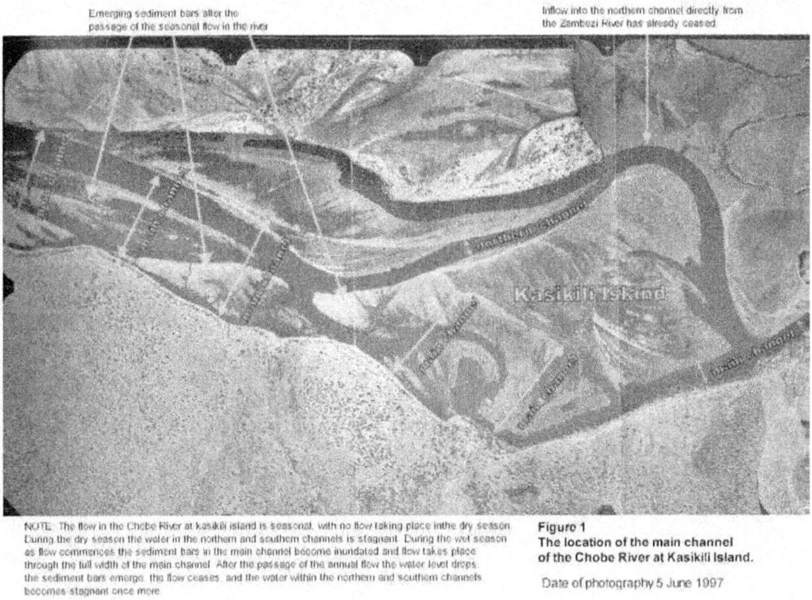

FIGURE 6.5. 'Figure 1 The location of the main channel of the Chobe River at Kasikili Island' in Namibia, 'Reply of the Republic of Namibia', 27 November 1998, the International Court of Justice, Kasikili/Sedudu Island (*Botswana v. Namibia*), following page 23, reproduced in black and white in *Kasikili/Sedudu Island* (*Botswana v. Namibia*) (*Judgment*) [1999] ICJ Rep 1045 at 1069.

territorial or maritime boundaries,[76] photographs have also been used to support claims of damage to land.[77] Written claims of genocide have been supported by photographic images of places, events and injuries to people.[78] Photographs submitted by the parties have also been reproduced by the Court in its written judgments (e.g., Figure 6.5).

[76] See, for example, *Maritime Delimitation and Territorial Questions between Qatar and Bahrain (Qatar v. Bahrain) (Judgment)* [2001] ICJ Rep 40, [109]; *Frontier Dispute (Benin/Niger) (Judgment)* [2005] ICJ Rep 90, [40]; see also Aguilar Mawdsley, 'Evidence before the ICJ', 547.

[77] See, for example, 'Memorial of the Republic of Nauru', *Certain Phosphate Lands in Nauru (Nauru v. Australia)*, International Court of Justice, vol. 1, April 1990, annex [96], [200]–[201], [211]–[213]; 'Memorial of The Republic of Hungary', *Gabčíkovo-Nagymaros Project (Hungary/Slovakia)*, International Court of Justice, vol. 1, 2 May 1994, Annex 2, 492; note also 'Memorial of Slovak Republic', *Gabčíkovo-Nagymaros Project (Hungary/Slovakia)* xi.

[78] See *Application of the Convention on the Prevention and Punishment of the Crime of Genocide (Bosnia and Herzegovina v. Serbia and Montenegro) (Judgment)* [2007] ICJ Rep 43, para. [52]; see also 'Counter-memorial of the Federal Republic of Yugoslavia', *Application of the Convention on the Prevention and Punishment of the Crime of Genocide (Bosnia and Herzegovina v. Serbia and Montenegro)* International Court of Justice, 23 July 1997, Chapter VII, Annex No. C 160, 1118.

The ready acceptance of visual images by the ICJ stems from the principle of free admissibility of evidence.[79] Owing its jurisdiction to the voluntary submission of states, the Court accepts all evidence presented in the written pleadings of the parties.[80] Allowing the images to be submitted to the Court does not necessarily mean, however, that it will take them into account in its judgments. The ICJ is more discerning in its *evaluation* of the evidence than in its acceptance of it. It appears from those cases in which the Court has explained the basis for its evaluation that the ICJ assesses relevance and accords different probative value to different categories of evidence.[81] Probative value has been identified as generally depending on 'the reliability and neutrality of the source of such evidence.'[82] The Court has explained that it will 'treat with caution' evidentiary materials that have been prepared specifically for the purposes of a case and 'materials emanating from a single source'.[83]

Imagistic evidence has not fared well in the ICJ's evaluations. Maps are generally considered to be circumspect or false: That maps were historically unreliable and self-serving has justified caution in their evaluation by the Court in the past.[84] Likewise, audio-visual materials have typically been afforded little if any weight. Particular scrutiny of the authenticity and purpose for which audio-visual material was made has led the Court to downgrade the relevance of such evidence in its judgment of the facts.[85] There is less judicial comment from which to assess the Court's approach to photographic images. However, similar considerations of relevance and probative value would likely apply.[86] ICJ *Practice Direction* IX*quater* explains when audio-visual or

79 See Quintana, *Litigation at the ICJ*, p. 385; Riddell and Plant, *Evidence before the ICJ*, p. 152; Aguilar Mawdsley, 'Evidence before the ICJ', 533–4, 539.

80 Note Articles 43(2) (supporting documentation) and 52 (power to refuse further evidence) of the *ICJ Statute*.

81 See Kolb, *Elgar Companion to the ICJ*, p. 314; Riddell and Plant, *Evidence Before the ICJ*, p. 234. Visual evidence is sometimes 'demonstrative or real evidence': Quintana, *Litigation at the ICJ*, p. 426.

82 Benzing, 'Evidentiary issues', 1405 [114].

83 *Armed Activities on the Territory of the Congo (Democratic Republic of the Congo v. Uganda) (Judgment)* [2005] ICJ Rep 168, para. [61]; *Application of the Genocide Convention*, para. [213].

84 See, for example, *Frontier Dispute (Burkina Faso/Republic of Mali) (Judgment)* [1986] ICJ Rep 554, para. [61]; *The Temple of Preah Vihear (Cambodia v. Thailand) (Judgment) (Merits)* [1962] ICJ Rep 6, pp. 70–1 (Judge Quintana); *Certain Activities Carried Out by Nicaragua in the Border Area (Costa Rica v. Nicaragua) (Judgment)* [2015] ICJ Rep 665. See Riddell and Plant, *Evidence Before the ICJ*, p. 256; Benzing, 'Evidentiary issues', 1410 [128].

85 See Riddell and Plant, *Evidence before the ICJ*, pp. 287–8.

86 The Court has requested the origin of photographs and of other visual material presented during oral proceedings: See, for example, *Application of the Genocide Convention*, p. 52.

photographic material not previously included in the written submissions may be allowed at a later stage in the proceedings, requiring for example that the source and circumstances of its making be specified.[87]

Whether the ICJ in *Whaling in the Antarctic* considered any of the images submitted by the parties in terms of evidence is not apparent from the Judgment: It is not uncommon for the Court's evaluation of evidence to go unstated.[88] On the last day of the oral proceedings in *Whaling in the Antarctic*, counsel for Japan made specific mention of the Court's *Practice Direction* IX*quater* as preventing him from projecting certain images in court.[89] Yet the Court had previously acquiesced to the projection of visual images during oral submissions, including photographs not previously included in written submissions, providing no insight into the Court's treatment of the images.[90] The photographs in the *Whaling in the Antarctic* proceedings would nevertheless appear to have little if any evidentiary value. Australia's photographs were presented in its written submissions with statements about lethal method being counter-productive to the collection of useful data. Lethal method, it claimed, can damage body tissue and organs and empty stomach contents. The photographs show some damaged tissue but they do not show damage to organs specifically required for scientific analysis. Instead, Australia's photographs show that whales were killed by harpoon, a fact that is not denied by Japan. The evidentiary value of Japan's photographs is similarly impugned. They were submitted in the written submissions with statements claiming that lethal method is necessary for the collection of data useful to the aims of the JARPA II programme. The photographs show a technical process. They do not prove that the tissue of whales caught by lethal method under the JARPA II programme was used in that technical process or that it generated data relevant to scientific analysis.

Presumably aware of the flawed nature of the photographs as evidence, the parties might have contemplated a broader purpose for the images they employed. They might, for example, have relied on the photographs as a form of legal rhetoric,[91] enabling their arguments as to the scientific merits, or otherwise, of lethal methods in the research of whales.

87 International Court of Justice, *Practice Direction IXquater*, 11 April 2013.

88 Benzing, 'Evidentiary issues', 1402 [103]. See generally Chen, 'Re-Assessing the Evidentiary Regime'.

89 See *Whaling in the Antarctic*, 'Verbatim record 2013/23', 17 (M. Alain Pellet).

90 See, for example, photographic montages of scientists at work in *Whaling in the Antarctic*, 'Verbatim record 2013/13', 14; *Whaling in the Antarctic*, 'Verbatim record 2013/16', 28.

91 See generally Sarat (ed.), *Rhetorical Processes and Legal Judgments*. Cf. Goodrich, *Legal Discourse*.

6.3.3 *Photographs as Rhetoric*

In practice, ICJ proceedings are dispassionate, typically devoid of 'drama' and emotion.[92] The rules and practice of the ICJ restrict the length and form of written and oral submissions,[93] possibly discouraging 'heated debate and pungent polemics' and instead fostering a 'courteous and business like atmosphere maintained throughout'.[94] To acknowledge rhetoric as a function of legal argument, and still further to characterise graphic image as a rhetorical device, might be a step too far for a dogmatic practitioner of international law. But from a perspective of aesthetic theory, there can be no practice of law without rhetoric.[95] Photographs can in this sense be used in the service of persuasive argument to posit meanings for law – meanings that can underscore or augment written and verbal arguments. In the clinical environs of the ICJ, graphic images can serve as a rhetorical device in a very practical sense, adding persuasive significance to legal argument that is otherwise expected to be unsentimental.[96]

Rhetoric for my purposes is the 'art' of persuasion in legal argument, or the 'art' in legal proceedings that contemplates style and performance of written or verbal language. I extend rhetoric to the style and performance of graphic images, including representational images such as photographs. Common law theorist James Boyd White describes rhetoric from the perspective of writing and reading law but,[97] as discussed in Chapter 4, critical legal scholars such as Costas Douzinas and Lynda Nead have interrogated legal rhetoric in terms of 'image', which can include graphic images.[98]

By 'rhetoric', I do not mean to invoke the rhetoric that is commonly associated with the meta-narratives of international law and politics.[99] I understand rhetoric in a more modest way, as the 'alchemy' of legal argument,[100] the advocate's deft use of image – verbal images in speech or graphic images displayed – to persuade. My characterisation of rhetoric concerns

92 See, for example, Eyffinger, *The International Court of Justice*, pp. 136–7. Cf. Higgins, 'Respecting Sovereign States', 130; Black, 'The Tasmanian Dam Case'.
93 Quintana, *Litigation at the ICJ*, p. 355.
94 Eyffinger, *The International Court of Justice*, pp. 136–7.
95 See, for example, Reichman, 'Narrative and rhetoric', 377. See also Scobbie, 'Rhetoric, persuasion and interpretation in international law'; Kotecha, 'The art of rhetoric'.
96 Cf. Simpson, *Sentimental Life of International Law.*
97 See White, 'Imagining the law', 29.
98 Douzinas and Nead, 'Introduction', 8–9. In the context of the common law in the United States, see Porter, 'Taking images seriously'.
99 See, for example, Koskenniemi, 'The politics of international law'.
100 See Johnson, 'The alchemy of style and law', 261.

persuasive argument elucidating rather than obfuscating the law.[101] It is for my purposes craft not bombast. This is arguably a classical conception of rhetoric as power in argument before a court,[102] where I position graphic image as exposition not exhibition. Immi Tallgren calls it simply the power of images.[103] I distinguish my characterisation of image as rhetoric from dogmatic characterisations of image as 'evidence' of fact. This is not to claim that rhetoric is irrelevant to the advocate's presentation of evidence. Rather, I maintain that graphic image can also serve a rhetorical function apart from the evidence of fact, in the presentation of the law.

The rhetorical purchase of the photographs submitted by Australia was indirectly acknowledged in a subsequent domestic legal proceeding. The Australian Government denied a freedom of information request for footage of Japanese whaling on the basis that it would 'harm relations with Japan'.[104] Overturning the decision, the review authority found that the photographs submitted to the ICJ by Australia in *Whaling in the Antarctic* had already put the imagery in the public domain.[105] However, advocates appearing before the ICJ might be loath to characterise images as rhetoric if the images can be admitted as evidence but function as rhetoric. There is otherwise a risk that judges of the ICJ would dismiss them as a distortion of the law,[106] or as a legitimate but ineffective rhetorical device.

Ultimately, there is no formal account of graphic image in ICJ practice that explains the parties' use of the photographs in the *Whaling in the Antarctic* proceedings. The photographs are, I explained earlier, not evidence but nor are they, in my analysis, necessarily irrelevant simply by virtue of being graphic images. In the next part, I use aesthetic method to illuminate a rhetorical function for the photographs. I situate the photographs in visual art in Australia and Japan to analyse the different ways they engage and disengage an aesthetic appeal of whales that is relevant to the parties' claims in the *Whaling in the Antarctic* dispute. While legal scholars such as Boyd White promote an understanding of verbal images in words and speech of legal

[101] See, for example, discussion of contrasting Platonic and Aristotelian traditions of rhetoric in Sarat and Kearns, 'Editorial introduction', 7.

[102] See generally Frost, *Introduction to Classical Legal Rhetoric*.

[103] Tallgren, 'Come and see?'. See also Rush and Elander, 'Working through the cinematography'. Note Nettel, 'The power of image'.

[104] *Sea Shepherd Australia and Department of Immigration and Border Protection (Freedom of information)* [2017] AICmr 48.

[105] Ibid.

[106] See Section 6.5.2.

argument as rhetoric, I attend to the photographic images as an object for rhetorical analysis.

6.4 REPRESENTATIONS OF ART IN THE PHOTOGRAPHS

Australia and Japan have a rich history of representing whales in visual art. As demonstrated below, an analysis of the photographs submitted by the parties in the *Whaling in the Antarctic* proceedings in light of select visual artworks representing whales in Australia and Japan, from the nineteenth to the present century, reveals aesthetic and other values of whales relevant to the depictions in the photographs. The aesthetic method adopted here is one of several strategies for analysing graphic images that was discussed in Chapter 4.[107] I use aesthetic methods relevant to visual art but I take account also of the philosophy of environmental aesthetics. The field of environmental aesthetics addresses the aesthetic value of whales as an animal in the natural environment as opposed to the aesthetic value of the artistic representations of whales. The role of art in understandings of environmental aesthetics concerning wild animals has been acknowledged in aesthetic philosophy,[108] a qualification to the position of those philosophers of environmental aesthetics who maintain a clear division in the aesthetic appreciation of the environment as opposed to the arts.[109]

6.4.1 *Australia's Representations of Whales in Art*

From the killing of the first whale off the Australian coast by British whalers in October 1791,[110] to the processing of the last whale at the Western Australian Cheynes Beach Whaling Company in 1978,[111] the image of whales in Australia has found artistic form in a massive and mystical creature of the sea, once to be conquered, now to be revered.[112] By the 1970s, humane considerations came to surpass the waning economic benefits of whaling, leading then Prime Minister Malcolm Fraser to announce the end to whaling in Australia by the close of that decade in the following terms:

107 See Levinson, 'Philosophical aesthetics', 3. See Section 4.3.
108 See Brady, 'Aesthetic value and wild animals', 188, 192, 199.
109 See Section 2.2.1.
110 'Letter from Thomas Melville, captain of ship Britannia'.
111 See Ellis, *Men and Whales*, p. 104.
112 See Kalland, *Unveiling the Whale*, p. 44. See, for example, Dakin, *Whalemen Adventurers*; Ellis, *Men and Whales*.

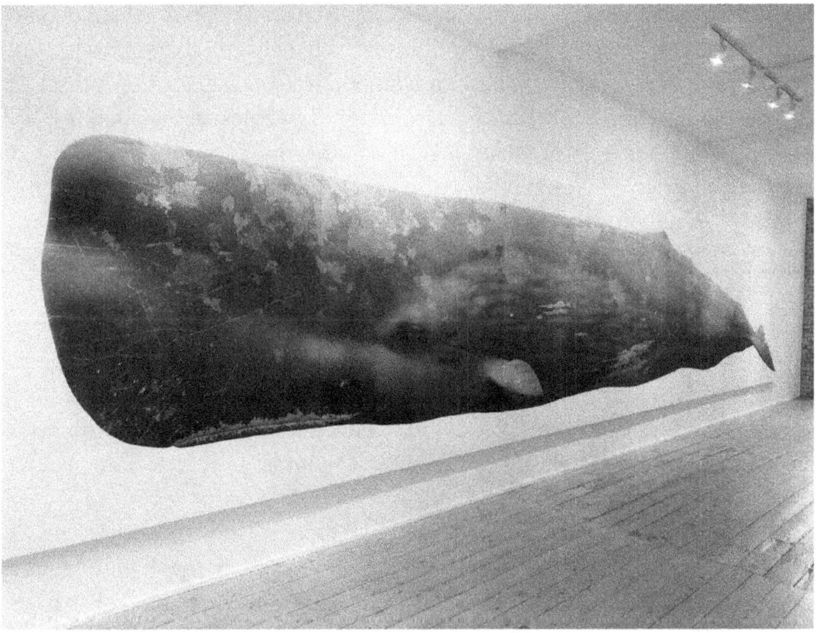

FIGURE 6.6. Jonathan Delafield Cook, *Sperm Whale II*, 2013. Charcoal on primed linen, 245 × 1200 cm. © Jonathan Delafield Cook. Courtesy the artist and Olsen Gallery, Sydney.

> There is a natural community concern about an activity which threatens the extinction of any species, particularly when it is directed against a species as special and intelligent as the whale and where there is a fear that the continued existence of these special forms of wildlife are threatened by continued exploitation. ... The harpooning of these mammals is offensive to many people who regard killing them as inconsistent with the ideals of mankind and without serving any valid economic purpose in mitigation.[113]

Jonathan Delafield Cook's 12-metre-long charcoal drawing of a sperm whale in 2013 depicts what was for the Australian Prime Minister a 'special and intelligent' mammal (Figure 6.6). Seemingly suspended in time and space, this delicate whale image goes beyond the *a situ* representations of eighteenth-century natural historians with the sense of wonder and serenity it invokes, its individual markings, the scars and scratches of a life at sea, its gaze.[114] The work's arresting scale recalls the actual size of the animal itself. The treatment

[113] Commonwealth of Australia, *Parliamentary Debates*, House of Representatives, 4 April 1979, 1481.
[114] Cf. Bonnaterre, 'Histoire naturelle: Cétacés' plate 7, Hand-coloured copper plate engraving.

of whales by humans has been described as a marker of a civilised nation and Delafield Cook's portrayal might well inspire a beneficent attitude towards all species and their habitats.[115] His work suits former leader of the Australian Greens party Bob Brown's understanding of whales as 'mysterious ... unthreatening, amiable or technologically innocent'.[116]

Philosopher of environmental aesthetics, Emily Brady has considered the nature of aesthetic value as it applies to wild animals, applying by analogy some of the theories developed for visual art to understand human responses to the expressiveness of wild animals.[117] She also contemplates the symbolic associations of wild animals as a cultural influence in aesthetic appreciation. Brady would likely characterise Delafield Cook's rendition of the sperm whale, and the political understandings of whales as 'special and intelligent',[118] as related to certain features of whales.[119] This might include their expressive qualities – such as their movement, their sounds and their eyes – as a semblance of human expression.[120]

The butchering of the mammal with the harpoon head seen in Australia's fourth photograph (Figure 6.2) would be jarring, possibly reprehensible, to a viewer more inured to a Delafield Cook-like presentation of whales (Figure 6.6). In its eighth photograph (Figure 6.7), Australia shows a whale being dragged up the blood-soaked slipway of the whaling vessel, the black ribbed hull of the ship a humpback's underbelly, the slipway a ravenous mouth. The photographs invite judgement on the ethical and aesthetic dimensions of killing whales, relying on the aesthetic of the whale as 'special and intelligent' to impugn Japan's claims that its whaling is for purposes of scientific research. This is the same aesthetic sensibility discussed at the beginning of this chapter that Captain Boomer invoked with its whale model in the Manzanares River (Figure 6.1).

But Delafield Cook's beneficent whale is a relatively recent contribution to artistic portrayals of whales in Australian waters. From the industry's beginnings in Australia, the legacy of European accounts of whales and whaling in

[115] See Kalland, *Unveiling the Whale*, pp. 18, 133. See also Vincent, *Blood & Guts*, pp. 40, 136, 193, 196.

[116] Brown, 'Letter to Sea Shepherd'.

[117] Brady, 'Aesthetic value and wild animals'; see also Rolston III, 'Beauty and the beast', 187; Parsons, 'The aesthetic value of animals'; Hettinger, 'Animal beauty, ethics'. Cf. Parsons and Carlson, *Functional Beauty*.

[118] Commonwealth of Australia, *Parliamentary Debates*, House of Representatives, 4 April 1979, 1481.

[119] Also 'mysterious ... unthreatening, amiable or technologically innocent': Brown, 'Letter to the Sea Shepherd'.

[120] Brady, 'Aesthetic value and wild animals'.

FIGURE 6.7. 'Photo 8: A harpooned whale being hauled up the stern slipway of Japan's factory ship, the Nisshin-Maru' in 'Memorial of Australia', vol. I, 103.

art and literature imbued the art of Europeans in Australia, from illustrated logbooks and scrimshaws to large-scale paintings.[121] Nineteenth-century

[121] This chapter does not address images of whales by Indigenous peoples in Australia, or the participation of Indigenous people in post-settlement whaling in Australia. See further Clode, *Killers in Eden*, p. 151. See also Newton, *A Savage History*, p. 40.

FIGURE 6.8. Oswald Brierly, *Whalers off Twofold Bay, New South Wales*, 1867. Watercolour with white highlights and scraping out, 86.3 × 147.5 cm. Collection of the Art Gallery of New South Wales.

British-born whaler and artist Oswald Brierly developed significant artistic accounts of Australia's whaling. Unlike JMW Turner, whose dramatic British whaling scenes were likely based on depictions from natural history sources,[122] Brierly's elaborate oil paintings command particular authority, drawing on his first-hand experience of whale hunts documented in his 'reminiscences' of whaling in colonial Australia. His recollections of the fear and courage inspired by the whale hunt are expressed in his 1867 painting *Whalers off Twofold Bay, New South Wales* (Figure 6.8).

Brierly's works depict a fervent heyday of whaling in Australian waters where '[l]ike gold-seeking, [whaling] gripped its men to the exclusion of all else'.[123] Danger and awe combined in the perfect subject for the Romantic painter. Brierly recalled: 'I shall never forget the new & sickening sensation of finding the whole boat suddenly lifted out of the water by the rising back of the whale, and the sliding gliding helplessly slipping motion of the boat as it shot down the back of the monster under us.'[124] This whaler's sentiment would persist in Australia's endemic whale tales and imagery for decades to come. The infamous Old Tom, an orca whale that reputedly assisted the whalers in

[122] See Hokanson, 'Turner's whaling pictures', 17.
[123] Dakin, *Whalemen Adventurers*, p. 11.
[124] See Brierly, 'The Cetacea or reminiscences of the sea', cited by Australian Art Department, 'Sir Oswald Brierly'.

Twofold Bay by herding baleen whales within reach of the harpoons in exchange for the hunted whales' lips and tongues,[125] was Australia's own ghoulish twist on the whale myth.

Yet the daring-do of the whale hunt seen in the nineteenth-century Australian paintings of Brierly and others is notably absent from the graphic scenes depicted in the whale photographs submitted by Australia in the *Whaling in the Antarctic* proceedings (e.g., Figure 6.2). Gone are the large-scale beasts against small-scale whalers in thrashing seas. Instead, in Australia's images, the dying but not yet dead mammals are diminished against the enormous ships that tow them from the water. Blood does not gush or spray, it ekes in a slow and presumably painful death that is inhumane and unethical and wholly inconsistent with aesthetic representations of whales in Australia today. Australia's photographs undo the legacy of whaling bravado in its aesthetic history with the close image of the gored whale (Figure 6.2) and the bloody carcass dragged away for dissection (Figure 6.7).

However, it was not all blood and courage in nineteenth-century Australian representations of whaling. British artist John Skinner Prout portrayed a more desolate Australian whaling image in his circa 1874 print 'Old Whaling Station' (Figure 6.9). Against the backdrop of a rugged Tasmanian skyline, the bleached whale skull abandoned in the shallows of calm water is far removed from the drama of skiffs on turbulent high seas, thrashing beasts and bloody spray of the whale hunt depicted by Brierly and others. Nor is this a stranded whale carcass, such a curiosity that whale skeletons would eventually become a staple of natural history museums.[126] This is the skull of a dismembered whale, the diminished and spent remains of the great creature that once was, abandoned on a remote shore. Skinner Prout's serene yet sinister image is perhaps a portentous comment on the industry's decline, a meditative musing on an exhausted resource, no longer flesh and blood, just bone, sharp and angular like the inanimate rocks and barren mountains around it. The whale skull would reappear, over a century later, in contemporary Australian artist Rick Amor's 1993 print 'The whale' (Figure 6.10). It was around this time, in 1992, that Australia had recognised a state of global environmental insecurity with its signing of two major international treaties

[125] See Dakin, *Whalemen Adventurers*, p. 155; see also Clode, *Killers in Eden*, pp. 8, 64. For still photographic image, see 'Old Tom, swimming alongside a whaling boat that is being towed by a harpooned whale (out of frame to the right). A whale calf can be seen between Old Tom and the boat', still from the 1910 documentary by C.E. Wellings & C.B. Jenkins, *Whale Chase in Twofold Bay*.

[126] The 'Ostend Whale' is purportedly the first touring whale skeleton: Ellis, *Men and Whales*, pp. 371–2.

FIGURE 6.9. John Skinner Prout, *Old Whaling Station*, c. 1874. Engraving by Edward Paxman Brandard. Image extracted from Edwin Carton Booth, *Australia … Illustrated with Drawings by Skinner Prout, N. Chevalier*, vol. 1, 39. Original held and digitised by the British Library. *Source*: Wikimedia Commons.

FIGURE 6.10. Rick Amor, *The whale*, 1993. Etching, 20 × 30.5 cm. © Rick Amor. Courtesy the artist and Niagara Galleries, Melbourne.

addressing climate change and the protection of biodiversity.[127] With the foreboding clouds above and rising waters below, Amor's whale skull could be seen to carry a significant message, the fate of the endangered mammal species a warning for humanity. It is the futility and desolation of the works by Skinner Prout and Amor – over a century apart – that Australia captures in its photographs submitted to the ICJ.

6.4.2 *Japanese Art on Whales*

Ironically, Japan's history of artistic representations of whales and whaling supports a claim of respect for whales in death.[128] In contrast to Australia's history of post-settlement whaling with harpoons, Japanese whalers practised artisanal whaling using nets over several centuries before expanding to modern whaling with mechanised harpoons in the early twentieth century.[129] Whales were predominantly hunted for their meat but modern whaling techniques saw them also processed for oil.[130] The Buddhist prohibition on the consumption of meat was avoided by naming whales 'brave fish' (isana) and, later, 'big fish' (kujira).[131] The sacrifice of a whale's life was nevertheless the subject of sacred rituals, with chants and dances an important feature of the whaling seasons.[132] Upon the death of a hunted whale, whalers would 'chant three times "May its soul rest in peace," and express their thanks to god and Buddha in a hymn for the capture of the most prized and great right whale'.[133]

Associated with religious beliefs, Japan's artistic depictions of whales through history are complex and varied. Buddhist-inspired understandings of whales prevalent in Japan honour and celebrate the life of whales. Shrines and monuments are dedicated to whales in Japan's coastal whaling

[127] *United Nations Framework Convention on Climate Change*, New York, 9 May 1992, in force 21 March 1994, 1771 UNTS 107 (Australia signed 4 June 1992 and ratified 30 December 1992); *Convention on Biological Diversity*, Rio de Janeiro, 5 June 1992, in force 29 December 1993, 1760 UNTS 79 (Australia signed 5 June 1992 and ratified 18 June 1993).

[128] See below. See also Utagawa Kuniyoshi, *Whaling Scene at Goto, Hirado or Kishu*.

[129] Ellis, *Men and Whales*, pp. 266–7. See also Kalland and Moeran, *Japanese Whaling: End of an Era?*

[130] Ellis, *Men and Whales*, pp. 266–7.

[131] Ibid., p. 82.

[132] Ibid., p. 87. See also Kalland, *Unveiling the Whale*, p. 155.

[133] Yosei, *Yogiotoru Eshi* [Pictures of whaling], cited in Ellis, *Men and Whales*, p. 86; see also Vincent, *Blood & Guts*, p. 124.

FIGURE 6.11. Katsushika Hokusai, *Whaling Scene on the Coast of Gotō*, c. 1830. Woodblock print. *Source*: Wikimedia Commons.

communities.[134] Nineteenth-century Japanese art celebrates the whale hunt in much the same way as Brierly and other European artists of that era. The ingenuity and industry of whalers is depicted in the works of Hokusai (Figure 6.11), Kuniyoshi (Figure 6.12), Koson and other *ukiyo-e* masters exploring landscape and legend through painting and woodblock prints in the 1800s.[135] The other-worldly creatures are shown overcome at sea or dissected near to shore. Whales are also a significant feature of Japanese folklore, with whale protagonists appearing in stories of courage and adversity. In Utagawa Kuniyoshi's woodblock print *Miyamoto no Musashi Attacking the Giant Whale* (Figure 6.12), a famed Japanese swordsman rides on the back of a whale performing the *ken kiri* or lancing of the whale. In real life, this would occur only after the whale had been weakened by hand-thrown harpoons. Described as a scene much anticipated by Japanese whalers, Yomada Yosei

[134] See Kalland and Moeran, *Japanese Whaling: End of an Era?*, 150–7. See also Vincent, *Blood & Guts*, pp. 109, 124–5.

[135] See, for example, The New Bedford Whaling Museum, *Pacific Encounters*, including Koson, *Hogei sogakari no zu* [Attacking a whale in unison], 10. On Ukiyoe art, see Edmonds et al., 'Japan, §VI, 4'.

FIGURE 6.12. Utagawa Kuniyoshi, *Miyamoto no Musashi Attacking the Giant Whale*, c. 1847–50. Triptych woodblock print. *Source*: Wikimedia Commons.

wrote in 1829 that this moment 'was terrible enough to make one break out in a cold sweat'.[136]

Australia's photographs can be seen in dialogue with Japanese aesthetics, belittling Japan for its lack of respect or reverence seen in its art history. In Australia's third photograph (Figure 6.13), instead of the famed Japanese swordsman Musashi astride the whale, a Japanese whaler – in Australia's counsel's words, 'the gentleman ... with the rifle'[137] – stands at the ready to deliver the *coup de grace*. A safe distance from the beast, rifle not sword in hand, the whaler is seen for Australia's purposes to be cowardly and merciless. Australia's eighth photograph (Figure 6.7) exploits the juxtaposition between the visual image of the savaged whale carcass and the written inscription 'Legal Research under the ICRW' on the Japanese whaling vessels, the written word presented here as a baseless expression of Japan's preferred interpretation of the images of its whaling practices as legitimate in international law. The words would later be removed when the same ship set sail to hunt whales in Japan's territorial waters.[138]

In contrast to Australia's images, the sanitised setting of the Japanese photographs – the laboratory emphasising the scientific purpose – de-animates the whale, creating an image that has no association with the visual history of whales in either Japan or Australia. Despite the glimpse of different whale

[136] Yosei, *Yogiotoru Eshi* [Pictures of whaling].
[137] 'Verbatim record 2013/8', 60 [12] (Philippe Sands QC).
[138] See Palmer, 'Absent images of international law'.

FIGURE 6.13. 'Photo 3 A harpooned whale being hauled to the side of one of Japan's whale catcher boats, while a Japanese whaler aims a rifle at it' in 'Memorial of Australia', vol. I, 98.

species on a chart in one image (Figure 6.14), the caption for the photographs of scientists at work might well read: 'This is not a whale.' To be effective as rhetoric, the photographs submitted by Japan would need to have no visual associations with the lives of mighty whales that have been celebrated in Japanese culture and grandly represented in the country's visual art. Yet even the method of combining two images, to make one composite photograph, employs Japanese artistic methods and aesthetic sensibility. Japan's photographic diptych recalls the segmented images of folding screens or double-page illustrations common to books presenting Japanese *manga* 'sketches' in the nineteenth century.[139] The original photograph of the ear plug tissue has been manipulated for the submission (Figure 6.3), stretched to complement the other image in the diptych, compromising the veracity of the photographs

139 Tinios, '2. Edo period'.

FIGURE 6.14. 'Photo 2: Analysis of mercury contained in muscle' (attributed to Institute of Cetacean Research) in 'Counter-memorial of Japan', vol. I, 177.

for the sake of aesthetic convention. The Japanese photographs reference aesthetic values despite themselves.

Japan's footnote references to photographs of incidents between activist Sea Shepherd vessels and Japanese whaling ships are also relevant to an analysis of the parties' use of photographic images.[140] The use of the word 'rammed' to describe the collisions, summons nineteenth-century visual art – in Australia and Japan – where whalers' boats are tossed in the air on the back of a whale. Whale as menace has been a constant in Japanese artistic imagery. Depicted in twentieth-century artist Shigeru Mizuki manga style,[141] the legend of *Bake Kujira* tells the story of a skeleton whale that roamed the seas terrorising whalers, unperturbed by the swords thrown by fearful sailors. Contemporary artist Takashi Murakami might well have created his own take on this whale demon in his painting 727 (Figure 6.15). Murakami's Mr DOB,[142] a formerly benevolent character recurring in his works, is transformed in this painting into a maniacal creature, all-seeing and all-knowing, riding waves painted in a style that recalls traditional Japanese artistic methods, its gaping mouth like that of a toothed whale species at the ready to swallow all in its path.

Looking at photographs on the website of the Japanese Institute of Cetacean Research,[143] however, a different image from the one provided by Japan in the text of its submission is revealed. The Sea Shepherd vessels hardly look set to

[140] *Whaling in the Antarctic*, 'Counter-memorial of Japan', 263, nn 729, 731.
[141] Shigeru Mizuki, *Bake-Kujira*, in *No Yōkai Jiten*, p. 19.
[142] See Falconer and Chou, 'Murakami, Takashi'.
[143] The URLs provided in *Whaling in the Antarctic*, 'Counter-memorial of Japan' 263, nn 729, 731 no longer function; images published by the Institute of Cetacean Research fit the description of those referenced in the submission: See www.icrwhale.org/08-AENG.html.

FIGURE 6.15. Takashi Murakami, 727, 1996. Acrylic on canvas mounted on board, three panels, 3000 × 4500 × 70 mm. © 1996 Takashi Murakami/Kaikai Kiki Co. Ltd. All Rights Reserved. Courtesy Blum & Poe.

overcome the Japanese whaling ships. In one photograph,[144] the dark shiny form of the activist ship flanks a Japanese vessel much like a whale rising up against assailant whalers. The bravado of the pirate symbol emerging from the sea spray, and the spectre of a 'ghost ship' tailing the Yushin Maru No 3 and the Bob Barker, casts Sea Shepherd at once as menacing – the skeletal *Bake Kujira* – and as fearless saviours of whales. Against the Japanese ships, however, Sea Shepherd remains the underdog, so that the photograph might well fail Japan's purpose of showing that it was a victim of interference that compromised its whale catch.

My analysis of the photographs submitted in the proceedings for *Whaling in the Antarctic* from aesthetic perspectives shows how the visual representations can be understood to support or undermine the parties' arguments as to the interpretation of the *Whaling Convention*. Next, I consider the relevance of aesthetic method to these and other proceedings before the ICJ.

[144] The Institute of Cetacean Research, '2010.02.06 Bob Barker rams the Yushin Maru No.3 port stern', www.icrwhale.org/gpandsea-img216ENG.html.

6.5 THE ART OF REPRESENTATION BEFORE THE ICJ

My analysis of the photographs in Section 6.4 demonstrates the ways in which aesthetic methods for analysing images can illuminate the rhetorical function of photographs. In this way, my analysis using aesthetic methods serves as rhetorical analysis. I argue that aesthetic theory can produce conceptions of image for law, and aesthetic method can be employed in the articulation of argument arising from images, in circumstances where no such method has been identified by the ICJ.[145] In this section, I consider the aesthetic significance of photographs of whales to the parties' claims in *Whaling in the Antarctic*. I then examine the rhetorical function of aesthetic significance, and the conception of image for the purposes of rhetorical analysis as distinct from the conception of image for the evaluation of evidence. My findings from my aesthetic analysis of the photographs in the *Whaling in the Antarctic* proceedings are relevant to future uses of photographs in proceedings before the ICJ in ways described below.

6.5.1 *Aesthetic Significance of Photographs*

Photographs have aesthetic significance – both outside and inside legal proceedings. Outside legal proceedings, anyone browsing the website photo gallery curated by the International Whaling Commission will find a collection of unlabelled images in a folder titled 'dead/injured whales'.[146] Like the actors attending to Captain Boomer's whale model (Figure 6.1), people are seen in one photograph beside a giant and inert beast dislodged from its natural habitat (Figure 6.16). Here, however, the whale is bound by ropes, mouth agape, as the people appear to make ready for flensing. Even in black and white – or possibly *because* it is drained of colour – the photograph can leave a viewer bereft. The purpose of these images on the website is unclear but it would be disingenuous to suggest that they do not speak to values and sentiment: Even the webmaster warns that 'viewer discretion is advised'.[147]

Inside the courtroom, no such warning accompanied Australia's use of images of dead or injured whales in *Whaling in the Antarctic* proceedings. Yet I have shown in Section 6.4 of this chapter how the photographs submitted by both parties speak to values and sentiment associated with whaling.

145 See, for example, Biber and San Roque, 'The trouble with pictures'. Cf. Reichman, 'Narrative and rhetoric', 377.
146 International Whaling Commission, 'Dead/injured whales'.
147 Ibid.

FIGURE 6.16. 'Caught blue whale south Georgia 1930s'. *Source*: International Whaling Commission.

Australia's images confront the mythic legacy of whaling, seen in nineteenth-century art in Australia and Japan, and show aesthetic sensibilities as they are for Australia today. They do not show a heroic fight to the death, but the slaughter of a sentient creature that is defenceless against Japan's unforgiving industrial might. Australia's choice of photographs substitutes the nineteenth-century narrative of the courageous whaler with an invocation of moral values, if not in respect of the life of the whale itself, at least in respect of the manner of its killing, an inhumane method where death is not immediate and someone must stand at the ready with a rifle to kill the harpooned whale.[148] Meanwhile, Japan was compelled by the terms of the exception in Article VIII of the *Whaling Convention* to present an image of scientific enterprise, deflecting away from cultural aspects of its whaling practices. It impugned Australia for doing otherwise, railing against Australia's quest to impose a Delafield Cook-style whale-sympathising sensibility on Japan. Japan's counsel referred, for example, to Australia's 'emotional anti-whaling moral crusade' and its attempt to impose 'the cultural preference of some at the expense of others'.[149]

[148] See further Mence, 'The cetacean right to life revisited'. See also Fitzmaurice, *Whaling and International Law*, p. 153.

[149] *Whaling in the Antarctic*, 'Verbatim record 2013/12', 16, 63 ('Australia cannot impose its will on other nations').

As well as providing an account of how the photographs support the parties' arguments in the *Whaling in the Antarctic* dispute, my use of aesthetic method to analyse the images also warns of the ways in which they could pervert the advocate's script: How the images might fail as a persuasive device. I show how, for example, Japan's use of an image of a Sea Shepherd vessel during oral proceedings might not be seen to support its claim that it was interference from the anti-whaling pirate organisation, rather than falling demand for whale meat, that was responsible for Japan failing to reach its 'scientifically' determined catch quota.[150] Conversely, the claims of aesthetic and ethical values, that can be constructed with aesthetic method from Australia's images of harpooned whales, might have undermined Australia's claims as to the lack of merit of Japan's science if the ICJ determined that such considerations were irrelevant to the resolution of the dispute. Also problematic for Australia's arguments, the inscription 'Legal Research under the ICRW' on the Japanese whaling vessels shown in Australia's photographs (e.g., Figure 6.7) confirm – in words – Japan's preferred interpretation of the images of its whaling practices as legitimate in international law.

I have used aesthetic method here to articulate the aesthetic significance of the photographs submitted by the parties in the *Whaling in the Antarctic* proceedings in a rhetorical sense. However, neither the parties' arguments nor the Court's Judgment acknowledged the photographs for their aesthetic affect or significance.

6.5.2 *Rhetorical Function of Photographs*

My analysis of the aesthetic significance of the photographs articulates a rhetorical function of the images in the *Whaling in the Antarctic* proceedings. With aesthetic method, I examine the means of persuasive communication through visual representations. I show how the photographs can be seen to depict Australia's claim of a lack of merit, or Japan's claim of merit, of lethal methods 'for purposes of scientific research' under Article VIII of the *Whaling Convention*. I argue that the photographs bring to the interpretation of Article VIII the values and sentiment that motivated the ban on commercial whaling to which Article VIII provides an exemption.[151] Yet, unspoken and unacknowledged, the aesthetic significance of the photographs was, I maintain, left to roam free about the parties' arguments and, ultimately, the Judgment. This is, I argue, inconsistent with jurisprudential consideration for the proper conduct

[150] Ibid., 60.
[151] See Section 3.4.

of law,[152] and the good administration of justice.[153] Not because aesthetic significance is not relevant to legal argument, interpretation and judgment – but because it is.

The majority of the members of the ICJ deciding *Whaling in the Antarctic* might have been unperturbed by the unbridled use of photographs in the proceedings. In the same way they claimed a capacity to isolate law from policy,[154] the majority might have invoked a Ulysses-inspired capacity to resist the aesthetic influence of the photographs. Dissenting, Judge Bennouna was openly wary of the aesthetic context of the dispute, acknowledging 'that the issue of whaling is one that carries a heavy emotional and cultural charge, nourished over the centuries by literature, mythology and religious writings'.[155] Though perhaps implicitly concerned that aesthetics had influenced the majority, he was confident of his own capacity to ring-fence the law from emotion and culture. His Honour stated that, although 'they cannot ignore' the emotional and cultural background evoked in the parties' submissions, judges of the ICJ 'are bound, by virtue of their function, to ensure that it does not impinge in any way on their strictly legal analysis'.[156]

The manner in which the photographs were presented by both parties mirrors, in different ways, Judge Bennouna's expectation of impartial authority in the practice of international law. The Japanese images support, in their literal and metaphorical sterility, the neutral claims of legal method, a possible case for their probative weight as evidence. For Australia, the dead pan unemotional descriptions that accompany the photographs, in the written submissions and in the oral proceedings,[157] perform rationality. However I, like critical legal scholars,[158] am sceptical that judges can be armoured against aesthetic influence, including the aesthetic affect of photographs. This is not the same as aesthetic philosopher Emily Brady's formulation of

[152] Cf. for common law, Porter, 'Taking images seriously'; Goodrich, 'Imago decidendi'; Goodrich, 'Retinal justice'.
[153] See Fuller, 'The forms and limits of adjudication'; cf. Simma, 'The ICJ and scientific expertise'; Voigt (ed.), *International Judicial Practice on the Environment.*
[154] *Whaling in the Antarctic* at para. [69]; see also at p. 405 (Judge Greenwood).
[155] Ibid., p. 341 (Judge Bennouna).
[156] Ibid.
[157] See Section 6.3.1.
[158] Related to the 'indeterminacy' thesis, see Bianchi, *International Law Theories*, p. 136; cf. legal realism of Frank, *Law and the Modern Mind*, cited in Bianchi, *International Law Theories*, pp. 91–2. On emotion, see generally Amaya and Del Mar (eds.), *Virtue, Emotion and Imagination*; Deigh, *Emotions, Values, and the Law*; Nussbaum, *Political Emotions*.

'disinterestedness' in aesthetic judgement.[159] Brady's disinterestedness puts distance between the judge and the thing judged; it does not remove that thing entirely from the realm of judgement.

I argue that, if it allows parties to submit photographs in proceedings, the ICJ should be capable of identifying the function of the photographs and addressing their aesthetic significance.[160] I maintain that jurisprudential consideration for the proper conduct of law, and the good administration of justice, demand such an account. If the ICJ evaluates the photographs as having no evidentiary weight, it should nevertheless consider other functions of the photographs, including as a persuasive device in the service of rhetoric with implications for its judgment. The judges might duly expect an explanation of the relevance of the images from the parties – as evidence, or as rhetoric – and then themselves reason the images into or, as the case may be, out of their judgment of the facts and law.

6.5.3 *Aesthetic Conceptions of Image*

An analysis of photographs for their rhetorical function requires a different conception of image from that which is implied in the evaluation of evidence. Aesthetic theory provides a basis for that distinction. To be considered as evidence in legal process, the photographs must be 'documents' – records of actual uncontrived events that serve to prove facts. From the perspective of aesthetic theory, this conceives of photographs as a 'transparent' medium to something imagined as 'real'.[161] As already explained in Chapter 4, the realism of photographs suggests impartiality, which, in turn, garners legitimacy.[162] It is this quality that I say makes photographs distinct from the informational graphics that were also presented by the parties in the *Whaling in the Antarctic* dispute.[163]

My aesthetic critique of the photographs submitted in the proceedings before the ICJ is founded, by contrast, on a conception of photographic

159 Brady, *Aesthetics of the Natural Environment*, p. 141; see further Section 2.3.3. In this book, 'judgment' refers to legal judgment and 'judgement' refers to aesthetic judgement. See generally Manderson, 'Judgment in law and the humanities'.

160 On US courts, see Porter, 'Taking images seriously'; Goodrich, 'Imago decidendi'; Goodrich, 'Retinal justice'. The ICJ's reliance on 'written evidence' has been attributed to the influence of civil law systems: Riddell and Plant, *Evidence before the ICJ*, p. 232. See also Quintana, *Litigation at the ICJ*, p. 426.

161 Walton, 'Transparent pictures'.

162 See Section 4.3.1.

163 Ibid.

images as 'representations'.[164] As discussed in Chapter 4,[165] aesthetic analysis explains how representations in photographs are constructed and reconstructed, with images laid upon other images in the mind of each viewer. The representations are mediated by each observer – including legal counsel or a judge of the ICJ who uses or gazes upon the image. Once conceived as representation, photographic images can be offered by parties, and analysed by judges, for their persuasive effect in law. They can be aided in their analysis of the images by aesthetic methods. In the case of the photographs of whales, those methods could enlighten an understanding of the aesthetic value of whales in terms of the philosophy of environmental aesthetics, which, I have argued, is relevant to an interpretation of the *Whaling Convention's* ban on commercial whaling and exceptions to it. If acknowledged and described as representations, photographs can be used in international legal process to develop arguments in ways that might be deemed effective rather than being eschewed for exerting improper influence.[166]

The use of photographic images in international legal proceedings should not be dismissed in international proceedings as visual distractions. Describing the use of some forms of visual aid in court as a 'needless distraction [that] can be extremely annoying', former judge and President of the Court, Sir Robert Jennings, nevertheless recognised that graphic images could be of 'great assistance' in court.[167] It was 'maps, charts and diagrams' contemplated in this instance.[168] However, I maintain that photographic images used in the practice of international law should also be properly exploited by advocates for their rhetorical purchase and formally recognised by judges for their representational import to legal argument, interpretation and judgment.

6.6 CONCLUSION

Limited to an understanding of photographic images as 'evidence', international legal practice before the ICJ lacks the concepts and methods for all that aesthetic scholarship tells us that photographs can do and say. An

164 See Savedoff, *Transforming Images*. See also Mnookin, 'The image of truth'; Torresi, 'The photographic image', 125; Haldar, 'The articles of law'.
165 See Section 4.3.2. Note especially Drenthen, 'Environmental hermeneutics', 162.
166 See generally Sherwin, *Visualising Law in the Age of the Digital Baroque*; Porter, 'Taking images seriously'.
167 Jennings, 'The work of the International Bar', 443, 456.
168 Ibid. See also Quintana, *Litigation at the ICJ*, p. 355.

aesthetic conception of photographs as depictions of a physical reality corresponds with the ICJ's treatment of photographs as evidence.[169] Both rely on a photographic capacity for verisimilitude. But aesthetic theory also identifies photographic images as representations that have aesthetic significance. Conceived as representations, the photographs used in ICJ proceedings can be analysed for their aesthetic significance using aesthetic concepts and methods of interpretation.

My analysis of the photographs submitted in *Whaling in the Antarctic* uses the histories of visual art to lay bare putative meanings of the visual representations to the Court. My analysis also relies on insights from the philosophical field of environmental aesthetics which, I argue, are relevant to representations of environments – including fauna – for their aesthetic value. In this regard, my findings in this chapter are peculiar to the use of environmental photographs in ICJ proceedings concerning international environmental agreements. My method of analysis could, however, serve international law more broadly by explaining the rhetorical function of any photograph that could, in turn, have a bearing on judicial interpretation and, ultimately, the ICJ's judgments.

With aesthetic methods at their disposal, judges could articulate and analyse a role for photographic images in circumstances where such images are currently presented to the Court, and tolerated in the proceedings, with no account of their aesthetic significance. To ignore or deny the aesthetic significance of photographs is, I say, to risk the consideration of matters admitted but not reasoned. I argue that a jurisprudential concern for the proper conduct of law, and the legal principle of good administration of justice, require an account of image for ICJ proceedings and judgments.

While my analysis of photographs in determinations of World Heritage in Chapter 5 considered the role of image as justifications for determinations of aesthetic value in the administration of a treaty, my analysis of images in this chapter has considered the aesthetics of image as it relates to legal argument and judgment in the enforcement of a treaty. Chapter 5 was important to my analysis in revealing conceptions of image as verbal and graphic while this chapter has been significant for its understanding of image as both verisimilitude and as representation. In Chapter 7, I will examine the role of photo-

[169] Cf. Bennouna, 'Experts before the International Court of Justice'; Mbengue, 'Scientific fact-finding at the International Court of Justice'.

graphs in the documents that inform decisions on the implementation of the *Biodiversity Convention*, a treaty that protects the aesthetic value of biodiversity as one of several values expressed in the preamble.[170] There I examine the images as vehicles for plural representations of biodiversity's aesthetic value, showing how a range of meanings can be identified through aesthetic method.

[170] First tiret of the preamble of the *Convention on Biological Diversity*. See Section 3.3.

7

Fragmented Aesthetics of Biodiversity

EXHIBIT: EMILY KAME KNGWARREYE, *EARTH'S CREATION* (1994)

FIGURE 7.1. Emily Kame Kngwarreye, *Earth's Creation*, 1994. Synthetic polymer paint on linen mounted on canvas, four panels, 275 × 632 cm. As exhibited at *La Biennale di Venezia: 56th International Art Exhibition: All the World's Futures* = 56. © Emily Kame Kngwarreye. Photo: Alice Palmer.

Emily Kame Kngwarreye's *Earth's Creation* (Figure 7.1) is both leaden and light, it falls and it rises. Held to a museum wall, its four conjoined panels make ready to tumble while its daubs effervesce. In European aesthetics, it is an insensible corruption of abstraction and figuration, formalism and expressionism.[1] But it is not clear that such aesthetic conceptions can be properly given to this work.[2] For its Anmatyerre Elder creator, *Earth's Creation* is perhaps better understood in terms of space, time, land, story, law or life.[3] Lying flat in the red desert, it grew out of the earth, absorbing and reflecting everything about it. As the painting was disassembled, wrapped and flown to Europe in 2015, the Alhalkere Country of its making went too, its hot days and cool nights filling the temperature-controlled exhibition space in Venice with home.

When one-time 'Young British Artist' Damien Hirst reportedly claimed never to have heard of the Utopia art collective,[4] excusing his vacuous simulation of the oeuvre of Kngwarreye and other peoples from Country in the central Australian desert, he displayed the credible ignorance of an Englishman so absorbed in himself and his empire that he sees nothing of the world about him. Not least the Aboriginal women artists among those First Nations peoples so long unseen in the Australian *terra nullius*. Hirst surely profits from this would-be appropriation.[5] But his ignorance is his loss. Hirst's product pales against *Earth's Creation*. A work that inspires – in ways cultural and aesthetic, among many, but most certainly in ways that matter.

7.1 INTRODUCTION

The complex relationship between 'aesthetic' and 'cultural' values of the natural environment inherent in my description of Kngwarreye's *Earth's Creation* (Figure 7.1) also arises in the implementation of the *Biodiversity Convention*.[6] Both values are in a suite of biodiversity values identified for protection in the preamble to the *Biodiversity Convention*,[7] and in the 'Aichi Targets' – goals set by the states parties to facilitate implementation of the treaty over a decade to 2020.[8] Aesthetic and cultural values are

1 See Neale, 'Emily Kame Kngwarreye'.
2 See, for example, Garneau, 'Indigenous art', 311. See generally McLean, *Rattling Spears*.
3 See Morphy, *Ancestral Connections*; Rose, *Nourishing Terrains*; Carty, *Balgo*; Yunkaporta, *Sand Talk*.
4 See Wahlquist, '"Uncanny similarity"'.
5 See Foley, 'When the circus came to town'; Elsdon, 'Protecting the intellectual and cultural property of Aboriginal art'.
6 *Convention on Biological Diversity*, Rio de Janeiro, 5 June 1992, in force 29 December 1993, 1760 UNTS 79.
7 First tiret of the preamble in ibid.
8 Conference of the Parties to the *Convention on Biological Diversity*, *The Strategic Plan for Biodiversity*, UN Doc. UNEP/CBD/COP/DEC/X/2, Annex. Cf. Post-2020, for example, *Report of the Open-ended Working Group on the Post-2020 Global Biodiversity Framework on its third meeting (Part II)*, UN Doc. CBD/WG2020/3/7. Cf. also regarding earlier decades, for example, Executive Secretary and Johnston, 'Ten years on'.

together distinguished by advisors to the states parties to the treaty from the 'material' economic value of biodiversity also listed for protection under the treaty.[9] Yet nowhere in the treaty are any of the values of biodiversity defined, and the states parties, working collectively as the Conference of the Parties, have not made it clear how one biodiversity value differs from another.

Many of the methods favoured by states parties to identify the values of biodiversity do little to differentiate them: Aesthetic value is characterised as a cultural value that has economic value in the valuation of 'services' provided to humans by biodiverse ecosystems.[10] The Conference of the Parties has recognised emerging methods aimed at evaluating 'non-material' values of biodiversity, including aesthetic value.[11] However, more nuanced understandings of how each value might be defined, as contemplated for 'aesthetic' value in the philosophy of environmental aesthetics,[12] have not been articulated by the governing body. Decisions by the Conference of the Parties do not, for example, make sense of distinctions between the cultural value of biodiversity expressed in the arts of First Nations peoples, such as *Earth's Creation* (Figure 7.1), and aesthetic values of biodiversity conceived by the many cultures of the nation states party to the treaty.[13]

Building on my findings in Chapter 5 on the *World Heritage Convention* and Chapter 6 on the *Whaling Convention*, this chapter considers how photographs used in the collective work of the states parties to the *Biodiversity Convention* can contribute to an understanding of aesthetic value and its relationship to other biodiversity values, particularly cultural value. For the reasons explained in Chapter 4,[14] I maintain that graphic images of the environment are relevant for the consideration of aesthetic value in terms of both the aesthetic philosophy of the arts and of environmental aesthetics. I argue that aesthetic insights into the meanings of biodiversity values represented in photographs could contribute to an understanding of those values

9 Leadley et al., *Progress towards the Aichi Biodiversity Targets*, p. 12.

10 Daily, 'Introduction', p. 3. See also Bell-James, 'Ecosystem services as a metaphor'. See Sections 7.2.2. and 7.3.1.2.

11 On 'nature's contribution to people', see Conference of the Parties to the *Convention on Biological Diversity, Resource Manual for the Sixth National Report*, UN Doc. UNEP/CBD/COP/13/21. See discussion in Section 7.2.2.

12 See Cooper et al., 'Aesthetic and spiritual values of ecosystems'. See further Section 2.2.

13 See generally Woodliffe, 'Biodiversity and indigenous peoples', 255. Note the terms 'First Nations' and 'Indigenous' peoples are used in this book interchangeably, but the *Biodiversity Convention* refers to indigenous communities, for example, Article 8(j).

14 See Section 4.3.2.

among the states parties to the *Biodiversity Convention* and, in turn, of their relevance to commitments under the treaty.

This chapter revisits in Section 7.2 the doctrinal approaches to defining aesthetic value under the *Biodiversity Convention* before proceeding in Section 7.3 with an aesthetic account of the photographs used in the fourth edition of the *Global Biodiversity Outlook* – a report that was prepared at the direction of the Conference of the Parties to the *Biodiversity Convention* to assess progress towards the Aichi Targets, including Targets that concern biodiversity values.[15] I close the chapter in Section 7.4 with a discussion of the relevance of the aesthetic analysis of photographic images to the implementation of the *Biodiversity Convention*.

7.2 DOCTRINAL MEANING OF BIODIVERSITY'S AESTHETIC VALUE

The *Biodiversity Convention* protects values of biodiversity. Specifically, the preamble to the treaty recognises the 'ecological, genetic, social, economic, scientific, educational, cultural, recreational and aesthetic values' of biodiversity and its components, as well as the 'intrinsic' value of biodiversity.[16] In this section, I explain the relevance of biodiversity values, including aesthetic value, to the implementation of the *Biodiversity Convention* before briefly revisiting my findings from doctrinal treaty interpretation in Chapter 3. The lack of clarity as to the meaning of aesthetic value from orthodox sources of treaty interpretation leads me in Section 7.3 to interrogate meanings of aesthetic value represented in photographs used in connection with the implementation of the *Biodiversity Convention*. It is there that I address critical perspectives on the issues raised by doctrinal interpretation, including those relevant to First Nations peoples.

7.2.1 *The Relevance of Biodiversity Values*

Biodiversity values inform the implementation of the parties' commitments in the *Biodiversity Convention*. When, for example, parties act under the treaty to establish a system of national areas for protection of biodiversity,[17] they do so as a matter of doctrinal treaty interpretation to protect the values of biological diversity listed in the preamble.[18] Biodiversity values would also be implicated

[15] Secretariat of the *Convention on Biological Diversity*, *Global Biodiversity Outlook 4*.
[16] First tiret of the preamble of the *Convention on Biological Diversity*.
[17] Ibid., Article 8(a).
[18] See Section 3.3.1.2.

in treaty commitments concerning such matters as the protection of Indigenous knowledge,[19] and in the creation of incentives for the private management of biodiversity.[20]

In 2010, the Conference of the Parties to the *Biodiversity Convention* decided on a strategic plan for the implementation of the treaty over a decade to 2020.[21] Associated with the strategic plan were the 'Aichi Targets', a set of goals for the states parties in their implementation of the *Biodiversity Convention*.[22] Three of the Aichi Targets made express mention of the 'values' of biodiversity.[23] They concerned: Raising awareness of the values of biodiversity (Target 1); the integration of biodiversity values into planning and accounting for economic development (Target 2); and the development of knowledge and technologies relevant to biodiversity, including values of biodiversity (Target 19). The specific values of biodiversity contemplated by the parties were not identified. The list of biodiversity values identified in a technical report on progress towards the Aichi Targets corresponded with those in the preamble to the *Biodiversity Convention*.[24]

The fourth edition of the *Global Biodiversity Outlook* ('GBO-4') examined in this chapter assessed the states parties' progress in achieving the Aichi Targets.[25] The *Global Biodiversity Outlook* is a periodic assessment of biodiversity approved by the Conference of the Parties to the *Biodiversity Convention*.[26] It is instigated by the states parties to gauge the achievement of the treaty objectives and to inform the implementation and development of treaty commitments.[27] Overall, *GBO-4* found 'that actions need to be stepped up and accelerated if the goals of the Strategic Plan are to be achieved'.[28] Regarding the three Aichi Targets 1, 2 and 19 specific to biodiversity values, parties were on track to achieve only part of Target 19. Progress towards the

19 Article 8(j) of the *Convention on Biological Diversity*.
20 Ibid., Article 11.
21 Conference of the Parties to the *Convention on Biological Diversity*, *The Strategic Plan for Biodiversity*.
22 Ibid., Annex.
23 Ibid., pp. 8–9.
24 Leadley et al., *Progress towards the Aichi Biodiversity Targets*, p. 11.
25 Secretariat of the *Convention on Biological Diversity*, *Global Biodiversity Outlook 4*.
26 Conference of the Parties to the *Convention on Biological Diversity*, *Report of the Second Meeting of the Conference of the Parties to the Convention on Biological Diversity*, UN Doc. UNEP/CBD/COP/2/19.
27 Subsidiary Body on Scientific, Technical and Technological Advice, *Report of the First Meeting of the Subsidiary Body on Scientific, Technical and Technological Advice*, UN Doc. UNEP/CBD/COP/2/5, p. 32; see also Secretariat of the *Convention on Biological Diversity*, *Global Biodiversity Outlook 4*, p. 27.
28 Secretariat of the *Convention on Biological Diversity*, *Global Biodiversity Outlook 4*, p. 130.

other part of Target 19, and Targets 1 and 2, was judged in the report as insufficient to meet the deadline of 2020.[29]

The fifth edition of the *Global Biodiversity Outlook* launched in September 2020 assessed the extent to which the Aichi Targets have been achieved.[30] As anticipated in *GBO-4*, it found that '[b]iodiversity is declining at an unprecedented rate, and the pressures driving this decline are intensifying. None of the Aichi Biodiversity Targets were fully met, in turn threatening the achievement of the Sustainable Development Goals and undermining efforts to address climate change.'[31] Efforts to negotiate new targets as part of a Post-2020 Global Biodiversity Framework were interrupted by the COVID-19 pandemic but were eventually adopted in 2022.[32]

7.2.2 *Doctrinal Meanings of Biodiversity's Aesthetic Value*

None of the values of biodiversity is defined in the *Biodiversity Convention*. In Chapter 3, I employed doctrinal methods of treaty interpretation, largely codified in the *Vienna Convention on the Law of Treaties*,[33] to develop a legal meaning for 'aesthetic' value expressed in the preamble to the *Biodiversity Convention*. As explained again briefly here, my doctrinal interpretation of aesthetic value in the *Biodiversity Convention* pointed to possible associations with 'natural beauty', but it did not clarify the relationship between aesthetic value and other biodiversity values, including cultural and economic value.

Looking first at the ordinary meaning of 'aesthetic' value, I identified in Chapter 3 dictionary definitions that referred to aesthetic value in terms of 'beauty' or 'perception by the senses'. I noted that the interpretative principle of effectiveness requires a meaning of 'aesthetic' value of biodiversity that can be distinguished from other values of biodiversity expressly identified in the treaty's preamble, including 'cultural' value. The distinction in aesthetic philosophy between environmental aesthetics, and the aesthetic philosophy of the arts, could assist to distinguish the aesthetic value of biodiversity from

29 Ibid., pp. 18, 22.

30 Secretariat of the *Convention on Biological Diversity*, *Global Biodiversity Outlook* 5; see also Conference of the Parties to the *Convention on Biological Diversity*, *Comprehensive and Participatory Process for the Preparation of the Post-2020 Global Biodiversity Framework*, UN Doc. CBD/COP/DEC/14/35.

31 Secretariat of the *Convention on Biological Diversity*, *Global Biodiversity Outlook* 5, p. 7.

32 See, for example, Conference of the Parties to the *Convention on Biological Diversity*, *Comprehensive and Participatory Process*; *Report of the Open-ended Working Group on the Post-2020 Global Biodiversity Framework on Its Third Meeting (Part II)*, UN Doc. CBD/WG2020/3/7.

33 *Vienna Convention on the Law of Treaties*, Vienna, 23 May 1969, 27 January 1980, 1155 UNTS 331, Articles 31–2.

aesthetic elements of the 'cultural' values of biodiversity associated with the arts. I also explained that the 'aesthetic' value of biodiversity could be informed by the term 'wilderness' expressed in annex I to the *Biodiversity Convention.*

The object valued – biological diversity or, in short form, biodiversity – is also part of the context that would be relevant to defining aesthetic value using doctrinal techniques. Biological diversity is defined in the treaty as 'the variability among living organisms'.[34] However, complexities around the concept of biodiversity, and the attribution of values to it, have been raised by scholars of international environmental law and philosophers of environmental aesthetics.[35] Reference to biodiversity as the object of aesthetic value might be further complicated by my finding in Chapter 3 as to the historical provenance of the values listed in the *Biodiversity Convention.*[36] The *Convention on the Conservation of Migratory Species of Wild Animals* ('*Bonn Convention*') contains a list of values that is the likely precedent for the values listed in the preamble to the *Biodiversity Convention.*[37] It is not apparent from the negotiating materials for the *Biodiversity Convention* what, if any, consideration was given to whether values applied to wild animals might differ when applied to biodiversity.

In Chapter 3, I also considered as an orthodox source for treaty interpretation the 'subsequent practice' of the parties. Under Article 31(3) of the *Vienna Convention*, interpreters of treaties can look to sources such as '[a]ny subsequent practice in the application of the treaty which establishes the agreement of the parties regarding its interpretation'.[38] I argued that the disparate understandings of aesthetic value apparent from a select number of national reports submitted by individual states parties under Article 26 of the *Biodiversity Convention* were not likely to establish the agreement of the parties for the purposes of treaty interpretation.[39]

I also considered as possible evidence of subsequent practice decisions of the Conference of the Parties to the *Biodiversity Convention* (COP decisions) and related reports. I noted that few COP decisions mention the 'aesthetic' value of biodiversity and, where they do, it is mentioned only as one in the

34 Article 2 of the *Convention on Biological Diversity*.
35 See Section 7.3.1.2. See also Scholtz, 'Ethical and humane use'.
36 See Section 3.3.3.
37 Third tiret of the preamble of the *Convention on the Conservation of Migratory Species of Wild Animals*, Bonn, 23 June 1979, in force 1 November 1983, 1651 UNTS 333 (does not list intrinsic value).
38 *Vienna Convention*, Article 31(3)(b).
39 Gardiner, *Treaty Interpretation*, p. 254.

suite of biodiversity values contained in the treaty preamble.[40] Other decisions refer to biodiversity values in general. The Aichi Targets, for example, referred to 'biodiversity values' or 'values of biodiversity' without specifying what they are. Methods of biodiversity valuation have been endorsed in decisions of the Conference of the Parties to the *Biodiversity Convention* and adopted by parties in their national jurisdictions.[41] They typically value biodiversity in terms of 'ecosystem services' where aesthetic, cultural and economic values of biodiversity appear to have been combined. These methods ascribe economic value to 'ecosystem services', including a category of 'cultural' ecosystem services serving aesthetic functions.[42] It is, however, recognised by advisors to the Conference of the Parties that prevalent methodologies for the economic valuation of biodiversity neglect the non-material values of biodiversity, including aesthetic value.[43] Economic valuation is criticised by experts for its potential to give greater emphasis to material values in assessments of the protection of biodiversity values under the treaty.[44]

Through its adoption of a resource manual in 2016,[45] the Conference of the Parties to the *Biodiversity Convention* encouraged states parties to use methodologies for assessing biodiversity in their national reports similar to those of the Intergovernmental Science-Policy Platform on Biodiversity and Ecosystem Services (IPBES). Created by over 100 states in 2012,[46] IPBES is adopting methodologies aimed at understandings of biodiversity values that are additional to economic value.[47] Specifically, IPBES assessments rely on a framework of valuation based on 'nature's contribution to people', which is intended to take account of perspectives on cultural value developed in social science.[48] However, no mention is made in the categories prescribed for this

40 See Section 3.3.2.2.

41 See ibid.

42 See Sukhdev et al., *The Economics of Ecosystems and Biodiversity*, Annex, p. 34. See generally Reid and Nsoh, *The Privatisation of Biodiversity?*.

43 See Leadley et al., *Progress towards the Aichi Biodiversity Targets*, p. 12. See also Secretariat of the *Convention on Biological Diversity*, *An Exploration of Tools and Methodologies*, p. 16.

44 See, for example, Cooper et al., 'Aesthetic and spiritual values of ecosystems'. Note Small, Munday and Durance, 'The challenge of valuing ecosystem services'; Turner et al., 'Valuing nature'; Prior, 'Economic valuation'.

45 The COP has encouraged states parties to adopt the IPBES approach to valuation in their sixth national reports on their implementation of the *Convention* due at the end of 2018: Conference of the Parties to the *Convention on Biological Diversity*, *Resource Manual*.

46 See IPBES, 'About', ipbes.net/history-establishment.

47 See Fischer et al. (eds.), *Summary for Policymakers of the Regional Assessment Report*, p. 7.

48 See, for example, ibid., Appendix 2.

methodology of concepts relevant to aesthetic philosophy.[49] There is no explanation of aesthetic value in terms, for example, of the philosophy of environmental aesthetics or in terms of the arts. Nor does the methodology appear to contemplate the use of photographs in the assessment of nature's contribution to people.

I concluded in Chapter 3 that none of the COP decisions and subsequent practices I identified appear likely to 'establish the agreement of the parties' as to the meaning of aesthetic value for the purposes of the *Vienna Convention* rules of interpretation.[50] My examination of sources of treaty interpretation did not, however, extend to the *Global Biodiversity Outlook*. Prepared by experts working in consultation with the Secretariat to the *Biodiversity Convention*, the *Global Biodiversity Outlook* is one of many resources that inform the parties in their collective oversight of treaty implementation. It synthesises information from other reports, including the national reports on treaty implementation noted above.[51] Commissioned by the Secretariat at the direction of the Conference of the Parties,[52] the *Global Biodiversity Outlook* arguably documents practice that is descriptive or indicative of the parties' understandings of treaty terms. Assessing the implementation of the Aichi Targets, including those specifically related to biodiversity values, *GBO-4* could be suggestive of meanings of those values. However, it provides only a broad overview of progress towards the Targets concerning biodiversity values, with no specific analysis of aesthetic value.[53] *GBO-5* also provides no explanation of the meaning of biodiversity values.[54] Moreover, the various editions of the *Global Biodiversity Outlook* could inform COP decisions but they would not necessarily determine their outcome. As such, it is not clear that it has any interpretative relevance for the purposes of the rules under the *Vienna Convention*.

In addition to the written text, *GBO-4* contains many visual representations of biodiversity in the form of photographs. In the ways explained in Chapter 4, and elaborated in Chapters 5 and 6 of this book, I maintain that photographs

49 Category 16, Table S1, Supplementary Material in Díaz et al., 'Assessing nature's contributions', 270–2.

50 Ibid.

51 See, for example, Secretariat of the *Convention on Biological Diversity*, *Global Biodiversity Outlook* 4, p. 3.

52 Conference of the Parties to the *Convention on Biological Diversity*, *Report of the Second Meeting*.

53 See, for example, Secretariat of the *Convention on Biological Diversity*, *Global Biodiversity Outlook* 4, pp. 32–9.

54 Secretariat of the *Convention on Biological Diversity*, *Global Biodiversity Outlook* 5.

used in the *Global Biodiversity Outlook* and other documents generated under the treaty can be analysed, from an aesthetic perspective, to develop understandings of biodiversity's aesthetic value. In the next part, I consider the extent to which photographs included in *GBO-4* can be analysed to provide an account of aesthetic and other values of biodiversity.

7.3 AESTHETIC VALUES OF BIODIVERSITY IN PHOTOGRAPHS

Photographs contained in *GBO-4* show lush forests, coral reefs of varied colours and charismatic fauna as well as people relying on the environment for their food, water and livelihoods.[55] The photographs also show damage done to the environment – by large-scale agriculture, industrial manufacturers and power generators.[56] In this part, I examine from an aesthetic perspective the six photographs in *GBO-4* that accompany the assessment of the three Aichi Targets concerning biodiversity values: Targets 1, 2 and 19.[57] I examine representations of aesthetic value in the photographs first in terms of 'natural beauty' and second in terms of 'cultural' value. I refer to the aesthetic value of the 'natural environment' and, in some instances, I identify specific issues arising from the philosophical literature for the aesthetic value of 'biodiversity'. Few philosophers of environmental aesthetics address questions specific to the aesthetic appreciation of 'biodiversity'.[58]

7.3.1 *Aesthetic Value of Biodiversity as Natural Beauty*

Doctrinal treaty interpretation suggests that the aesthetic value contemplated for the *Biodiversity Convention* could be synonymous with 'natural beauty'.[59] As discussed in Chapter 2,[60] 'natural beauty' is variously conceived in aesthetic philosophy. It can be understood, for example, in terms of 'scenic' qualities exploited in landscape painting. Natural beauty is also associated in aesthetic

55 See, e.g., Figures 7.2, 7.3, 7.8, 7.9, 7.12, 7.13.
56 See, e.g., Secretariat of the *Convention on Biological Diversity*, *Global Biodiversity Outlook 4*, pp. 41, 43, 66.
57 Conference of the Parties to the *Convention on Biological Diversity*, *The Strategic Plan for Biodiversity*, pp. 8–9. See n23 and accompanying text.
58 Cf. Brady, 'Aesthetics in practice', 285. Note the significance of attributing values to biodiversity as distinct from the natural environment is not specifically addressed in Norton (ed.), *The Preservation of Species*.
59 See Section 7.2.2; see also Section 3.3.
60 See Section 2.4.1.

philosophy with the notion of 'wilderness'. Below I consider the relevance of these two conceptions of natural beauty to photographs in *GBO-4*.

7.3.1.1 Scenic Landscapes

The relationship between the aesthetic value of the environment and 'scenic' qualities stems from developments in Western European landscape painting.[61] Art historian Simon Schama identifies a seventeenth-century emblem, 'Rura Mihi et Silentium', as the quintessential bucolic scene in the Western landscape tradition, depicting the countryside as 'the moral corrective to the ills of court and city'.[62] By the eighteenth century, a portable tinted convex mirror known as a 'Claude glass' was being used by artists to create a sense of a greater distance between the viewer and a feature in the landscape, such as a lake or hillside. Natural spaces were framed by the mirror's edge and viewed in their entirety from a vantage point. An eighteenth-century guide book to the Lake District of England encouraged use of the Claude glass by visitors to the area to give 'the finished picture, in highest colouring, and just perspective.'[63] People were encouraged to visit natural spaces for leisure and to view those places as if they were a landscape painting, conscious of formal 'scenic' qualities in the environment – contrasts in shapes, colours and lines – and perspective.[64]

Two photographs that appear with the discussion of biodiversity values in *GBO-4* can be readily analysed from an aesthetic perspective in terms of 'scenic' landscapes. One of the photographs, included with the discussion of Aichi Target 1 on raising awareness of biodiversity values, shows SCUBA divers ascending from a coral reef (Figure 7.2). The other photograph, featured in the section of *GBO-4* assessing Aichi Target 19 on the development of knowledge of biodiversity values, shows an expansive view of rice paddy terraces (Figure 7.3).

Both photographs suggest a scenic aesthetic. The photograph of the coral reef depicts a picturesque scene, highlighting the irregular shapes and colours of the reef. The dark foregrounding of coral formations and schools of fish, with the divers in the background ascending upwards towards the light, provides a scenic vantage, albeit in an aquatic environment. The divers look

61 See generally Berleant, 'Scenic beauty in a global context', 79.

62 Schama, *Landscape and Memory*, p. 10.

63 West, A *Guide to the Lakes*, pp. 15, 131, quoted by Odgen, 'From spatial to aesthetic distance', 67.

64 See Brady, *Aesthetics of the Natural Environment*, pp. 20–1, 43. See also Carlson, *Aesthetics and the Environment*, pp. 32, 45.

FIGURE 7.2. Untitled (reef), Secretariat of the *Convention on Biological Diversity, Global Biodiversity Outlook* 4, p. 32. Photo under license of Shutterstock to Secretariat of *the* Convention on Biological Diversity.

FIGURE 7.3. Untitled (rice paddies), Secretariat of the *Convention on Biological Diversity, Global Biodiversity Outlook* 4, p. 118. Photo under license of Shutterstock to Secretariat of the *Convention on Biological Diversity.*

on – through them we see ourselves seeing the reef. The elevated view in the photograph of the rice paddy terraces accentuates the patterns and contrasts in the scene – the pastel colours, organic lines and concertina shapes have visual appeal. It has the semblance of pastoral tranquillity: The huts, modest versions

FIGURE 7.4. Eugène von Guérard, *Mr Clark's Station, Deep Creek, near Keilor*, 1867. Oil on canvas, 68.4 × 122.0 cm. National Gallery of Victoria, Melbourne. Purchased with funds donated by Mr and Mrs Solomon Lew and with the assistance of the National Gallery Society of Victoria, 1986. Photo: National Gallery of Victoria.

of Eugène von Guérard's station estate (Figure 7.4), suggest a peaceful country life. Both images depict diversity as it has been conceived for the arts – a concept that has been appropriated by Western science in the conception of biological diversity.[65]

However, aesthetic conceptions of scenic environments have been criticised in aesthetic philosophy for their limited characterisation of the aesthetic experience of nature.[66] Aesthetic philosopher Emily Brady observes that: 'Scenic value is used all the time in conservation literature, yet it designates an outmoded way of understanding the environment which ignores the special *environing* qualities of environments.'[67] As discussed in Chapter 2,[68] this is one of the grounds on which environmental aestheticians reject models for appreciating art as an analogy for the aesthetic appreciation of nature.

Yet I have argued that visual art can inform critical understandings of scenic representations of the environment.[69] Contemporary painter Mandy Martin

65 See Brady, 'Aesthetics in practice', 285; see also below n81 (ecological impacts of rice cultivation), n84 (concept of biodiversity).

66 See Section 2.4.1. See also Berleant, 'Scenic beauty'.

67 Brady, *Aesthetics of the Natural Environment*, p. 21 (emphasis in original). See further Jenkins, 'In defence of natural beauty'.

68 See Section 2.2.1.

69 See Section 4.3.2.

embraces the genres of eighteenth- and nineteenth-century scenic landscapes but she manipulates them to draw attention to the fragility of the natural environment.[70] In her painting *O-B-L-I-V-I-O-N*,[71] for example, Martin depicts a sublime tempest while letters mark the textured surface with a word – a mark of human intervention – that is both a literal description and a portent of environmental collapse. Similar themes can be understood from Janet Laurence's artwork *Deep Breathing: Resuscitation for the Reef* (Figure 4.3) discussed earlier in Chapter 4 of this book.[72] These contemporary landscapes are possibly examples of what Simon Schama calls the 'anti-landscape' – a reaction, he said, to 'the annexation of nature by culture'.[73] He offers René Magritte's painting *The Human Condition* as an example of that annexation rejected by contemporary landscapists.[74] It is, however, also possible that Magritte lamented the constraints of artistic convention in Western European landscape tradition. The artist said of his work in 1938 that '[w]e see [the world] as being outside ourselves even though it is only a mental representation of what we experience on the inside'.[75]

I maintain that visual art, and ways of understanding visual art, can be used to examine issues for biodiversity values that arise from scenic landscapes in light of the philosophy of environmental aesthetics. The SCUBA divers in the *GBO-4* photograph of the coral reef (Figure 7.2), literally immersed in the aquatic environment, suggest the kind of sensory and imaginative engagement with the environment theorised by many philosophers of environmental aesthetics such as Emily Brady.[76] But the image also combines aesthetic value with another environmental value – recreational value.

The association of aesthetic and recreational values is problematic for the implementation of the *Biodiversity Convention*. Both values are listed separately as values of biodiversity in the preamble to the treaty and, as such, they should be conceived as distinct values for the purposes of effective treaty interpretation.[77] Yet problems arising from any conflation of those values are also philosophical. As Emily Brady and other philosophers of environmental

[70] See Soboslay, 'Mandy Martin: Eco-worrying', 32.
[71] Mandy Martin, *O-B-L-I-V-I-O-N*.
[72] See Section 4.2.3.
[73] Schama, *Landscape and Memory*, p. 12.
[74] Ibid.
[75] René Magritte, quoted in ibid. Cf. characterisation of this work by Graham, 'This is not a thing', 396.
[76] Cf. imagination from above the water's surface: Brady, *Aesthetics of the Natural Environment*, p. 57.
[77] See Section 3.3.1.2.

FIGURE 7.5. Marie Voignier, *Standing Still* (*Les Immobiles*), 2013 (still). HD film. © Marie Voignier. Courtesy Marcelle Alix.

aesthetics observe,[78] the association with recreational value ends by trivialising and tainting aesthetic value. Recreational value has a complex history, evolving from the hunting of animals in game reserves to hiking in natural environments protected for their biodiversity.[79] This is a biodiversity value associated with leisure, a hedonistic luxury for the few, readily transposed into economic value born of income from tourism.

It is the harmful aspects of recreational value that Marie Voignier explores in her video artwork, *Standing Still* (*Les Immobiles*) (Figure 7.5).[80] In it, the recollections of a safari guide narrate still photographs of trophy hunters, highlighting the dissociative capacity of people insensitive to the impacts of their recreational sport. The artwork reveals the ways in which recreational value is different from the aesthetic appreciation of the environment conceived by philosophers of environmental aesthetics and – possibly – by parties to the *Biodiversity Convention*. The subtitle caught on the still (Figure 7.5) corresponds to the narration, stated without flourish, as a simple fact of the recreational big game hunt: 'Each person was allowed 15 animals.'

78 See Brady, *Aesthetics of the Natural Environment*, p. 129. See generally Section 2.2.3.

79 See Gillespie, *International Environmental Law, Policy and Ethics*, 2nd edn, p. 18. Note a more extensive examination of 'recreational value' in relation to wilderness and aesthetic value in the first edition: Gillespie, *International Environmental Law, Policy and Ethics*, 1st edn, pp. 102–6.

80 See Macel, Gyalui and Margutti (eds.), *Esposizione Internationale d'Arte*, pp. 264–7.

The photograph of the rice paddy terraces (Figure 7.3) can also be examined from critical perspectives debated among philosophers of environmental aesthetics. By framing the environment as a scene, placing it at a distance from the human viewer, the image of the rice paddies fails to convey the spatial, immersive quality of being in and part of environmental spaces as understood in contemporary environmental aesthetics. The rice paddy photograph is also notable for its depiction of a cultivated environment. Vegetation has been cleared from the foothills and the terraces have been constructed and flooded, presumably with water diverted from a natural watercourse.[81] For some environmental aestheticians, the human intervention in that environment would disqualify it from aesthetic appreciation altogether. The converse of the 'positive' aesthetic developed by philosopher Allen Carlson and others, for example, is that an unnatural, cultivated or otherwise altered environment is not capable of being understood in terms of environmental aesthetics.[82] The cultivated nature of the rice paddies exposes underlying tensions in the conception of 'biodiversity' appreciated for its aesthetic value under the *Biodiversity Convention*. The forms of variability apparent in the image of the rice paddies – the colours and contours produced by the human manipulation of the land – might not be the forms of variability contemplated for the treaty, which conceives of biodiversity 'within species, between species and of ecosystems'.[83] The aesthetic elements of the image attest to human intervention that could be at odds with the treaty's own definition of biodiversity. Through an aesthetic examination of the image, it becomes apparent that the object valued under the *Biodiversity Convention* – biodiversity – must also be understood in the task of defining the values protected under the treaty.[84]

Enriched by critical insights from art and the philosophy of environmental aesthetics, the photographs of the coral reef and the rice paddies suggest a disjuncture between the aesthetic qualities in the images and the aesthetic value or values of biodiversity protected under the *Biodiversity Convention*. In Section 7.3.1.2, I consider photographs in *GBO-4* from the perspective of another aesthetic concept related to natural beauty: 'Wilderness'.

[81] See Bambaradeniya and Amerasinghe 'Biodiversity associated with the rice field agroecosystem'. Cf. cultural elements in rice cultivation: Descola, *Beyond Nature and Culture*, p. 44; Chapeskie, 'Culture, landscape and diversity', 76.

[82] Carlson, *Aesthetics and the Environment*, p. 73. See Section 2.2.1.

[83] Article 2 of the *Convention on Biological Diversity*.

[84] See, for example, Bowman, 'The nature, development and philosophical foundations of the biodiversity concept', 5; Takacs, *The Idea of Biodiversity*; Scholtz, 'Animal culling', 11.

7.3.1.2 Wilderness Untouched

As discussed in Chapter 2, the concept of 'wilderness' is an environmental aesthetic that in the twentieth century was adopted into law in the United States and other countries around the world.[85] It imagines the environment in terms of wild spaces and species untouched by humans, valued for its capacity to transport people to an existential realm. Associated with American Transcendentalism,[86] the idea of wilderness reimagined notions of Arcadia, as well as Romantic understandings of the sublime and picturesque, for the twentieth century.[87] It is also related to the philosophical theory of positive aesthetics,[88] limiting the aesthetic appreciation of natural environments to those places undisturbed by humans. Wilderness is a conception of the natural environment from which humans are absent save the person who is immersed in the appreciation of it. It is also related to the recreational value discussed above in relation to scenic landscapes, with 'wilderness' valued by people for purported physical and psychological benefits.[89]

The two photographs in *GBO-4* that accompany the discussion of the integration of biodiversity values into planning and accounting for economic development (Aichi Target 2) can be analysed from an aesthetic perspective in terms of 'wilderness'. They depict, respectively, a mangrove forest (Figure 7.6) and an elephant herd grazing on a savannah plain (Figure 7.7). The ancient and pristine mangrove forest, with twisted buttress roots wending their way into clear water reflecting the trunks and leafy mass above, appears as a wilderness untouched by humans. Cool shaded interiors contrast with the stark light that pierces the tree canopy. It is a wild space to inspire and to be conserved. The photograph of the elephants invites the viewer to marvel at the size, strength and resilience of the wandering pachyderms. The rising horizon in the background suggests the fertile legacy of a volcano crater, a bountiful wilderness.

These wilderness photographs in *GBO-4* conjure the Romantic landscape imagery of nineteenth-century European and British painters discussed in

[85] See Woods, 'Federal wilderness preservation'; Hargrove, 'The historical foundations of American environmental attitudes', 29; Gillespie, *International Environmental Law, Policy and Ethics*, 2nd edn, pp. 18–19. On the global construction of environmental laws, see Godden, Peel and McDonald, *Environmental Law*, p. 26.

[86] Brady, *Aesthetics of the Natural Environment*, p. 46. See Section 4.2.1.

[87] Cf. Stephens, 'What is the point of international environmental law scholarship', 129.

[88] Carlson, *Aesthetics and the Environment*, p. 73.

[89] See Gillespie, *International Environmental Law, Policy and Ethics*, 1st edn, p. 104.

FIGURE 7.6. Untitled (mangroves), Secretariat of the *Convention on Biological Diversity*, *Global Biodiversity Outlook* 4, p. 37. Photo under license of Shutterstock to Secretariat of the *Convention on Biological Diversity*.

FIGURE 7.7. Untitled (elephants), Secretariat of the *Convention on Biological Diversity*, *Global Biodiversity Outlook* 4, p. 38. Photo under license of Shutterstock to Secretariat of the *Convention on Biological Diversity*.

Chapter 4,[90] as well as the landscape aesthetic of many contemporary artists around the world today. The idea of wilderness and the Romantic rejection of industrial 'progression' as an aesthetic value of the environment persists, for example, in the contemporary art of Raymond Arnold. His composite etching, *Mt Lyell (Expanded Field)*,[91] zooms out from meticulous studies of gnarled tree trunks, and bejewelled rock faces, to reveal a vast and rugged landscape damaged by mining but 'returned to nature'. Finding resonance in a poem by Seamus Heaney – 'An elsewhere world, beyond Maps and atlases' – Arnold's work is a nostalgic invocation of a reclaimed wilderness.[92] It is a reassurance that nature will prevail.

The wilderness aesthetic is, however, the subject of significant critique among aesthetic scholars, environmental aestheticians and art critics alike.[93] For philosophers of environmental aesthetics such as Emily Brady, an environment absent humans is not an environment appreciated for its aesthetic value.[94] Aesthetic value is necessarily an anthropocentric value of the environment, perceived by humans in and part of the environment that is valued.[95] Brady's characterisation of the natural environment capable of aesthetic appreciation is consistent with the concept of biological diversity developed for Western science. It is a concept founded in biology on connections between all elements of the environment, from habitats to species and their genes – *including* human beings.[96] As such, wilderness photographs of environments, devoid of humans, can be understood as anachronistic and antagonistic to the very concept of biodiversity.

It is perhaps instead intrinsic value that is represented in the wilderness apparent in the *GBO-4* photographs for Aichi Target 2. Intrinsic value is a value of biodiversity that is distinguished from other values – including aesthetic value – in the *Biodiversity Convention*.[97] It is a value that is generally understood to serve no instrumental application for humans: It is the value of

90 See Section 4.2.1. Cf. Bowman, 'Law, legal scholarship and the conservation of biological diversity', 13.
91 Arnold, *Mt. Lyell (Expanded Field)*.
92 Arnold, *Elsewhere World*.
93 See generally Woods, *Rethinking Wilderness*; Bartel et al. (eds.), *Rethinking Wilderness and The Wild*. See also Cronon, 'The trouble with wilderness', 471; Delaney, *Law and Nature*, pp. 178–9.
94 Brady, *Aesthetics of the Natural Environment*, p. 53.
95 Gillespie, *International Law, Policy and Ethics*, 2nd edn, p. 13.
96 See Sarkar, 'Approaches to biodiversity', 43.
97 First tiret of the preamble of the *Convention on Biological Diversity*.

the environment in its own right.[98] But scholars have pointed out that it is conceptually difficult to apply the notion of intrinsic value to biodiversity – the 'diversity' of genes, species and ecosystems is not necessarily a subject of 'intrinsic' worth in and of itself. Freya Dawson, for example, questions the extent to which scientific knowledge is relevant to conceptions of intrinsic value.[99] She maintains that science 'does not recognize the intrinsic value of biodiversity. We must always look to cultural factors to identify value.'[100]

Analysing the photographs from an eco-critical perspective,[101] situating them for example in socio-political discourse, can help to develop an aesthetic account of concepts and values relevant to the implementation of the *Biodiversity Convention*. For example, one of the elephants in the *GBO-4* photo has extended ears, a defensive gesture asserting authority and claiming territory. Likely an African elephant,[102] it stands on soil over which wars have been waged, with or between colonial pretenders, with or between the first human inhabitants of planet Earth. Claims and counter-claims to land are indifferent to biodiversity, though not to biological resources. As sovereign, states decide for themselves how to use the resources of the realm. Again, an understanding of the object of value under the treaty is significant to an understanding of the values – both biological diversity and 'its components' are named as objects of aesthetic value in the preamble to the *Biodiversity Convention*.[103]

The relationship between the aesthetic and economic value of biodiversity is also apparent in the photographs. Economic value attributed to the ecosystem services provided by a pristine mangrove, for example, might be different, in terms of biodiversity protection, from the economic value to be gained from hunting elephants – whether permitted or illegal. Yet such distinctions are not obvious from the general call in Aichi Target 2 for the integration of the values of biodiversity into planning for economic development.[104] Fiona Hall's artwork, *Tender*,[105] takes aim at economies of the environment in ways that can illuminate understandings of biodiversity's value. Adopting a title

98 See Fosci and West, 'In whose interest?', 55; Scholtz, 'Ethical and humane use'; Bell-James, 'Ecosystem services as a metaphor'. See debate among legal scholars in Section 2.3.2.1.
99 Dawson, 'What is the value of biodiversity?', 93.
100 Ibid., 107.
101 See Section 4.3.3.
102 Sikes, *The Natural History of the African Elephant*.
103 First tiret of the preamble of the *Convention on Biological Diversity*.
104 Conference of the Parties to the *Convention on Biological Diversity*, *The Strategic Plan for Biodiversity*, Annex.
105 Hall, *Tender*.

ambiguously referencing both love and money, the artist has woven birds' nests from shredded US dollar bills in a blatant critique of the monetary values promoted over aesthetics and, possibly, at nature's expense. The delicate shape she gives to the nests, a symbol of a fragile natural habitat, is undermined by the hard currency that constitutes them.

The impacts of commerce are acknowledged in the written text of the *GBO-4* – agricultural subsidies are, for example, identified as one of the significant causes of harm to biodiversity.[106] However, such impacts are largely absent from the photographic imagery of nature's aesthetic ideal.[107] Recreational hunts for the rich, and poaching by the poor, will see elephant populations decimated for trophies and ivory.[108] But through the *GBO-4* photograph (Figure 7.7), we are not meant to see the elephants for their ivory tusks, a valuable commodity that sees them poached to near extinction. Nor are we to see in the mangrove image (Figure 7.6) biodiversity as either vulnerable to rising sea levels or as protective of the land. Instead, the photographs speak to biodiversity as wilderness, cherished by those who have created it as an escape from modernity.

States parties might contest the extent to which the 'wilderness' projected by the photographs correlates with the aesthetic value protected under the *Biodiversity Convention*. The inclusion of photographs representing biodiversity as wilderness in reports on biodiversity could be a departure from the decisions of the Conference of the Parties of the *Biodiversity Convention* to conserve biodiversity in a way that respects the human communities that live with it. For example, the reconceptualization of nature inhabited by humans was central to work under the *Biodiversity Convention* to produce the *Akwé: Kon Guidelines*.[109] These voluntary guidelines were agreed by the Conference of the Parties in 2004 to better integrate the concerns of those people living in biodiverse places – Indigenous and local communities – in assessments of development impacts on biodiversity. The acknowledgement by the states parties of these human concerns is, possibly, consistent with the social value

106 Secretariat of the *Convention on Biological Diversity*, *Global Biodiversity Outlook* 4, p. 41.

107 Cf. ibid., pp. 40 (tractor), 43 (silos), 59 (fish nets), 65 (aquaculture), 66 (chimneys), 122 (erosion).

108 See *Convention on International Trade in Endangered Species of Wild Fauna and Flora* (CITES), 'African elephant poaching down'; Barbier et al., *Elephants, Economics and Ivory*.

109 Conference of the Parties to the *Convention on Biological Diversity*, *Akwé: Kon Voluntary Guidelines*, UN Doc. UNEP/CBD/COP/DEC/VII/16; see also Subsidiary Body on Scientific, Technical and Technological Advice, *Managing Biodiversity Is about People*, UN Doc. UNEP/CBD/SBSTTA/17/INF/1.

of biodiversity recognised in the treaty's preamble but not suited to an idea of aesthetic value as wilderness.

Ultimately, my aesthetic analysis of the mangrove and elephant images in *GBO-4* (Figures 7.6 and 7.7) serves to identify aesthetic legacies and contradictions embedded in visual representations of biodiversity in the work of the *Biodiversity Convention*. With no humans in view, the photographic images are not a comprehensive representation of the concept of biological diversity that is the foundation of the treaty. The images facilitate critical understandings of aesthetic value showing how ideas of natural beauty portrayed in the photographs are culturally situated as scenic beauty and wilderness. The photographs can also be analysed from an aesthetic perspective to highlight differences between biodiversity's aesthetic value and other values – intrinsic, or economic. Aesthetic analysis also illuminates understanding of the object of value – biodiversity. In Section 7.3.2, I will reflect on aesthetic perspectives of another environmental value – cultural value – revealed in photographs in *GBO-4* as one that can be distinguished from the aesthetic value of biodiversity despite their conflation in treaty practice.

7.3.2 *Aesthetic Value of Biodiversity as Culture*

The 'aesthetic' value of biodiversity is listed separately from 'cultural' value in the preamble to the *Biodiversity Convention*.[110] I have, however, noted links between aesthetic and cultural value that have been made by the parties to the *Biodiversity Convention*.[111] Methods for the valuation of biodiversity on the basis of 'ecosystem services', for example, include various environmental functions described as 'aesthetic' in the category of 'cultural' services.[112] In this section, I analyse the aesthetic value of the environment understood from the photographs in terms of culture. Specifically, I examine cultural elements of biodiversity's aesthetic value and aesthetic elements of biodiversity's cultural value.

7.3.2.1 Cultural Elements of Biodiversity's Aesthetic Value

Some philosophers of environmental aesthetics distinguish the aesthetic appreciation of the natural environment from that of culture, such as built

[110] First tiret of the preamble of the *Convention on Biological Diversity*.
[111] See Section 7.2.2, in the context of ecosystem services.
[112] See Cooper et al., 'Aesthetic and spiritual values'.

environments and artefacts.[113] The natural environment is not considered a product of human craft, enabling a distinction between the aesthetic appreciation of the natural environment, on the one hand, and cultivated landscapes as artificial design, on the other hand. Similarly, an aesthetic appreciation of art depicting the natural environment, or made from materials sourced from the natural environment – what I discussed as 'environmental art' in Chapter 4 – is not generally contemplated for the kind of aesthetic appreciation conceived by philosophers of environmental aesthetics.[114]

Several philosophers of environmental aesthetics nevertheless argue that a person's aesthetic appreciation of the environment is a function of culture.[115] That culture is one shared among a community of people, whether defined by language, ethnicity or nationality. For this purpose, it remains the case that the object of appreciation – the natural environment – is not a cultural object in the way that art or architecture is a cultural object. Instead, the person appreciating the natural environment is a cultural subject. *Earth's Creation* (Figure 7.1), the artwork discussed at the outset of this chapter, can be seen as a cultural object but it could also be characterised for the philosophy of environmental aesthetics as a manifestation of the artist's aesthetic appreciation of the environment, as informed by her culture.[116] Western science could also be characterised as a form of cultural knowledge that informs a human subject's aesthetic appreciation of the environment.[117] As discussed earlier in this chapter,[118] the appreciation of the natural environment in terms of natural beauty defined by scenic and wilderness qualities is understood with reference to culture, Western European and Anglo-American culture, depicted in the form of scenic beauty in landscape art and concepts of wilderness.

In this section, I analyse two photographs in *GBO-4* to explain philosophical aspects of the relationship between aesthetic and cultural values of biodiversity protected by the treaty. Like the other photographs I have analysed, no titles or captions are used in *GBO-4* to describe the subject matter of the images. One of the photographs (Figure 7.8) shows a man with a wooden rod over his shoulders, tin cans strung from each end – a possible water-carrier. It is included with the discussion of Aichi Target 1 on raising awareness of

[113] See further Section 2.2.1. See also Maskit, 'On universalism and cultural historicism', 41.
[114] See Section 4.2.2.
[115] See Maskit. 'On universalism and cultural historicism'.
[116] On Indigenous perspectives, see discussion of Julie Gough, 'Observance' (Figure 8.1) in Chapter 8.
[117] See, for example, Brady, *Aesthetics of the Natural Environment*, p. 77.
[118] See Section 7.3.1.

FIGURE 7.8. Untitled (man), Secretariat of the *Convention on Biological Diversity*, *Global Biodiversity Outlook* 4, 35. Photo under license of Shutterstock to Secretariat of the *Convention on Biological Diversity*.

FIGURE 7.9. Untitled (men), Secretariat of the *Convention on Biological Diversity*, *Global Biodiversity Outlook* 4, p. 120. Photo under license of Shutterstock to Secretariat of the *Convention on Biological Diversity*.

biodiversity values.[119] Another photograph (Figure 7.9) shows a man in a natural environment who appears to be fishing. It is featured in the section

[119] Secretariat of the *Convention on Biological Diversity*, *Global Biodiversity Outlook* 4, p. 35.

of *GBO-4* assessing Aichi Target 19 on the development of knowledge of biodiversity values.[120]

The *GBO-4* photographs of the water-carrier and the fisherman can be analysed together to develop a particular understanding of cultural value for the aesthetic appreciation of the environment that is theorised in the philosophy of environmental aesthetics.[121] Both photographs are portraits of men standing in what might be seen as a rural environment. The water-carrier looks up and out at the world. He is alone, contemplating the environment around him, an environment that extends outside the frame of the image. In the other image, the fisherman is introspective, focused on the detail of a fishing line that renders all around it irrelevant. He has a sarong tied around his waist, a naked torso and wears a turban. There are other people behind him. Like them, the main figure appears to be balanced on stilts, a method of fishing common in Sri Lanka.[122]

From the two images, it could be said that the human subjects see their environments differently, from their own vantage points, with their own aesthetic sensibility. The water-carrier could be characterised for the purposes of the philosophy of environmental aesthetics as an archetype of a subjectivist aesthetic experience. But the fisherman, from his clothing and his method of fishing, appears as a product of his culture. He could be seen as appreciating the natural environment around him from a specific cultural vantage.[123] He has a like-minded community of people about him who share that cultural perspective and the elements of the aesthetic experience that come with it. In this way, the fisherman is perhaps closer to the objectivists in the philosophy of environmental aesthetics,[124] where traditional knowledge, as opposed to Western science, could be seen to lend an objective frame of reference to his aesthetic experience of the environment. This is not to say that the aesthetic experience of the environment is necessarily all or only cultural. Some philosophers of aesthetics maintain that it is.[125] However, for others such as Emily Brady, cultural value is one element that joins others, such as emotion and imagination, to shape the aesthetic value of the environment.[126]

[120] Ibid., p.120.
[121] See, for example, Brady, *Aesthetics of the Natural Environment*, p. 52.
[122] Alexander, *Sri Lankan Fishermen*.
[123] However, see my discussion of 'subsistence' value in Section 7.3.2.3.
[124] See, for example, Carlson, *Aesthetics and the Environment*; see also Brady, *Aesthetics of the Natural Environment*, p. 191.
[125] See Maskit, 'On universalism and cultural historicism'.
[126] Brady, *Aesthetics of the Natural Environment*, p. 146.

FIGURE 7.10. John Glover, *The River Nile, Van Diemen's Land, from Mr Glover's farm*, 1837. Oil on canvas, 76.4 × 114.6 cm. National Gallery of Victoria, Melbourne. Felton Bequest, 1956. Photo: National Gallery of Victoria.

An aesthetic analysis of the *GBO-4* photographs can be instructive in explaining cultural elements of the aesthetic appreciation of the environment for the philosophy of environmental aesthetics. But the photographs can also inspire eco-critical reflections on the vision of 'undeveloped' landscapes embedded in the cultural legacy of Western art. The contemplative gaze of the water-carrier, and the balletic poise of the fisherman, both men of colour, could be seen as suggestive of the hunters and gatherers of societies that were so frequently depicted as primitive in British and European art from colonial encounters.[127] Portrayals of 'native' communities and the 'noble savage' – such as those apparent in paintings depicting an Australian 'Aboriginal Arcadia' – have long been critiqued for the oppression they engender.[128] Nineteenth-century British painter John Glover imagined Indigenous peoples into his paintings of the Tasmanian landscape (Figure 7.10) long after so many had been killed or exiled from their country by the colonial settlers.[129] Glover and

[127] See Leahy and Ryan (eds.), *Colony*, p. 190. On 'noble savage', see Gillespie, *International Environmental Law, Policy and Ethics*, p. 84. Cf. Chalmers, 'Native dignity'.

[128] See Edwards, 'A delightful and difficult art', 178; Staszak, 'Primitivism and the Other'; Broude (ed.), *Gauguin's Challenge*.

[129] Hansen and Timms (eds.), *John Glover and the Colonial Picturesque*. In relation to law, see Neale, 'Duplicity of meaning';

FIGURE 7.11. Danie Mellor, *Et in arcadia ego (of landscape and memory)*, 2011. Wax pastel, pencil, glitter, Swarovski crystal and wash on Saunders Waterford paper, 152 × 226 cm. Private collection. © Danie Mellor. Courtesy the artist and Tolarno Galleries, Melbourne.

other artists of the time show Indigenous peoples as naïve, so enmeshed with their natural environments that they are not seen – not recognised apart from the exotic environment – by the European invaders of the territory.[130]

Contemporary artists have highlighted such critical elements through their works.[131] Artist Danie Mellor, for example, critiques depictions of pre-contact Australia as a savage nirvana: Indigenous people 'at play', living with and on the continent's fauna and flora.[132] Mellor's artwork, *Et in arcadia ego (of landscape and memory)* (Figure 7.11), evokes with its title the seventeenth-century French Baroque painting by Nicolas Poussin.[133] But in Mellor's work, the pasture green is blue, and the shepherd in death takes a very different form. The scene shows an Indigenous man, poised on a fallen tree trunk, returning from a hunt with marsupials draped around his shoulders. A white

[130] McLean, 'The Australianness of the English Claude'; Gough et al., *Fugitive History*.

[131] See McMillan, *Contemporary Art and Unforgetting in Colonial Landscapes*.

[132] Palmer, 'Introduction', 17.

[133] Ibid., 52–3. See Nicolas Poussin, *Et in arcadia ego* (also known as *Les bergers d'Arcadie* or *The Arcadian Shepherds*).

man, also standing on a fallen tree in the rainforest but dressed for the city, aims a rifle at the tangled tree canopy. Fauna endemic to Australia – though not all from a rainforest habitat – are off-scale icons in a post-settlement imaginary, pasted on a seemingly alien forest in this conjured Eden and memorialised within a gilded floral frame. Both humans are visible, distinct from the landscape. But only one knows the value of place. Only one belongs. If anyone is naïve in this image, it is the hapless European, soon to be entombed – not the First Nations man who knows the place and is sure to survive.

Casting the fisherman in the *GBO-4* photograph (Figure 7.9) in similar terms, the man is no longer the culturally embedded appreciator of a natural environment. Nor is he primitive. He and the water-carrier (Figure 7.8) could instead be seen as symbols of resilience, wise and well-practised stewards of a fragile environment. Rather than seeing the *GBO-4* photographs as perpetuating disingenuous tropes, aesthetic analysis can be used to redeem the images as a depiction of cultural knowledge of biodiversity protected under the *Biodiversity Convention*. In the next section, I address the cultural value of biodiversity expressed in the aesthetic practices of Indigenous peoples that can – and I argue should – be distinguished from cultural elements that inform aesthetic appreciation of biodiversity.

7.3.2.2 Aesthetic Elements of Biodiversity's Cultural Values

Like aesthetic value, the 'cultural' value of biodiversity and its components acknowledged in the preamble to the *Biodiversity Convention* is not defined. It might include the value of knowledges of Indigenous and local communities, relevant to the conservation of biodiversity, which is protected under the treaty.[134] It is these forms of knowledge that give rise to 'biocultural rights'.[135] *Cultural and Spiritual Values of Biodiversity* is an edited compendium of essays produced for the United Nations Environment Programme that has been cited in work of the Secretariat to the *Biodiversity Convention*.[136] The editor of the compendium associates 'cultural value' with, among other things, 'the beliefs and practices of indigenous and traditional peoples in relation to

[134] Articles 8(j) (traditional knowledge) and 10(c) (customary use) of the *Convention on Biological Diversity*.

[135] Bavikatte and Bennett, 'Community stewardship'.

[136] See, for example, Conference of the Parties to the *Convention on Biological Diversity*, *Report of the Sixth Meeting of the Conference of the Parties to the Convention on Biological Diversity*, UN Doc. UNEP/CBD/COP/6/20, Annex 1.

their use and conservation of biodiversity'.[137] The cultural value of biodiversity is also described by other contributors to the compendium with reference to aesthetic values associated with the arts.[138] Particular mention is made of the creative arts of Indigenous and traditional communities, including stories, dances and songs.[139] Photographs used in the publication depict scenes of First Nations lands at risk from human pollution embroidered on fabric, as well as 'bark-cloth' paintings representing animals and hunting methods.[140]

Characterisations in *Cultural and Spiritual Values of Biodiversity* of the cultural value of biodiversity as 'aesthetic' suggests a Western European and Anglo-American conception of aesthetics related to the arts. But it is not clear from that compendium how artistic expressions of cultural value might also relate to the aesthetic value of biodiversity in terms conceived by philosophers of environmental aesthetics. Nor is it clear if the conception of aesthetic value in Western European and Anglo-American philosophy – as it relates to either the arts or to the natural environment – is appropriately extended to cultural or other appreciations of the environment among First Nations communities. The use of non-Indigenous aesthetic concepts to describe what some identify as 'Indigenous art', and relationships of First Nations peoples to the natural environment apparent in art, is contested and would require explanation and qualification.[141]

In contrast to *Cultural and Spiritual Values of Biodiversity*, there are no images in *GBO-4* of creative arts as an expression of the cultural value of biodiversity, Indigenous or otherwise. The image of the fisherman (Figure 7.9) is, arguably, an image of artisanal fishing practice that might be born of traditional knowledge that is protective of biodiversity. But in the photographic images included in *GBO-4*, no one is seen painting with ochre hues on bark, no one fashions twigs and leaves into artefact, no one dons decorative feathers for a hunt or ceremonial dance. With the absence of such images, *GBO-4* has avoided tropes that can stereotype and oppress. Yet *GBO-4* might have also missed an opportunity to address connections made by the parties themselves between biodiversity's aesthetic value and culture[142] – and to

[137] Posey, 'Introduction'. See also Gillespie, *International Environmental Law, Policy and Ethics*, 2nd edn, p. 86. Cf. Godden, 'Indigenous heritage and the environment'.

[138] See McLean, 'Art and environment', 439; Chernela, 'Indigenous knowledge', at 423 (see also colour plates 22–4 after 284); Hillman, 'Where is the environment?', at 486–7.

[139] See, for example, Whitt, 'Indigenous peoples', 69; Montes, 'Spirit, story and medicine', 276.

[140] See Posey (ed.), *Cultural and Spiritual Values of Biodiversity*, colour plates after p. 284.

[141] See Garneau, 'Indigenous art'.

[142] See Section 7.2.2.

FIGURE 7.12. Abel Rodríguez, *Annual cycle of the flooded rainforest*, 2009–10 (one of a series of 12). Ink, graphite, watercolour on paper, 50 × 70 cm. Courtesy Tropenbos Colombia.

reconceive the dominant aesthetic of Britain and Western Europe from perspectives of First Nations peoples.

Some examples of art by First Nations peoples can be seen to express the cultural knowledge of biodiversity, and the value of that knowledge, through aesthetic practices familiar to a Western European and Anglo-American conception of aesthetics related to the arts. In ways explained below, these works can be seen as aesthetic translations of Indigenous values of biodiversity aimed at educating non-Indigenous communities so that they might also value and protect biodiversity on that basis.

The meticulous ink, graphite and watercolour drawings of Nonuya elder, Abel Rodríguez, are an example of knowledge communicated across Indigenous and European imaginaries of biodiversity. They are an artistic representation of Indigenous knowledge of the natural environment in ways that can be understood in terms of biodiversity. Select drawings from the series 'Annual cycle of the flooded rainforest' (Figure 7.12) and 'Studies of trees' (Figure 7.13) show trees, and details of leaves, as well as fauna, from the Cahuinari region in Colombia. Notations in Nonuya and Spanish languages explain the structures or properties of plants. With written annotations reminiscent of the botanical records of the naturalists that would accompany

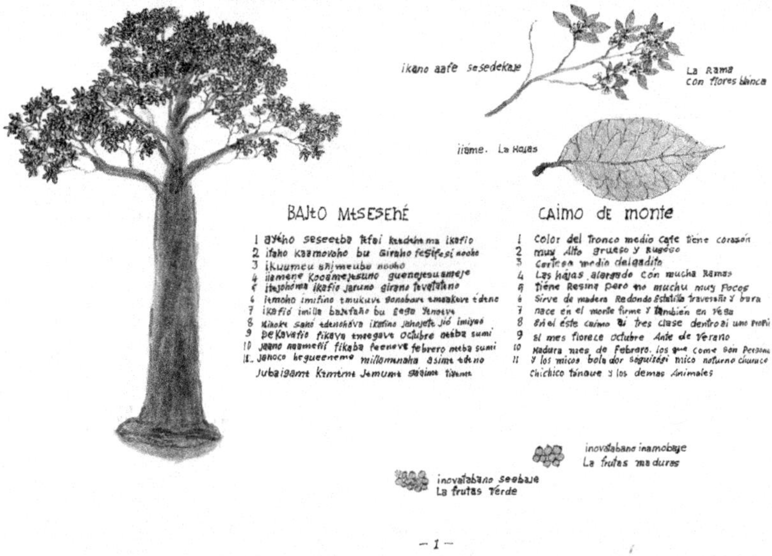

FIGURE 7.13. Abel Rodríguez, *Caimo de monte*, 2008 (from the series *Studies of trees*). Ink on paper, 23 × 34 cm. Courtesy Tropenbos Colombia.

colonial explorers,[143] Rodríguez' delicate portrayals of flora and fauna display an intimate knowledge of both the parts and processes that make habitats whole. He has an expertise apart from Western natural science that is highly sensitive to the variability and interdependence of life's elements and peculiar to his community's land. Rodríguez' willingness to provide open access to Nonuya knowledge of nature's instrumental qualities is unnerving for those viewers concerned about any piratic dispositions of corporations.[144] For Rodríguez, however, this may well facilitate an elder's task in the preservation of nature for future generations.[145]

The artistic collaboration of Mulkun Wirrpanda and John Wolseley provides further reflection on the relationship between aesthetics and First Nations culture in connection with biodiversity.[146] The artists' contrapuntal

[143] See Brunton (ed.), *The Endeavour Journal of Joseph Banks*; Fornasiero, Monteath and West-Sooby, *Encountering Terra Australis*.

[144] See Gillespie, *Conservation, Biodiversity and International Law*, p. 501. See also Eckstein and Schwarz (eds.), *Postcolonial Piracy*; Elsdon, 'Protecting the intellectual and cultural property of Aboriginal art'.

[145] See Roca, 'Abel Rodríguez'; Rodríguez, *Las Plantas Cultivadas*.

[146] See Stubbs and Wolseley (eds.), *Midawarr Harvest*. See also Mandy Martin's 'extensive immersion projects': Haynes, *Mandy Martin*, p. 10; and Fiona Hall's collaboration with Tjanpi Desert Weavers: Hall, *Wrong Way Time*.

visions of the environment's aesthetics facilitate a dual conception of culture as, on the one hand, traditional knowledge of biodiversity and, on the other hand, aesthetic convention for representations of the environment.[147] Wirrpanda communicates her Indigenous knowledge of biodiversity to Wolseley through art and he 'repeats' the catechism through an European aesthetic tradition. The resulting hybridised environmental aesthetic could be critiqued by those wary of the 'assimilation' of Aboriginal imaginaries,[148] but this collaboration sees a Western aesthetic value of biodiversity led by an Indigenous knowledge that is vital to the protection of biodiversity.

My aesthetic examination of artworks representing traditional knowledge of the natural environment shows how images can contribute to a conceptualisation of the cultural value of biodiversity for the *Biodiversity Convention*. The use of such images in *GBO-4* could have served the states parties in their understanding of aesthetic elements of biodiversity's cultural value as distinct from the cultural elements of the aesthetic value of biodiversity. Distinctions between cultural and aesthetic value in these terms could have implications for the implementation of the treaty – for what is protected, and how it is protected, in ways informed by and protective of Indigenous values. While I have for the purposes of this analysis identified values in *images* absent from *GBO-4*, I now turn to consider how the *GBO-4* images present a *value* absent from the express terms of the treaty: Subsistence value.

7.3.2.3 Subsistence Value of Biodiversity through Aesthetics

Missing from the list of biodiversity values in the preamble to the *Biodiversity Convention* is an environmental value essential to the very concept of biological diversity – the subsistence value of biodiversity. Described in a technical report used as a basis for *GBO-4* as a non-monetary value,[149] subsistence is eerily absent from the intrinsic, ecological, genetic, social, economic, scientific, educational, cultural, recreational or aesthetic biodiversity values expressly protected under the treaty.[150] Some of the values could perhaps be interpreted to include subsistence. The mention of 'intrinsic' value might stretch to a right of survival of all species, and 'ecological' value rests on an

[147] See, for example, Wirrpanda and Wolseley, *Midawarr Harvest.*
[148] See, for example, Leslie, *Aboriginal Art*, p. 43.
[149] See Leadley et al., *Progress towards the Aichi Biodiversity Targets*, p. 17. See also at p. 23. See generally Maass, *The Cultural Context of Biodiversity Conservation*, p. 315.
[150] First tiret of the preamble of the *Convention on Biological Diversity*. There is no reference to subsistence value in the treaty.

awareness of the interdependence of all life.[151] But none quite speaks to the value of biodiversity for human survival.[152]

The subsistence value of biodiversity is one particularly relevant to developing country states, sometimes contrasted with and elevated above biodiversity's aesthetic value.[153] In his contribution to *Cultural and Spiritual Values of Biodiversity*, for example, Clark Peteru observed that '[d]espite the turmoil [in Western Samoa], people still survive from their own plot of land rather than the supermarket shelf.'[154] He described 'Western Samoan views of the environment' in terms of subsistence as opposed to aesthetic value:

> Survival requires pragmatism not aestheticism, and for that reason Samoans have a utilitarian view of nature. Nature exists to feed, to house, then to satisfy cultural obligations. Usually it is only at the end of the day that one can relax and enjoy one's surroundings and the coolness of the approaching evening. To my knowledge the environment is neither revered nor protected for its own sake.[155]

Artist Amar Kanwar's video artwork *The Scene of Crime* (Figure 7.14) speaks to the relationship between the subsistence value of the natural environment and environmental conservation in developing countries. Various scenes and sounds are combined in the work to portray the resistance of people displaced from subsistence farming lands earmarked for industrial development in the Indian state of Odisha. The video is part of a larger multimedia installation called *The Sovereign Forest* (2011), comprising books, documents, soundscapes, a collection of seeds and various artefacts that, the artist says, are evidence of crimes against people and the environments that sustain them.[156]

The absence of subsistence value from the biodiversity values listed for protection under the *Biodiversity Convention* is difficult to reconcile with the account often given of the treaty as having marked a shift in international environmental law in favour of the 'developing' Global South.[157]

[151] See Fosci and West, 'In whose interest?', 75.

[152] See Cardinale et al., 'Biodiversity loss'.

[153] See generally Roe, Fancourt and Sandbrook, 'Biodiversity conservation and poverty reduction'.

[154] Peteru, 'Western Samoan views of the environment', 422.

[155] Ibid., 421.

[156] See TarraWarra Museum of Art, *TarraWarra International* 2013.

[157] See Kotsakis, 'The historical roots of the north-south dynamic', 44. I variously refer to 'developing countries' and the 'Global South' to refer to countries with low- and middle-income economies or that otherwise identify as 'developing countries' in the work of the *Convention on Biological Diversity*. I distinguish them from so-called developed countries of the 'North' that have high-income economies. See further Anghie, *Imperialism, Sovereignty and the Making of International Law*.

FIGURE 7.14. Amar Kanwar, *The Scene of Crime*, 2011 (still). HD video installation (colour, sound), 42 min, part of the *Sovereign Forest* multimedia installation. © Amar Kanwar. Courtesy Marian Goodman Gallery.

The equitable sharing of 'benefits' flowing from the exploitation of genetic resources, recognised in the objectives and expressed through Articles 15 and 19 of the *Biodiversity Convention*, had been a demand of developing countries.[158] With developing countries constituting many of the centres of diversity for genetic resources that are desired for pharmaceutical and other development by countries of the 'developed' North,[159] the Global South succeeded in asserting a claim to the benefits associated with the exploitation of this natural resource within their jurisdictions. The adoption of the treaty was, ultimately, an assertion of sovereign equality in name and in practice. It was a move away from the international administration of environmental protections under, for example, the *World Heritage Convention*, to nationalised processes of biodiversity conservation.

Despite there being no express reference to subsistence value in the *Biodiversity Convention*, the photographs of the water-carrier and fisherman in *GBO-4* (Figures 7.8 and 7.9) can be analysed in such terms. Both men are engaged in tasks of subsistence, one (I have assumed) collecting freshwater,

[158] See further *Nagoya Protocol on Access to Genetic Resources and the Fair and Equitable Sharing of Benefits Arising from their Utilization to the Convention on Biological Diversity*, Nagoya, 29 October 2010, in force 12 October 2014, 3008 UNTS 3.

[159] See Gillespie, *Conservation, Biodiversity and International Law*, p. 501.

the other hoping to catch a fish for an evening meal. These photographic images of people living from the natural environment highlight the subsistence value of biodiversity in ways vital for people of the Global South. As such, they evoke an 'environmentalism of the poor' to describe values of the environment common to many living in developing countries.[160] This articulation of environmentalism rejects a conception of the Global South as favouring economic development over environmental protection. Indeed, Rob Nixon says the North's focus on the conservation of 'charismatic megafauna' in a 'masculinist tradition' is at odds with the environmental values of the South.[161] The *GBO-4* photographs could be seen to recognise instead the value of clean environments to poor communities for sustenance.

The photographs of the water-carrier and the fisherman (Figures 7.8 and 7.9), understood in terms of the subsistence value of biodiversity, is a repost to the photographs in *GBO-4* of natural beauty.[162] My aesthetic analysis of the images serves to highlight subsistence as a value of biodiversity that is additional to those expressly contemplated by the states parties in the treaty. It understands the images from a position of the Global South, addressing Nixon's concern that eco-criticism as a scholarly endeavour has focused on North American culture.[163] In doing so, however, my analysis risks perpetuating stereotypes about attitudes towards the environment in developing countries. It also underplays the relevance of the images to all parties to the *Biodiversity Convention*, as biodiversity's subsistence value must also pertain to people in cities and in the industrialised countries of the North. Ultimately, an analysis of the photographs for their representations shows that the selection of images for their portrayal of the biodiversity values protected by the *Biodiversity Convention* must be mindful of different perspectives and the many meanings that can be seen to arise from images using aesthetic methods.

7.3.3 *Fragmented Aesthetics of Biodiversity*

My doctrinal interpretation of aesthetic value for the *Biodiversity Convention* from orthodox written sources in Chapter 3 concluded that aesthetic value might be synonymous with 'natural beauty', and that it is in the practice of the states parties conflated with cultural values of biodiversity.[164] Turning instead

[160] See Guha, *Environmentalism*. See Section 2.4.3.
[161] Nixon, *Slow Violence*, p. 139.
[162] See Section 7.3.1.
[163] Nixon, *Slow Violence*, p. 234.
[164] See Section 3.3.2.2.

to the photographic images used in *GBO-4*, I have used aesthetic methods to examine meanings of biodiversity's aesthetic value from the perspective of aesthetic philosophy – both as it concerns the arts and the natural environment. My aesthetic analysis of the images has revealed critical perspectives on 'natural beauty' as scenic landscapes and wilderness. It also provided an account of the relationship between biodiversity's aesthetic value and its cultural value, identifying distinctions important to the protection of each value of biodiversity in its own right.

For meanings of 'aesthetic' value under the *Biodiversity Convention*, the photographs in *GBO-4* support an understanding of natural beauty as scenic landscape or wilderness. But they also facilitate a critique of aesthetic value as natural beauty, associating the value with cultural values of Britain, Western Europe and North America. Aesthetic analysis, whether from the perspective of environmental aesthetics or art theory, can reveal the ways in which the concepts and values evoked in the photographs in *GBO-4* might ultimately undermine the objectives of the *Biodiversity Convention*. How, for example, the aesthetic appeal of a rice paddy scene (Figure 7.3) is not necessarily indicative of the aesthetic value of biodiversity.

My aesthetic analysis also raises the prospect that the 'aesthetic' value of biodiversity contemplated in the *Biodiversity Convention* is separate from the 'cultural' value inherent in, or manifested by, the traditional knowledge and cultural practices of Indigenous peoples and local communities protected under the treaty. An understanding of the *cultural elements* of aesthetic values applied to biodiversity allows for pluralised definitions of aesthetic value appropriate for a treaty, with states parties representing a wide range of cultural perspectives. Separately, an understanding of the *aesthetic elements* of the cultural value of biodiversity in terms of the arts can take proper account of Indigenous values in articulations of that value for the implementation of a treaty that protects aesthetic and cultural values as distinct values of biodiversity.

Ultimately, my analysis of the photographic images in *GBO-4* reveals fragmented understandings of biodiversity's aesthetic value. It highlights complex intersections with other values named in the treaty, such as recreational, cultural and economic values, and values not named, such as subsistence value. It points to issues arising from the application of values to biodiversity as distinct from the natural environment. It does not resolve the ambiguity of meaning left by doctrinal interpretation but it could inform a critical understanding of aesthetic value for the collective oversight by the Conference of the Parties of the implementation of the *Biodiversity Convention*.

7.4 USING AESTHETIC ANALYSIS OF IMAGES FOR THE *BIODIVERSITY CONVENTION*

I have shown in this and previous chapters how photographs of the natural environment can be analysed from an aesthetic perspective to develop understandings of terms relevant to the implementation of international environmental treaties. Specifically, I have used images to understand the meaning of the environment's aesthetic value to such treaties.[165] In this section, I argue that meanings from photographic images could also be identified and used to inform decisions of the Conference of the Parties to the *Biodiversity Convention* and the implementation of the treaty by states parties.

Editions of the *Global Biodiversity Outlook* have, over time, made increasing use of photographic images.[166] Other reports to the Conference of the Parties to the *Biodiversity Convention*, such as national reports prepared under the treaty by individual states parties,[167] also contain photographic images. The Maldives Fifth National Report, for example, is replete with photographs, most depicting vivid scenes associated with the archipelago's biodiversity.[168] As I noted in Chapter 5 on the *World Heritage Convention*,[169] photographs that represent the natural environment can be seen to document for international environmental treaty regimes determinations of aesthetic value in their administration of the treaty. There is, however, no guidance from the Conference of the Parties to the *Biodiversity Convention* on the use and purpose of photographs in reports prepared under the treaty.[170] Existing guidance issued by the Secretariat to the *Biodiversity Convention* on the preparation of national reports has encouraged parties 'to include illustrative tables, figures and images',[171] but no reason or requirements are provided for photographs.

Recognising the capacity for photographs to convey meanings, the Conference of the Parties could in the future endorse and facilitate the use of photographic images for their substantive relevance to the implementation

165 See Chapter 5 for the *World Heritage Convention* and Chapter 6 for the *Whaling Convention*.
166 See Secretariat of the *Convention on Biological Diversity*, 'Global Biodiversity Outlook (GBO)'.
167 Article 26 of the *Convention on Biological Diversity*.
168 Maldives, 'Fifth national report'. Cf. photographs in Uganda, 'Fifth national report'.
169 See Section 5.5.1.
170 Secretariat of the *Convention on Biological Diversity*, *Use of Cameras and Audio/Video Recording Devices*.
171 Conference of the Parties to the *Convention on Biological Diversity*, *National Reporting: Review of Experience and Proposals for the Fifth National Report*, UN Doc. UNEP/CBD/COP/DEC/X/10, p. 6; see also Secretariat of the *Convention on Biological Diversity*, 'Guidelines for the fourth national report'.

of the *Biodiversity Convention*. It could, for example, produce guidance to states parties and the Secretariat on the presentation of photographic images in reports prepared under the *Biodiversity Convention*. Formal guidance could ensure that images consistent with the parties' understanding of the terms of the treaty – including biodiversity's 'aesthetic' value – are used to portray or explain the meaning of such terms in those reports. Guidance could in turn facilitate a discussion among the parties as to the meaning of aesthetic and other biodiversity values with reference to such photographs.

Guidance would need to address such matters as the quality of images used, and the nature of any written commentary accompanying the image. As discussed in Chapter 5 on the *World Heritage Convention*,[172] the capacity of an image to activate an imaginative or emotional response to the environment it represents could be compromised by its small size or low resolution. The content and quality of the written text accompanying images, such as descriptions of properties in files nominating sites for World Heritage status and Statements of Outstanding Universal Value, could also steer aesthetic analysis of the images for the *Biodiversity Convention*. Marie Voignier's visual footage is one aspect of her artwork (Figure 7.5), the narration is another ('Each person was allowed 15 animals.'). In the case of *GBO-4* studied for this chapter, large-format and high-resolution photographs appeared with the written text. No captions or written text described the content of the photographs or explained their relevance to the findings in the report.[173] The high quality of the images facilitated my aesthetic analysis but the absence of any written explanation might have meant that assumptions I made for the purposes of aesthetic analysis were not accurate.

It would also be appropriate for guidance on the use of photographs in reports prepared under the *Biodiversity Convention* to explain the purpose of using images. Guidance could, for example, address the relevance of the images to interpretations of the parties' commitments under the treaty. Considerations that determine whether written documents are appropriate sources for doctrinal treaty interpretation, such as evidence of subsequent practice,[174] could also be used by interpreters to determine whether images qualify as an interpretative source. I argued in Chapter 5 that photographs used in documents nominating properties for World Heritage status were a

[172] See Section 5.5.2.

[173] See Secretariat of the *Convention on Biological Diversity*, 'Global Biodiversity Outlook (GBO)'. *Global Biodiversity Outlook 2* included captions while *Global Biodiversity Outlook 3* provided explanatory text or captions for only some photographs.

[174] Gardiner, *Treaty Interpretation*, p. 255.

lawful source of interpretation;[175] in Chapter 6 I argued that photographs included in the submissions of parties to the International Court of Justice could also be understood for their meaning in a legal judgment.[176] For the purposes of interpreting the *Biodiversity Convention*, my finding that *GBO-4* does not 'establish the agreement of the parties' as to the meaning of aesthetic value might also disqualify images contained in *GBO-4* from formal consideration in interpretation. However, formal guidance developed by the states parties to the *Biodiversity Convention* could clarify the circumstances in which such images would inform the states parties in their implementation of the treaty.

As an alternative to guidance, the Conference of the Parties to the *Biodiversity Convention* could expressly state that images in their documentation are excluded from substantive considerations in its work. The IPBES, to which the Secretariat to the *Biodiversity Convention* is an observer,[177] has on occasion expressly claimed to have excluded photographic images from substantive conclusions.[178] This would not, however, prevent substantive conclusions being drawn from images as a matter of practice. Relegating images to an unspecified decorative function does not mean that they cannot be seen for their aesthetic significance. Such relegation would serve only to dismiss the critical insights that might come from an overt analysis of the images in light of biodiversity values and other matters relevant to the implementation of commitments under the *Biodiversity Convention*.

Finally, where the Conference of the Parties to the *Biodiversity Convention* endorses valuation methodologies, it should also propose the use of aesthetic methods of assessment. For example, the interdisciplinary premise for the assessment of 'nature's contribution to people', employed by IPBES and endorsed by the Conference of the Parties,[179] could be extended to take account of the philosophy of environmental aesthetics and aesthetic methods for developing meanings from photographs, including meanings of aesthetic value.[180] As I argued in Chapter 2,[181] understandings of the aesthetic value of the natural environment developed in the philosophy of environmental

[175] See Section 5.5.3.
[176] See Section 6.5.3.
[177] See IPBES, 'Members and observers'.
[178] Cf. a disclaimer accompanying photographs provided with Intergovernmental Science-Policy Platform on Biodiversity and Ecosystem Services (IPBES), 'Dangerous decline'.
[179] See explanation above, Section 7.2.2.
[180] See, for example, UK National Ecosystem Assessment Follow-on Phase, 'Cultural ecosystem services and indicators', Annex 1.
[181] See Section 2.4.

aesthetics have a role in the valuation of the natural environment in public policy settings and, by extension, in law.[182] Understandings of the environment's aesthetic value in terms of a sensorial experience, as developed by philosophers such as Emily Brady,[183] could be employed to articulate a meaning for the aesthetic valued under the *Biodiversity Convention* as distinct from other biodiversity values that must also be protected under the treaty. The aesthetic analysis of images of the natural environment could also be employed in the valuation of biodiversity to enlighten conceptions of biodiversity values, particularly non-material values such as aesthetic value, in the implementation and development of the *Biodiversity Convention*.

7.5 CONCLUSION

By many accounts, a failure to achieve the objectives of the *Biodiversity Convention* will have devastating impacts on all life on earth.[184] But a lack of visibility of species and habitat diversity in the daily lives of many people is thought to contribute to complacency in its protection. Executive Secretary for the *Biodiversity Convention*, Cristiana Paşca Palmer, has for example referred to biodiversity loss as a 'silent killer', different from climate change 'where people feel the impact in everyday life'.[185] Indeed, it is the imperceptibility of the significance of biodiversity to people that prompted the Conference of the Parties to the *Biodiversity Convention* to use the first of their Aichi Targets to call on states to raise the awareness of biodiversity values.[186]

Images of biodiversity could be used in institutional publications such as the *Global Biodiversity Outlook* and other materials produced under the *Biodiversity Convention* to explain and foster the protection of biodiversity values in a manner that is openly acknowledged and properly explained in aesthetic terms. Campaigns of environmental organisations, such as *Love Not*

[182] See, for example, Brady, *Aesthetics of the Natural Environment*; see also Sepänmaa, 'From theoretical to applied environmental aesthetics', 87.

[183] See Brady, *Aesthetics of the Natural Environment*, 237–8.

[184] See, for example, Fischer et al. (eds.), *Summary for Policymakers of the Regional Assessment Report*.

[185] Cristiana Paşca Palmer, quoted in Watts, 'Stop biodiversity loss'. See also Conference of the Parties to the *Convention on Biological Diversity*, 'Opening statement by Ms. Cristiana Paşca Palmer, Executive Secretary of the *Convention on Biological Diversity*' in *Report of the Conference of the Parties to the Convention on Biological Diversity on its Fourteenth Meeting*, UN Doc. CBD/COP/14/14, Annex II, p. 292.

[186] Secretariat of the *Convention on Biological Diversity*, *Global Biodiversity Outlook*. See also Lloyd, 'Reconsidering the species-specific approach'.

Loss, deliberately use images to raise awareness of the value of biodiversity to people.[187] However, the Conference of the Parties has produced no formal guidance that identifies the purpose of images, or articulates meanings for images, to its formal decisions under the *Biodiversity Convention*. My aesthetic analysis of the photographs in *GBO-4* in this chapter shows why and how this could be done.

Aesthetic insights from photographic images of biodiversity can be used to develop understandings of biodiversity values that are deemed so fundamental to the implementation of the *Biodiversity Convention* that they are expressly named in the treaty's preamble. I have shown how aesthetic analysis is useful to an understanding of aesthetic value as a value of biodiversity that is both important and distinct from other values of biodiversity, including cultural value. My analysis has also shown that critical perspectives applied to images through aesthetic methods such as eco-criticism can be used to identify and exclude images that undermine or are otherwise inconsistent with the objectives of the treaty. In the next and final chapter, I will address my conclusions in this chapter with reference to my findings throughout the book.

[187] See International Union for Conservation of Nature, 'Love not loss'.

8

Beyond the Frame: A Conclusion

International law is made with words and it has methods for understanding their meanings.[1] But it is also made with graphic images – including photographs – in decision-making processes under treaties that protect the environment's aesthetic value.[2] My focus in this book has been a particular source of international law: The international environmental treaties that account for much of what is called international environmental law.[3] Specifically, I have paid attention to the photographs that populate the practices of nation states under the *World Heritage Convention*,[4] the *Whaling Convention*[5] and the *Biodiversity Convention*.[6] The procedural rules concerning the use of photographs in decision-making processes under those treaties conceive of photographs as records of fact.[7] Aesthetic philosophy, by contrast, recognises them as representations.[8] With no methods in international law to guide my understanding of the photographs for their meanings, I turned to aesthetic methods that have been developed by aesthetic scholars and practitioners for the visual arts.[9] This is a way of thinking about images for law that has been developed

1 See Chapter 3. See generally Bianchi, Peat and Windsor (eds.), *Interpretation in International Law*.

2 See Chapters 5–7. Following Mitchell, *Iconology*, references to 'graphic' image refer to form as opposed to e.g. vivid images: See Section 4.4.1.

3 See generally Sands and Peel, *Principles of International Environmental Law*.

4 *Convention for the Protection of the World Cultural and Natural Heritage*, Paris, 16 November 1972, in force 17 December 1975, 1037 UNTS 151.

5 *International Convention on the Regulation of Whaling*, Washington, 2 December 1946, in force 10 November 1948, 161 UNTS 72.

6 *Convention on Biological Diversity*, Rio de Janeiro, 5 June 1992, in force 29 December 1993, 1760 UNTS 79.

7 See Chapters 5–7.

8 See Chapter 4. See generally Davies and Alperson, *The Philosophy of Art*.

9 Ibid. See also Levinson, 'Philosophical aesthetics', 3.

largely by scholars of common and civil law as 'visual jurisprudence',[10] or as what Desmond Manderson describes as 'imaginal law'.[11]

My analysis of the photographs as if they were art had a particular aim: I went looking for representations of the environment's aesthetic value. Aesthetic value is one of several environmental values protected by the three treaties but it is variously understood in the scholarship on international environmental law,[12] and in the practices of the states parties to the treaties.[13] There, it is oftentimes conflated with other values, maligned for its subjective basis, and imagined as universal in the image of Western European and Anglo-American landscape art and mannered conceptions of wilderness.[14] These characterisations of aesthetic value were also apparent from my eco-critical analysis of the photographs.[15] These meanings are problematic for the protection of aesthetic value under international environmental law. They render it hedonistic, hegemonic – either way ill-suited practically and ideologically to protection under international treaties accepted by diverse nation states.[16] They are also at odds with a characterisation of the environment's aesthetic value among philosophers of environmental aesthetics,[17] an orientation in aesthetic philosophy that is concerned with the aesthetic appreciation of the natural environment as distinct from the arts. Several propose pluralised meanings for the environment's aesthetic value associated with such things as sensation, imagination, emotion and knowledge from different cultures.[18] One philosopher in particular, Emily Brady, has formulated an integrated aesthetic model that relies on 'disinterestedness' to develop an understanding of the environment's aesthetic value.[19] This, I argue, could be adapted for common methods of evaluation for international law. In respect of hedonism, Brady's model stresses the profound nature of a multi-sensory experience as opposed to one limited to the visual field; and, in respect of hegemony, Brady

[10] See Douzinas and Nead, 'Introduction'.

[11] Manderson, 'Introduction: Imaginal law', 4, citing Bottici, *Imaginal Politics*. Cf. for international law, Goodrich, 'International signs'; Miles, 'Visuality of a treaty'. See Chapter 4.

[12] See Chapter 2.

[13] See Chapter 3.

[14] See Chapter 4. See generally Braddock and Irmscher (eds.), *A Keener Perception*; Elkins, *The End of Diversity in Art Historical Writing*.

[15] See Chapters 5–7.

[16] See Chapter 3. See generally Maskit, 'On universalism'.

[17] See Chapter 2. See generally Fisher, 'Environmental aesthetics', 667; Carlson, 'Ten steps', 13.

[18] See Chapters 5 and 7. See generally Brady, 'Aesthetic value, nature, and environment', 186.

[19] Brady, *Aesthetics of the Natural Environment*, adapting Kantian concept: p. 140. See further Chapter 2.

acknowledges the plural cultures that shape aesthetic appreciations of the natural environment.

Together, my aesthetic conceptions of image, my methods for analysing those images, and the meanings of aesthetic value I construct with those methods, combine to make a jurisprudence of aesthetics for the practice of international law. The book has explained ways to conceive of graphic images as representations – rather than as records of fact – and how to develop meanings from them relevant to a particular source of international law: International environmental treaties. Through a critical lens, I have uncovered issues in the conception of the environment's aesthetic value in international law. And in a normative orientation, I have proposed meanings that are both sensitive to critical understandings of international law and well-suited to international legal practice. In that task, I show how aesthetic method can be repurposed to give significance to representations from photographs for international environmental treaties and, by extension, to other international laws. In the book, I bring theory to international legal practice for good ends.[20] For an international legal practice adept with images. And for international laws that protect the environment. Where other environmental values might mean something to nation states, I maintain that the environment's aesthetic value could mean more.

In this final chapter, I look beyond the frame of my analysis to consider its wider implications for international legal practice. I explain my conclusions in terms of interpretative 'method' and interpreted 'meanings'. My proposed methods are described in Section 8.1 as aesthetic ways of knowing graphic images in international law. Aesthetic methods for the arts are 'interpretative' in a dual sense. They define images as representations of meaning as well as defining the meanings that arise from images. In Section 8.2, I explain how I have used aesthetic method to interpret the meanings of the environment's aesthetic value through the photographs used in decision-making processes under the three international environmental treaties studied for the book. The relevance of aesthetic philosophy to environmental law is an emerging field.[21] My analysis introduces the philosophy of environmental aesthetics to the interdisciplinary study of law and image, expanding the role of images in international law. In Section 8.3, I address the relevance of my findings and arguments to international legal practice. I propose that decision-makers could accommodate aesthetic methods in rules of treaty interpretation, procedural practices and methods of judgement. I end the chapter as preceding chapters

[20] See Harcourt, *Critique and Praxis*.

[21] See Section 4.2. See, for example, Richardson, *The Art of Environmental Law*.

have begun, with an aesthetic analysis of an exhibit – an artwork by Julie Gough from the past for the future. There I demonstrate one last time the methods and meanings I propose for photographs of the environment's aesthetic value in international environmental law.

8.1 KNOWING PHOTOGRAPHS IN INTERNATIONAL LAW: THE ARTS

International law's contemplation of meaning is limited to words: The principal sources of international law are grounded in written and verbal language,[22] and international law's methods for interpreting that language are constructed with words in written texts.[23] In Chapter 3, I engaged written sources for a doctrinal legal interpretation of aesthetic value under the three treaties examined in the book: Two making express mention of aesthetic value, the *World Heritage Convention* and the *Biodiversity Convention*, and one that I argued is informed by aesthetic value, the *Whaling Convention*.[24] Having applied techniques of treaty interpretation using written reference materials and documentation generated under treaties, I then turned to photographs to identify and interrogate meanings of the environment's aesthetic value.[25]

8.1.1 *Aesthetic Value in Treaty Practice*

My application of the international rules of treaty interpretation generated a variable account of the meaning of the environment's 'aesthetic' value.[26] I found that the international bodies established to administer the treaties have characterised 'aesthetic' value in ways that give the term only limited, if any, significance in the implementation of those treaties.

One limitation is through the conflation of aesthetic value with other environmental values. In the case of the *World Heritage Convention*, the parties and the World Heritage Committee appear to treat aesthetic value as being synonymous with 'natural beauty'.[27] Understandings of aesthetic value

[22] See Section 3.5. On the written sources of international law generally, see Besson, 'Theorizing the sources of international law', 163; Dupuy and Viñuales, *International Environmental Law*, p. 38. Cf Staubach, *The Rule of Unwritten International Law*.
[23] Article 31 of the *Vienna Convention on the Law of Treaties*, Vienna, 23 May 1969, in force 27 January 1980, 1155 UNTS 331. See 'Interpretative material generated in making treaties' in Gardiner, *Treaty Interpretation*, p. 81. On documentation of 'subsequent practice', see 255. See Chapter 3.
[24] See Chapter 3.
[25] See Chapters 5–7.
[26] See Chapter 3.
[27] Ibid.

in the administration of the *Biodiversity Convention* are associated with 'cultural' value.[28] The treaties respectively express natural beauty and cultural value as environmental values in addition to aesthetic value but distinctions between the values are not explained. The conflation of aesthetic value with other environmental values also expressed in the treaty might constitute a misinterpretation of the term 'aesthetic': The international principle of effective treaty interpretation requires that each term in a treaty be distinguished from other terms.[29] However, the conflated meanings might also amount to the 'subsequent agreement' of the parties as to the meaning of 'aesthetic' value under the *Vienna Convention on the Law of Treaties*.[30] My analysis of 'aesthetic' value in relation to the *Whaling Convention* took me to debates before the International Whaling Commission that suggest that aesthetic value is among several environmental values that inform the maintenance of the ban on commercial whaling under the treaty.[31] However, the states parties variously present the aesthetic value of whales as a cultural or ethical concern. There is no stated understanding of aesthetic value independent of those values, and no explanation of how aesthetic value might relate to the ethical, scientific and economic values expressly protected under the *Whaling Convention*.[32]

Another way in which aesthetic value appears to have no significance in treaty practice is through its displacement by other environmental values. These other values are quantified in purportedly objective terms, such as scientific and economic values, while aesthetic value is characterised as a subjective value.[33] For the *World Heritage Convention*, scientific values are articulated in decisions of the World Heritage Committee to inscribe natural properties in the World Heritage List on the basis of 'aesthetic' or 'natural beauty' points of view.[34] The scientific matters relevant to the express provisions of the *Whaling Convention* at issue in the *Whaling in the Antarctic* case saw the parties to the dispute, and the International Court of Justice (ICJ), adhere to science over other values that might have also expressly informed the ICJ's reasoning of the law.[35] In valuation methods employed by the states

28 Ibid.

29 See Gardiner, *Treaty Interpretation*, pp. 168 and 179ff. See Chapter 3.

30 *Vienna Convention*.

31 Clause 10(e) of the Schedule to the *Whaling Convention* (commercial whaling ban).

32 See Section 3.4. See discussion in Section 8.3.1.

33 See Brady, *Aesthetics of the Natural Environment*, p. 100.

34 See Chapter 5.

35 *Whaling in the Antarctic (Australia v Japan; New Zealand intervening) (Judgment)* [2014] ICJ Rep 226. See Chapter 6.

parties to the *Biodiversity Convention*, aesthetic value is conceived in terms of its economic value – another value readily determined on objective grounds.[36]

8.1.2 *Photographs as Representations and Records*

Meanings of the environment's aesthetic value could be constructed from the photographs submitted by nation states in the decision-making processes of international bodies under the three treaties studied for this book.[37] For example, meanings developed from photographs could substantiate a claim by a state party, or justify a decision of the World Heritage Committee, as to the outstanding universal value of natural heritage from an 'aesthetic' point of view under the *World Heritage Convention*.[38] Meanings from photographs presented by states in their submissions to the ICJ – such as those used in the *Whaling in the Antarctic* dispute under the *Whaling Convention* – could be acknowledged for their role in legal argument as rhetoric and a legitimate basis upon which judges might develop their legal interpretations and develop their reasons for judgment.[39] Additionally, meanings from photographs employed in the practices of the parties to the *Biodiversity Convention* could be used to explain the significance of the 'aesthetic' value of biodiversity for a decision of the Conference of the Parties.[40]

However, photographs are not formally recognised in the procedural rules and practices of international bodies under the treaties as images that represent meanings. In this book, I examined the rules and practices of the international bodies that are empowered to make decisions under the three treaties, finding that the photographs are conceived instead as records of fact.[41] The rules of procedure and practices on the use of photographs in submissions to the World Heritage Committee, and to the ICJ, as well as the practices of using photographs in material requested by the Conference of the Parties to the *Biodiversity Convention*, appear to treat photographs as a proxy for what would have been seen in a place, at a time, by the naked eye.[42]

36 See Chapter 7. See discussion in Section 8.3.2.
37 See Chapter 5–7.
38 See Chapter 5.
39 See Chapter 6.
40 See Chapter 7.
41 See Chapters 5–7.
42 See Chapters 5–7.

8.1.3 *Aesthetic Values from Photographs*

In contrast to the formal rules and practices of the international bodies that judge the environment's aesthetic value for the treaties, aesthetic philosophers conceive of photographs as representations, and they develop meanings from those representations using a range of interpretative methods.[43] In Chapter 4, I explained how 'image' can be variously conceived for this purpose. For example, there is 'graphic' image – the photograph printed on paper or projected on screen; there is also 'representational' image – images constitutive of meanings constructed by viewers of the graphic image;[44] and there is the factual or recorded image – the image perceived in physical terms as light to the eye of a viewer at a given time and place. Art historian WJT Mitchell describes this last type of image as an 'optical' image, distinguishing it from graphic, verbal, mental and perceptual images.[45]

In Chapters 5 through 7, I engaged different aesthetic methods to construct and interrogate meanings of aesthetic value from the images represented in the photographs used in the decision-making processes under the *World Heritage Convention*, the *Whaling Convention* and the *Biodiversity Convention*. These included methods that reference precedents in art history.[46] My aesthetic methods also developed critical reflections that drew on socio-political, economic, scientific and cultural contexts.[47] These methods are associated with 'eco-criticism', which has been extended from literature to visual art,[48] and from North American contexts to the arts of cultures around the world.[49]

My aesthetic analysis of the photographs was premised on an understanding that concepts and methods developed for the arts can be employed in the study of graphic images in legal process regardless of whether those images could be characterised as 'art'.[50] Graphic images as aesthetic subjects in law have been theorised for common and civil law traditions.[51] With my analysis of the photographs submitted in treaty processes, I have extended that visual

43 See generally Savedoff, *Transforming Images*. Note discussion of environmental hermeneutics in Chapter 4.
44 See further Chapter 4. See generally Davies, *The Philosophy of Art*, p. 159.
45 Mitchell, *Iconology*, p. 10; for concepts of 'image' by visual jurisprudents, see Section 4.4.1.
46 See Chapter 4.
47 Ibid.
48 See Braddock and Irmscher, *A Keener Perception*.
49 See Nixon, *Slow Violence*. Note Elkins, *The End of Diversity in Art Historical Writing*.
50 See Stecker, 'What is art?', 95.
51 On visual jurisprudence, see further Chapter 4.

jurisprudence to the practice of international environmental law. However, as explained next, my aesthetic analysis of photographs to develop meanings of the environment's aesthetic value might be problematic for the philosophy of 'environmental aesthetics'.[52]

8.2 MEANINGS OF AESTHETIC VALUE IN PHOTOGRAPHS: ENVIRONMENTAL AESTHETICS

Two orientations in Western European and Anglo-American aesthetic philosophy are relevant to my aesthetic analysis of the photographs used in the international decision-making processes under the three treaties. As well as employing theories in aesthetic philosophy for the visual arts described in Section 8.1, my analysis of the photographs also engaged philosophical theories from 'environmental aesthetics', a field in aesthetic philosophy that concerns the aesthetic appreciation of the natural environment.[53]

8.2.1 *Environmental Aesthetics*

My articulation of the environment's aesthetic value has relied principally on the model of environmental aesthetics developed by philosopher Emily Brady, the proponent of an integrated aesthetic model developed for application in environmental policy.[54] Brady understands that the aesthetic value of the natural environment is necessarily pluralised, derived from sensorial experience and shaped by imagination, emotion and knowledge from different cultures.[55] She considers, however, that within communities that share certain knowledge, there are common elements to aesthetic value that are capable of being communicated to others.[56] For Brady and other philosophers of environmental aesthetics, this aesthetic appreciation of the natural environment comes from a multi-sensory experience that is profound – not trivial, superficial, hedonistic or indulgent – producing what I name for the book an 'exquisite' affect.[57]

For many philosophers of environmental aesthetics, the aesthetic appreciation of the environment is different from an aesthetic evaluation of visual

[52] See Fisher, 'Environmental aesthetics'.
[53] See Chapter 2.
[54] Brady, *Aesthetics of the Natural Environment*, p. 3.
[55] Ibid., pp. 237–8.
[56] See Chapter 2.
[57] Brady, *Aesthetics of the Natural Environment*, pp. 142, 170, 185. See also Hepburn, 'Trivial and serious', 65.

art.[58] Those philosophers maintain that an appreciation of the environment requires a physical immersion in the environment as distinct from the observation of an art object.[59] But I argue for an adaptation of this position for international law. First, the decision-making processes described in this book are institutional processes. It is not necessarily feasible or desirable for the decision-makers to undertake site visits for a physical experience of the environment on which to judge its aesthetic value under a treaty.[60] In addition, the decision-making processes of the three treaties analysed for the book are governed by international law, and they also produce international law. Graphic representations of the environment judged as having aesthetic value are necessary in legal processes that document reasons for decisions in order to communicate, evaluate and, in some cases, replicate those reasons.[61] Finally, visual art can in any event communicate the kinds of aesthetic values of the natural environment contemplated by philosophers of environmental aesthetics.[62] My analyses of select photographs in terms of sensorial perception demonstrate how graphic images conceived as representation can be understood in terms beyond visual perception. To be sure, aesthetic value imagined from a photograph is necessarily different from a physical experience of place. However, aesthetic analysis of the photograph provides an approximation of aesthetic experience adapted for the institutional nature of legal process.

8.2.2 *Critical and Normative Accounts of Aesthetic Value*

My analysis of the environmental images in photographs provided accounts of the environment's aesthetic value that were both critical and normative. Through a critical lens, I identified the aesthetic values evident in some of the photographs used under the three treaties as those associated with landscape art. In what I described as conventional conceptions of Western European and British landscape, I found that the environment's aesthetic value had been limited in photographs to 'scenes' that are visually apparent and objectified by reference to formal qualities associated with the

[58] See Section 2.2.1.

[59] Brady, *Aesthetics of the Natural Environment*, p. 237; Berleant, 'Art, environment and the shaping of experience', 7–8.

[60] See, for example, Becker and Rose, 'Investigating the value of site visits'.

[61] On 'settled jurisprudence', see Gardiner, *Treaty Interpretation*, pp. 285–7. I argue that photographs could have precedential import for World Heritage inscriptions: See Section 5.3.3.1.

[62] Note Berleant, 'Art, environment and the shaping of experience'. See Section 4.3.2 regarding Fisher, 'Environmental aesthetics', 674.

appreciation of art.[63] This conventional landscape connotes smooth and delicate qualities with 'natural beauty', immense features and vast horizons with the 'sublime', and irregular and vibrant environments with the 'picturesque'.[64] These aesthetic conventions were developed in nineteenth-century Western European and British landscape, derived from Chinese and Japanese landscapes, and adapted by landscape artists in European and British colonies in Africa, Australia and North and South America.[65] Prevalence of the landscape convention is, however, not necessarily an indication of a preference shared globally across cultures.[66] I critiqued the landscape aesthetic, through the photographs, as insensitive to pluralised conceptions of the environment's aesthetic value likely held by the many states parties to the multilateral treaties.[67]

Separate from my critical analysis, I also analysed the photographs to develop normative renderings of the environment's aesthetic value. Those accounts understood the environment's aesthetic value in terms of multi-sensory and multi-cultural perceptions, as contemplated by environmental aestheticians such as Emily Brady.[68] As I have explained, Brady describes the environment's aesthetic value in terms of sensation, imagination, emotion and knowledge.[69] This normative construction is what I term a 'now-world' aesthetic value of the environment. It can evolve with changing environments, and be adapted for different places and for different people. Distinguishable from other environmental values, the now-world aesthetic eschews the limited and singular representation of the environment's aesthetic value in nineteenth-century Western European and British landscape art.

My critical account of the environment's aesthetic value suggests an aesthetic imperialism that resonates with observations made in post-colonial critiques of international environmental law.[70] I maintain that aesthetic value understood in terms of an Anglo-European conventional landscape aesthetic is not necessarily representative of the aesthetic values of developing countries of the Global South that make up the majority of the states parties to the

[63] See below as to the cultural context for these landscape conventions.
[64] Brady, *Aesthetics of the Natural Environment*, p. 32.
[65] See Chapter 4. See also Danto, 'Can it be the "most wanted painting"'; cf. Dutton, *The Art Instinct*.
[66] See Section 4.2.1. Cf. Berleant, 'Scenic beauty in a global context'.
[67] See Chapters 5 and 7.
[68] Brady, *Aesthetics of the Natural Environment*; see further Chapter 2.
[69] See Section 8.2.1.
[70] See generally Natarajan and Khoday, 'Locating nature'; Mickelson, 'South, north'.

World Heritage Convention and the *Biodiversity Convention*.[71] Charges of aesthetic imperialism do not stop, however, at North–South relationships. In the *Whaling in the Antarctic* dispute, Japan's submissions to the ICJ criticised Australia for using the *Whaling Convention* to impose its cultural views of whales on Japan – cultural views that I show in Chapter 6 of the book to have an aesthetic dimension for both parties to the dispute.[72]

My normative construction of a now-world aesthetic developed from photographs addresses some of the concerns arising from critical accounts of the images. Specifically, my analysis of photographs used in the contexts of the *World Heritage Convention* and the *Biodiversity Convention* identified aesthetic appreciation of the natural environment as culturally relative. I pointed out that the subjective nature of this account is, however, antithetical to constructions of aesthetic value ripe for comparison with other environmental values, as required in the administration of international environmental law. I discussed the extent to which the Kantian concept of 'disinterestedness', as imagined by Brady for her theory of integrated aesthetics of the environment,[73] could be adopted to avoid idiosyncratic or arbitrary formulations of the environment's aesthetic value in decision-making processes of international law.[74] Critical perspectives could be a function of disinterestedness but it is not clear that such disinterestedness could be achieved in an institutional process for making aesthetic judgements. The concept might not be something that can be commonly adopted by the people responsible for making decisions based on judgements of aesthetic value under the treaties. The subjective nature of an aesthetic appreciation of the environment is, however, no reason to abandon its protection under international environmental law: Brady and other philosophers of environmental aesthetics contribute a common language for a pluralised value that can be articulated for legal process and, I maintain, expressed through images.

Lastly, the theories of environmental aesthetics are themselves culturally situated in Anglo-American – and to a degree Western European – philosophical discourse.[75] Indeed, Jonathan Maskit is critical of much of the philosophy of environmental aesthetics for its cultural bias towards Anglo-American aesthetic preferences.[76] However, to the extent that scholars such as Emily Brady advance theories that take account of cultural pluralism, philosophical

[71] See Maskit, 'On universalism'. See also Brady, 'Aesthetic value, nature, and environment'.
[72] See Chapter 6.
[73] Brady, *Aesthetics of the Natural Environment*, p. 140.
[74] See Section 2.4.3.
[75] See Maskit, 'On universalism'.
[76] Ibid., 41–2.

theories of environmental aesthetics contemplate and embrace diverse ontological understandings of the environment and its aesthetic value.[77]

8.2.3 *Taking Aesthetics to the Practice of International Law*

There are both similarities and differences in the meanings of the environment's aesthetic value arising from, on the one hand, my doctrinal interpretation from orthodox written materials and, on the other hand, my aesthetic accounts constructed and analysed from photographs. Both written and graphic sources suggest understandings of the environment's 'aesthetic' value in terms of natural beauty portrayed in conventional landscape art in nineteenth-century Western Europe and Britain. Yet such an understanding risks protecting the aesthetic values of only some of the states parties in the implementation of international environmental treaties that otherwise purport to protect aesthetic value for all parties.[78] This is at odds with dogmatic law: The legal principle *pacta sunt servanda*, for example, requires that all parties abide by their treaty commitments.[79] And from a jurisprudential perspective – or for the prudent conduct of law – the reasoned and responsible practice of law demands an understanding and explanation of the role of graphic images in the formulation of meanings for treaty terms.[80]

With my identification of the photographs, and the meanings they convey, I was not claiming that the images were in fact understood as such in the practice of international environmental law.[81] Images in photographs are used by advocates for their meanings, and those intended and other meanings would register in the minds of the decision-makers that view them.[82] But the work in this book did not extend to demonstrating which meanings were intended by the states using them, or which meanings decision-makers took from photographs, or how they were in fact reflected in the decisions of international bodies on aesthetic value. Instead, my findings showed that

77 Cf. ibid., 50. See Chapter 2.

78 See Chapter 3.

79 See Shaw, *International Law*, p. 788.

80 On concepts of 'modern' and 'postmodern' jurisprudence, see Douzinas, Warrington and McVeigh, *Postmodern Jurisprudence*, pp. 25–8.

81 On literature, see generally Morgan, *The Aesthetics of International Law*; Simpson, *Sentimental Life of International Law*. On literature and performance, see O'Connell, *The Art of Law in the International Community*.

82 Cf. legal realism of Frank, *Law and the Modern Mind*, cited in Bianchi, *International Law* Theories, pp. 91–2.

decision-makers have not been attentive to graphic images. The capacity for photographs to be understood for their representations demands an account of such images in both the conception, and practice, of international law – for the sake of law done well and, in the case of understanding the environment's aesthetic value, for the sake of international laws that protect the environment.

I walk a fine line between theories from different disciplines both critical and normative – what images are, are not, and should be; what aesthetic value is, is not, and should be – towards a call for those theories to be applied in the practice of international law. And where it is the philosophy of environmental aesthetics that I seek to engage for law, mine is a call that should appeal to those philosophers who seek to activate their thinking in applied contexts.[83] But international law as a critical and a practical endeavour has been historically, if not still, difficult to parse.[84] It has been decades since Deborah Cass wrote of 'the potential to create a productive dialogue between the bearers of the international tradition and its challengers'.[85] I maintain, however, that my proposals for the practice of international law are necessary for the proper conduct of law in jurisprudential terms and for the good administration of justice as a matter of doctrine.[86] With that, I am mindful of Bernard Harcourt's entreaty to engage in 'critical praxis',[87] at a time of crisis brought on by nation states reckless in their responsibility to protect the environment.

8.3 AESTHETIC METHOD FOR IMAGES IN INTERNATIONAL LAW: LEGAL PRACTICE

My aesthetic methods for making meaning from images are relevant to future practices of international law. Below, I consider how the analysis of photographic images through aesthetic concepts and methods could be taken into account for: International rules of interpretation for treaties; procedures governing the use of photographs in international decision-making processes; and methods by which the environment's aesthetic value is identified and judged by states parties and decision-makers for, and in accordance with, international law. The contexts for my proposals are the decision-making processes under the three international environmental treaties that

[83] Described as 'empirical' and 'speculative' aesthetics in Drenthen and Keulartz, 'Introduction', 1. See also Sepänmaa, 'From theoretical to applied environmental aesthetics', 87.
[84] See, for example, Orford and Hoffmann, 'Introduction', 1; Bianchi, *International Law Theories*.
[85] Cass, 'Navigating the newstream', 342–3.
[86] See Fuller, 'The forms and limits of adjudication'; cf. Simma, 'The International Court of Justice'.
[87] Harcourt, *Critique and Praxis*, p. 18.

I examined for the book – the administration of a treaty, in the case of the World Heritage Committee, the enforcement of a treaty in the case of the ICJ, and the implementation of a treaty, in the case of the Conference of the Parties to the *Biodiversity Convention*. But, as explained here, a need for aesthetic methods to develop meanings from photographs of the environment could have analogous relevance to images in the practices of other international laws, in any field.[88]

8.3.1 *Interpretation of 'Aesthetic' Value for Treaties*

As explained earlier, my aesthetic analysis of the photographs of the environment highlights meanings relevant to 'aesthetic' value for the *World Heritage Convention*, the *Biodiversity Convention* and the *Whaling Convention*.[89] However, aesthetic methods could also be employed to analyse photographs as sources of treaty interpretation in the practice of international law more broadly.

8.3.1.1 Photographs as Sources for Legal Interpretation

Photographs could be accommodated in what are described as 'evolutive', 'dynamic' or 'sociological' interpretation techniques which take account of meanings that develop after the adoption of a treaty among the states parties or the international community more generally.[90] I will, however, focus here on how the photographs could be conceived for the purposes of the *Vienna Convention on the Law of Treaties* as indications of the 'subsequent practice in the application of the treaty which establishes the agreement of the parties regarding its interpretation'.[91]

'Subsequent practice' has been understood for doctrinal treaty interpretation in various ways but only in connection with written texts.[92] Several factors might determine whether states parties would be willing to accept

88 For understandings of image for other international laws, see generally Ainley, Humphreys and Tallgren, 'International criminal justice on/and film'; Manderson, 'Not drowning, waving', 159; Miles, 'Visuality of a treaty'.

89 For other treaties protecting the environment's aesthetic value, see, for example, Article 3 of the *Protocol on Environmental Protection to the Antarctic Treaty*, Madrid, 4 October 1991, in force 14 January 1998, 402 UNTS 71. See further Chapter 2.

90 See Chapter 3.

91 Article 31(3)(b) of the *Vienna Convention*.

92 Gardiner describes 'subsequent practice' as 'what can be shown to have been done systematically or repeatedly in implementation and application of a treaty': Gardiner, *Treaty Interpretation*, p. 254. On written texts, see p. 255.

photographs as constitutive of subsequent practice. In the case of decisions on aesthetic value under international environmental treaties, photographs used to justify or explain a finding of aesthetic value could, I argue, qualify as subsequent practice. Another factor relevant to the status of photographs as subsequent practice might be the juridical nature of the judgement of aesthetic value that has relied on photographs.[93] A photograph used to justify a decision of the World Heritage Committee might amount to an 'agreement' of the parties. By contrast, a photograph in a report produced by expert advisors, such as the periodic *Global Biodiversity Outlook* (GBO), might not. Unlike a determination of world heritage status, the GBO informs only a hortatory decision of the Conference of the Parties to the *Biodiversity Convention*, such as the decision agreeing the Aichi Targets.[94] Photographs in such a report could, however, be relevant more broadly to the development of meanings for the treaty over time, were such meanings articulated for and by the states parties in the administration of their commitments.

8.3.1.2 Adapting Legal Methods of Interpretation

This book considered issues of treaty interpretation in the contexts of treaties being administered by experts, implemented by nation states, and enforced by judges. However, all manner of state representatives, bureaucrats and experts having responsibilities to make or implement international law must interpret the terms of international law.[95] I maintain that decision-makers tasked with treaty interpretation for these purposes could engage aesthetic methods to articulate meanings from photographs used in their decision-making processes.

As explained in Chapter 3, aesthetic methods and graphic images have not been formally used in the customary international legal practices of treaty interpretation codified in the *Vienna Convention on the Law of Treaties*.[96] Yet because graphic images can represent meanings, those practices could be adapted for the many images that populate the decision-making processes of international laws. The interpretation of treaties is described as an art not a science.[97] As such, it could readily accommodate new sources for interpretation, such as photographs and other graphic images.

93 On 'establishing' agreement, see ibid., p. 269.

94 Conference of the Parties to the *Convention on Biological Diversity*, *The Strategic Plan for Biodiversity* 2011-2020, UN Doc. UNEP/CBD/COP/DEC/X/2, Annex, para. [13].

95 Gardiner, *Treaty Interpretation*, p. 123; see also Klabbers, 'Virtuous interpretation', 37.

96 See, for example, Gardiner, *Treaty Interpretation*, Section 8.1.

97 See Waldcock, 'Third report on the law of treaties'. See also Klabbers, *International Law*, p. 58.

Critical understandings of terms, developed from photographs through aesthetic method, will inevitably lead to different interpretations. But, as they do with words, treaty interpreters could articulate those different meanings, and explain why one is justified over another. They would do so with reference to legal principles and rules of treaty interpretation adapted for graphic images as sources of interpretation. Treaty interpreters already navigate the many meanings that can arise from a term in a treaty: Photographic images can be seen as another source, and aesthetic method seen as another technique, to provide a reasoned basis for the interpretation of international law.

8.3.2 *Procedures for Decisions on Aesthetic Value*

Procedural rules and practices are developed by international bodies to ensure fair and transparent decision-making processes under international law.[98] Each of the international bodies making decisions under the treaties studied in the book have rules of procedure and documented practices of their decision-making. Below, I discuss the implications of my findings for the procedures of the World Heritage Committee, the ICJ, and the Conference of the Parties to the *Biodiversity Convention*. However, my findings could also be applied to the procedures of other international bodies using graphic images in their decision-making processes.

8.3.2.1 World Heritage Committee Procedures

The *Operational Guidelines* for the World Heritage Committee currently contemplate the use of photographs in documents made by states to nominate properties to the World Heritage List.[99] Specifically, states are encouraged to 'provide a sufficient number of recent images (prints, slides and, where possible, electronic formats, videos and aerial photographs) to give a good general picture of the property'.[100] In addition, states are advised to provide 'documentation necessary to substantiate the nomination', including 'images

[98] See Klabbers, *An Introduction to International Organizations Law*; Sands and Klein, *Bowett's Law of International Institutions*, p. 297. See also Kingsbury, 'Global environmental governance'.

[99] World Heritage Committee, *Operational Guidelines for the Implementation of the World Heritage Convention*, UN Doc. WHC.21/01, para. [77]. See Section 5.5.3.

[100] Ibid., Annex 5 ('Properties for inscription on the World Heritage List' nomination format) para. [7a] 113; see also World Heritage Centre, 'Preparing World Heritage nominations', 121.

of a quality suitable for printing'.[101] However, the *Operational Guidelines* do not properly explain the purpose of the photographs or the methods used for analysing them.

Given the range of meanings of the environment's aesthetic value that can arise from photographs, the *Operational Guidelines* should be amended to explain how photographs relate to determinations of a property's aesthetic value by the World Heritage Committee. This would apply to both natural and cultural properties, but I have argued in Chapter 5 that photographs have particular relevance to understandings of the environment's aesthetic value as one distinct from aesthetic values that are associated with cultural heritage. The *Operational Guidelines* are regularly revised by the World Heritage Committee and a possible amendment could be considered in the context of future reviews.[102] Any consideration given to the use of photographs, and aesthetic expertise, by states parties in the process of nominating properties for World Heritage, should take account of necessary resources, corresponding costs and likely impacts on developing country parties.[103]

8.3.2.2 International Court of Justice Procedures

Like the World Heritage Committee, the ICJ has also developed formal rules of procedure. However, those rules do not address the submission of photographs in legal proceedings. The ICJ has, as a matter of practice, allowed photographs in written submissions as evidence and it has made formal mention of photographs in its *Practice Direction* IX*quater*.[104] My aesthetic analysis of the photographs in the *Whaling in the Antarctic* case in Chapter 6 nevertheless demonstrates for states, and the ICJ, that photographs and other graphic images can be understood for their 'representations' of meaning.

Parties to legal proceedings properly conducted should be required to account for their use of graphic images in their submissions to the ICJ. This would be consistent with principles of the good administration of justice.[105] My findings are based on an analysis of photographs of whales in the *Whaling*

[101] *WHC Operational Guidelines*, para. [132]. See also World Heritage Centre, 'Preparing World Heritage nominations', 60 ('providing attractive photographs is inadequate'), 98 ('[p]oor quality images are of no use').
[102] See also World Heritage Policy Compendium.
[103] See, for example, through the 'upstream process': World Heritage Committee, 'Upstream process', UN Doc. WHC/19/43.COM/9A.Rev. See Section 5.5.2.
[104] International Court of Justice, *Practice Direction* IX*quater*, 11 April 2013. See Section 6.3.2.
[105] See Fuller, 'The Forms and limits of adjudication'; cf. Simma, 'The International Court of Justice'.

in the Antarctic dispute. However, the potential for photographs to have what I describe as legitimate rhetorical import – with implications for legal interpretation and judgment – warrants procedures that acknowledge the aesthetic relevance of graphic images to legal reasoning for all proceedings. The use of photographs and other visual material for purposes other than evidence could be addressed by the ICJ, for example in future proceedings on a case-by-case basis, or through a future practice direction.[106] Similar considerations would apply to other international courts and tribunals allowing photographs in submissions.[107]

8.3.2.3 Procedures of the Conference of the Parties to the *Biodiversity Convention*

Rules of procedure govern the decision-making of the Conference of the Parties to the *Biodiversity Convention*. However, my research for Chapter 7 did not identify any publicly available guidance on the use of photographs in material generated in connection with decisions of the Conference of the Parties.[108] Other international bodies appear to have rules or protocols governing the use of photographs in their reports,[109] but it is not clear that such rules would be relevant to decisions of the Conference of the Parties that rely on those reports.

There are at least two reasons for the Conference of the Parties to the *Biodiversity Convention* to develop rules or guidance on the use of photographs for its decision-making processes. First, to explain the role and relevance of photographs currently used in documentation. Second, to strengthen understandings of biodiversity values in general, and aesthetic value in particular. A lack of understanding of those values has been identified as an impediment to the implementation of the *Biodiversity Convention*.[110] With the extensive and rapid loss of biodiversity acknowledged by the Conference of the Parties and other bodies,[111] initiatives that might assist implementation of the treaty should be explored.

[106] On the role of image in rhetoric, see Chapter 6.

[107] On images in evidence for other international courts and tribunals, see, for example, Amerasinghe, *Evidence in International Litigation*, p. 394.

[108] Cf. Conference of the Parties to the *Convention on Biological Diversity*, *Rules of Procedure*, UN Doc. UNEP/CBD/COP/DEC/I/1, Annex (amended by Decision V/20).

[109] Note disclaimer accompanying photographs provided with Intergovernmental Science-Policy Platform on Biodiversity and Ecosystem Services (IPBES), 'dangerous decline'.

[110] Secretariat of the *Convention on Biological Diversity*, *Global Biodiversity Outlook 4*.

[111] See, for example, ibid.; Brondizio et al. (eds.), *Global Assessment Report on Biodiversity and Ecosystem Services*.

8.3.3 *Judgements of the Environment's Aesthetic Value*

An understanding of the 'judgement' of environmental values in a legal context – in a decision-making process under international law that is itself governed by international law – can be distinguished from 'judgment' as the outcome of a judicial process.[112] I maintain that each of the international bodies making decisions under the three treaties studied in this book, including the ICJ, undertake a process of judgement in their assessment, evaluation or determination of environmental values invoked by states under the treaties that is relevant to their legal or juridical judgments. For example, the World Heritage Committee and the Conference of the Parties to the *Biodiversity Convention* undertake judgements in their administrative assessments or evaluations of aesthetic value; and the ICJ exercises judgement of aesthetic value for the interpretation of international law. Below I argue that the relevance of photographs used in the decision-making processes of these bodies should be expressly addressed for, and in, decisions made under treaties.

8.3.3.1 Administrative Determinations

Criterion (vii) for assessing the outstanding universal value of natural heritage, set out in the *Operational Guidelines* of the World Heritage Committee,[113] is based on the 'natural beauty' and 'aesthetic' points of view protected under the *World Heritage Convention*.[114] A study commissioned by the International Union for Conservation of Nature (IUCN) anticipated that experts in environmental aesthetics could be consulted on 'clear evidence' of natural beauty and aesthetic importance in the course of the World Heritage Committee's evaluation of natural properties for inscription on the World Heritage List.[115] The study also suggested that experts in aesthetics be consulted on the development of a landscape typology.[116] There is, however, no mention of the role of photographs in such assessments of aesthetic value. My analysis in Chapter 5 concludes that the relevance of photographs to determinations of outstanding universal value should be addressed in any future work of the World Heritage

[112] See Manderson, 'Judgment in law and the humanities', 43–62; cf Carlson, 'Nature, aesthetic judgment', 54; Brady, *Aesthetics of the Natural Environment*, p. 191.
[113] *WHC Operational Guidelines*, para. 77. See Chapter 5.
[114] Article 2 of the *World Heritage Convention*.
[115] IUCN, *Study on the Application of Criterion (vii)*, 57–8.
[116] Ibid.

Committee on the application of criterion (vii). My findings on the conflation of the aesthetic and natural beauty points of view in the practices of the World Heritage Committee should also be considered in the context of any reforms to the *Operational Guidelines*.[117]

Models of evaluation that assign monetary values to 'ecosystem services' are commonly used by states in their characterisation of biodiversity values for the implementation of the *Biodiversity Convention*.[118] The governing body of the *Biodiversity Convention*, the Conference of the Parties, has encouraged states parties to use methods of valuation for biodiversity based on 'nature's contribution to people' alongside their fiscal evaluations of ecosystem services.[119] This approach recognises that valuation models for biodiversity commonly employed by the parties do not properly account for non-material values such as aesthetic value.[120] However, concepts and methods from aesthetic philosophy are not currently expressed in the prescribed categories of 'nature's contribution to people'.[121] The interdisciplinary premise for this emerging approach to valuation should be extended to take account of aesthetic methods for developing meanings of aesthetic value from photographs.[122]

8.3.3.2 Judicial Judgment

As explained above, my aesthetic analysis of the photographs used in the *Whaling in the Antarctic* proceedings demonstrates that photographs and other graphic images can be understood for their 'representations' of meaning. If ICJ procedures were adapted for graphic images used for their representations in parties' submissions, an understanding of the relevance of those images to ICJ judgments would also need to be developed.[123] Understandings of the ways in which those representations are taken into account in judgments should be articulated for the proper conduct of law

[117] See Chapters 3 and 5.

[118] See Chapter 7. See, for example, Sukhdev et al., *The Economics of Ecosystems and Biodiversity*; or United Nations, *System of Economic and Environmental Accounting*.

[119] For example, states parties were encouraged to adopt the IPBES approach in their 6th national reports on the implementation of the *Convention on Biological Diversity*: See further Conference of the Parties to the *Convention on Biological Diversity*, *Resource Manual for the Sixth National Report*, UN Doc. UNEP/CBD/COP/13/21.

[120] Fischer et al. (eds.), *Summary for Policymakers of the Regional Assessment Report*, p. 7.

[121] Category 16, Table S1, Supplementary Material in Díaz et al., 'Assessing nature's contributions'.

[122] See, for example, UK National Ecosystem Assessment Follow-on Phase, 'Cultural ecosystem services and indicators', Annex 1.

[123] Scobbie, 'Rhetoric, persuasion, and interpretation'.

and the good administration of justice.[124] Where graphic images are reproduced in judgments, the ICJ should be capable of explaining the significance of the images to its decision – with the possibility of the Court making a distinction between graphic images seen as representations in an aesthetic sense, and those seen for their presentation of facts as evidence.

8.3.4 *Aesthetic Expertise*

These proposals for formal recognition of photographs for their meanings are premised on a knowledge of aesthetic concepts and method. However, aesthetic philosophy, like international law, is an academic and professional discipline.[125] As such, expertise or expert advice in aesthetic philosophy would be necessary for decision-makers to work with aesthetic concepts and method in the practice of international law. This is not a remarkable claim. Extra-disciplinary analysis is typical in international law,[126] particularly international environmental law. The complex nature of environmental issues requires decision-makers to engage in such matters as science and economics.[127] The World Heritage Committee is, for example, advised on ecology and anthropology by advisory bodies, including by the International Union for Conservation of Nature (IUCN).[128] Judges of the ICJ acquired an understanding of scientific principles, and relied on scientific experts, for their decision in the *Whaling in the Antarctic* case.[129] The periodic *Global Biodiversity Outlook* is prepared by experts in ecology,[130] including scientific experts, whose findings guide the Conference of the Parties to the *Biodiversity Convention*.[131] In the same way that these decision-makers are currently advised and instructed by scientists and other experts, they can also rely on the advice of experts in aesthetic philosophy to understand graphic images, and acquire an appreciation of the relevance of graphic image to decisions made under international law.

[124] Note in the context of common law: Porter, 'Taking images seriously'; Goodrich, 'Imago decidendi'; Goodrich, 'Retinal justice'. Note also that common law courts address international law: On international environmental law in domestic courts, see Palmer and Robb (eds.), *International Environmental Reports*.

[125] See, for example, Pateman, *Key Concepts*; cf d'Aspremont et al. (eds.), *International Law as a Profession*.

[126] See Bennouna, 'Experts before the International Court of Justice'.

[127] See Sands and Peel, *Principles of International Environmental Law*, p. 6.

[128] Article 14 of the *World Heritage Convention*.

[129] See Mbengue, 'Scientific fact-finding at the International Court of Justice'.

[130] Secretariat of the *Convention on Biological Diversity*, *Global Biodiversity Outlook* 4.

[131] Conference of the Parties to the *Convention on Biological Diversity*, *Report of the Second Meeting of the Conference of the Parties to the Convention on Biological Diversity*, UN Doc. UNEP/CBD/COP/2/19.

EXHIBIT: JULIE GOUGH, *OBSERVANCE* (2012)

FIGURE 8.1. Julie Gough, *Observance*, 2012 (still). Video projection HDMI, H264, colour, sound, 17:09 mins, edition of 10. Edited by Jemma Rea © Julie Gough. Courtesy the artist.

Panneebothi, temtoryer, teeburrickar, lillerclapperlar, noermernar . . . flour, sheep, soldier, whale boat, white man. These are the names of things introduced to lutruwita/Tasmania with the arrival of Europeans that are written over coastal scenes in artist Julie Gough's video *Observance* (2012) (Figure 8.1). From a distance – among trees, behind boulders, atop a hill – Gough's camera surveys the land as it meets Australia's southern seas. Wombats graze on a verge. Wallabies swat flies. Plovers dart over sand. And all the while ecotourists decked in hiking gear and saddled with backpacks come in and out of view, picking their way over the sand and rocks. They stumble, stop, stare out to sea. They take photographs or reach for curios in the flotsam. Some of the intrepid travellers appear delighted, others weary, as they live the promise of an adventure in this remote and wild place.

Yet from Gough's vantage, these people are objects, not subjects in their own experience of nature. They are avatars for the white colonisers who invaded this place, each step they take an encroachment on Aboriginal territory.[132] The artist turns the sounds of nature on and off, the interval between marking a moment's silence for her fallen people. Layering text on the picture, Gough lists the first words for new things to this old place,

[132] Gough, 'Observance', 268–9; see also Ryan, 'Disquiet and resistance'.

translating them into English, the foreign language of their provenance, to reveal them as agents of destruction in a 'parallel world'.[133] An excerpt from British lay preacher George Augustus Robinson's journal of 1830 is featured at the start of the video. As I reflect on his journal entry, I can only wonder at the vantage of my own convict ancestor when he was finally set free in 'this country and other parts equally barren'.[134]

There is much to appreciate in this artwork. Relevant to my conclusions in this book, I can interrogate different features of the environment's 'aesthetic' value that are debated in aesthetic philosophy as it concerns the natural environment and the arts. I can imagine the sensory engagement of the tourists depicted in this natural place in the philosophical terms of environmental aesthetics. At the same time, I have a critical understanding of the aesthetic pleasure of these people as an imposition on others – notably, Australia's First Nations peoples. At best, it is a pleasure not shared with some or even many and available to only a few. At worst, it is a relentless violation of the law of Indigenous peoples.

Also relevant to my conclusions, I am conscious of the many ways in which an aesthetic sense of the environment is mediated, starting with the very form in which the original moving image is presented here on the page: A photographic still. Between the picture I see (and think I know), and the word I read (but do not understand), I comprehend 'image' as veils of graphic expression, representation and contested facts. Perhaps most of all, I am struck by an intimacy between image, the environment and law in an Indigenous conception of 'Country' that is so distinct from understandings of environmental images for international law.[135] Next to this, international law – protecting the environment through the treaties, rules and principles of states that comprise 'international environmental law' – appears to me an impoverished and misguided endeavour. But one I am not ready to abandon as a tool used by states to protect the planet.

So I propose that jurisprudents and legal practitioners return to the values that underlie the particular body of laws conceived as international environmental law. Understanding that scientific, economic and ethical values of the environment have been well-accommodated in the practice and theory of the discipline, I look elsewhere, to aesthetic value, to see what it might do to make

133 Gough, 'Observance'.
134 Robinson, 'Journal', cited in Julie Gough, 'Observance'.
135 Watson, *Aboriginal Peoples, Colonialism and International Law*; Black, *The Land Is the Source of the Law*. See also Godden, 'Indigenous heritage and the environment'; Dorsett and McVeigh, 'Just so'; Watson, 'Aboriginal relationships to the natural world'; Dorsett and McVeigh, 'Conduct of laws'; McMillan et al., 'Obligations of conduct'.

international law work to protect the environment. To know what aesthetic value of the environment means for international environmental treaties, I use image – starting with the photographic images that already populate the practice of those treaties.

With these *graphic images* already there in treaty practice, I maintain as jurisprudent that international bodies should know what work such visual images are doing in their decision-making processes governed by international law. I say the expertise of art scholars well-versed in understandings of image in aesthetic philosophy can and should guide the thinking and practice of international law with visual images. With these graphic images of the *environment* already there in treaty practice, I also see an opportunity to understand aesthetic value for international environmental law in terms redeemed by the philosophy of environmental aesthetics: Away from a conventional aesthetic in Western European and British landscape to what I call a pluralised now-world aesthetic of sensory affect, imagination, emotion and knowledge, including personal and cultural knowledges. A value that is meaningful – to people, states and international bodies – in ways that justify international laws for the natural environments represented in those photographs, places which, for now at least, are still experienced in myriad but exquisite ways in real lives.

Bibliography

ARTICLES AND BOOKS

Abrahams, Guy, Bronwyn Johnson and Kelly Gellatly (eds.), *Art+Climate=Change* (Carlton: Melbourne University Press, 2016)

Abrams, Meyer H., *The Mirror and the Lamp: Romantic Theory and the Critical Tradition* (New York: Oxford University Press, 1953)

Aguilar Mawdsley, Andrés, 'Evidence before the International Court of Justice' in Ronald St John Macdonald (ed.), *Essays in Honour of Wang Tieya* (Dordrecht: Martinus Nijhoff, 1993)

Ainley, Kirsten, Stephen Humphreys and Immi Tallgren, 'International criminal justice on/and film' (2018) 6(1) *London Review of International Law* 3

Akhtar-Khavari, Afshin, 'Fear and ecological (in)justice in Edvard Munch's *The Scream of Nature*' (2015) 2(6) *Naveiñ Reet: Nordic Journal of Law and Social Research* 93

Alam, Shawkat et al. (eds.), *International Environmental Law and the Global South* (New York: Cambridge University Press, 2015)

Alexander, Paul, *Sri Lankan Fishermen: Rural Capitalism and Peasant Society* (Canberra: Australian National University, 1982)

Allott, Philip, 'Language, method and the nature of international law' (1971) 45 *British Yearbook of International Law* 79

Amaya, Amalia and Maksymilian Del Mar (eds.), *Virtue, Emotion and Imagination in Law and Legal Reasoning* (Oxford: Hart, 2020)

Amerasinghe, Chittharanjan F., *Evidence in International Litigation* (Leiden and Boston: Martinus Nijhoff, 2005)

Principles of the Institutional Law of International Organizations, 2nd ed. (Cambridge: Cambridge University Press, 2005)

Anghie, Antony, *Imperialism, Sovereignty and the Making of International Law* (Cambridge: Cambridge University Press, 2005)

Arato, Julian, 'Subsequent practice and evolutive interpretation: Techniques of treaty interpretation over time and their diverse consequences' (2010) 9 *Law and Practice of International Courts and Tribunals* 443

Argyrou, Vassos, *The Logic of Environmentalism: Anthropology, Ecology and Postcoloniality* (New York and Oxford: Berghahn Books, 2005)

Attfield, Robin, *Environmental Ethics: An Overview for the Twenty-First Century* (Cambridge and Malden, MA: Polity Press, 2003)

Aust, Anthony, *Modern Treaty Law and Practice* (Cambridge: Cambridge University Press, 2013)

Bagnall, Gary, *Law as Art* (Aldershot and Brookfield: Dartmouth, 1996)

Bakken, Kaitlin, 'The value of wildlife in international environmental law' (2021) 46(1) *Alternative Law Journal* 71

Bańkowski, Zenon, Maksymilian Del Mar and Paul Maharg (eds.), *The Arts and the Legal Academy beyond Text in Legal Education* (Farnham and Burlington: Ashgate, 2013)

Bannister, John, *Great Whales* (Collingwood: CSIRO, 2008)

Bannon, Bryan E., 'Re-envisioning nature: The role of aesthetics in environmental ethics' (2011) 33(4) *Environmental Ethics* 415

Barbier, Edward B. et al., *Elephants, Economics and Ivory* (London: Earthscan, 2009)

Barr, Olivia, *A Jurisprudence of Movement: Common Law, Walking, Unsettling Place* (Abingdon and New York: Routledge, 2016)

Barrett, Jonathan, 'Copying artistic works: Copyright, aesthetics, and artistic practice' in Jani McCutcheon and Fiona McGaughey (eds.), *The Research Handbook on Art and Law* (Northampton: Edward Elgar, 2020)

Bartel, Robyn et al. (eds.), *Rethinking Wilderness and the Wild: Conflict, Conservation and Co-existence* (Abingdon and New York: Routledge, 2021)

Bavikatte, Kabir Sanjay and Tom Bennett, 'Community stewardship: The foundation of biocultural rights' (2015) 6(1) *Journal of Human Rights and the Environment* 7

Bazin, André, 'The ontology of the photographic image' (1945), reprinted in André Bazin (tr. Hugh Grey), *What Is Cinema?*, vol. 1 (Berkeley: University of California Press, 1967, 2005)

Becker, Michael A. and Cecily Rose, 'Investigating the value of site visits in inter-state arbitration and adjudication' (2017) 8(2) *Journal of International Dispute Settlement* 219

Behrmann, Carolin, 'Law, visual studies, and image history' in Simon Stern, Maksymilian Del Mar and Bernadette Meyler (eds.), *The Oxford Handbook of Law and Humanities* (New York: Oxford University Press, 2020)

Bell-James, Justine, 'Ecosystem services as a metaphor in environmental law: Balancing intrinsic and instrumental values' (2020) 39(3) *University of Queensland Law Journal* 525

Ben-Dor, Oren (ed.), *Law and Art: Justice, Ethics and Aesthetics* (Abingdon and New York: Routledge, 2011)

Bennouna, Mohamed, 'Experts before the International Court of Justice: What for?' (2018) 9(3) *Journal of International Dispute Settlement* 345

Benson, John, 'Aesthetic and other values in the rural landscape' (2008) 17(2) *Environmental Values* 221

Benzing, Markus, 'Evidentiary issues' in Andreas Zimmermann et al. (eds.), *The Statute of the International Court of Justice: A Commentary*, 3rd ed. (Oxford: Oxford University Press, 2019)

Berleant, Arnold, *Aesthetics and Environment: Theme and Variations on Art and Culture* (Aldershot and Burlington: Ashgate, 2005)

Aesthetics beyond the Arts: New and Recent Essays (Farnham and Burlington: Ashgate, 2012)
'Art, environment and the shaping of experience' in Arnold Berleant (ed.), *Environment and the Arts: Perspectives on Environmental Aesthetics* (Aldershot: Ashgate, 2002)
'Scenic beauty in a global context' in Arnold Berleant (ed.), *Aesthetics beyond the Arts: New and Recent Essays* (Farnham and Burlington: Ashgate, 2012)
'The aesthetics of art and nature' in Salim Kemal and Ivan Gaskell (eds.), *Landscape, Natural Beauty and the Arts* (Cambridge and New York: Cambridge University Press, 1993)
(ed.), *Environment and the Arts: Perspectives on Environmental Aesthetics* (Aldershot: Ashgate, 2002)
Besson, Samantha, 'Theorizing the sources of international law' in Samantha Besson and John Tasioulas (eds.), *The Philosophy of International Law* (Oxford and New York: Oxford University Press, 2010)
Bianchi, Andrea, *International Law Theories: An Inquiry into Different Ways of Thinking* (Oxford: Oxford University Press, 2016)
Theory and Philosophy of International Law: An Edward Elgar Research Review (Cheltenham: Edward Elgar, 2017)
Bianchi, Andrea, Daniel Peat and Matthew Windsor (eds.), *Interpretation in International Law* (Oxford: Oxford University Press, 2015)
Biber, Katherine, 'Photographs and labels: Against a criminology of innocence' (2005) 10 *Law Text Culture* 19
Biber, Katherine and Mehera San Roque, 'The trouble with pictures' (2006) 10 *Law Text Culture* 1
Birnie, Patricia (ed.), *International Regulation of Whaling: From Conservation of Whaling to Conservation of Whales and Regulation of Whale-Watching*, 2 vols. (New York: Oceana, 1985), vol. I
Bishop, Claire, *Artificial Hells: Participatory Art and the Politics of Spectatorship* (Brooklyn: Verso, 2012)
Bjorge, Eirik, *The Evolutionary Interpretation of Treaties* (Oxford: Oxford University Press, 2014)
Black, CF, *A Mosaic of Indigenous Legal Thought: Legendary Tales and Other Writings* (Abingdon and New York: Routledge, 2017)
The Land Is the Source of the Law: A Dialogic Encounter with Indigenous Jurisprudence (London and New York: Routledge, 2010)
Black AC QC, The Hon Michael, 'The Tasmanian Dam Case: An advocate's memoir' (2015) 24(1) *Griffith Law Review* 22
Blanc, Nathalie, 'Ethics and aesthetics of environmental engagement' in Emily Brady and Pauline Phemister (eds.), *Human-Environment Relations: Transformative Values in Theory and Practice* (Dordrecht and New York: Springer, 2012)
Bodansky, Daniel, *The Art and Craft of International Environmental Law* (Cambridge: Harvard University Press, 2010)
Bodansky, Daniel, Jutta Brunnée and Ellen Hey, 'International environmental law: Mapping the field' in Daniel Bodansky, Jutta Brunnée and Ellen Hey (eds.),

Oxford Handbook of International Environmental Law (Oxford: Oxford University Press, 2008)

Bonyhady, Tim, *Images in Opposition: Australian Landscape Painting 1801–1890* (Melbourne: Oxford University Press, 1985)

Places Worth Keeping: Conservationists, Politics and Law (St Leonards: Allen & Unwin, 1993)

Bonyhady, Tim and Tom Griffiths (eds.), *Words for Country: Landscape & Language in Australia* (Sydney: University of New South Wales Press, 2002)

Bos, Maarten, 'Theory and practice of treaty interpretation', part I (1980) 27(1) *Netherlands International Law Review* 3

'Theory and practice of treaty interpretation', part II (1980) 27(2) *Netherlands International Law Review* 135

Bosse, Joanna, 'Nature/revelation: Ian Potter Museum of Art, University of Melbourne' in Guy Abrahams, Bronwyn Johnson, and Kelly Gellatly (eds.), *Art +Climate=Change* (Carlton: Melbourne University Press, 2016)

Bottici, Chiara, *Imaginal Politics* (Columbia University Press, 2014)

Bowman, Michael, 'Biodiversity, intrinsic value and the definition and valuation of environmental harm' in Michael J. Bowman and Alan E. Boyle (eds.), *Environmental Damage in International and Comparative Law: Problems of Definition and Valuation* (Oxford: Oxford University Press, 2002)

'Law, legal scholarship and the conservation of biological diversity: 2020 vision and beyond' in Michael Bowman, Peter Davies and Edward Goodwin (eds.), *Research Handbook on Biodiversity and Law* (Cheltenham and Northampton: Edward Elgar, 2016)

'"Normalizing" the *International Convention for the Regulation of Whaling*' (2008) 29 *Michigan Journal of International Law* 293

'The nature, development and philosophical foundations of the biodiversity concept in international law' in Michael Bowman and Catherine Redgwell (eds.), *International Law and the Conservation of Biological Diversity* (London and Boston: Kluwer Law International, 1996)

Bowman, Michael, Peter Davies and Catherine Redgwell, *Lyster's International Wildlife Law*, 2nd ed. (Cambridge: Cambridge University Press, 2010)

Bowman, Michael and Catherine Redgwell (eds.), *International Law and the Conservation of Biological Diversity* (London and Boston: Kluwer Law International, 1996)

Boyle, Alan, and Catherine Redgwell, *Birnie, Boyle & Redgwell's International Law and the Environment*, 4th ed. (Oxford, U.K.: Oxford University Press, 2021)

Bracker, Alison (ed.), *Vita Vitale: La Biennale di Venezia, 2015* (Heydar Aliyev Foundation, 2015)

Braddock, Alan C., 'Ecocritical art history' (2009) 23(1) *American Art* 24

'From nature to ecology: The emergence of ecocritical art history' in John Davis, Jennifer Greenhill and Jason LaFountain (eds.), *A Companion to American Art* (Malden: Wiley-Blackwell, 2015)

Braddock, Alan C. and Christoph Irmscher (eds.), *A Keener Perception: Ecocritical Studies in American Art History* (Tuscaloosa: University of Alabama Press, 2009)

Braddock, Alan C. and Renée Ater, 'Art in the anthropocene' (2014) 28(3) *American Art* 2

Brady, Emily 'Aesthetic value and wild animals' in Martin Drenthen and Jozef Keulartz (eds.), *Environmental Aesthetics: Crossing Divides and Breaking Ground* (New York: Fordham University Press, 2014)

'Aesthetic value, nature, and environment' in Stephen M. Gardiner and Allen Thompson (eds.), *The Oxford Handbook of Environmental Ethics* (New York: Oxford University Press, 2017)

'Aesthetics in practice: Valuing the natural world' (2006) 13(3) *Environmental Values* 277

Aesthetics of the Natural Environment (Edinburgh: Edinburgh University Press, 2003)

'Imagination and the aesthetic appreciation of nature' (1998) 56(2) *Journal of Aesthetics and Art Criticism* 139

The Sublime in Modern Philosophy: Aesthetics, Ethics and Nature (New York: Cambridge University Press, 2013)

'The ugly truth: Negative aesthetics and environment' (2012) 69 *Philosophy and Environment: Royal Institute of Philosophy Supplements* 83

Broude, Norma (ed.), *Gauguin's Challenge: New Perspectives After Postmodernism* (London and New York: Bloomsbury Visual Arts, 2018)

Broughton, Robert, 'Aesthetics and environmental law' (1972) 7 *Land and Water Law Review* 451

Brown, Andrew, *Art and Ecology Now* (London: Thames and Hudson, 2014)

Brown, Chris and Robyn Eckersley, 'International political theory and the real world' in Chris Brown and Robyn Eckersley (eds.), *The Oxford Handbook of International Political Theory* (Oxford: Oxford University Press, 2018)

Brunnée, Jutta, 'Common areas, common heritage, and common concern' in Daniel Bodansky, Jutta Brunnée and Ellen Hey (eds.), *The Oxford Handbook of International Environmental Law* (Oxford: Oxford University Press, 2008) p. 550

'COPing with consent: Law-making under multilateral environmental agreements' (2002) 15(1) *Leiden Journal of International Law* 1

Brunton, Paul (ed.), *The Endeavour Journal of Joseph Banks: The Australian Journey* (Pymble, NSW: HarperCollins, 1998)

Budd, Malcolm, *The Aesthetic Appreciation of Nature: Essays on the Aesthetics of Nature* (Oxford: Clarendon Press 2005)

'Objectivity and the aesthetic value of nature: Reply to Parsons' (2006) 46(3) *British Journal of Aesthetics* 267

Buell, Lawrence, *The Environmental Imagination: Thoreau, Nature Writing, and the Formation of American Culture* (Cambridge, MA: Belknap Press of Harvard University Press, 1995)

Bunge, John and Adrienne Freeman-Gallant, 'Blue world order?: A post hoc statistical analysis of art preference surveys from ten countries' in JoAnn Wypijewski (ed.), *Painting by Numbers: Komar and Melamid's Scientific Guide to Art* (New York: Farrar Straus Giroux, 1997)

Callicott, J Baird, *Earth's Insights: A Survey of Ecological Ethics from the Mediterranean Basin to the Australian Outback* (Berkeley: University of California Press, 1994)

'On the intrinsic value of nonhuman species' in Bryan G Norton (ed.), *The Preservation of Species: The Value of Biological Diversity* (Princeton: Princeton University Press, 1986)

Cameron, Christina and Mechtild Rössler, *Many Voices, One Vision: The Early Years of the World Heritage Convention* (Farnham: Ashgate, 2013)

Cardinale, Bradley J. et al., 'Biodiversity loss and its impact on humanity' (2012) 486 *Nature* 59

Carlson, Allen, 'Appreciation and the natural environment' (1979) 37 *Journal of Aesthetics and Art Criticism* 267

Aesthetics and the Environment: The Appreciation of Nature, Art and Architecture (London: Routledge, 2000)

'Environmental aesthetics' in Edward Craig (ed.), *Routledge Encyclopedia of Philosophy* (Online: Taylor & Francis, 2021)

'Is environmental art an aesthetic affront to nature?' in Allen Carlson (ed.), *Aesthetics and the Environment: The Appreciation of Nature, Art and Architecture* (London: Routledge, 2000)

Nature and Landscape: An Introduction to Environmental Aesthetics (New York: Columbia University Press, 2009)

'Nature: Contemporary thought' in Michael Kelly (ed.), *Encyclopedia of Aesthetics* (Online: Oxford Art Online, 1998)

'Ten steps in the development of Western environmental aesthetics' in Martin Drenthen and Jozef Keulartz (eds.), *Environmental Aesthetics: Crossing Divides and Breaking Ground* (New York: Fordham University Press, 2014)

Carlson, Allen and Arnold Berleant (eds.), *The Aesthetics of Natural Environments* (Peterborough and Plymouth: Broadview, 2004)

Carty, Anthony, *Philosophy of International Law* (Edinburgh: Edinburgh University Press, 2007)

Carty, John, *Balgo: Creating Country* (Crawley: UWA, 2021)

Cass, Deborah, 'Navigating the Newstream: Recent critical scholarship in international law' (1996) 65 *Nordic Journal of International Law* 341

Chalmers, Shane, 'Native dignity' (2020) 29(2) *Griffith Law Review* 175

Charlesworth, Hilary, 'The travels of human rights: The UNESCO human rights exhibition 1950–1953' in Shane Chalmers and Sundhya Pahuja (eds.), *The Routledge Handbook of International Law and the Humanities* (Abingdon: Routledge, 2021)

Chen, Siyuan, 'Re-assessing the evidentiary regime of the International Court of Justice: A case for codifying its discretion to exclude evidence' (2015) 13 *International Commentary on Evidence* 1

Churchill, Robin R. and Geir Ulfstein, 'Autonomous institutional arrangements in multilateral environmental agreements: A little-noticed phenomenon in international law' (2000) 94(4) *American Journal of International Law* 623

Clark, Kenneth, *Landscape into Art* (Harmondsworth: Pelican Books, 1956)

Clingerman, Forrest et al. (eds.), *Interpreting Nature: The Emerging Field of Environmental Hermeneutics* (New York: Fordham University Press, 2013)

Clode, Danielle, *Killers in Eden: The True Story of the Killer Whales and Their Remarkable Partnership with the Whalers of Twofold Bay* (Crows Nest: Allen & Unwin, 2002)

Collins, Lynda, 'The United Nations, human rights and the environment' in Anna Grear and Louis J. Kotzé (eds.), *Research Handbook on Human Rights and the Environment* (Cheltenham: Edward Elgar, 2015)

Cooper, David E., 'The intimacy of art and nature' in Emily Brady and Pauline Phemister (eds.), *Human-Environment Relations: Transformative Values in Theory and Practice* (Dordrecht and New York: Springer, 2012)

Cooper, Nigel et al., 'Aesthetic and spiritual values of ecosystems: Recognising the ontological and axiological plurality of cultural ecosystem services' (2016) 21 *Ecosystem Services* 218

Corten, Olivier, and Pierre Klein (eds.), *The Vienna Conventions on the Law of Treaties: A Commentary*, vol. I (Oxford: Oxford University Press, 2011)

Corten, Olivier et al. (tr. Christopher Sutcliffe), *A Critical Introduction to International Law* (Brussels: Editions de l'Université de Bruxelles, 2020)

Costello, Diarmuid and Dominic Willsdon (eds.), *The Life and Death of Images: Ethics and Aesthetics* (Ithaca: Cornell University Press, 2008)

Costonis, John J, *Icons and Aliens: Law, Aesthetics, and Environmental Change* (Urbana: University of Illinois Press, 1989)

'Law and aesthetics: A critique and a reformulation of the dilemmas' (1982) 80 *Michigan Law Review* 335

Couacaud, Sally, *After Nature: Lauren Berkowitz, Rosemary Laing, Janet Laurence, Louise Weaver* (Booragul: Lake Macquarie City Art Gallery, 2005)

Cronon, William, 'The trouble with wilderness or getting back to the wrong nature' in J. Baird Callicott and Michael P. Nelson (eds.), *The Great New Wilderness Debate* (Athens: University of Georgia Press, 1998)

Curtis, David J., 'Creating inspiration: The role of the arts in creating empathy for ecological restoration' (2009) 10(3) *Ecological Management & Restoration* 174

Dahlberg, Leif, Klaus Stierstorfer and Daniela Carpi (eds.), *Visualizing Law and Authority: Essays on Legal Aesthetics* (Berlin and Boston: Walter de Gruyter, 2012)

Daily, Gretchen C, 'Introduction: What are ecosystem services?' in Gretchen C Daily (ed.), *Nature's Services: Societal Dependence on Natural Ecosystems* (Washington DC: Island Press, 1997)

Dakin, WJ, *Whalemen Adventurers: The Story of Whaling in Australian Waters and Other Southern Seas Related thereto from the Days of Sails to Modern Times* (Sydney: Sirius Books, 1963)

Danilenko, G. M., *Law-Making in the International Community* (Dordrecht and Boston: Martinus Nijhoff, 1993)

Danto, Arthur C., *After the End of Art: Contemporary Art and the Pale of History* (Princeton: Princeton University Press, 1997)

'Can it be the "most wanted painting" even if nobody wants it?' in JoAnn Wypijewski (ed.), *Painting by Numbers: Komar and Melamid's Scientific Guide to Art* (New York: Farrar Straus Giroux, 1997)

What Art Is (New Haven and London: Yale University Press, 2013)

d'Aspremont, Jean, *International Law as a Belief System* (Cambridge and New York: Cambridge University Press, 2017)

'Towards a new theory of sources in international law' in Anne Orford and Florian Hoffmann with Martin Clark (eds.), *The Oxford Handbook of the Theory of International Law* (New York: Oxford University Press, 2016)

'Wording in international law' (2012) 25 *Leiden Journal of International Law* 575
d'Aspremont, Jean and Eric De Brabandere, 'Paintings of international law' in Jessie Hohmann and Daniel Joyce (eds.), *International Law's Objects* (Oxford: Oxford University Press, 2018)
d'Aspremont, Jean et al. (eds.), *International Law as a Profession* (Cambridge and New York: Cambridge University Press, 2017)
Davies, Margaret, *Asking the Law Question*, 4th ed. (Pyrmont: Thomson Reuters, 2017)
'Consciousness of trees' (2015) 27(2) *Law & Literature* 217
Law Unlimited: Materialism, Pluralism, and Legal Theory (Abingdon and New York: Routledge, 2017)
Davies, Margaret, Lee Godden and Nicole Graham, 'Situating property within habitat: Reintegrating place, people, and the law' (2021) 6 *Journal of Law, Property and Society* 1
Davies, Stephen and Philip Alperson, 'Pictorial representation and the visual arts' in Stephen Davies and Philip Alperson, *The Philosophy of Art* (Chichester: Wiley Blackwell, 2016)
The Philosophy of Art (Chichester: Wiley Blackwell, 2016)
Davis, John, Robert Owen and Ken Unsworth, *Venice Biennale 1978: From Nature to Art, from Art to Nature: Australia* (Sydney: Visual Arts Board, 1978)
Dawson, Freya, 'What is the value of biodiversity? Scientific and philosophical perspectives' in Nicole Rogers (ed.), *Green Paradigms and the Law* (Lismore: Southern Cross University Press, 1998)
De Lucia, Vito, 'Competing narratives and complex genealogies: The ecosystem approach in international environmental law' (2015) 27 *Journal of Environmental Law* 91
Deigh, John, *Emotions, Values, and the Law* (Oxford and New York: Oxford University Press, 2008)
Delaney, David, *Law and Nature* (Cambridge: Cambridge University Press, 2003)
Del Mar, Maksymilian, 'Thinking in images in legal theory' in M Del Mar and C Michelson (eds.), *The Anxiety of the Jurist* (Farnham: Ashgate, 2013)
Del Mar, Maksymilian and Peter Goodrich (eds.), *Legal Theory and the Humanities* (Farnham and Burlington: Ashgate, 2014)
Demos, TJ, 'Contemporary art and the politics of ecology: An introduction' (2013) 27(1) *Third Text* 1
Demos, T.J., Emily Eliza Scott, and Subhankar Banerjee (eds.), *The Routledge Companion to Contemporary Art, Visual Culture, and Climate Change* (New York, N.Y.: Routledge, 2021)
Descola, Philippe (tr. Janet Lloyd), *Beyond Nature and Culture*, (Chicago and London: The University of Chicago Press, 2013)
de Saussure, Ferdinand (tr. Roy Harris), *Course in General Linguistics* (London: Bloomsbury, 2013)
de Zegher, Catherine and Gerald McMaster (eds.), *18th Biennale of Sydney 2012: All Our Relations* (Woolloomooloo: Biennale of Sydney, 2012)
Díaz, S. et al., 'Assessing nature's contributions to people' (2018) 359 *Science* 270
Dombrovskis, Peter and Ellen Miller, *The Quiet Land* (Sandy Bay: Peter Dombrovskis, 1977)

Dorsett, Shaunnagh and Shaun McVeigh, 'Just so: "The law which governs Australia is Australian law"' (2002) 13(3) *Law and Critique* 289
'The persona of the jurist in Salmond's jurisprudence: On the exposition of "what law is . . ."' (2007) 38 *Victoria University of Wellington Law Review* 771
'Conduct of laws: Native title, responsibility, and some limits of jurisdictional thinking' (2012) 36(2) *Melbourne University Law Review* 470
Dorsey, Kurkpatrick, *Whales & Nations: Environmental Diplomacy on the High Seas* (Seattle: University of Washington Press, 2013)
Douzinas, Costas, 'A legal phenomenology of images' in Oren Ben-Dor (ed.), *Law and Art: Justice Ethics and Aesthetics* (Abingdon and New York: Routledge, 2011)
'A short history of the British Critical Legal Conference or, the responsibility of the critic' (2014) 25(2) *Law and Critique* 187
'The legality of the image' (2000) 63 *Modern Law Review* 813
Douzinas, Costas and Lynda Nead, 'Introduction' in Costas Douzinas and Lynda Nead (eds.), *Law and the Image: The Authority of Art and the Aesthetics of Law* (Chicago: The University of Chicago Press, 1999)
Douzinas, Costas and Ronnie Warrington, *Justice Miscarried: Ethics and Aesthetics in Law* (London and New York: Harvester Wheatsheaf, 1994)
Douzinas, Costas and Ronnie Warrington with Shaun McVeigh, *Postmodern Jurisprudence: The Law of the Text in the Texts of the Law* (London and New York: Routledge, 1991)
Drenthen, Martin, 'Environmental hermeneutics and the meaning of nature' in Stephen M. Gardiner and Allen Thompson (eds.), *The Oxford Handbook of Environmental Ethics* (New York: Oxford University Press, 2017)
Drenthen, Martin and Jozef Keulartz, 'Introduction' in Martin Drenthen and Jozef Keulartz (eds.), *Environmental Aesthetics: Crossing Divides and Breaking Ground* (New York: Fordham University Press, 2014)
Drenthen, Martin and Jozef Keulartz (eds.), *Environmental Aesthetics: Crossing Divides and Breaking Ground* (New York: Fordham University Press, 2014)
Dunaway, Finis, *Natural Visions: The Power of Images in American Environmental Reform* (Chicago: University of Chicago Press, 2005)
'Reframing the last frontier' in Alan C Braddock and Christoph Irmscher (eds.), *A Keener Perception: Ecocritical Studies in American Art History* (Tuscaloosa: University of Alabama Press, 2009)
Seeing Green: The Use and Abuse of American Environmental Images (Chicago and London: University of Chicago Press, 2015)
'The ecological sublime' (2005) 25(2) *Raritan* 78
Dunoff, Jeffrey L., and Mark A. Pollack (eds.), *Interdisciplinary Perspectives on International Law and International Relations: The State of the Art* (Cambridge: Cambridge University Press, 2013)
Dupuy, Pierre-Marie, 'Evolutionary interpretation of treaties: Between memory and prophecy' in Enzo Cannizzaro (ed.), *The Law of Treaties Beyond the Vienna Convention* (Oxford: Oxford University Press, 2011)
Dupuy, Pierre-Marie and Jorge E. Viñuales, *International Environmental Law: A Modern Introduction*, 2nd ed. (Cambridge: Cambridge University Press, 2018)

Dutton, Denis, *The Art Instinct: Beauty, Pleasure and Human Evolution* (Oxford and New York: Oxford University Press, 2009)

Duvic-Paoli, Leslie-Anne, 'Trees' in Jessie Hohmann and Daniel Joyce (eds.), *International Law's Objects* (Oxford: Oxford University Press, 2018)

Eckstein, Lars and Anja Schwarz (eds.), *Postcolonial Piracy: Media Distribution and Cultural Production in the Global South* (London: Bloomsbury Academic, 2014)

Edelman, Murray, *From Art to Politics: How Artistic Creations Shape Political Conceptions* (Chicago: Chicago University Press, 1995)

Edmonds, Richard Louis et al., 'Japan, §VI, 4: Late painting' in *Grove Art Online* (Online: Oxford University Press, 2003)

Edwards, Rebecca, 'A delightful and difficult art' in Cathy Leahy and Judith Ryan (eds.), *Colony: Australia 1770–1861/Frontier Wars* (Melbourne: National Gallery of Victoria, 2018)

Ehrlich, Ludwik, 'The development of international law as a science' (1962) 105 *Recueil des Cours* 173

Elder, Klaus (tr. Mark Ritter), *The Social Construction of Nature: A Sociology of Ecological Enlightenment* (London and Thousand Oaks: Sage, 1996)

Eldridge, Richard, *An Introduction to the Philosophy of Art* (New York: Cambridge University Press, 2003)

Elkins, James, *The End of Diversity in Art Historical Writing: North Atlantic Art History and its Alternatives* (Berlin and Boston: De Gruyter, 2021)

Elliot, Robert, *Environmental Ethics* (Oxford and New York: Oxford University Press, 1995)

Faking Nature: The Ethics of Environmental Restoration (London and New York: Routledge, 1997)

Ellis, Richard, *Men and Whales* (New York: Knopf, 1991)

Elsdon, Lee, 'Protecting the intellectual and cultural property of Aboriginal art' (April 2019) *The Bulletin* 20

Executive Secretary, Convention on Biological Diversity and Sam Johnston, 'The Convention on Biological Diversity: Ten years on and the strategic plan' (2001) 4(2) *Journal of International Wildlife Law & Policy* 147

Eyffinger, Arthur, *The International Court of Justice* (The Hague and Boston: Kluwer Law International, 1996)

Fagan, Brian, 'Alaska's rock art' (2008) 27 *Current World Archaeology* (online)

'CWA travels to the petroglyphs of Bangudae' (2014) 63 *Current World Archaeology* (online)

Falconer, Morgan and Mary Chou, 'Murakami, Takashi' in *Grove Art Online* (Online: Oxford University Press, 2003)

Farley, Christine Haight, 'Imagining the law: Art' in Austin Sarat, Matthew Anderson and Cathrine O. Frank (eds.), *Law and the Humanities: An Introduction* (Cambridge and New York: Cambridge University Press, 2010)

Feagin, Susan, 'Painting' in Jerrold Levinson (ed.), *The Oxford Handbook of Aesthetics* (New York: Oxford University Press, 2003)

Finchett-Maddock, Lucy and Eleftheria Lekakis, 'Introduction' in Lucy Finchett-Maddock and Eleftheria Lekakis (eds.), *Art Law Power: Perspectives on Legality and Resistance in Contemporary Aesthetics* (Oxford: Counterpress 2020) 1

Fisher, DE, 'Can the law protect landscape values?' (2005) 9 *New Zealand Journal of Environmental Law* 1
Fisher, John A., 'Environmental aesthetics' in Jerrold Levinson (ed.), *The Oxford Handbook of Aesthetics* (New York: Oxford University Press, 2003)
Fitter, Christopher, 'Landscape from the ancients to the seventeenth century' in Michael Kelly (ed.), *Encyclopedia of Aesthetics*, 2nd ed. (New York: Oxford University Press, 2014)
et al., 'Landscape' in Michael Kelly (ed.), *Encyclopedia of Aesthetics* (New York: Oxford University Press, 2014)
Fitzmaurice, Sir Gerald, '*Vae victis* or woe to the negotiators! Your treaty or our "interpretation" of it?' (1971) 65(2) *American Journal of International Law* 358
Fitzmaurice, Malgosia, 'Dynamic (evolutive) interpretation of treaties, part I' (2008) 21 *Hague Yearbook of International Law* 101
'Dynamic (evolutive) interpretation of treaties, part II' (2009) 22 *Hague Yearbook of International Law* 3
'Some reflections on legal and philosophical foundations of international environmental law' (2012) 32 *Polish Yearbook of International Law* 89
'Whale' in Jessie Hohmann and Daniel Joyce (eds.), *International Law's Objects* (Oxford: Oxford University Press, 2018)
Whaling and International Law (Cambridge: Cambridge University Press, 2015)
Foley, Fiona, 'When the circus came to town' (November, 2011) 245 *Art Monthly* 5
Fornasiero, Jean, Peter Monteath and John West-Sooby, *Encountering Terra Australis: The Australian Voyages of Nicolas Baudin and Matthew Flinders* (Kent Town: Wakefield Press, 2004)
Forster, Honore (ed.), *The South Sea Whaler: An Annotated Bibliography of Published Historical, Literary, and Art Material Relating to Whaling in the Pacific Ocean in the Nineteenth Century* (Sharon: Kendall Whaling Museum, 1985)
Fosci, Mattia and Tom West, 'In whose interest? Instrumental and intrinsic value in biodiversity law' in Michael Bowman, Peter Davies and Edward Goodwin (eds.), *Research Handbook on Biodiversity and Law* (Northampton: Edward Elgar, 2016)
Foster, Cheryl, 'The narrative and the ambient in environmental aesthetics' (1998) 56 *Journal of Aesthetics and Art Criticism* 2
Foster, Hal, *The Return of the Real: The Avant-Garde at the End of the Century* (Cambridge, MA: MIT Press, 1996)
Franck, Thomas M., *Fairness in International Law and Institutions* (Oxford: Clarendon Press and New York: Oxford University Press, 1995)
Judging the World Court (New York: Priority Press, 1986)
Frank, Jerome, *Law and the Modern Mind* (London: Taylor & Francis, 2017) (first published in 1930)
Frost, Michael H, *Introduction to Classical Legal Rhetoric: A Lost Heritage* (London: Routledge, 2016)
Fuller, Lon L, 'The forms and limits of adjudication' (1978) 92 *Harvard Law Review* 353
Gardiner, Richard, *Treaty Interpretation*, 2nd ed. (Oxford: Oxford University Press, 2016)
Gardiner, Stephen M, and Allen Thompson (eds.), *The Oxford Handbook of Environmental Ethics* (New York: Oxford University Press, 2017)

Garneau, David, 'Indigenous art: From appreciation to art criticism' in Ian McLean (ed.), *Double Desire: Transculturation and Indigenous Contemporary Art* (Newcastle upon Tyne: Cambridge Scholars, 2014)

Garrard, Greg, *Ecocriticism*, 2nd ed. (Abingdon and New York: Routledge, 2012)

Gearey, Adam, *Law and Aesthetics* (Oxford and Portland: Hart, 2001)

Genovese, Ann, Shaun McVeigh and Peter Rush, 'Lives lived with law: An introduction' (2016) 20 *Law Text Culture* 1

Giddens, Thomas, *On Comics and Legal Aesthetics: Multimodality and the Haunted Mask of Knowing* (Abingdon and New York: Routledge, 2018)

Gillespie, Alexander, *Conservation, Biodiversity and International Law* (Cheltenham: Edward Elgar, 2011)

'Ethical considerations' in Lavanya Rajamani and Jacqueline Peel (eds.), *The Oxford Handbook of International Environmental Law* (Oxford: Oxford University Press, 2021)

International Environmental Law, Policy and Ethics (Oxford: Clarendon Press and New York: Oxford University Press, 1997)

International Environmental Law, Policy and Ethics, 2nd ed. (Oxford: Oxford University Press, 2014)

The Long Road to Sustainability: The Past, Present, and Future of International Environmental Law and Policy (Oxford: Oxford University Press, 2018)

Glotfelty, Cheryll and Harold Fromm (eds.), *The Ecocriticism Reader: Landmarks in Literary Ecology* (Athens: University of Georgia Press, 1996)

Godden, Lee, 'Indigenous heritage and the environment: "Legal categories are only one way of imagining the Real"' (2002) 19 *Environmental and Planning Law Journal* 258

'Preserving natural heritage: Nature as other' (1998) 22 *Melbourne University Law Review* 719

Godden, Lee, Jacqueline Peel and Jan McDonald, *Environmental Law*, 2nd ed. (Docklands: Oxford University Press, 2019)

Goehr, Lydia, 'Art and politics' in Jerrold Levinson (ed.), *The Oxford Handbook of Aesthetics* (New York: Oxford University Press, 2003)

Gombrich, Ernst Hans, *Art and Illusion: A Study in the Psychology of Pictorial Representation*, 5th ed. (London: Phaidon, 1977)

Goodman, Nelson, *Languages of Art: An Approach to a Theory of Symbols* (Indianapolis: The Bobbs-Merrill Co Inc, 1968)

Goodrich, Peter, *Advanced Introduction to Law and Literature* (Cheltenham: Edward Elgar, 2021)

'Imago decidendi: On the common law of images' (2017) 1(1) *Art and Law* 1

'Jurisliterature and transgression' (2019) 36(2) *Law in Context: A Socio-Legal Journal* 10

Languages of Law: From Logics of Memory to Nomadic Masks (London: Weidenfeld and Nicolson, 1990)

'Law by other means' (1998) 10 *Cardozo Studies in Law and Literature* 111

Legal Discourse: Studies in Linguistics, Rhetoric and Legal Analysis (London: Macmillan, 1987)

Legal Emblems and the Art of Law: Obiter Depicta as the Vision of Governance (New York: Cambridge University Press, 2014)

'Retinal justice: Rats, maps and masks' (2021) 47(2) *Critical Inquiry* 241

'The international signs law' in Anne Orford and Florian Hoffmann with Martin Clark (eds.), *The Oxford Handbook of the Theory of International Law* (New York: Oxford University Press, 2016)

Goodrich, Peter and Valérie Hayaert (eds.), *Genealogies of Legal Vision* (London and New York: Routledge, 2015)

Gough, Julie, 'Observance' in Cathy Leahy and Judith Ryan (eds.), *Colony: Australia 1770–1861/Frontier Wars* (Melbourne: National Gallery of Victoria, 2018)

et al., *Fugitive History: The Art of Julie Gough* (Crawley, Western Australia: UWA, 2018)

Graham, Gordon, *Philosophy of the Arts: An Introduction to Aesthetics*, 3rd ed. (London and New York: Routledge, 2005)

Graham, Nicole, 'This is not a thing: Land, sustainability and legal education' (2014) 26 *Journal of Environmental Law* 395

Grear, Anna et al. (eds.), *Posthuman Legalities: New Materialism and Law Beyond the Human* (Cheltenham and Northampton: Edward Elgar, 2021)

Grossman, Michele (ed.), *Blacklines: Contemporary Critical Writing by Indigenous Australians* (Carlton: Melbourne University Press, 2003)

Grosz, Elizabeth, *Chaos, Territory, Art: Deleuze and the Framing of the Earth* (New York: Columbia University Press, 2008)

Guha, Ramachandra, *Environmentalism: A Global History* (Longman, 2000)

'Radical American environmentalism and wilderness preservation: A Third World critique' (1989) 11(1) *Environmental Ethics* 71

Guha, Ramachandra and Joan Martinez-Alier, *Varieties of Environmentalism: Essays North and South* (London: Earthscan 1997)

Gulliver, Robyn et al., 'Testing the impact of images in environmental campaigns' (2020) 71 *Journal of Environmental Psychology* 101468

Guyer, Paul, 'History of modern aesthetics' in Jerrold Levinson (ed.), *The Oxford Handbook of Aesthetics* (New York: Oxford University Press, 2003)

Gyalui, Luz (ed.), *La Biennale di Venezia: 56th International Art Exhibition: All the World's Futures* = 56, vol. 1 (Venice: Marsilio Editori, 2015)

Haapala, Arto, 'The interplay of works of art and natural phenomena' in Arnold Berleant (ed.), *Environment and the Arts: Perspectives on Environmental Aesthetics* (Ashgate, 2002)

Haldar, Piyel, 'The articles of law: Renaissance theories of evidence and the poetic life of facts' (2016) 10(2) *Law and Humanities* 281

'The tongue and the eye: Eloquence and office in Renaissance emblems' in Peter Goodrich and Valérie Hayaert (eds.), *Genealogies of Legal Vision* (London and New York: Routledge, 2015)

Halsey, Mark, 'Majesty and monstrosity: Deleuze and the defence of nature' in Andreas Philippopoulos-Mihalopoulos (ed.), *Law and Ecology: New Environmental Foundations* (New York: Routledge, 2011)

Hanne, Michael and Robert Weisberg (eds.), *Narrative and Metaphor in the Law* (Cambridge: Cambridge University Press, 2018)

Hansen, David and Peter Timms (eds.), *John Glover and the Colonial Picturesque* (Hobart: Tasmanian Museum and Art Gallery, 2003)

Harcourt, Bernard, *Critique and Praxis: A Critical Philosophy of Illusions, Values, and Action* (New York: Columbia University Press, 2020)

Hargrove, Eugene C., 'An overview of conservation and human values: Are conservation goals merely cultural attitudes?' in David Western and Mary C. Pearl (eds.), *Conservation for the Twenty-First Century* (New York: Oxford University Press, 1989) p. 227

Foundations of Environmental Ethics (Englewood Cliffs: Prentice Hall, 1989)

'The historical foundations of American environmental attitudes' in Allen Carlson and Sheila Lintott (eds.), *Nature, Aesthetics, and Environmentalism: From Beauty to Duty* (New York: Columbia University Press, 2008) p. 29

Harlow, Carol, 'Global administrative law: The quest for principles and values' (2006) 17(1) *European Journal of International Law* 187

Harris, Alexandra, Alan Hollinghurst and Ali Smith, *Tacita Dean: Landscape, Portrait, Still Life* (London: Royal Academy of Arts, the National Portrait Gallery and the National Gallery, 2018)

Haynes, Peter, *Mandy Martin: Painting 1981–2009* (Civic Square: Canberra Museum and Gallery, 2008)

Heartney, Eleanor, 'Art for the anthropocene era: Four artists take on the challenges of our environmental crisis' (2014) *Art in America* 76

Hegel, Georg Wilhelm Friedrich (tr. Bernard Bosanquet), *The Introduction to Hegel's Philosophy of Fine Art* (Oxford: Routledge, 2016)

Hepburn, Ronald, 'Contemporary aesthetics and the neglect of natural beauty' in Bernard Williams and Alan Montefiore (eds.), *British Analytical Philosophy* (New York: Humanities Press, 1966)

'Nature humanised: Nature respected' (1998) 7 *Environmental Values* 267

'Trivial and serious in aesthetic appreciation of nature' in Salim Kemal and Ivan Gaskell (eds.), *Landscape, Natural Beauty and the Arts* (Cambridge and New York: Cambridge University Press, 1993)

Hettinger, Ned, 'Allen Carlson's environmental aesthetics and the protection of the environment' (2005) 27 *Environmental Ethics* 57

'Animal beauty, ethics, and environmental preservation' (2010) 32(2) *Environmental Ethics* 115

Higgins, Judge Rosalyn, 'Respecting sovereign states and running a tight courtroom' (2001) 50(1) *International and Comparative Law Quarterly* 121

Hills, Richard L., *Power in the Industrial Revolution* (Manchester: Manchester University Press, 1970)

Hiltner, Ken (ed.), *Ecocriticism: The Essential Reader* (New York: Routledge, 2014)

Hirose, Iwao and Jonas Olson, 'Introduction to value theory' in Iwao Hirose and Jonas Olson (eds.), *The Oxford Handbook of Value Theory* (New York: Oxford University Press, 2015)

Hohmann, Jessie and Daniel Joyce (eds.), *International Law's Objects* (Oxford: Oxford University Press, 2018)

Hokanson, Alison, 'Turner's whaling pictures' (2016) 73(4) *The Metropolitan Museum of Art Bulletin* 1

Hosseinnejad, Katayoun, 'On the nature of interpretation in international law' (2015) 4 (2) *UCL Journal of Law and Jurisprudence* 225

Humby, Tracy-Lynn, 'Evaluating the value of TWAIL, environmental justice, and decolonization discourses as framing lenses for international environmental law' (2017) 26(2) *Transnational Law and Contemporary Problems* 317

Humphreys, Stephen and Yuriko Otomo, 'Theorizing international environmental law' in Anne Orford and Florian Hoffmann with Martin Clark (eds.), *The Oxford Handbook of the Theory of International Law* (New York: Oxford University Press, 2016)

Hunter, David, James Salzman and Durwood Zaelke, *International Environmental Law and Policy*, 5th ed. (St Paul: Foundation Press, 2015)

Huygebaert, Stefan et al. (eds.), *The Art of Law: Artistic Representations and Iconography of Law and Justice in Context, from the Middle Ages to the First World War* (Cham, Switzerland: Springer, 2018)

Isenberg, Andrew C. (ed.), *The Oxford Handbook of Environmental History* (Oxford and New York: Oxford University Press, 2014)

Jagodzinski, Jan (ed.), *Interrogating the Anthropocene: Ecology, Aesthetics, Pedagogy, and the Future in Question* (Cham, Switzerland: Palgrave Macmillan, 2018)

Jasanoff, Sheila, 'A new climate for society' (2010) 27(2–3) *Theory, Culture and Society* 233

'Heaven and earth: The politics of environmental images', in Sheila Jasanoff and M. Martello (eds.), *Earthly Politics: Local and Global in Environmental Governance* (Cambridge, MA: MIT Press, 2004)

'Image and imagination: The formation of global environmental consciousness' in Clark A. Miller and Paul N. Edwards (eds.), *Changing the Atmosphere: Expert Knowledge and Environmental Governance* (Cambridge, MA: MIT Press, 2001)

Jenkins, Victoria, 'In defence of natural beauty: Aesthetic obligation and the law on the designation of protected landscapes in England and Wales' (2020) 22(1) *Environmental Law Review* 7

Jennings, Sir Robert, 'The work of the International Bar' in Lal Chand Vohrah et al. (eds.), *Man's Inhumanity to Man, Essays on International Law in Honour of Antonio Cassese* (Leiden and Boston: Martinus Nijhoff, 2003)

Johns, Fleur, 'International legal theory: Snapshots from a decade of international legal life' (2009) 10(1) *Melbourne Journal of International Law* 1

Johnson, Barbara, 'The alchemy of style and law' in Austin Sarat and Thomas R. Kearns (eds.), *The Rhetoric of Law* (Ann Arbor: The University of Michigan Press, 1994)

Johnson, Bronwyn and Kelly Gellatly (eds.), *Art+Climate=Change II* (Carlton: Melbourne University Publishing, 2022)

Johnston, Sam, 'The role of science' in Lavanya Rajamani and Jacqueline Peel (eds.), *The Oxford Handbook of International Environmental Law* (Oxford: Oxford University Press, 2021)

Johnstone, Ian, 'Treaty interpretation: The authority of interpretive communities' (1991) 12(1) *Michigan Journal of International Law* 371

Jonas, Silvia, *Ineffability and Its Metaphysics: The Unspeakable in Art, Religion, and Philosophy* (Houndmills and New York: Palgrave Macmillan, 2016)

Joseph, Sarah, 'Art and human rights law' in Jani McCutcheon and Fiona McGaughey (eds.), *The Research Handbook on Art and Law* (Northampton: Edward Elgar, 2020)

Junker, Kirk W. (ed.), *Environmental Law Across Cultures* (Abingdon and New York: Routledge 2020)

Kalland, Arne, *Unveiling the Whale: Discourses on Whales and Whaling* (New York: Berghahn Books, 2009)

Kalland, Arne and Brian Moeran, *Japanese Whaling: End of an Era?* (London: Curzon Press, 1992)

Kammerhofer, Jörg, 'International legal positivism' in Anne Orford and Florian Hoffmann with Martin Clark (eds.), *The Oxford Handbook of the Theory of International Law* (New York: Oxford University Press, 2016)

Kang, Hyo Yoon, 'Law's materiality: Between concrete matters and abstract forms, or how matter becomes material' in Andreas Philippopoulos-Mihalopoulos (ed.), *Routledge Handbook of Law and Theory* (Abingdon: Routledge, 2019)

Kant, Immanuel (tr. Werner S. Plurar), *Critique of Judgment* (Indianapolis: Hackett, 1987)

Karp, JP, 'The evolving meaning of aesthetics in land use regulation' (1990) 15 *Colombia Journal of Environmental Law* 307

Keating, Adrian and Camilla B. Andersen, 'A graphic contract: Taking visualisation in contracting a step further' (2016) 2 *Journal of Strategic Contracting and Negotiation* 10

Keller, David R. (ed.), *Environmental Ethics: The Big Questions* (Malden: Wiley-Blackwell, 2010)

Kelsey, Robin, 'Ecology, sustainability, and historical interpretation' (2014) 28(3) *American Art* 8

Kemal, Salim, and Ivan Gaskell, 'Nature, fine arts, and aesthetics' in Salim Kemal and Ivan Gaskell (eds.), *Landscape, Natural Beauty and the Arts* (Cambridge and New York: Cambridge University Press, 1993)

Kennedy, David, 'A new stream of international law scholarship' (1988) 7(1) *Wisconsin International Law Journal* 1

'Critical legal theory' in Susan Tiefenbrun (ed.), *Law and the Arts* (Westport: Greenwood Press, 1999)

Kenyon, Andrew T. and Peter D. Rush (eds.), *An Aesthetics of Law and Culture: Text, Images, Screens* (Amsterdam and London: Elsevier JAI, 2004)

Kieran, Matthew, 'Aesthetic value: Beauty, ugliness and incoherence' (1997) 72(281) *Philosophy* 383

Kim, Rak E. and Klaus Bosselmann, 'International environmental law in the anthropocene: Towards a purposive system of multilateral environmental agreements' (2013) 2 *Transnational Environmental Law* 285

Kingsbury, Benedict, 'Global environmental governance as administration: Implications for international law' in Daniel Bodansky, Jutta Brunnée and Ellen Hey (eds.), *The Oxford Handbook of International Environmental Law* (Oxford: Oxford University Press, 2008)

'The concept of "law" in global administrative law' (2009) 20 *European Journal of International Law* 23

Kingsbury, Benedict, Nico Krisch and Richard B. Stewart, 'The emergence of global administrative law' (2005) 68(3–4) *Law and Contemporary Problems* 15

Kitcher, Philip, *Science, Truth and Democracy* (Oxford and New York: Oxford University Press, 2001)

Klabbers, Jan, *An Introduction to International Organizations Law*, 4th ed. (Cambridge: Cambridge University Press, 2022)
International Law, 3rd ed. (Cambridge: Cambridge University Press, 2021)
'The paradox of international institutional law' (2008) 5 *International Organizations Law Review* 151
'Virtuous interpretation' in Malgosia Fitzmaurice, Olufemi Elias and Panos Merkouris (eds.), *Treaty Interpretation and the Vienna Convention on the Law of Treaties: 30 Years On* (Leiden and Boston: Martinus Nijhoff, 2010)
Klaver, Irene J., 'Landscapes of the environmental imagination: Ranging from NASA and Cuyahoga images to Kiefer and O'Keeffe paintings' in Martin Drenthen and Jozef Keulartz (eds.), *Environmental Aesthetics: Crossing Divides and Breaking Ground* (New York: Fordham University Press, 2014)
Kolb, Robert, *The Elgar Companion to the International Court of Justice* (Cheltenham: Edward Elgar, 2014)
Koskenniemi, Martti, *From Apology to Utopia: The Structure of International Legal Argument* (Cambridge: Cambridge University Press, 1989)
The Gentle Civilizer of Nations: The Rise and Fall of International Law, 1870–1960 (Cambridge and New York: Cambridge University Press, 2002)
'The politics of international law' (1990) 1 *European Journal of International Law* 4
'What is international law for?' in Malcolm D Evans (ed.), *International Law*, 5th ed. (Oxford: Oxford University Press, 2018)
Koskenniemi, Martti and Päivi Leino, 'Fragmentation of international law? Postmodern anxieties' (2002) 15 *Leiden Journal of International Law* 553
Kotecha, Birju, 'The art of rhetoric: Perceptions of the International Criminal Court and legalism' (2018) 31(4) *Leiden Journal of International Law* 939
Kotsakis, Andreas, 'The historical roots of the north–south dynamic in biodiversity conservation and its imprint on the *Convention on Biological Diversity*' in Jona Razzaque and Elisa Morgera (eds.), *Biodiversity and Nature Protection Law* (Northampton: Edward Elgar, 2017)
Kreitner, Roy, Anat Rosenberg and Christopher Tomlins, 'Arts and the aesthetic in legal history' 2(2) *Critical Analysis of Law* (2015) 315
Kritsiotis, Dino, 'The power of international law as language' (1998) 34(2) *California Western Law Review* 397
Labadi, Sophia, *UNESCO, Cultural Heritage, and Outstanding Universal Value Value-Based Analyses of the World Heritage and Intangible Cultural Heritage Conventions* (Lanham, Md: AltaMira Press, 2013)
Lange-Berndt, Petra, 'White cube ecologies' in Omar Kholeif (ed.), *Lynette Yiadom-Boakye: Natures, Natural and Unnatural* (London: Whitechapel Gallery, 2015)
Latimer, Quinn and Adam Szymczyk (eds.), *The Documenta 14 Reader* (Munich: Prestel Verlag, 2017)
Leahy, Cathy with Helen McDonald and John Wolseley, *John Wolseley: Heartlands & Headwaters* (Melbourne: National Gallery of Victoria, 2015)
Leahy, Cathy and Judith Ryan (eds.), *Colony: Australia 1770–1861/Frontier Wars* (Melbourne: National Gallery of Victoria, 2018)
Leslie, Donna, *Aboriginal Art: Creativity and Assimilation* (South Yarra: Macmillan Art, 2008)

Letsas, G., *A Theory of Interpretation of the European Convention on Human Rights* (Oxford: Oxford University Press, 2007)

'Letter from Thomas Melville, captain of ship Britannia, to Sam. Enderby & Sons, 22 November 1791,' extracted in WJ Dakin, *Whalemen Adventurers: The Story of Whaling in Australian Waters and Other Southern Seas Related thereto from the Days of Sails to Modern Times* (Sydney: Sirius Books, 1963)

Levinson, Jerrold, 'Aesthetic contextualism' in Jerrold Levinson (ed.), *Aesthetic Pursuits: Essays in Philosophy of Art* (Oxford: Oxford University Press, 2016)

'Artistic worth and personal taste' in Jerrold Levinson, *Aesthetic Pursuits: Essays in Philosophy of Art* (Oxford: Oxford University Press, 2016)

'Philosophical aesthetics: An overview' in Jerrold Levinson (ed.), *The Oxford Handbook of Aesthetics* (New York: Oxford University Press, 2003)

Liivoja, Rain and Jarna Petman (eds.), *International Law-Making: Essays in Honour of Jan Klabbers* (London: Routledge, 2014)

Lloyd, Sophie, 'Reconsidering the species-specific approach: Insects and the *Environment Protection and Biodiversity Conservation Act*' (2020) 37(2) *Environmental and Planning Law Journal* 242

Lowenthal, David, 'Not every prospect pleases: What is our criterion for scenic beauty?' (1962–63) 12 *Landscape* 19

Macel, Christine, Luz Gyalui and Flavia Fossa Margutti (eds.), *57 Esposizione Internationale d'Arte: La Biennale di Venezia: Viva Arte Viva*, (New York: Rizzoli International, 2017), vol. I

MacKenzie, John M., *The Empire of Nature: Hunting, Conservation, and British Imperialism* (Manchester and New York: Manchester University Press, 1997)

Maloney, Michelle and Peter Burden (eds.), *Wild Law: In Practice* (Oxford and New York: Routledge, 2014)

Manderson, Desmond, 'Bodies in the water: On reading images more sensibly' (2015) 27(2) *Law and Literature* 279

Danse Macabre: Temporalities of Law in the Visual Arts (Cambridge and New York: Cambridge University Press, 2019)

'Force of wall' (2021) 33(3) *Law & Literature* 365

'Here and now: From "aestheticizing politics" to "politicizing art"' (2016) 13 *No Foundations* 1

'Introduction: Imaginal law' in Desmond Manderson (ed.), *Law and the Visual: Representations, Technologies and Critique* (Toronto: University of Toronto Press, 2018)

'Judgment in law and the humanities' (2013) 1 *Revista Forumul Judecatorilor* 43

'Not drowning, waving: Images, history, and the representation of asylum seekers' in Marianne Dickie, Dorota Gozdecka and Sudrishti Reich (eds.), *Unintended Consequences — The Impact of Migration Law and Policy* (Acton: ANU Press, 2016)

Songs without Music: Aesthetic Dimensions of Law and Justice (Berkeley: University of California Press, 2000)

Mannison, Don, 'A prolegomenon to a human chauvinistic aesthetic' in Don Mannison, Michael McRobbie and Richard Routley (eds.), *Environmental Philosophy* (Canberra: ANU, 1980)

Margutti, Flavia Fossa (ed.), *Viva Arte Viva: Biennale Art 2017 Short Guide, 57 Esposizione Internazionale d'Arte curated by Christine Macel* (Venice: La Biennale di Venezia, 2017)

May You Live in Interesting Times: Biennale Arte 2019 Short Guide, 58 Esposizione Internazionale d'Arte curated by Ralph Rugoff (Venice: La Biennale di Venezia, 2019)

Markussen, Michael et al. (eds.), *Valuation and Conservation of Biodiversity: Interdisciplinary Perspectives on the Convention on Biological Diversity* (Berlin and New York: Springer, 2005)

Maskit, Jonathan, 'On universalism and cultural historicism in environmental aesthetics' in Martin Drenthen and Jozef Keulartz (eds.), *Environmental Aesthetics: Crossing Divides and Breaking Ground* (New York: Fordham University Press, 2014)

Maass, Petra, *The Cultural Context of Biodiversity Conservation* in Michael Markussen et al. (eds.), *Valuation and Conservation of Biodiversity: Interdisciplinary Perspectives on the Convention on Biological Diversity* (Berlin and New York: Springer, 2005)

Maswood, S. Javed, 'Kakadu and the politics of World Heritage listing' (2000) 54(3) *Australian Journal of International Affairs* 357

Matilsky, Barbara C., *Fragile Ecologies: Contemporary Artists' Interpretations and Solutions* (New York: Rizzoli International, 1992)

'The survival of culture and nature' in *Art & Design Magazine, Art & Design Profile No. 36: Art and the Natural Environment* (London: Academy Editions, 1994)

Matthews, L. Harrison, *The Whale* (London: Allen & Unwin, 1968)

Matthews, Patricia, 'Scientific knowledge and the aesthetic appreciation of nature' (2002) 60 *Journal of Aesthetics and Art Criticism* 37

Maynard, Patrick, *The Engine of Visualization: Thinking through Photography* (Ithaca: Cornell University Press, 1997)

Mbengue, Makane Moïse, 'Scientific fact-finding at the International Court of Justice: An appraisal in the aftermath of the Whaling Case' (2016) 29(2) *Leiden Journal of International Law* 529

McCutcheon, Jani and Fiona McGaughey (eds.), *The Research Handbook on Art and Law* (Northampton: Edward Elgar, 2020)

McCutcheon, Jani and Natalie Skead, 'The art of crime: The application of literary proceeds of crime confiscation legislation to visual art' (2018) 22(3) *Media and Arts Law Review* 253

McDougal, Myres S., Harold D. Lasswell and James C. Miller, *The Interpretation of Agreements and World Public Order: Principles of Content and Procedure* (New Haven: Yale University Press, 1967)

McLean, Ian (ed.), *How Aborigines Invented the Idea of Contemporary Art* (Brisbane: Institute of Modern Art/Power, 2011)

Rattling Spears: A History of Indigenous Australian Art (London: Reaktion Books, 2016)

'The Australianness of the English Claude: Nation and empire in the art of John Glover' (2006) 7(1) *Australian and New Zealand Journal of Art* 125

McMillan, Kate, *Contemporary Art and Unforgetting in Colonial Landscapes: Islands of Empire* (Cham, Switzerland: Palgrave Macmillan, 2019)

McMillan, Mark et al., 'Obligations of conduct: Public law — treaty advice' (2021) 44 (2) *Melbourne University Law Review* 602

McVeigh, Shaun, 'Jurisprudent of London: Arts of association' (2016) 20 *Law Text Culture* 189

'Law as (more or less) itself: On some not very reflective elements of law' (2014) 4 *UC Irvine Law Review* 471

Meeker, Joseph W., *The Comedy of Survival: Studies in Literary Ecology* (New York: Scribner, 1974)

Mence, David, 'The cetacean right to life revisited' (2015) 11(1) *International Journal of Law in Context* 17

Merkouris, Panos, 'Introduction: Interpretation is a science, is an art, is a science' in Malgosia Fitzmaurice, Olufemi Elias and Panos Merkouris (eds.), *Treaty Interpretation and the Vienna Convention on the Law of Treaties: 30 Years on* (Leiden and Boston: Martinus Nijhoff, 2010)

Merrills, JG, 'Two approaches to treaty interpretation' (1968–1969) *Australian Yearbook of International Law* 55

Mickelson, Karin, 'South, north, international environmental law, and international environmental lawyers' (2000) 11(1) *Yearbook of International Environmental Law* 52

Miles, Kate, 'Painting international law as universal: Imperialism and the co-opting of image and art' (2020) 8(3) *London Review of International Law* 367

'Visuality of a treaty: Reflection on Versailles' (2020) 8(1) *London Review of International Law* 7

Miles, Malcolm, *Eco-Aesthetics: Art, Literature and Architecture in a Period of Climate Change* (London: Bloomsbury Academic, 2014)

Miller, Angela, 'The fate of wilderness in American landscape art' in Alan C. Braddock and Christoph Irmscher (eds.), *A Keener Perception: Ecocritical Studies in American Art History* (Tuscaloosa: University of Alabama Press, 2009)

Milne, Sandy, 'Threat to the rule of international law in the Antarctic?' (2019) 36 *Environmental and Planning Law Journal* 153

Mitchell, WJT, *Iconology: Image, Text, Ideology* (Chicago: University of Chicago Press, 1986)

Landscape and Power (Chicago: University of Chicago Press, 1992)

'Pictorial turn' in Roland Bleiker (ed.), *Visual Global Politics* (London: Taylor and Francis, 2018)

The Reconfigured Eye: Visual Truth in the Post-Photographic Era (Cambridge, MA: MIT Press, 1994)

What Do Pictures Want?: The Lives and Loves of Images (Chicago: University of Chicago Press, 2005)

Mizuki, Shigeru, *no yōkai jiten* [水木しげるの妖怪事典] (Tōkyō: Shōwa 56, 1981)

Mnookin, Jennifer L., 'The image of truth: Photographic evidence and the power of analogy' (1998) 10 *Yale Journal of Law and the Humanities* 1

Moloo, Rahim, 'When actions speak louder than words: The relevance of subsequent party conduct to treaty interpretation' (2013) 31(1) *Berkeley Journal of International Law* 39

Monani, Salma and Joni Adamson (eds.), *Ecocriticism and Indigenous Studies: Conversations from Earth to Cosmos* (New York and London: Routledge, 2017)

Moore, Ronald, 'Appreciating natural beauty as beautiful' in Allen Carlson and Arnold Berleant (eds.), *The Aesthetics of Natural Environments* (Peterborough and Plymouth: Broadview Press, 2004)

Moran, Leslie, *Law, Judges and Visual Culture* (Abingdon and New York: Routledge 2020)

Morgan, David, *Images at Work: The Material Culture of Enchantment* (New York: Oxford University Press, 2018)

Morgan, Ed, *The Aesthetics of International Law* (Toronto and Buffalo: University of Toronto Press, 2007)

Morgera, Elisa and Elsa Tsioumani, 'Yesterday, today, and tomorrow: Looking afresh at the *Convention on Biological Diversity*' (2010) 21(1) *Yearbook of International Environmental Law* 3

Morishita, Joji and Dan Goodman, 'The IWC moratorium on commercial whaling was not a value judgement and was not intended as a permanent prohibition' (2011) 1(2) *Aegean Review of the Law of the Sea and Maritime Law* 30

Morphy, Howard, *Ancestral Connections: Art and an Aboriginal System of Knowledge* (Chicago: University of Chicago Press, 1991)

Mulcahy, Linda, 'Eyes of the law: A visual turn in socio-legal studies?' (2017) 44 S1 *Journal of Law and Society* S111

Munsterberg, Hugo, *The Landscape Painting of China and Japan* (Rutland: CE Tuttle Co, 1955)

Nagtzaam, Gerry, 'Righting the ship? Australia, New Zealand and Japan at the ICJ and the barbed issue of "scientific whaling"' (2014) 1(1) *Australian Journal of Environmental Law* 71

The Making of International Environmental Treaties: Neoliberal and Constructivist Analyses of Normative Evolution (Cheltenham and Northampton: Edward Elgar, 2009)

Nasar, Jack L. (ed.), *Environmental Aesthetics: Theory, Research, and Applications* (Cambridge and New York: Cambridge University Press, 1988)

Natarajan, Usha, 'Third world approaches to international law (TWAIL) and the environment' in Andreas Philippopoulos-Mihalopoulos and Victoria Brooks (eds.), *Research Methods in Environmental Law: A Handbook* (Northampton: Edward Elgar, 2017)

Natarajan, Usha and Kishan Khoday, 'Locating nature: Making and unmaking international law' (2014) 27 *Leiden Journal of International Law* 573

Neale, Margo, 'Emily Kame Kngwarreye: The impossible modernist' (2017) 37(2) *Artlink* 42

Neale, Timothy, 'Duplicity of meaning: Wildness, indigeneity and recognition in the *Wild Rivers Act* debate' (2011) 20 *Griffith Law Review* 310

Neff, Stephen, 'A short history of international law' in Malcolm D. Evans (ed.), *International Law*, 5th ed. (Oxford: Oxford University Press, 2018)

Neill, Alex and Aaron Ridley (eds.), *Arguing About Art: Contemporary Philosophical Debates* (London and New York: Routledge, 2008)

Nettel, Ana Laura, 'The power of image and the image of power: The case of law' (2005) 21 *Word & Image* 136

Newton, John, *A Savage History: Whaling in the Pacific and Southern Oceans* (Sydney: NewSouth, 2013)

Nickel, James and Daniel Magraw, 'Philosophical issues in international environmental law' in Samantha Besson and John Tasioulas (eds.), *The Philosophy of International Law* (Oxford and New York: Oxford University Press, 2010)

Nicolson, Marjorie Hope, *Mountain Gloom and Mountain Glory: The Development of the Aesthetics of the Infinite* (Seattle and London: University of Washington Press, 1997)

Nixon, Rob, *Slow Violence and the Environmentalism of the Poor* (Cambridge, MA: Harvard University Press, 2011)

Nnamdi, Basil Sunday, Obari Gomba and Frank Ugiomoh, 'Environmental challenges and eco-aesthetics in Nigeria's Niger Delta' (2013) 27(1) *Third Text* 65

Norton, Bryan G. (ed.), *The Preservation of Species: The Value of Biological Diversity* (Princeton: Princeton University Press, 1986)

Nussbaum, Martha C., *Political Emotions: Why Love Matters for Justice* (Cambridge, MA: The Belknap Press of Harvard University Press, 2013)

O'Connell, Mary-Ellen, *The Art of Law in the International Community* (Cambridge and New York: Cambridge University Press, 2019)

Odgen, JT, 'From spatial to aesthetic distance in the eighteenth century' (1974) 35 *Journal of the History of Ideas* 63

O'Neill, Saffron J., and Nicholas Smith, 'Climate change and visual imagery' (2014) 5(1) *WIREs Climate Change* 73

Orakhelashvili, Alexander and Sarah Williams (eds.), *40 Years of the Vienna Convention on the Law of Treaties* (London: British Institute of International and Comparative Law, 2010)

Orford, Anne and Florian Hoffmann, 'Introduction: Theorizing international law' in Anne and Florian Hoffmann with Martin Clark (eds.), *The Oxford Handbook of the Theory of International Law* (New York: Oxford University Press, 2016)

Osborne, Harold, 'The use of nature in art' (1962) 2 *British Journal of Aesthetics* 318

Paden, Roger, Laurlyn K. Harmon and Charles R. Milling, 'Ecology, evolution, and aesthetics: Towards an evolutionary aesthetics of nature' (2012) 52(2) *British Journal of Aesthetics* 123

'Picturesque landscape painting and environmental aesthetics' (2015) 49(2) *The Journal of Aesthetic Education* 39

Pahuja, Sundhya, 'Conserving the world's resources?' in James Crawford and Martti Koskenniemi (eds.), *The Cambridge Companion to International Law* (Cambridge: Cambridge University Press, 2012)

Decolonising International Law: Development, Economic Growth and the Politics of Universality (Cambridge and New York: Cambridge University Press, 2011)

Palmer, Alice, 'Absent images of international law' in Shane Chalmers and Sundhya Pahuja (eds.), *The Routledge Handbook of International Law and the Humanities* (Abingdon: Routledge, 2021)

'Image and art in the *Whaling in the Antarctic Case*' in Jani McCutcheon and Fiona McGaughey (eds.), *The Research Handbook on Art and Law* (Northampton: Edward Elgar, 2020)

'Legal dimensions to valuing aesthetics in World Heritage decisions' (2017) 26(5) *Social & Legal Studies* 581

Palmer, Alice and Cairo Robb (eds.), *International Environmental Law Reports, Volume 4: International Environmental Law in National Courts* (Cambridge: Cambridge University Press, 2004)

Palmer, Maudie, 'Introduction' in Maudie Palmer and Samantha Littley, *Danie Mellor: Exotic Lies Sacred Ties* (Brisbane: University of Queensland Art Museum, 2014)

Panofsky, Erwin, *Studies in Iconology* (New York: Oxford University Press, 1939)

Parker, James E. K., *Acoustic Jurisprudence: Listening to the Trial of Simon Bikindi* (Oxford: Oxford University Press, 2015)

Parsons, Glenn, 'Freedom and objectivity in the aesthetic appreciation of nature' (2006) 46(1) *British Journal of Aesthetics* 17

'The aesthetic value of animals', (2007) 29 *Environmental Ethics* 151

Parsons, Glenn and Allen Carlson, *Functional Beauty* (Oxford: Oxford University Press, 2008)

Pateman, Trevor, *Key Concepts: A Guide to Aesthetics, Criticism and the Arts in Education* (London and New York: Routledge, 2016)

'Photography' in Trevor Pateman, *Key Concepts: A Guide to Aesthetics, Criticism and the Arts in Education* (London and New York: Routledge, 2016)

Pedersen, Ole, 'The limits of interdisciplinarity and the practice of environmental law scholarship' (2014) 26 *Journal of Environmental Law* 423

Pepper, David with John Perkins and Martyn Youngs, *The Roots of Modern Environmentalism* (London and Dover: Croom Helm, 1984)

Petersen, Laura, 'Foot notes. Reflections on method and form' in Shane Chalmers and Sundhya Pahuja (eds.), *The Routledge Handbook of International Law and the Humanities* (Abingdon: Routledge, 2021)

Petroski, Karen, 'Visual legal commentary' in Anne Wagner and Richard K. Sherwin (eds.), *Law, Culture and Visual Studies* (Dordrecht and New York: Springer, 2013)

Philippopoulos-Mihalopoulos, Andreas, 'Critical legal thinking in environmental law' in Andreas Philippopoulos-Mihalopoulos (ed.), *Law and Ecology: New Environmental Foundations* (New York: Routledge, 2011)

'The sound of a breaking string: Critical environmental law and ontological vulnerability' (2011) 2(1) *Journal of Human Rights and the Environment* 5

Phillips, Dougal, 'The dilemma of artistic works: How can the court make aesthetic decisions?' (2014) 32(1) *Copyright Reporter* 1

Pitlo, Adriaan, *Evolutie in het privaatrecht* [Evolution in private law] (Haarlem: HD Tjeenk Willink, 1969)

Porteous, J. Douglas, *Environmental Aesthetics: Ideas, Politics and Planning* (London: Routledge, 1996)

Porter, Elizabeth, 'Taking images seriously' (2014) 114 *Columbia Law Review* 1687

Prior, Michael, 'Economic valuation and environmental values' (1998) 7(4) *Environmental Values* 423

Prost, Mario and Alejandra Torres Camprubí, 'Against fairness? International environmental law, disciplinary bias, and pareto justice' (2012) 25 *Leiden Journal of International Law* 379

Purdy, Jedediah, *After Nature: A Politics for the Anthropocene* (Cambridge, MA: Harvard University Press, 2015)

Quintana, Juan José, *Litigation at the International Court of Justice: Practice and Procedure* (Leiden and Boston: Brill Nijhoff, 2015)

Rajamani, Lavanya and Jacqueline Peel, 'International environmental law: Changing context, emerging trends, and expanding frontiers' in Lavanya Rajamani and Jacqueline Peel (eds.), *The Oxford Handbook of International Environmental Law* (Oxford: Oxford University Press, 2021)

Rampley, Matthew, *The Seductions of Darwin: Art, Evolution, Neuroscience* (University Park: Pennsylvania State University Press, 2017)

Ramshaw, Sara, *Justice as Improvisation: The Law of the Extempore* (Oxford: Routledge, 2013)

Rancière, Jacques (tr. Steven Cocoran), *Dissensus: On Politics and Aesthetics*, (London and New York: Continuum, 2010)

(tr. Gregory Elliott), *The Future of Image* (London and New York: Verso, 2007)

Raz, Joseph, *The Morality of Freedom* (New York: Oxford University Press, 1986)

Redgwell, Catherine, 'Article 2 definition of natural heritage' in Francesco Francioni (ed.), *The 1972 World Heritage Convention: A Commentary* (Oxford: Oxford University Press, 2008)

'Life, the universe and everything: Critique of anthropocentric rights' in Alan Boyle and Michael Anderson (eds.), *Human Rights Approaches to Environmental Protection* (Oxford: Clarendon Press, 1996)

Reichman, Ravit, 'Narrative and rhetoric' in Austin Sarat, Matthew Anderson and Cathrine O. Frank (eds.), *Law and the Humanities* (Cambridge and New York: Cambridge University Press, 2010)

Reid, Colin T. and Walters Nsoh, *The Privatisation of Biodiversity?: New Approaches to Conservation Law* (Northampton: Edward Elgar, 2016)

Richardson, Benjamin J., 'Aesthetics and environmental law: Valuing Tasmania's "Ordinary" nature' (2018) 27(1) *Griffith Law Review* 1

'Climate change law: Encounters with aesthetics and art' (2018) 3–4 *Climate Law* 279

The Art of Environmental Law: Governing with Aesthetics (Oxford: Hart, 2019)

Richardson, Benjamin J., Emily Barritt and Megan Bowman, 'Beauty: A lingua franca for environmental law?' (2019) 8(1) *Transnational Environmental Law* 59

Riddell, Anna and Brendan Plant, *Evidence Before the International Court of Justice* (London: British Institute of International & Comparative Law, 2009)

Robidoux, Meghan and Jason F Kovacs, 'Public art as a tool for environmental outreach: Insights on the challenges of implementation' (2018) 48(3) *Journal of Arts Management, Law and Society* 159

Roca, José, 'Abel Rodríguez' in Quinn Latimer and Adam Szymczyk (eds.), *documenta 14: Daybook* (Munich: Prestel Verlag, 2017)

Rodríguez, Abel, *Las Plantas Cultivadas por la Gente de Dentro en la Amazonia Colombiana* [The plants cultivated by the people from the center in the Colombian Amazon] (Bogotá: Tropenbos Internacional Colombia, 2013)

Roele, Isobel, 'We Are Making a New World' in Shane Chalmers and Sundhya Pahuja (eds.), *The Routledge Handbook of International Law and the Humanities* (Abingdon: Routledge, 2021)

Rolland, Sonia E., '*Whaling in the Antarctic (Australia v. Japan: New Zealand Intervening)*' (2014) 108 *American Journal of International Law* 496

Rolston III, Holmes, 'Beauty and the beast: Aesthetic experience of wildlife', in Daniel J Decker and R. Gary Goff (eds.), *Valuing Wildlife: Economic and Social Perspectives* (Boulder: Westview Press, 1987)

'Does aesthetic appreciation of nature need to be science based?' (1995) 35 *British Journal of Aesthetics* 374

'Landscape from the eighteenth century to the present' in Michael Kelly (ed.), *Encyclopedia of Aesthetics*, 2nd ed. (New York: Oxford University Press, 2014)

Rose, Deborah Bird, *Nourishing Terrains: Australian Aboriginal Views of Landscape and Wilderness* (Canberra: Australian Heritage Commission, 1996)

Rose, Justin, Margaretha Wewerinke-Singh and Jessica Miranda, 'Primal scene to anthropocene: Narrative and myth in international environmental law' (2019) 66 (3) *Netherlands International Law Review* 441

Rosenne, Shabtai, 'Conceptualism as a guide to treaty interpretation' in Shabtai Rosenne, *An International Law Miscellany* (Dordrecht: Martinus Nijhoff, 1993)

Ross Kiester, A., 'Aesthetics of biological diversity' (1996) 3(2) *Human Ecology Review* 151

Ross, Stephanie, 'Gardens, earthworks, and environmental art' in Salim Kemal and Ivan Gaskell (eds.), *Landscape, Natural Beauty and the Arts* (Cambridge and New York: Cambridge University Press, 1993)

Rush, Peter D., 'A sense of place with landmark judgments: Anthropogenic justice, wildlife extinction, and climate change' (2022) 9(2) *Asian Journal of Law and Society* 228.

Rush, Peter D. and Andrew T. Kenyon 'Alter egos: The mise-en-scène of law and aesthetics' in Andrew T. Kenyon and Peter D. Rush (eds.), *An Aesthetics of Law and Culture: Text, Images, Screens* (Amsterdam and London: Elsevier JAI, 2004)

Rush, Peter D. and Maria Elander, 'Working through the cinematography of international criminal justice: Procedures of law and images of atrocity' (2018) 6(1) *London Review of International Law* 17

Ryan, Judith, 'Disquiet and resistance in the art of Julie Gough' (June 2013) 33(2) *Artlink* 72

Sadler, Barry and Allen Carlson (eds.), *Environmental Aesthetics: Essays in Interpretation* (Victoria: Department of Geography, University of Victoria, 1982)

Saito, Yuriko, 'Environmental directions for aesthetics and the arts' in Arnold Berleant (ed.), *Environment and the Arts: Perspectives on Environmental Aesthetics* (Aldershot: Ashgate, 2002)

'The aesthetics of unscenic nature' (1998) 56(2) *Journal of Aesthetics and Art Criticism* 101

Sands, Philippe and Jacqueline Peel, *Principles of International Environmental Law*, 4th ed. (Cambridge: Cambridge University Press, 2018)

Sands, Philippe and Pierre Klein, *Bowett's Law of International Institutions* (London: Sweet & Maxwell, 2009)

Sarat, Austin (ed.), *Rhetorical Processes and Legal Judgments: How Language and Arguments Shape Struggles for Rights and Power* (New York: Cambridge University Press, 2016)

Sarat, Austin, Matthew Anderson and Cathrine O. Frank (eds.), *Law and the Humanities: An Introduction* (Cambridge and New York: Cambridge University Press, 2010)

Sarat, Austin and Thomas R. Kearns, 'Editorial introduction' in Austin Sarat and Thomas R. Kearns (eds.), *The Rhetoric of Law* (Ann Arbor: University of Michigan Press, 1994) 7

Sarkar, Sahotra, 'Approaches to biodiversity' in Justin Garson, Anya Plutynski, and Sahotra Sarkar (eds.), *The Routledge Handbook of Philosophy of Biodiversity* (New York: Routledge, 2017)

Biodiversity and Environmental Philosophy: An Introduction (Cambridge and New York: Cambridge University Press, 2005)

Savedoff, Barbara, *Transforming Images: How Photography Complicates the Picture* (Ithaca: Cornell University Press, 2000)

Schachter, Oscar, *International Law in Theory and Practice* (Dordrecht and Boston: Martinus Nijhoff, 1991)

Schama, Simon, *Landscape and Memory* (London: HarperCollins, 1995)

Wordy: Sounding Off on High Art, Low Appetite and the Power of Memory (London: Simon & Schuster, 2019)

Schermers, Henry G. and Niels M. Blokker, *International Institutional Law: Unity Within Diversity*, 6th ed. (Leiden and Boston: Brill Nijhoff, 2018)

Schlag, Pierre, 'The aesthetics of American law' (2002) 115 *Harvard Law Review* 1047

Scholtz, Werner, 'Animal culling: A sustainable approach or anthropocentric atrocity? Issues of biodiversity and custodial sovereignty' (2005) 2(2) *Macquarie Journal of International and Comparative Environmental Law* 9

'"Ethical and humane use", intrinsic value and the *Convention on Biological Diversity*: Towards the reconfiguration of sustainable development and use' (2021) 30(1) *Review of European, Comparative & International Environmental Law* 73

Scholtz, Werner (ed.), *Animal Welfare and International Environmental Law: From Conservation to Compassion* (Northampton: Edward Elgar, 2019)

Schorr, David B., 'Art and the history of environmental law' (2015) 2(2) *Critical Analysis of Law* 322

Scobbie, Iain, 'Rhetoric, persuasion, and interpretation in international law' in Andrea Bianchi, Daniel Peat and Matthew Windsor (eds.), *Interpretation in International Law* (Oxford: Oxford University Press, 2015)

'A view of Delft: Some thoughts about thinking about international law' in Malcolm D. Evans (ed.), *International Law*, 5th ed. (Oxford: Oxford University Press, 2018)

Scruton, Roger, 'Photography and representation' in Roger Scruton, *The Aesthetic Understanding: Essays in The Philosophy of Art and Culture* (Manchester: Carcanet, 1983)

Seel, Martin, *Eine Ästhetik der Natur* (Frankfurt: Suhrkamp, 1991)

Sepänmaa, Yrjö, 'From theoretical to applied environmental aesthetics: Academic aesthetics meets real-world demands' in Martin Drenthen and Jozef Keulartz (eds.), *Environmental Aesthetics: Crossing Divides and Breaking Ground* (New York: Fordham University Press, 2014)

'Human nature and aesthetic ecosystem services: Nature in the service of humankind and humankind in the service of nature' (2016) 14 *Contemporary Aesthetics* (online)

'The two aesthetic cultures: The great analogy of art and the environment' in Arnold Berleant (ed.), *Environment and the Arts: Perspectives on Environmental Aesthetics* (Aldershot: Ashgate, 2002)

Shaw, Malcolm N., 'Documents in support' in *Rosenne's Law and Practice of the International Court: 1920–2015* (Leiden and Boston: Brill Nijhoff, 2016), vol. III

International Law, 9th ed. (Cambridge and New York: Cambridge University Press, 2021)

Sherwin, Richard K., 'Introduction: Law, culture, and visual studies' in Anne Wagner and Richard K. Sherwin (eds.), *Law, Culture and Visual Studies* (Dordrecht and New York: Springer, 2013)

'Visual jurisprudence' (2012–13) 57 *New York Law School Law Review* 11

Visualizing Law in the Age of the Digital Baroque: Arabesques and Entanglements (London: Routledge 2011)

'What authorises the image' in Desmond Manderson (ed.), *Law and the Visual: Representations, Technologies and Critique* (Toronto: University of Toronto Press, 2018)

Sibley, Frank, 'Some notes on ugliness' in John Benson, Betty Redfern and Jeremy Roxbee Cox (eds.), *Approach to Aesthetics: Collected Papers on Philosophical Aesthetics* (New York: Oxford University Press, 2001)

Sikes, Sylvia K., *The Natural History of the African Elephant* (London: Weidenfeld & Nicolson, 1971)

Silbey, Jessica, 'Images in/of law' (2012–13) 57 *New York Law School Law Review* 171

Simma, Bruno, 'The International Court of Justice and scientific expertise' (2012) 106 *Proceedings of the ASIL Annual Meeting* 230

Simpson, Gerry, *Sentimental Life of International Law: Literature, Language and Longing in World Politics* (Oxford: Oxford University Press, 2021)

'The sentimental life of international law' (2015) 3(1) *London Review of International Law* 3

Simus, Jason B., 'Ecological art and environmental citizenship' (2008) 30 *Environmental Ethics* 21

'Environmental art and ecological citizenship' in Martin Drenthen and Jozef Keulartz (eds.), *Environmental Aesthetics: Crossing Divides and Breaking Ground* (New York: Fordham University Press, 2014)

Slijper, E. J. (tr. AJ Pomerans), *Whales* (London: Hutchinson, 1962)

Slovic, Scott, Swarnalatha Rangarajan and Vidya Sarveswaran (eds.), *Ecocriticism of the Global South* (Lanham: Lexington Books, 2015)

Small, N., M. Munday and I. Durance, 'The challenge of valuing ecosystem services that have no material benefits' (2017) 44 *Global Environmental Change* 57

Smith, Jeffrey J., 'Evolving to conservation: The International Court's decision in the Australia/Japan Whaling Case' (2014) 45(4) *Ocean Development and International Law* 301

Snyder, Joel and Neil Walsh Allen, 'Photography, vision and representation' (1975) 2(1) *Critical Inquiry* 143

Soboslay, Zsuzsanna, 'Mandy Martin: Eco-worrying' (2010) 226 *Art Monthly Australia* 30

Sommer, Laura Kim and Christian A. Klöckner, 'Does activist art have the capacity to raise awareness of audiences?—A study on climate change art at the

ArtCOP21 event in Paris' (2021) 15(1) *Psychology of Aesthetics, Creativity, and the Arts* 60

Soper, Kate, *What is Nature? Culture, Politics and the Non-Human* (Oxford and Cambridge, MA: Blackwell, 1995)

Staszak, Jean-François, 'Primitivism and the other: History of art and cultural geography' (2004) 60 *GeoJournal* 353

Staubach, Peter G., *The Rule of Unwritten International Law: Customary Law, General Principles, and World Order* (London: Taylor & Francis, 2018)

Stecker, Robert, 'Definition of art' in Jerrold Levinson (ed.), *The Oxford Handbook of Aesthetics* (New York: Oxford University Press, 2003)

'What is art?' in Robert Stecker, *Aesthetics and the Philosophy of Art: An Introduction*, 2nd ed. (Lanham: Rowman & Littlefield, 2010)

Stephens, Tim, 'What is the point of international environmental law scholarship in the Anthropocene?' in Ole W Pedersen (ed.), *Perspectives on Environmental Law Scholarship: Essays on Purpose, Shape and Direction* (Cambridge and New York: Cambridge University Press, 2018)

Stone, Christopher D, 'Ethics and international environmental law' in Daniel Bodansky, Jutta Brunnée and Ellen Hey (eds.), *The Oxford Handbook of International Environmental Law* (Oxford: Oxford University Press, 2008)

Stubbs, Will and John Wolseley (eds.), *Midawarr Harvest: The Art of Mulkuṉ Wirrpanda and John Wolseley* (Canberra: National Museum of Australia, 2018)

Tafalla, Marta, 'From Allen Carlson to Richard Long: The art-based appreciation of nature' (2010) 2 *Proceedings of the European Society for Aesthetics* 491

Takacs, D., *The Idea of Biodiversity: Philosophies of Paradise* (Baltimore: Johns Hopkins University Press, 1996)

Tallgren, Immi, 'Come and see? The power of images and International Criminal Justice' (2016) 17 *International Criminal Law Review* 259

Thompson, Janna, 'Aesthetics and the value of nature' (1995) 17(3) *Environmental Ethics* 291

Thorsell, James, 'Scenic natural beauty: How can it be judged?' (2012) 63 *World Heritage* 8

Tiefenbrun, Susan, *Decoding International Law: Semiotics and the Humanities* (New York: Oxford University Press, 2010)

Tinios, Ellis, '2. Edo period (1600–1868) and after: Books' in Richard Louis Edmonds et al. (eds.), 'Japan, §X: prints and books' in *Grove Art Online* (Online: Oxford University Press, 2003)

Torresi, Ira, 'The photographic image: Truth or sign?' in Anne Wagner and Richard K. Sherwin (eds.), *Law, Culture and Visual Studies* (Dordrecht and New York: Springer, 2013)

Tsing, Anna Lowenhaupt, *The Mushroom at the End of the World: On the Possibility of Life in Capitalist Ruins* (Princeton: Princeton University Press, 2015)

Turner, R. K. et al., 'Valuing nature: Lessons learned and future research directions' (2003) 46 *Ecological Economics* 493

Urquhart, F., 'Found at last: The Monarch's winter home' (1976) *National Geographic Magazine* 161

Vadi, Valentina, 'Power, law and images: International law and material culture' (2018) 45(2) *Syracuse Journal of International Law and Commerce* 215

Valencia-Ospina, Eduardo, 'Evidence before the International Court of Justice' (1999) 1(4) *International Law FORUM du droit international* 202

Van Alstine, Michael P., 'Dynamic treaty interpretation' (1997–1998) 146 *University of Pennsylvania Law Review* 687

van Heijnsbergen, Pieter, *International Legal Protection of Wild Fauna and Flora* (Amsterdam and Washington: IOS Press, 1997)

van Klink, Bart and Sanne Taekema, *Law and Method: Interdisciplinary Research into Law* (Tübingen: Mohr Siebeck, 2011)

Van Veeren, Elspeth, 'Layered wanderings: Epistemic justice through the art of Wangechi Mutu and Njideka Akunyili Crosby' (2019) 21(3) *International Feminist Journal of Politics* 488

Veitch, Scott, Emilios Christodoulidis and Lindsay Farmer, *Jurisprudence: Themes and Concepts* (London: Routledge, 2012)

Verhoeven, Joe, Philippe Sands and Maxwell Bruce (eds.), *The Antarctic Environment and International Law* (London and Boston: Graham & Trotman, 1992)

Vincent, Sam, *Blood & Guts: Dispatches from the Whale Wars* (Collingwood: Black Inc, 2014)

Vogel, Steven, *Thinking Like a Mall: Environmental Philosophy after the End of Nature* (Cambridge, MA and London: MIT Press, 2015)

Voigt, Christina (ed.), *International Judicial Practice on the Environment: Questions of Legitimacy* (Cambridge: Cambridge University Press, 2019)

Waibel, Michael, 'Interpretive communities in international law' in Andrea Bianchi, Daniel Peat and Matthew Windsor (eds.), *Interpretation in International Law* (Oxford: Oxford University Press, 2015)

Waldcock, Sir Humphrey, 'Third report on the law of treaties' (1964) II *Yearbook of the International Law Commission* 54, UN Doc. A/CN.4/167

Wallen, R., 'Ecological art: A call for visionary intervention in a time of crisis,' (2012) 45 (3) *Leonardo* 234

Walsh, David et al., *On the Origin of Art* (Hobart: Tasmania Museum of Old and New Art, 2016)

Walton, Kendall, 'Transparent pictures: On the nature of photographic realism' (1984) 11(2) *Critical Inquiry* 246

Warburton, Nigel, 'Photography' in Jerrold Levinson (ed.), *The Oxford Handbook of Aesthetics* (New York: Oxford University Press, 2003)

'Seeing through "Seeing through photographs"' (1988) 28 *British Journal of Aesthetics* 173

Watson, Irene, *Aboriginal Peoples, Colonialism and International Law: Raw Law* (Oxford and New York: Routledge, 2014)

'Aboriginal relationships to the natural world: Colonial "protection" of human rights and the environment' (2018) 9(2) *Journal of Human Rights and the Environment* 119

Weintraub, Linda, *To Life! Eco-Art in Pursuit of a Sustainable Planet* (Berkeley: University of California Press, 2012)

Weiss, Edith Brown, 'International environmental law: Contemporary issues and the emergence of a New World Order' in R. N. Wells Jr. (ed.), *Law, Values, and the Environment: A Reader and Selective Bibliography* (Lanham: Scarecrow Press, 1996) p. 495

West, Kate, 'Feeling things: From visual to material jurisprudence' (2020) 31 *Law and Critique* 113

West, Thomas, A *Guide to the Lakes, in Cumberland, Westmorland, and Lancashire* (London: Richardson and Urquhart, 1778)

White, James Boyd, 'Imagining the law' in Austin Sarat and Thomas R. Kearns (eds.), *The Rhetoric of Law* (Ann Arbor: University of Michigan Press, 1994)

Whitfield, Roderick, 'Landscape: China, People's Republic of' in *Grove Art Online* (Online: Oxford University Press, 2003)

Widener, Michael and Mark S. Weiner, *Law's Picture Books: The Yale Law Library Collection* (Clark: Talbot, 2017)

Wilson, Emma-Kate, 'Lauren Berkowitz's Fragile Structures' (2019) 314 *Art Monthly Australasia* 36

Woodliffe, John, 'Biodiversity and indigenous peoples' in Michael Bowman and Catherine Redgwell (eds.), *International Law and the Conservation of Biological Diversity* (London and Boston: Kluwer Law International, 1996)

Woods, Mark, 'Federal wilderness preservation in the United States: The preservation of wilderness?' in J. Baird Callicott and Michael Nelson (eds.), *The Great New Wilderness Debate* (Athens: University of Georgia Press, 1998)

Rethinking Wilderness (Peterborough, Ont: Broadview Press, 2017)

Wypijewski, JoAnn (ed.), *Painting by Numbers: Komar and Melamid's Scientific Guide to Art* (New York: Farrar Straus Giroux, 1997)

Xue, Fuxing, 'Two types of a doctrine of objectivity in the aesthetic appreciation of nature' (2018) 6 *Contemporary Aesthetics* 13

Young, Alison, *Judging the Image: Art, Value, Law* (London and New York: Routledge, 2004)

'Aesthetic vertigo: Disgust and the illegitimate touching of art' in Alison Young, *Judging the Image: Art, Value, Law* (London and New York: Routledge, 2004)

Young, Margaret A. and Sebastian Rioseco Sullivan, 'Evolution through the duty to cooperate: Implications of the Whaling Case at the International Court of Justice' (2015) 16(2) *Melbourne Journal of International Law* 311

Yunkaporta, Tyson, *Sand Talk: How Indigenous Thinking Can Save The World* (Melbourne: Text Publishing, 2019)

Zacharias, Diana, 'The UNESCO regime for the protection of world heritage as prototype of an autonomy-gaining international institution' (2008) 9 *German Law Journal* 1833

REPORTS

Brondizio, E. S. et al. (eds.), *Global Assessment Report on Biodiversity and Ecosystem Services of the Intergovernmental Science-Policy Platform on Biodiversity and Ecosystem Services* (Bonn, Germany: IPBES Secretariat, 2019)

Chernela, Janet M., 'Indigenous knowledge and Amazonian blackwaters of hunger' in Darrell Addison Posey (ed.), *Cultural and Spiritual Values of Biodiversity: A Complementary Contribution to the Global Biodiversity Assessment* (United Nations Environment Programme and Intermediate Technology, 1999)

Context Pty. Ltd., *Defining the Aesthetic Values of the Great Barrier Reef* (Australian Government, Department of Sustainability, Environment, Water, Population and Communities, February 2013)

Fischer, M. et al. (eds.), *Summary for Policymakers of the Regional Assessment Report on Biodiversity and Ecosystem Services for Europe and Central Asia of the Intergovernmental Science-Policy Platform on Biodiversity and Ecosystem Services* (IPBES Secretariat, 2018)

Herman, Ottó, *International Convention for the Protection of Birds Concluded in 1902: and Hungary: Historical Sketch*. (V. Hornyánszky, Court Printer, 1907)

Hillman, James, 'Where is the environment?' in Darrell Addison Posey (ed.), *Cultural and Spiritual Values of Biodiversity: A Complementary Contribution to the Global Biodiversity Assessment* (United Nations Environment Programme and Intermediate Technology, 1999)

IUCN, *Study on the Application of Criterion (vii): Considering Superlative Natural Phenomena and Exceptional Natural Beauty within the World Heritage Convention* (International Union for Conservation of Nature, 2013)

Leadley, Paul W, et al., *Progress Towards the Aichi Biodiversity Targets: An Assessment of Biodiversity Trends, Policy Scenarios and Key Actions* (Secretariat of the *Convention on Biological Diversity*, 2014)

McLean, Margot, 'Art and environment, or look here' in Darrell Addison Posey (ed.), *Cultural and Spiritual Values of Biodiversity: A Complementary Contribution to the Global Biodiversity Assessment* (United Nations Environment Programme and Intermediate Technology, 1999)

Millennium Ecosystem Assessment, 'Cultural and amenity services' in Millennium Ecosystem Assessment, Ecosystems and Human Well-Being: Current State and Trends (Washington: Island Press, 2005), www.millenniumassessment.org/documents/document.286.aspx.pdf

Ecosystems and Human Well-Being: Biodiversity Synthesis, UN Doc. UNEP/CBD/SBSTTA/11/INF/22, www.cbd.int/doc/meetings/sbstta/sbstta-11/information/sbstta-11-inf-22-en.pdf

Summary for decision makers of the Biodiversity Synthesis Report, UN. Doc UNEP/CBD/SBSTTA/11/7/Add.1, www.cbd.int/doc/meetings/sbstta/sbstta-11/official/sbstta-11-07-add1-en.pdf

Montes, Francisco (Kathleen Harrison, tr. and ed.), 'Spirit, story and medicine: Sachamama — an example of the ancient beings of the Amazon rainforest' in Darrell Addison Posey (ed.), *Cultural and Spiritual Values of Biodiversity: A Complementary Contribution to the Global Biodiversity Assessment* (United Nations Environment Programme and Intermediate Technology, 1999)

Mulongoy, K. J. and S. B. Gidda, *The Value of Nature: Ecological, Economic, Cultural and Social Benefits of Protected Areas* (Secretariat of the *Convention on Biological Diversity*, 2008)

Nolte, Georg, 'Treaties over time in particular: Subsequent agreement and practice' in International Law Commission, Report of the International Law Commission on the Work of its Sixtieth Session, UN Doc. A/63/10, 2008

Peteru, Clark, 'Western Samoan views of the environment' in Darrell Addison Posey (ed.), *Cultural and Spiritual Values of Biodiversity: A Complementary*

Contribution to the Global Biodiversity Assessment (United Nations Environment Programme and Intermediate Technology, 1999)

Posey, Darrell Addison (ed.), *Cultural and Spiritual Values of Biodiversity: A Complementary Contribution to the Global Biodiversity Assessment* (United Nations Environment Programme and Intermediate Technology, 1999)

'Introduction' in Darrell Addison Posey (ed.), *Cultural and Spiritual Values of Biodiversity: A Complementary Contribution to the Global Biodiversity Assessment* (United Nations Environment Programme and Intermediate Technology, 1999)

Sukhdev, Pavan, et al., *The Economics of Ecosystems and Biodiversity: Mainstreaming the Economics of Nature: A Synthesis of the Approach, Conclusions and Recommendations of TEEB* (Progress Press, 2010)

UK National Ecosystem Assessment Follow-on Phase, 'Cultural ecosystem services and indicators' in Peter Coates et al., *Arts & Humanities Perspectives on Cultural Ecosystem Services: Arts & Humanities Working Group (AHWG) Final Report* (April 2014)

Whitt, Laurie Anne, 'Indigenous peoples, their environments and territories: Metaphor and power in indigenous and Western knowledge systems' in Darrell Addison Posey, (ed.), *Cultural and Spiritual Values of Biodiversity: A Complementary Contribution to the Global Biodiversity Assessment* (United Nations Environment Programme and Intermediate Technology, 1999)

CASES AND PLEADINGS

Application of the Convention on the Prevention and Punishment of the Crime of Genocide (Bosnia and Herzegovina v. Serbia and Montenegro) (Judgment) [2007] ICJ Rep 43

Armed Activities on the Territory of the Congo (Democratic Republic of the Congo v. Uganda) (Judgment) [2005] ICJ Rep 168

'Audio-visual record', *Whaling in the Antarctic (Australia v. Japan; New Zealand intervening)*, International Court of Justice, General List No 148, 26 June 2013

Whaling in the Antarctic (Australia v. Japan; New Zealand intervening), International Court of Justice, General List No 148, 27 June 2013

Certain Activities Carried Out by Nicaragua in the Border Area (Costa Rica v. Nicaragua) (Judgment) [2015] ICJ Rep 665

'Counter-memorial of Japan', *Whaling in the Antarctic (Australia v. Japan; New Zealand intervening)*, International Court of Justice, General List No 148, 9 March 2012, vol. I

'Counter-memorial of the Federal Republic of Yugoslavia', *Application of the Convention on the Prevention and Punishment of the Crime of Genocide (Bosnia and Herzegovina v. Serbia and Montenegro)*, International Court of Justice, 23 July 1997

Feldbrugge v. Netherlands (appl. no. 8562/79) [1986] Eur Court HR (ser A) 99, joint dissenting opinion

Frontier Dispute (Benin/Niger) (Judgment) [2005] ICJ Rep 90

Frontier Dispute (Burkina Faso/Republic of Mali) (Judgment) [1986] ICJ Rep 554

Kasikili/Sedudu Island (Botswana v. Namibia) (Judgment) [1999] ICJ Rep 1045
Maritime Delimitation and Territorial Questions Between Qatar and Bahrain (Qatar v. Bahrain) (Judgment) [2001] ICJ Rep 40
'Memorial of Australia', *Whaling in the Antarctic (Australia v. Japan; New Zealand intervening)*, International Court of Justice, General List No 148, 9 May 2011 vol. I
'Memorial of Slovak Republic', *Gabčíkovo-Nagymaros Project (Hungary/Slovakia)*, International Court of Justice, 2 May 1994, vol. I
'Memorial of the Republic of Hungary', *Gabčíkovo-Nagymaros Project (Hungary/Slovakia)*, International Court of Justice, 2 May 1994, vol. I
'Memorial of the Republic of Nauru', *Certain Phosphate Lands in Nauru (Nauru v. Australia)*, International Court of Justice, April 1990, vol. I
'Memorial of the United Kingdom', *Corfu Channel (United Kingdom of Great Britain and Northern Ireland v. Albania)*, International Court of Justice, 30 September 1947
Sea Shepherd Australia and Department of Immigration and Border Protection (Freedom of information) [2017] AICmr 48
The Temple of Preah Vihear (Cambodia v. Thailand) (Merits) [1962] ICJ Rep 6
'Verbatim record 2013/8', *Whaling in the Antarctic (Australia v. Japan; New Zealand intervening)*, International Court of Justice, General List No 148, 26 June 2013
'Verbatim record 2013/10', *Whaling in the Antarctic (Australia v. Japan; New Zealand intervening)*, International Court of Justice, General List No 148, 27 June 2013
'Verbatim record 2013/12', *Whaling in the Antarctic (Australia v. Japan; New Zealand intervening)*, International Court of Justice, General List No 148, 2 July 2013
'Verbatim record 2013/13', *Whaling in the Antarctic (Australia v. Japan; New Zealand intervening)*, International Court of Justice, General List No 148, 3 July 2013
'Verbatim record 2013/16', *Whaling in the Antarctic (Australia v. Japan; New Zealand intervening)*, International Court of Justice, General List No 148, 4 July 2013
'Verbatim record 2013/19', *Whaling in the Antarctic (Australia v. Japan; New Zealand intervening)*, International Court of Justice, General List No 148, 10 July 2013
'Verbatim record 2013/23', *Whaling in the Antarctic (Australia v. Japan; New Zealand intervening)*, International Court of Justice, General List No 148, 16 July 2013
Whaling in the Antarctic (Australia v. Japan; New Zealand intervening) (Judgment) [2014] ICJ Rep 226

TREATIES

African Convention on the Conservation of Nature and Natural Resources, Algiers, 15 September 1968, in force 16 June 1969, 1001 UNTS 3
African Convention on the Conservation of Nature and Natural Resources (Revised), Maputo, 11 July 2003, in force 23 July 2016 (available at African Union Treaties website: https://au.int/en/treaties)
Agreement on the Conservation and Management of the Alaska-Chukotka Polar Bear Population, Washington, 16 October 2000, in force 23 September 2007, 40 ILM 397
Agreement on the Conservation of African-Eurasian Migratory Waterbirds, The Hague, 15 August 1996, in force 1 November 1999, 2365 UNTS 203

ASEAN *Agreement on the Conservation of Nature and Natural Resources*, Kuala Lumpur, 9 July 1985 (available at ASEAN Legal Documents Collection: https://asean.org/library-of-asec/legal-documents-collection/)

Cartagena Protocol on Biosafety to the Convention on Biological Diversity, Montreal, 29 January 2000, in force 11 September 2003, 2226 UNTS 208

Convention for the Protection of the World Cultural and Natural Heritage, Paris, 16 November 1972, in force 17 December 1975, 1037 UNTS 151

Convention for the Safeguarding of the Intangible Cultural Heritage, Paris, 17 October 2003, in force 20 April 2006, 2368 UNTS 3

Convention on Biological Diversity, Rio de Janeiro, 5 June 1992, in force 29 December 1993, 1760 UNTS 79

Convention on International Trade in Endangered Species of Wild Fauna and Flora, Washington, 3 March 1973, in force 1 July 1975, 993 UNTS 243

Convention on Nature Protection and Wildlife Preservation in the Western Hemisphere, Washington, 12 October 1940, in force 1 May 1942, 161 UNTS 193

Convention on the Conservation of European Wildlife and Natural Habitats, Bern, 19 September 1979, in force 1 June 1982, ETS No. 104

Convention on the Conservation of Migratory Species of Wild Animals, Bonn, 23 June 1979, in force 1 November 1983, 1651 UNTS 333

Convention on the Conservation of Nature in the South Pacific, Apia, 12 June 1976, in force 26 June 1990, [1990] ATS 41

Convention on Wetlands of International Importance Especially as Waterfowl Habitat, Ramsar, 2 February 1971, in force 21 December 1975, 996 UNTS 245

Convention Relative to the Preservation of Fauna and Flora in their Natural State, London, 8 November 1933, in force 14 January 1936, 172 LNTS 241

Convention to Protect Birds Useful to Agriculture, Paris, 19 March 1902, in force 6 December 1905 in Bernd Rüster and Bruno Simma (eds.), *International Protection of the Environment: Treaties and Related Documents*, 10 vols. (Dobbs Ferry, New York: Oceana Publications, 1975–1982) vol. IV, p. 1615

Council of Europe, Convention for the Protection of Human Rights and Fundamental Freedoms, Rome, 4 November 1950, in force 3 September 1953, 213 UNTS 222

International Convention on the Regulation of Whaling, Washington, 2 December 1946, in force 10 November 1948, 161 UNTS 72

Nagoya Protocol on Access to Genetic Resources and the Fair and Equitable Sharing of Benefits Arising from their Utilization to the Convention on Biological Diversity, Nagoya, 29 October 2010, in force 12 October 2014, 3008 UNTS 3

Protocol Concerning Specially Protected Areas and Biological Diversity in the Mediterranean, to the Convention for the Protection of the Mediterranean Sea against Pollution, Barcelona, 10 June 1995, in force 12 December 1999, 2102 UNTS 181

Protocol Concerning Specially Protected Areas and Wildlife to the Convention for the Protection and Development of the Marine Environment of the Wider Caribbean Region, Kingston, 18 January 1990, in force 17 June 2000, 2180 UNTS 101

Protocol on Environmental Protection to the Antarctic Treaty, Madrid, 4 October 1991, in force 14 January 1998, 2941 UNTS 3

Protocol on Integrated Coastal Zone Management in the Mediterranean to the *Convention for the Protection of the Marine Environment and the Coastal*

Region of the Mediterranean, Madrid, 21 January 2008, in force 24 March 2011, 2742 UNTS 197
United Nations Framework Convention on Climate Change, New York, 9 May 1992, in force 21 March 1994, 1771 UNTS 107
Vienna Convention on the Law of Treaties, Vienna, 23 May 1969, in force 27 January 1980, 1155 UNTS 331

DOCUMENTS OF INTERNATIONAL INSTITUTIONS

Biodiversity

Ad Hoc Working Group of Legal and Technical Experts on Biological Diversity, *Elements for Possible Inclusion in a Global Framework Legal Instrument on Biological Diversity*, UN Doc. UNEP/Bio.Div/WG.2/1/3, 24 September 1990
Draft Convention on Biological Diversity, UN Doc. UNEP/BIO.Div/WG.2/2/2, 22 January 1991
Antigua and Barbuda, 'Antigua and Barbuda's first national report to the *Convention on Biological Diversity*', March 2001
Australia, 'Australia's fifth national report to the *Convention on Biological Diversity*', May 2014
Brazil, 'Fourth national report to the *Convention on Biological Diversity*', October 2010
Cambodia, 'The fifth national report to the *Convention on Biological Diversity*', 2014
Canada, 'Canada's 4th national report to the United Nations *Convention on Biological Diversity*', undated, circa 2010
Conference of the Parties to the *Convention on Biological Diversity*, *Comprehensive and Participatory Process for the Preparation of the Post-2020 Global Biodiversity Framework*, Decision 14/34, UN Doc. UNEP/CBD/COP/DEC/14/34, 30 November 2018
'Opening statement by Ms. Cristiana Paşca Palmer, Executive Secretary of the *Convention on Biological Diversity*' in *Report of the Conference of the Parties to the* Convention on Biological Diversity *on its Fourteenth Meeting*, UN Doc. CBD/COP/14/14, 20 March 2019
National Reporting: Review of Experience and Proposals for the Fifth National Report, Decision X/10, UN Doc. UNEP/CBD/COP/DEC/X/10, 29 October 2010
Report of the Second Meeting of the Conference of the Parties to the Convention on Biological Diversity, Decision II/1, UN Doc. UNEP/CBD/COP/2/19, 30 November 1995
Report of the Open-ended Working Group on the Post-2020 Global Biodiversity Framework on its third meeting (Part II), UN Doc. CBD/WG2020/3/7, 29 March 2022
The Strategic Plan for Biodiversity 2011–2020 and the Aichi Biodiversity Targets, Decision X/2, UN Doc. UNEP/CBD/COP/DEC/X/2, 29 October 2010
Akwé: Kon Voluntary Guidelines, Decision VII/16 F, UN Doc. UNEP/CBD/COP/DEC/VII/16, 13 April 2004
Resource Mobilization, Decision XII/3, UN Doc. UNEP/CBD/COP/DEC/XII/3, 17 October 2014

Impact Assessment: Voluntary Guidelines on Biodiversity-Inclusive Impact Assessment, Decision VIII/28, UN Doc. UNEP/CBD/COP/DEC/VIII/28, 15 June 2006

Incentive Measures (Article 11), Decision IX/6, UN Doc. UNEP/CBD/COP/DEC/9/6, 30 May 2008

Ecosystem Approach, Decision VII/11, UN Doc. UNEP/CBD/COP/DEC/VII/11, 13 April 2004

Implications of the Findings of the Millennium Ecosystem Assessment, Decision VIII/9, UN Doc. UNEP/CBD/COP/DEC/VIII/9, 15 June 2006

Ecosystem Approach, Decision IX/7, UN Doc. UNEP/CBD/COP/DEC/IX/7, 9 October 2008

Follow-up to the Millennium Ecosystem Assessment, Decision IX/15, UN Doc. UNEP/CBD/COP/DEC/IX/15, 9 October 2008

Report of the Sixth Meeting of the Conference of the Parties to the Convention on Biological Diversity, Decision VI/10, UN Doc. UNEP/CBD/COP/6/20, 27 May 2002

Comprehensive and Participatory Process for the Preparation of the Post-2020 Global Biodiversity Framework, Decision 14/35, UN Doc. CBD/COP/DEC/14/35, 30 November 2018

'Note by the Executive Secretary' in Conference of the Parties to the *Biodiversity Convention, Resource Manual for the Sixth National Report, Including Annotated Reporting Templates*, UN Doc. UNEP/CBD/COP/13/21, 20 September 2016

Rules of Procedure for the Conference of the Parties, Decision I/1, UN Doc. UNEP/CBD/COP/DEC/I/1, 28 February 1995

Estonia, 'V national report to the *Convention on Biological Diversity*' undated

Georgia, 'Second national report to the *Convention on Biological Diversity*,' 2010

Intergovernmental Negotiating Committee for a Convention on Biological Diversity, *Fifth Revised Draft Convention on Biological Diversity*, UN Doc. UNEP/Bio.Div/N7-INC.5/2, 20 February 1992

IPBES, 'Members and observers', ipbes.net/members-observers

IUCN, 'Love not loss', www.iucn.org/commissions/commission-education-and-communication/resources/love-not-loss

Kenya, 'Fourth national report to the Conference of Parties of the *Convention on Biological Diversity*', July 2009

Kyrgyz Republic, 'Fourth national report on conservation of biodiversity of the Kyrgyz Republic', 2008

Indonesia, 'The fifth national report of Indonesia to the *Convention on Biological Diversity*', 2014

Lao People's Democratic Republic, 'Fifth national report to the United Nations *Convention on Biological Diversity*', 2016

Lebanon, 'Fifth national report of Lebanon to the *Convention on Biological Diversity*', August 2015

Malawi, 'Fifth national report to the *Convention on Biological Diversity*', July 2014

Maldives, 'Fifth national report to the United Nations *Convention on Biological Diversity*', 2015

Malta, 'Fourth national report to the *Convention on Biological Diversity*', 2010

Secretariat of the *Convention on Biological Diversity*, 'Guidelines for the fourth national report', www.cbd.int/reports/guidelines/default.shtml

Use of Cameras and Audio/Video Recording Devices by Participants at Meetings of the Convention on Biological Diversity, 15 August 2012

Global Biodiversity Outlook 4, 2014

Global Biodiversity Outlook 5, 2020

'Global biodiversity outlook (GBO)', www.cbd.int/gbo

'National reports', www.cbd.int/reports

An Exploration of Tools and Methodologies for Valuation of Biodiversity and Biodiversity Resources and Functions, 2007

Protected Areas in Today's World: Their Values and Benefits for the Welfare of the Planet, 2008

Seychelles, 'Fifth national report to the *Convention on Biological Diversity*', 2014

Subsidiary Body on Scientific, Technical and Technological Advice, *Managing Biodiversity is about People*, UN Doc. UNEP/CBD/SBSTTA/17/INF/1, 4 September 2013

Report of the First Meeting of the Subsidiary Body on Scientific, Technical and Technological Advice, Recommendation I/6, UN Doc. UNEP/CBD/COP/2/5, 21 September 1995

Tuvalu, 'Tuvalu national biodiversity strategy and action plan: Fifth national report to the *Convention on Biological Diversity*', 2016

Uganda, 'Fifth national report to the *Convention on Biological Diversity*', March 2014

Yemen, 'Fifth national report to the *Convention on Biological Diversity* (2010–2014)', 2014

International Court of Justice

International Court of Justice, *Practice Direction IXquater*, 11 April 2013

Rules of Court, 14 April 1978

Japan, *Declaration Recognizing as Compulsory the Jurisdiction of the International Court of Justice under Article 36, paragraph 2, of the Statute of the Court 15 October 1946*, October 6, 2015

Statute of the International Court of Justice, San Francisco, 26 June 1945, in force 24 October 1945, USTS 993

Whaling

Eustice, George, 'Outcomes from the 67th meeting of the International Whaling Commission', 2018 HC WS1055

International Whaling Commission, *Chair's Report of the 67th Meeting*, 10–14 September 2018

'Caught blue whale south Georgia 1930s' in International Whaling Commission, 'Dead/injured whales'

'Dead/injured whales', iwc.int/dead-injured-whales-gallery

'Florianópolis declaration on the role of the International Whaling Commission in the conservation and management of whales in the 21st century' in International Whaling Commission, *Chair's Report of the 67th Meeting*, 10–14 September 2018

Japan, 'The way forward of the IWC – IWC reform proposal including a draft resolution and proposed schedule amendment' in International Whaling Commission, *Chair's Report of the 67th Meeting*, 10–14 September 2018

'Note verbale', 26 December 2018 (concerning withdrawal from the *Whaling Convention*)

Ruston, Senator Anne, 'Opening statement at the 67th meeting of the International Whaling Commission' in International Whaling Commission, *Chair's Report of the 67th Meeting*, 10–14 September 2018

UN Conference on the Human Environment, *Report*, UN Doc. A/CONF.48/14/Rev.1, 5–16 June 1972

'Verbatim record', International Whaling Commission, 31st annual meeting, 9–13 July 1979

'Verbatim record', International Whaling Commission, 33rd annual meeting, 20 July 1981

'Verbatim record', International Whaling Commission, 34th annual meeting, 19–24 July 1982

World Heritage

Australia, 'Draft Retrospective Statement of Outstanding Universal Value' in *State Party Report on the State of Conservation of the Tasmanian Wilderness World Heritage Area (Australia)* (2010)

'Draft retrospective statement of Outstanding Universal Value' in International Council on Monuments and Sites and International Union for Conservation of Nature, *Reactive Monitoring Mission to the Tasmanian Wilderness, Australia: Mission Report*, 23–29 November 2015

State Party Report on the State of Conservation of the Great Barrier Reef World Heritage Area, 25 November 2019

State Party Report on the State of Conservation of the Tasmanian Wilderness World Heritage Area (Australia), 2022

Nomination of the Tasmanian Wilderness by the Government of Australia for Inclusion in the World Heritage List, Request, 15 September 1989

Nomination of Western Tasmania Wilderness National Parks by the Commonwealth of Australia for Inclusion in the World Heritage List, 11 November 1981

Chad, *Proposition d'Inscription des Lacs d'Ounianga sur la Liste du Patrimone Mondial* [Nomination of Lakes of Ounianga], January 2011

China, *Mount Sanqingshan National Park*, Nomination, assessed 2008

International Council on Monuments and Sites (ICOMOS) et al., *Guidance on the Preparation of Retrospective Statements of Outstanding Universal Value for World Heritage Properties*, July 2010

IUCN, 'Terms of reference for the IUCN World Heritage panel', approved November 2015

Outstanding Universal Value Standards for Natural World Heritage: A Compendium on Standards for Inscriptions of Natural Properties on the World Heritage List (Gland, Switzerland: IUCN, 2008)

Reactive Monitoring Mission Report for Monarch Butterfly Biosphere Reserve (Mexico) (Paris, France: World Heritage Committee, 2018)

Kenya, *Nomination Proposal: Kenya Lake System in the Great Rift Valley*, 2010

Mexico, *World Heritage Site Nomination Document: Monarch Butterfly Biosphere Reserve*, January 2007

Rules of Procedure of the World Heritage Committee, WHC-2015/5, July 2015

UNESCO, 'World Heritage Convention: States parties', whc.unesco.org/en/statesparties

UNESCO Special Committee of Government Experts to Prepare a Draft Convention and a Draft Recommendation to Member States Concerning the Protection of Monuments, Groups of Buildings and Sites, *Working Document Prepared by the Working Group II: Draft Convention Concerning the Protection of Cultural and Natural World Heritage*, UN Doc. SHC-72/CONF.37/8, 11 April 1972

Drafting Committee, UN Doc. SHC.72/CONF.37/RED/1

Draft Report, UN Doc. SHC.72/CONF.37/19, 21 April 1972

Projet d'amendement, présenté par la délégation de la France, UN Doc. SHC.72/CONF.37/DR.21, 10 April 1972

Working Document Prepared by the Working Group: Draft Convention Concerning the Protection of Cultural and Natural World Heritage, UN Doc. SHC-72/CONF.37/4, 7 April 1972

World Health Organisation, *Global Ambient Air Quality Database*, summary results of the database, 2018

World Heritage Centre, 'Preparing World Heritage nominations' *World Heritage Resource Manual*, 2nd ed. (UNESCO, 2011)

World Heritage Committee, *Białowieża Forest (Belarus/Poland)*, Decision 38 COM 8B.12, UN Doc. WHC-14/38.COM/16, 7 July 2014

Great Barrier Reef (Australia), Decision 38 COM 7B.63, UN Doc. WHC-14/38/COM/16, 7 July 2014

Item 9 of the Provisional Agenda: Global Strategy for a Representative, Balanced and Credible World Heritage List: 9A. Upstream Process, UN Doc. WHC/19/43.COM/9A.Rev, 19 June 2019

Kenya Lake System in the Great Rift Valley (Kenya), Decision 35 COM 8B.6, UN Doc. WHC-11/35.COM/20, 7 July 2011

Kenya Lake System in the Great Rift Valley (Kenya), Statement of Outstanding Universal Value, Decision 35 COM 8B.6, UN Doc. WHC-11/35.COM/20, 7 July 2011

Lakes of Ounianga (Chad), Decision 36 COM 8B.7, UN Doc. WHC-12/36.COM/19

Lakes of Ounianga (Chad), Statement of Outstanding Universal Value, Decision 36 COM 8B.7, UN Doc. WHC-12/36.COM/19

Monarch Butterfly Biosphere Reserve (Mexico), Decision 32 COM 8B.17, UN Doc. WHC-08/32.COM/24Rev, 31 March 2009

Monarch Butterfly Biosphere Reserve (Mexico), Decision 43 COM 7B.27, UN Doc. WHC/19/43.COM/18, 23 July 2019

Monarch Butterfly Biosphere Reserve (Mexico), Statement of Outstanding Universal Value, Decision 32 COM 8B.17, UN Doc. WHC-08/32.COM/24Rev, 31 March 2009
Monarch Butterfly Biosphere Reserve, Mexico: Agenda Item 7B State of Conservation of Properties Inscribed on the World Heritage List, Decision 41 COM 7B.16, UN Doc. WHC/17/41.COM/18, 12 July 2017
Mount Sanqingshan National Park (China), Decision 32 COM 8B.6, UN Doc. WHC-08/32.COM/24Rev, 31 March 2009
Mount Sanqingshan National Park (China), Statement of Outstanding Universal Value, Decision 32 COM 8B.6, UN Doc. WHC-08/32.COM/24Rev, 31 March 2009
Operational Guidelines for the Implementation of the World Heritage Convention, UN Doc. CC-77/CONF.001/8, 30 June 1977
Operational Guidelines for the Implementation of the World Heritage Convention, UN Doc. WHC/2/Revised, 27 March 1992
Operational Guidelines for the Implementation of the World Heritage Convention, UN Doc. WHC/2/Revised, February 1994
Operational Guidelines for the Implementation of the World Heritage Convention, UN Doc. WHC. 05/2, 2 February 2005
Operational Guidelines for the Implementation of the World Heritage Convention, UN Doc. WHC.21/01, 31 July 2021
Reflection on the Preparation of the Next Cycle of Periodic Reporting, Decision 31 COM 11D.1, UN Doc. WHC-07/31.COM/24, 31 July 2007
Report, UN Doc. WHC-92/CONF.002/12, 14 December 1992
Tasmanian Wilderness (Australia), Decision CONF 004 XV.A, UN Doc. SC-89/CONF.004/12, 22 December 1989
Tasmanian Wilderness (Australia), Decision 42 COM 7B.61, UN Doc. WHC/18/42.COM/18, 4 July 2018
Western Tasmania Wilderness National Parks (Australia), Decision CONF 015 VIII.20, UN Doc. CLT-82/CH/CONF.015/8, 17 January 1983
World Heritage List, whc.unesco.org/en/list
World Heritage Policy Compendium, whc.unesco.org/en/compendium
World Heritage List, *Monarch Butterfly Biosphere Reserve (Mexico)*, whc.unesco.org/en/list/1290/gallery

ARTWORKS AND EXHIBITIONS

Akomfrah, John, *Four Nocturnes*, Venice, 2019
Vertigo Sea, Venice, 2015
Amor, Rick, *The whale*, 1993
Arnold, Raymond, *Elsewhere World*, 2017
Mt. Lyell (Expanded Field), 2017
ARTCOP21, September–December 2015, www.artcop21.com
Artwise Curators, *Here Today*, artwisecurators.com/exhibitions/13/overview
Ballard, Thea, 'Portfolio: Diana Thater' (2015) 27(1) *Modern Painters* 17

Berkowitz, Lauren, 'Work', www.laurenberkowitz.com.au/Lauren_Berkowitz_Work.html
Bonnaterre, Pierre Joseph (Abbé), 'Histoire naturelle: Cétacés' in *The Encyclopédie Méthodique par ordre des matières* [Methodical Encyclopedia by Order of Subject Matter], 1789
Brierly, Oswald, *Whalers off Twofold Bay, New South Wales*, 1867
Cai, Guo-Qiang, *Falling Back to Earth*, Brisbane, 2014
Pulse (Mountain), National Gallery of Victoria, 2019
Captain Boomer, *The Why of the Whale*, Madrid, 2018
CarbonArts-World Health Organisation, *Breathe*, 19 May 2015, www.carbonarts.org/projects/breathe
CLIMARTE Festival 2019, *Peter Dombrovskis: Journeys into the Wild*, Monash Gallery of Art, Melbourne, 9 March 2019–12 Mary 2019
Dean, Tacita, 'Interview with artist' *accompanying Majesty (Portrait)*, Paris, 2006
Delafield Cook, Jonathan, *Sperm Whale II*, Sydney, 2013
Ghana Pavilion, Biennale Arte 2019, Venice, 2019, web.archive.org/web/20190524224035/, https://ghanainvenice.org/
Glover, John, *A mountain torrent*, c. 1837
The River Nile, Van Diemen's Land, from Mr Glover's farm, 1837
Gough, Julie, *Observance*, 2012
Hall, Fiona, *Tender*, 2003–05
Wrong Way Time, Australian Pavilion, Biennale Arte 2015, Venice, 2015
Hokusai, Katsushika, *Whaling Scene on the Coast of Gotō*, c. 1830
Huyghe, Pierre, *A Journey That Wasn't*, Paris, 2005
After ALife Ahead, 2017
Ian Potter Museum of Art, *Nature/Revelation*, Melbourne, 2015
Not as the Songs of Other Lands: 19th Century Australian and American Landscape Painting (Melbourne: Ian Potter Museum of Art, University of Melbourne, 2017)
Kanwar, Amar, *The Scene of Crime*, 2011
Kngwarreye, Emily Kame, *Earth's Creation*, 1994
Koson, *Hogei Sogakari No Zu* [Attacking a whale in unison], 1895
Kuniyoshi, Utagawa, *Miyamoto no Musashi Attacking the Giant Whale*, c. 1847–50.
Whaling Scene at Goto, Hirado or Kishu, c. 1840
Laurence, Janet, *Deep Breathing: Resuscitation for the Reef*, Paris, 2015–16
Ma, Lesley, Cai Guo-Qiang and Yuko Hasegawa, *The Transient Landscape*, National Gallery of Victoria, Melbourne, 2019
Magritte, René, *La condition humaine*, 1933
Martin, Mandy, *O-B-L-I-V-I-O-N*, 1993
Mellor, Danie, *Et in arcadia ego (of landscape and memory)*, 2011
Mizuki, Shigeru, *Bake-Kujira in No Yōkai Jiten* [Encyclopedia of monsters] (Tōkyō, Shōwa 56, 1981)
Morrison, James, *Sepik River*, 2012
Murakami, Takashi, 727, 1996
Museum of Contemporary Art, *In the Balance: Art for a Changing World*, Sydney, 2010
Mutu, Wangechi, *The End of carrying All*, New York, 2015

National Gallery of Victoria, *Triennial*, Melbourne, 2020, www.ngv.vic.gov.au/exhibition/triennial-2020
National Gallery of Victoria, Cathy Leahy and Helen McDonald, *John Woseley: Heartlands and Headwaters*, Melbourne, 2015
New Bedford Whaling Museum, *Pacific Encounters*, 2004–5
Phillips, Justy and Margaret Woodward, *Fall, Now a River*, 2016, from *Fall of the Derwent*, Glenorchy, 2015–16, www.apublishedevent.net/projects/fall-of-the-derwent
Poussin, Nicolas, *Et in arcadia ego (Les berges d'Arcadie)*, 1637–8
Prout, John Skinner, *Old Whaling Station*, c. 1874
Queensland Art Gallery/Gallery of Modern Art, *My Country, I Still Call Australia Home: Contemporary Art from Black Australia* (Brisbane: Queensland Art Gallery/Gallery of Modern Art, 2013)
Roca, José, *rīvus*, Biennale of Sydney, 2022, www.biennaleofsydney.art/biennale/23rd-biennale-of-sydney-2022
Rodríguez, Abel, Annual cycle of the flooded rainforest, 2009–10
Caimo de monte, 2008 in *Studies of trees*
Rousseau, Henri J, *Exotic Landscape*, 1908. Oil on canvas, 116 × 89 cm. Private collection. Reproduced in Roger Shattuck et al., *Henri Rousseau* (New York: Museum of Modern Art, 1985) p. 209
Royal Collection Trust, 'Manchester from Kersal Moor', www.rct.uk/collection/920223/manchester-from-kersal-moor
Sands, Philippe, 'East-west street: A song of good and evil', Hamer Hall, Melbourne, 21 February 2018
Saraceno, Tomás, *Aerocene*, aerocene.org
'Studio Tomás Saraceno', studiotomassaraceno.org
Simon, Taryn, *Paperwork and the Will of Capital*, 2015
Skulptur Projekte Münster 2017, www.skulptur-projekte-archiv.de/en-us/2017
TarraWarra Museum of Art, *TarraWarra International 2013: Animate/Inanimate*, Healesville, TarraWarra Museum of Art 2013
Thater, Diana, *Untitled Videowall (Butterflies)*, 2008
Voignier, Marie, *Standing Still* (Les Immobiles), 2013
von Guérard, Eugène, *Mr Clark's Station, Deep Creek*, near Keilor, 1867
Wellings, CE and CB Jenkins, *Whale Chase in Twofold Bay*, 1910, web.archive.org/web/20220214105106/, https://en.wikipedia.org/wiki/File:Killer_Whale_(Old_Tom)_and_whalers.jpeg
Wirrpanda, Mulkuṉ and John Wolseley, *Midawarr Harvest*, 2017
Wyld, William, *Manchester from Kersal Moor*, 1852
Yosei, Yamada, *Yogiotoru Eshi* [Pictures of whaling]

OTHER

Bambaradeniya, Channa N. B. and Felix P. Amerasinghe, 'Biodiversity associated with the rice field agroecosystem in Asian countries: A brief review' (Colombo, Sri Lanka: International Water Management Institute, 2003)
Bonyhady, Tim, 'When a picture packs punch' *Sydney Morning Herald*, 10 June 2004

Brierly, Oswald, 'The Cetacea or reminiscences of the sea', 1800s

Brown, Bob, 'Letter to the 120 Sea Shepherd crew in the Southern Ocean', 4 February 2013, www.facebook.com/Bob.Brown.Foundation/posts/415222831898940

Buchanan, Rachel, 'Agnes Denes' public sculpture neglected', Sydney Morning Herald online, 30 November 2014, www.smh.com.au/entertainment/art-and-design/agnes-denes-public-sculpture-neglected-20141125-11kaxu.htm

Christoff, Peter, 'The poster is political: How artists are challenging climate change', *The Conversation online*, 5 May 2016, theconversation.com/the-poster-is-political-how-artists-are-challenging-climate-change-58740

CLIMARTE, 'Art provokes and inspires at climate conference', 21 December 2015, web.archive.org/web/20160208081207/, http://climarte.org/art-provokes-and-inspires-at-climate-conference

'Arts for a safe climate', climarte.org

Commonwealth of Australia, *Parliamentary Debates*, House of Representatives, 4 April 1979, 1481 (Prime Minister Malcolm Fraser)

Convention on International Trade in Endangered Species of Wild Fauna and Flora (CITES) 'African elephant poaching down, ivory seizures up and hit record high', October 2017, cites.org/eng/news/pr/African_elephant_poaching_down_ivory_seizures_up_and_hit_record_high_24102017

Denyer, Susan, 'The cultural value of nature: A world heritage perspective' in Christina Cameron and Judith Herrmann (eds.) *Exploring the Cultural Value of Nature: A World Heritage Context*, proceedings of round table organized by the Canada Research Chair on Built Heritage, Faculty of Environmental Design (Université de Montréal, 12–14 March 2014 Montréal, Québec)

Dia Art Foundation, '*Most wanted* and *least wanted* paintings', awp.diaart.org/km/painting.html

Doherty, Sophie, 'Susanna the slut: Depictions of rape victims in law and in art' (Conference Paper, Art in Law in Art Conference, UWA, Perth, 4–5 July 2017)

Hoare, Philip, 'The lonely Thames beluga whale is an anomaly – and an omen' *The Guardian*, 26 September 2018

Intergovernmental Science-Policy Platform on Biodiversity and Ecosystem Services (IPBES), 'Important disclaimer' with visual material to IPBES, 'Biodiversity and nature's contributions continue dangerous decline, scientists warn', 28 March 2018, goo.gl/oJ4DRq

Jones, Sam, '"A riddle from the deep": Hyper-real whale found beached in Madrid' *The Guardian*, 14 September 2018

Kent, Rachel, 'Janet Laurence: *After Nature*', MCA Sydney, 2019, www.mca.com.au/artists-works/exhibitions/829-janet-laurence

l'Académie française, 9th ed. atilf.atilf.fr/academie9.htm

Lloyd, Joe, 'Skulptur Projekte Münster 2017' *Studio International*, online, 3 July 2017, www.studiointernational.com/index.php/skulptur-projekte-munster-2017-review-germany

Macquarie Dictionary Online (Macmillan Australia)

McEoin, Ewan, 'Some notes on conservation', National Gallery of Victoria, 15 January 2021, www.ngv.vic.gov.au/essay/some-notes-on-conservation

OED Online (Oxford University Press, 2019)

Philippopoulos-Mihalopoulos, Andreas, 'Lighter-than-air: The law of the anthropocene' in Tomas Saraceno's *Monument to the Anthropocene*, 2014

Readfearn, Graham, 'Whaling vote: Australia tells Japan it has lost argument for killings', *The Guardian*, 14 September 2018

Robertson, George Augustus, 'Journal', North-East Tasmania, 2 November 1830

Roe, Dilys, Max Fancourt and Chris Sandbrook, 'Biodiversity conservation and poverty reduction: What's the connection? A systematic mapping of the evidence' (London: International Institute for Environment and Development, 2015)

Stevenson, Angus and Christine A. Lindberg (eds.) *New Oxford American Dictionary*, 3rd ed. (Oxford University Press, 2011)

Sustainable Living Festival, 'Art climate ethics: What role for the arts?', Federation Square, 27 February 2014, climarte.org/project/art-climate-ethics-what-role-for-the-arts

Tipping, Marjorie J., 'Chevalier, Nicholas (1828–1902)', *Australian Dictionary of Biography*, vol. III (Macquarie University Press, 1969)

United Nations Environment Programme, '12 art installations to be unveiled across Asia-Pacific to mark World Environment Day', 30 May 2018

United Nations, *System of Economic and Environmental Accounting*, seea.un.org

United Nations Treaty Collection, 'Depository: Status of treaties', treaties.un.org

United States Department of State, 'Status list for the *Whaling Convention*', www.state.gov/international-convention-for-the-regulation-of-whaling

'Status lists for treaties for which the United States is depository', www.state.gov/depositary-status-lists

Wahlquist, Calla, '"Uncanny similarity": New Damien Hirst works in spot of bother in Australia', *The Guardian*, 29 March 2018

Watts, Jonathan, 'Stop biodiversity loss or we could face our own extinction, warns UN', *The Guardian*, 7 November 2018

Wen, Jun, 'Mt Sanqingshan, a botanical treasure' (*The Plant Press*, 2007) nmnh.typepad.com/the_plant_press/2007/10/mt-sanqingshan-a-botanical-treasure-vol-10-issue-4.html

Wiseman, John and Fay Chomley, 'Wrong Way Time: Climate change, ecology and art at the Venice Biennale' *ClimArte Newsletter*, 18 December 2015

World Environment Day, 'Turning air pollution into art', 24 May 2019, www.unep.org/news-and-stories/story/turning-air-pollution-art

World Heritage Centre, 'Documents: Establishment of the Convention', whc.unesco.org/en/documents

'Sadness and concern at the death of Mr Homero Gómez González', 31 January 2020, whc.unesco.org/en/news/2080

Index

For EU product safety concerns, contact us at Calle de José Abascal, 56–1°, 28003 Madrid, Spain or eugpsr@cambridge.org.

www.ingramcontent.com/pod-product-compliance
Lightning Source LLC
LaVergne TN
LVHW010916300926
849194LV00025B/254
* 9 7 8 1 0 0 9 3 5 0 0 7 5 *